D1757631

Dublin City Libraries
Withdrawn From Stock

Descendancy

This book examines Protestant loss of power and self-confidence in Ireland since 1795. David Fitzpatrick charts the declining power and influence of the Protestant community in Ireland and the strategies adopted in the face of this decline, presenting rich personal testimony that illustrates how individuals experienced and perceived 'descendancy'. Focusing on the attitudes and strategies adopted by the eventual losers rather than victors, he addresses contentious issues in Irish history through an analysis of the appeal of the Orange Order, the Ulster Covenant of 1912, and 'ethnic cleansing' in the Irish Revolution. Avoiding both apologetics and sentimentality when probing the psychology of those undergoing 'descendancy', the book examines the social and political ramifications of religious affiliation and belief as practised in fraternities, church congregations, and isolated sub-communities.

DAVID FITZPATRICK is Professor of Modern History at Trinity College, Dublin.

Front cover illustration: *Belfast under Home Rule. Making a Site for the Statue of King John the First of Ireland.* Postcard by unidentified artist (Belfast, W. & G. Baird, c.1912; author's collection). Behind the descendant Albert Memorial in Queen's Square (1869) are Lanyon's Northern Bank (1852) and Custom House (1857). As the monument to John Redmond is trundled in, the bank has become a 'Protestant Emigration Office' offering tickets 'to New York or anywhere', surmounted by the 'national' flag and an office of the AOH ('Molly Maguires'). The former Custom House is now a 'Poor House Annex', its replacement being a small green shed.

Back cover illustration: *Protestant Descendency: a pull at the Church.* Etching by the Northumbrian William Heath, pseud. Paul Pry (London, 26 Haymarket, T. McLean, 19 March 1829). Daniel O'Connell, the Duke of Wellington, and his Home Secretary Sir Robert Peel lead the tug as the parish church topples on the green hill marked 'Protestant Ascendency'. Meanwhile, bishops and clergy process from a chapel towards a basilica (roughly suggesting St Peter's), and a sinister friar unchains barrels of gunpowder in the 'Cave of Catholic Ascendency'. O'Connell exclaims 'By St Patrick I've got the rope over at last', Wellington cries 'Down with it, never mind the People', and Lord Eldon, the former Lord Chancellor, emerges from the underworld to say 'Look to your selves People'. This nightmarish vision of Catholic Emancipation was probably a model for 'Belfast under Home Rule'. © Trustees of the British Museum.

Descendancy: Irish Protestant Histories since 1795

David Fitzpatrick

Trinity College, Dublin

CAMBRIDGE
UNIVERSITY PRESS

University Printing House, Cambridge CB2 8BS, United Kingdom

Cambridge University Press is part of the University of Cambridge.

It furthers the University's mission by disseminating knowledge in the pursuit of education, learning and research at the highest international levels of excellence.

www.cambridge.org
Information on this title: www.cambridge.org/9781107080935

© David Fitzpatrick 2014

This publication is in copyright. Subject to statutory exception and to the provisions of relevant collective licensing agreements, no reproduction of any part may take place without the written permission of Cambridge University Press.

First published 2014

A catalogue record for this publication is available from the British Library

Library of Congress Cataloguing in Publication data
Fitzpatrick, David (David Patrick Brian)
Descendancy : Irish Protestant histories since 1795 / David Fitzpatrick, Trinity College Dublin.
   pages   cm
Includes bibliographical references and index.
ISBN 978-1-107-08093-5 – ISBN 978-1-107-44029-6 (pbk.)
1. Protestants – Ireland – History – 19th century.   2. Protestants – Ireland – History – 20th century.   3. Protestants – Ireland – Political aspects.   4. Protestants – Ireland – Social conditions.   I. Title.
DA950.F44   2014
305.6'80409415–dc23

2014025968

ISBN 978-1-107-08093-5 Hardback
ISBN 978-1-107-44029-6 Paperback

Cambridge University Press has no responsibility for the persistence or accuracy of URLs for external or third-party internet websites referred to in this publication, and does not guarantee that any content on such websites is, or will remain, accurate or appropriate.

Contents

Charts

Acknowledgements

This book was assembled in the serene surroundings of Magdalene College, Cambridge, during my gratifying tenure as Parnell Fellow in Irish Studies in 2013. The last and longest essay is a vastly expanded version of my Parnell Lecture. I am most grateful to my Cambridge mentors, especially Eamon Duffy, John Kerrigan, Máire Ní Mhaonaigh, and Eugenio Biagini, for their hospitality and support. I am no less indebted to indulgent colleagues in the Department of History at Trinity College, Dublin, particularly to the ever thoughtful and supportive David Ditchburn. For permission to include the six chapters based on articles that originally appeared in journals, I wish to thank the editors and publishers of the *Irish Sword* (Chapter 2), *Irish Historical Studies* (Chapters 3 and 8), the *Review of English Studies* and Oxford Journals (Chapter 4), and the *Bulletin of the Methodist Historical Society of Ireland* (Chapters 5 and 9). Among the many libraries and archives where I have worked on Irish Protestant history, two deserve special mention. For access to the archives of the Grand Orange Lodge of Ireland, and advice on how to interpret them, I am grateful to my hosts in Belfast, especially George Patton, David Hume, David Scott, Jonathan Mattison, Cecil Kilpatrick, and David Cargo. The unforeseen Methodist infiltration of my recent research is attributable to the encouragement and enthusiasm of the Revd Robin Roddie, archivist of the Methodist Historical Society of Ireland, who introduced me to a remarkable collection of records unmatched by other churches in Ireland. Michael Watson and his colleagues at the Cambridge University Press have made production of the book a pleasure. Julia and Hannah Fitzpatrick have put up with my historical preoccupations and even helped me to give musical expression to the spectre of 'ethnic cleansing'. My deepest thanks and apologies are due to Jane Leonard, who has endured, challenged, or abetted so many of my explorations of 'descendancy'. *Garde ta foy*!

Abbreviations

APCK	Association for the Promotion of Christian Knowledge
AR	*Annual Report*
BNL	*Belfast News-Letter*
BT	*Belfast Telegraph*
BWN	*Belfast Weekly News*
CA	*Christian Advocate* (Belfast)
CC	*Cork Constitution*
CCE	*Cork County Eagle* (Skibbereen)
CE	*Cork Examiner*
CGL	County Grand (Orange) Lodge
CIG	*Church of Ireland Gazette* (Dublin)
CIHS	Church of Ireland Historical Society
Co.	County
DED	District Electoral Division
DGC	Deputy Grand Chaplain
DGS	Deputy Grand Secretary
DM	*Daily Mail* (London)
FJ	*Freeman's Journal* (Dublin)
GBC	Grand Black Chapter
GC	Grand Chaplain
GLI	Grand Lodge of Ireland (Freemasons)
GOLE	Grand Orange Lodge of England
GOLI	Grand Orange Lodge of Ireland
GOLIA	GOLI Archive and Library (Belfast)
HCP	House of Commons Papers
HYR	*Report of the Proceedings of the Grand Orange Lodge of Ireland at the General Half-Yearly Meeting*
ICA	*Irish Christian Advocate* (Belfast)
IFA	Irish Folklore Archive (UCD)
IGC	Irish Grants Committee (London)
II	*Irish Independent* (Dublin)
IIS	Institute of Irish Studies (Queen's University of Belfast)

IMP	'Index of Methodist Preachers', unpublished database (MHSIA)
IRA	Irish Republican Army
IT	*Irish Times* (Dublin)
LOL	Loyal Orange Lodge
MCI	Methodist Church in Ireland
MCM	*Minutes of the . . . Conference of People Called Methodists*
MCR	Monthly Confidential Report (Crime Special Branch) by County Inspector, RIC
MHSIA	Methodist Historical Society of Ireland Archive (Edgehill College, Belfast)
MN	*Methodist Newsletter* (Belfast)
NAD	National Archives (Dublin)
NAL	National Archives (London)
NLI	National Library of Ireland (Dublin)
NW	*Northern Whig* (Belfast)
OBLDA	Orange, Black, and Loyalist Defence Association of Ireland
OS	*Orange Standard* (Birmingham)
OTC	Officers Training Corps
PCI	Presbyterian Church in Ireland
PHSI	Presbyterian Historical Society of Ireland
PWMM	*Primitive Wesleyan Methodist Magazine* (Dublin)
RIA	Royal Irish Academy (Dublin)
RIC	Royal Irish Constabulary
SS	*Southern Star* (Skibbereen)
TA	Total Abstinence
TCD	Trinity College, Dublin
UCD	University College, Dublin
UDC	Ulster Day Committee
UG	*Ulster Guardian* (Belfast)
USC	Ulster Special Constabulary
UUC	Ulster Unionist Council
UVF	Ulster Volunteer Force
UWUC	Ulster Women's Unionist Council
WS	Witness Statement (Bureau of Military History)

Prologue

1   Protestant descendancy in Ireland

I

One of the most abusive and abused terms in Irish historical parlance is 'the Protestant Ascendancy', signifying a privileged group defined by religious profession and exercising undue legal, political, administrative, economic, social, and moral power. It is undeniable that 'Roman Catholics' and 'Dissenters' were excluded from certain offices and civic rights under the 'penal laws' until the late eighteenth century, so that a relatively small group of men (but not women) adhering to the established church controlled most of Ireland's material and moral assets. Long after the extension of the county franchise to qualified Catholics in 1793 and even after 'Emancipation' in 1829, local ascendancies retained control of urban corporations and Protestants virtually monopolised senior state appointments. Yet, even at its height, the 'Ascendancy' was utterly unrepresentative of Irish Protestants. Apart from the exclusion of Presbyterians and Nonconformists, it was restricted to the small minority of Churchmen with sufficient wealth or pedigree to claim access to landed estates or public office, or to vote in parliamentary and local elections. Poorer Protestants gained little or no material benefit from supporting an 'Ascendancy' to which they did not in practice belong: they needed to be bribed, wooed, and bullied to secure their political and moral support in times of crisis.

During the two centuries of Irish history straddled by the chapters that follow, the foundations of legal, economic, and social ascendancy were inexorably undermined through repeal of discriminatory laws and professional barriers, broadening of patronage, Church disestablishment, and acquisition of landed estates by the state on behalf of tenant occupiers. More profoundly, state-sponsored mass education and an increasingly global outlook, fostered by mass emigration, placed all élites (whether Protestant or Catholic) under increasing pressure. Those who had endorsed or benefited from the former Ascendancy were acutely aware that the 'tide of history' was against them, and reacted to this awareness in different ways. Some clung to privilege and resisted reform to the bitter end; some invested the substantial compensation accompanying each reform in enterprises designed to reinforce their social or political influence; some kept their heads down and tried to protect their personal and communal interests by avoiding collision with the emerging nationalist élite.

In assembling this book I have raided a drawerful of unpublished and rather obscure published articles, reflecting my struggle in recent years to make sense of the often quixotic and perplexing history of Irish Protestantism. My aim has been to identify new sources to tackle familiar questions, and new questions to apply to familiar sources. My work concerns the social and political ramifications of religious affiliation and belief, rather than ecclesiastical organisation or religious doctrine. Part I consists of detailed studies associated with my unfinished study of the Loyal Orange Institution.[1] It examines aspects of the military, political, literary, and religious history of the 'Orange Order', the most dogged incarnation of Protestant determination to preserve 'Protestant Ascendancy in church and state', and subsequently to resist and impede what was viewed as a new Roman Catholic ascendancy. It is truly remarkable that so many brethren, who had never enjoyed access to legal or social privileges, were prepared to fight the Ascendancy's battles and supply a much-needed moral and popular basis for conservative politics.

Chapter 2 ('Orangeism and Irish military history') demonstrates the ubiquity of Orange lodges in the armed services of the Crown, often in defiance of military regulations, and the importance of militarism in the minds and memories of Orangemen ever since 1795.[2] Military service, whether against foreign powers or domestic rebels, offered powerful evidence of the Order's loyalty to the Crown (as distinct from government) and its ability to mobilise thousands of Protestants in practical support of 'law and order'. Chapter 3 ('The Orange Order and the border') examines the diminishing appeal of Orangeism in southern counties and the Order's

---

[1] Variants of the essays on Orangeism (Chapters 2–5) previously appeared respectively in the *Irish Sword*, xxii, no. 89 (2001), 268–80; *Irish Historical Studies*, xxxiii, no. 129 (2002), 52–67; *Review of English Studies*, lxiv, no. 263 (2012), 127–44; and *Bulletin of the MHSIA*, xvii (2012), 5–38. I am indebted to those who discussed preliminary presentations to the Military History Society of Ireland, Dublin (13 Oct. 2000), the Belfast Natural History and Philosophical Society (8 Feb. 2001), a conference on 'Living with the Border, 1922–5', Ulster Museum, Belfast (7–8 Nov. 2000), the Cambridge Group for Irish Studies, Magdalene College, Cambridge (1 Mar. 2011), and the Methodist History Society of Ireland Edgehill College, Belfast (14 Oct. 2011).

[2] In the twelve years since my findings were published, my research on military Orangeism has multiplied. Whereas most other chapters have been fairly lightly revised, I have here incorporated a statistical analysis of the Orange Yeomanry, a detailed account of one of the military lodges established during the Great War, and reference to some additional studies of the topic.

response to partition, which called into question the very nature of 'loyalty' for an Orangeman who chose to remain in southern Ireland after 1922. Chapter 4 ('The gardener and the stable boy') analyses the concealed impact of a partly Orange background on the lives and writings of two great Irish poets, W. B. Yeats and Louis MacNeice. Though neither joined the Order, both carried traces of Orangeism to their graves, detectable not only in Yeats's anti-Catholic rhetoric and glorification of violence, but also in MacNeice's latter-day nostalgia for the sober verities of his childhood in Belfast and Carrickfergus. Chapter 5 ('Methodism and the Orange Order') documents the importance of religion in the lives of brethren, concentrating on the little-known but deepening involvement of Methodist ministers in the Order as it diversified from its primarily Episcopalian origins. Orange lodges were not just convivial clubs with submerged political and economic functions, but sites for popular evangelisation and moral improvement. Even liberal clergy, for whom the battle with Rome was secondary to spreading the gospel among the indifferent masses, often chose to become Orange chaplains.

Part II comprises two unpublished studies of the Ulster Covenant, occasioned by centennial conferences held in Armagh and London in 2012.[3] These originated in my biographical pursuit of MacNeice's remarkable rector-father (at once a loyalist, an Orangeman, an evangelical, a reconciler, and a conspicuous non-Covenanter).[4] Chapter 6 ('Ulster's Covenanters') examines the rationale for Ulster Protestant resistance to Home Rule in 1912, based on the hope that some sort of Protestant ascendancy could be restored in part of the island as a reward for abandoning the 'South and West of Ireland' to Rome Rule. Particular attention is paid to both positive and negative responses by Protestant clergymen, in a period of evangelical revival and religious optimism facilitated by church disestablishment. No episode did more to unify the disparate Protestant communities and classes of Ulster, and more to divide Ulster Protestants from their southern brethren, than Carson's campaign in 1912. Even those who disapproved in principle of the Covenant, with its implicit threat of violence, were awed by the communal solidarity and social cohesion that it temporarily inspired. Chapter 7 ('Ulster's non-Covenanters') shows how hazardous it was for clergymen to oppose or stand apart from the popular will, and how courageously a few men like Frederick MacNeice confronted that challenge.

---

[3] Covenant conferences at the Robinson Library, Armagh, 28 Apr. 2012 (Church of Ireland Historical Society) and King's College, London, 7 Sept. 2012 (Irish Historians in Britain).
[4] David Fitzpatrick, 'Solitary and Wild': Frederick MacNeice and the Salvation of Ireland (Dublin, Lilliput Press, 2012).

Part III is the outcome of my recent attempt to advance the prolonged and often bitter debate on sectarianism in the Irish revolution.[5] Chapter 8 ('Protestant depopulation and the Irish revolution') reassesses the factors leading to the reduction by one-third of southern Ireland's Protestant population between 1911 and 1926, using fresh evidence from Methodist records to demonstrate the limited impact of forced emigration. This demographic study is complemented by Chapter 9 ('The spectre of "ethnic cleansing" in revolutionary Ireland'), which examines in minute human detail the impact of the revolution on the lives of Methodists in West Cork. It illustrates the resilience of southern Protestant communities when attacked, their refusal to succumb to campaigns sometimes categorised as 'ethnic cleansing', and the process by which these communities regrouped and rebuilt themselves within the Irish Free State. Since its first publication in 2013, this chapter has been enriched by access to some captivating intelligence files.

Together, the essays in this book offer a fresh perspective on what I have termed 'descendancy'.[6] By this I mean the states of mind engendered by shared awareness of the declining power and influence of a past ascendancy that was in many respects imaginary. 'Descendancy' also connotes descent from a common stock, conferring entitlements that seemed perpetually under threat. Most studies of Irish history since the 1790s have focused on the processes by which ascendancy was dismantled and a new governing élite created. My concern here is with the attitudes and strategies adopted by the eventual losers rather than the victors. In doing so, I have tried to avoid either apologetics or sentimentality when probing the psychology of those undergoing 'descendancy'. Rather than dimly illuminating 'the twilight of the Ascendancy', the decline of the 'big house', or Yeatsian fantasies of 'Anglo-Irish solitude', I concentrate on Protestant democracy as practised in fraternities, church congregations, and isolated sub-communities. At a period when more Irish people than ever before are trying to understand and reimagine 'the other side', I hope this book will help readers to think more dispassionately about alternative meanings

---

[5] See Trinity History Workshop, *Terror in Ireland, 1916–1923*, ed. David Fitzpatrick (Dublin, Lilliput Press, 2012); David Fitzpatrick, 'Ethnic Cleansing, Ethical Smearing and Irish Historians', *History*, xcviii, no. 329 (2013), 136–45. Variants of Chapters 8 and 9 appeared in *Irish Historical Studies*, xxxviii, no. 152 (2013), 643–70, and *Bulletin of the MHSIA*, xviii (2013), 5–70. These publications emerged from my Parnell Lecture in Irish Studies, Magdalene College, Cambridge, 11 Feb. 2013, and associated seminars in Hertford College, Oxford, the Institute of English Studies, University of London, and the University of Edinburgh; I am indebted to the organisers and participants for fruitful suggestions and criticisms.

[6] Though rarely used, this label has been appositely applied to the period 1790–1830 by Thomas Bartlett in *Ireland: A History* (Cambridge University Press, 2010), 206–66.

of the word 'Christian'. The voices of the 'descendancy', however strident or muted, deserve to be heard.

II

The notion of a unified 'Protestant community' in Ireland has always been an aspiration rather than a credible representation of reality. Many factors tended to divide those professing some variant of 'reformed' Christianity. The doctrinal and organisational differences between Presbyterians, Methodists, and Episcopalians, and also between competing factions within those general labels, were often no less marked and passionately contested than those between any individual Protestant denomination and the 'Church of Rome'. The resentments engendered by church establishment did not expire with disestablishment, despite the attempt of many bishops and parochial clergy after 1871 to remould their church into an evangelical body appealing rather than dictating to Irish souls. Many nominal Protestants, especially in cities, had little or no connection with any formal religious practice apart from rituals of baptism, marriage, and burial. Distrust and distaste for various aspects of Roman Catholicism was of course an important unifying factor, since these sentiments were the very basis of the Reformation and constantly reinforced in sermons, tracts, and informal exchanges. Yet shared negativity towards a rival and much larger community, if not accompanied by the development of supportive institutions and structures, offered a very shaky foundation for proclaiming the existence of an Irish Protestant community.

Throughout the era of 'descendancy', strenuous attempts were made by Protestant visionaries to create a truly communal basis for anti-Catholicism. Religious revivals, especially that of 1859, transcended denominational boundaries and offered the promise of immediate enlight-enment, for anyone not blinkered by clerical interference with the revela-tion of God's will through the medium of the 'Open Bible'. Shared aversion to nationalism, portrayed as the political incarnation of Catholicism, was deployed by Episcopalian, Presbyterian, and Methodist leaders as a tool for combining and mobilising their followers in a social as well as political movement. Though primary schooling remained predominantly confes-sional, being mainly under clerical management, institutions such as Trinity College, Dublin and a growing range of boarding and secondary schools catered for most varieties of Protestants but relatively few Catholics.

A widening array of societies dominated by laymen (and increasingly women) gave substance to this ecumenical aspiration: temperance cru-sades, youth movements, sporting clubs, self-improvement groups, and especially fraternities. Though the Orange Order was by far the most effective of Irish Protestant fraternities, there were several other 'loyal institutions' more or less closely connected with Orangeism. These included the Royal Arch Purple and Grand Black chapters, confined to active Orangemen and representing something of a moral élite, as well as the Apprentice Boys of Derry and many smaller clubs or networks whose membership was restricted to Protestants. Even the Freemasons (Free and Accepted Masons), despite their non-sectarian doctrine and extensive Catholic membership in Ireland up to the early nineteenth century, became almost exclusively Protestant as a result of papal and clerical condemnation. Such organisations provided practical opportunities for hundreds of thousands of male Protestants of many creeds to act and socialise together. For many participants, these fraternal activities were more important than attachment to any particular church.

Yet Protestant communalism remained amorphous and undisciplined by comparison with its Catholic counterpart, in which a much larger proportion of nominal adherents was prepared to adhere to a common discipline and direction, justified by doctrine and implemented by an increasingly cohesive parochial network. The Catholic Church in Ireland was by no means the fearsome monolith portrayed by its adversaries, being riven by episcopal, factional, and local disputes and fragmented by endemic tensions between prelates and pastors, parish priests and curates, secular and regular clergy, and lay and clerical leaders. Nevertheless, the Catholic Church proved far more effective than any Protestant agencies in applying communal discipline. Such was its power that most children of 'mixed' marriages (when tolerated) were brought up as Catholics, while 'perverts' to Protestantism faced social ostracism condoned and often led by priests. Even most of the supposedly non-denominational 'national' schools became in practice Catholic schools funded by the state, yet managed by priests, with Catholic teachers and Catholic religious instruction (delivered outside normal school hours). The very success of the clergy and hierarchy in insulating the Catholic community from contamination had the unintended side-effect of strengthening pan-Protestant communal bonds. But for the spectacular tightening of Catholic discipline and expansion of Catholic institutional provision in the course of the nineteenth century, the Protestant community would have been even more fractured and ineffectual.

The rhetorical insistence of both religious parties on the need to patrol and fortify intercommunal boundaries papered over an obvious subtext: the persistence of intermarriage and therefore 'hybridity' on both sides, the continued if limited availability of non-exclusive schooling, and the existence of non-sectarian societies and clubs. If these transgressions had not continued, there would have been no need for either Catholic or Protestant zealots to ceaselessly condemn and counteract such practices. But the communal exclusivists faced an even more fundamental problem – the extraordinary affinities between the mentality and culture of Irish Catholics and Protestants. However vehemently these affinities were denied by most protagonists, the underlying differences often appeared trivial when viewed by outsiders applying British, European, or American standards. Irish Catholic and Protestant demographic practices alike were remarkable for high marital fertility, low illegitimacy, and heavy emigration. Both communities showed an unusual level of conformity to the prevailing moral code, and a strong sense of mutual obligation within families and neighbourhoods. Communal division was further mitigated by the shared antagonisms of Protestant and Catholic tenant farmers to exploitative landlords, and of workers to ruthless employers. Such shared interests always threatened to break down communal boundaries, necessitating further (increasingly effective) attempts to stifle intercommunal solidarity on class lines. Religious polarisation was not a faithful and timeless reflection of the unbridgeable gulf between two races, nations, or cultures, but a carefully fostered strategy for defending the group interests of two competing but surprisingly similar subpopulations.[7]

III

A central theme of this book is sectarianism, as perceived and practised by Protestants. By 'sectarianism', I mean actions and attitudes calculated to advance the common interests of a 'sect' or religious group, implicitly or explicitly at the expense of rival sects or groups. Though sectarian rhetoric is deeply offensive to educated and liberal-minded readers today, it was ubiquitous in past religious, political, and social discourse. My aim is to treat past rhetoric as a useful signifier of underlying attitudes and interests, to avoid the reductive assumption that all manifestations of sectarianism are abhorrent and irrational, and above all to clarify its functions and why it appealed so widely, even to otherwise liberal minds. This approach should allow some insight into the mentality and hopes of Irish Protestants during the era of 'descendancy', as they struggled to counteract or at least retard the unmistakable decline in Protestant power after the 1790s.

---

[7] Donald Harman Akenson has done more than most to illuminate the underlying affinities of the rival Irish communities, especially in *Small Differences: Irish Catholics and Irish Protestants, 1815–1922: An International Perspective* (Kingston, Ont., McGill-Queen's University Press, 1988); see also David Fitzpatrick, *The Two Irelands, 1912–1939* (Oxford University Press, 1998).

The most obvious attraction of sectarian mobilisation was the promise of preferential access to employment, property, marriage partners, or other desirable goods and services in short supply. There is nothing peculiar to Ireland about combining in groups for such purposes. Yet the incentives for group-based competition were particularly forceful in a perennially sluggish economy characterised by century-long depopulation and notoriously inflexible property and marriage markets. Sectarianism was one of many discriminants encouraging individuals to advance their material interests through collective action. There is no inherent logical difference between choosing locality, occupation, class, political affiliation, or religious profession as the basis for joining a collective enterprise. In each case, participants are motivated not merely by the material benefits of working within a group, but by a sense of entitlement and moral superiority. Those combining under the banners of nationalism or socialism believed they were fighting a righteous as well as an advantageous cause in their struggle against colonialism or capitalism. The righteous generally identified themselves as victims of oppression and discrimination, even when outsiders and opponents took the opposite view.

Of all these categories, religion was probably the most likely to inspire long-term loyalty to the common cause. An individual might change residence, occupation, or political affiliation more or less at will, so that loyalties based on such connections tended to be temporary and reversible. Religion, however, was widely regarded as a bequest of birth and heritage rather than a matter of merely individual choice. Protestants might move fairly freely between reformed denominations but, as already argued, the costs associated with conversion to or from Catholicism were high. In an age when religious faith remained central to self-identification for most Irish people, combinations grounded in religion were more likely to endure. It follows that the incentive to associate on sectarian lines was exceptionally strong, driven by a particularly acute sense of moral superiority. Remarkably, Protestants were no less inclined than Catholics to regard themselves as victims of a ruthless and powerful opponent, despite their reputation as beneficiaries of an ascendancy. From the historian's perspective, Catholic and Protestant combinations might appear as mirror images. For participants, they were contending in a Manichean struggle for the very soul of Ireland.

For convinced Protestants, there was no contradiction between working collectively in the Protestant cause and in the cause of Ireland, Britain, or humanity. Since Protestantism embodied freedom of individual conscience, as against Catholic submission to restrictions imposed by an external spiritual authority, the triumph of Protestantism was essential for human liberation. Once freed from the spiritual 'despotism of a foreign

power', Catholics would likewise be free to make responsible civic decisions, to take full advantage of economic opportunities, and to participate
whole-heartedly in humanity's progress towards a higher state of civili-
sation. Sectarian campaigns could thus be construed as steps towards
general spiritual and material improvement, being ultimately beneficial
to Catholics as well as Protestants. Within the broad Protestant community, collective actions also promised spiritual as well as material benefits.
Collaboration in shared political or economic campaigns enhanced the
sense of moral solidarity among Protestants of all sects, helping each
participant to love his neighbour as himself. Unfortunately, the usual
corollary of enhanced Protestant solidarity was even more acute sectarian
polarisation between Protestants and Catholics.

The assumptions and attitudes underpinning Protestant sectarianism
were remarkably consistent over most of the past two centuries, because
they were grounded in a powerful historical myth. It was widely believed
that Irish Protestants over several centuries had pursued progress and
enlightenment, only to be resisted at every stage by rebellious, priest-
deluded, primitive, and ignorant Catholics. Even today, when Ulster's
industrial revolution and Catholic power in Ireland have long since
accompanied each other into oblivion, the imagination of Orangemen
still dwells upon the mighty *Titanic* and the wiles of the Scarlet Woman.
Episodes of Protestant victory or heroic sacrifice, such as the Battle of the
Boyne or the Battle of the Somme, continue to provide a moral example
and reassurance that virtue can prevail even in unpropitious circumstances. Concentration on an idealised past has made it easier for Protestants
to face an uncertain future with confidence, if also more difficult for them
to respond rationally to changed conditions.

Yet Protestant sectarianism was not impervious to the momentous
transfers of social and political power associated with the dismantling
of landed estates, the growth of a prosperous and self-confident Catholic
middle class, the ever closer identification between nationalism and
Catholicism, and ultimately the partition of Ireland into two more or
less confessional states. As the Catholic community advanced on every
front, aided by significant if intermittent legislative and administrative
reforms, the Protestant sense of victimhood intensified. Irish Catholics
were increasingly viewed as the next ascendancy, deploying the advantages of a close-knit religious community to exclude Protestants not
merely from accustomed privileges, but also from fair access to social
and economic opportunities. This attitude persisted even in Northern
Ireland under Home Rule, when Orange spokesmen regularly com-
plained of official discrimination in favour of Catholics despite the belief
of Catholics that they were mere helots in an 'Orange' state. Today's

sectarian loyalists in Northern Ireland are even more self-pitying and plaintive than their predecessors, reflecting a genuine loss of Protestant (and post-Protestant) power, and alarm at the obvious political, economic, and cultural resurgence of the Catholic (and post-Catholic) community.

Orangeism represented an extreme and alarmingly explicit variety of sectarianism, to which most Irish Protestants have never fully subscribed. Though nationalists routinely equated all manifestations of anti-nationalism and anti-Catholicism with Orangeism, many firm Protestants felt just as strong a revulsion for a fraternity widely blamed for inflaming intercommunal passions, dividing neighbours, and blocking social and economic cooperation. Even many who privately shared the Orangeman's distrust of Rome and 'Romans' objected to public denunciations of their neighbours' religious beliefs and civic values. Few members of the Protestant élite were happy with the implications of trying to develop a sealed and separated Protestant community. Manufacturers, merchants, and traders were typically averse to limiting their markets and customers to co-religionists; most landlords abhorred any attempt to divide their tenantries according to religion, so encouraging communal strife within estates; many magistrates were appalled at any suggestion that Protestant loyalists were above the law. Yet, at moments of crisis, such qualms did not prevent massive mobilisation of all Protestant classes on religious lines. All too easily, the civic virtues of good sense, tolerance, and even-handedness were brushed aside when Rome was perceived to be on the march. Great communal enterprises such as the Ulster Covenant exhilarated even the doubters, giddy with the excitement and novelty of Protestants straining together in a common cause.

These tropes of victimhood and discrimination suggest a vulnerable community, always uncertain that the chosen people and the Protestant citadel could withstand the unending Catholic siege, abetted by increasingly Godless and immoral British politicians. Yet Protestant sectarianism also has a more menacing aspect, arising from phases of communal arrogance and bullish self-confidence. The early Orangemen were shameless in their attempts to assert and maintain the supposed Ascendancy, morale being bolstered by the eventual rout of their United Irish opponents. The manufacturers and merchants of post-Famine Ulster interpreted their economic success as proof of the irresistible benefits of Protestantism. Just as the collective morale of Protestant Ulster was enhanced by the region's spectacular if short-lived economic miracle, so the political solidarity and optimism of southern Catholics was bolstered by undeniable economic and social advance. This coincidence added extra volatility to the crisis of 1912–14, when two supremely self-confident parties came close to collision in a sectarian civil war. To understand Protestant sectarianism, we must take into account the contradictory psychological consequences of experiencing 'descendancy', reflected in wild fluctuations between arrogance and self-doubt.

IV

After the catastrophe of the 1790s, the distinction between Irish political and religious affiliations became ever more blurred. In the aftermath of 1798, the imperative for Protestants to attest their loyalty to the Crown made it dangerous and uncomfortable to advocate republican or radical views, but the Protestant community remained deeply divided over issues of religious, social, and political reform. The effect of O'Connell's campaigns was to diminish Protestant influence among the reformers, and to intensify the identification of nationalism with Catholicism. Despite Protestant domination of the early Home Rule movement, that too became an overwhelmingly Catholic enterprise even under the nominally Protestant leadership of Parnell. Meanwhile, the apparent imminence of Home Rule created a remarkably strong consensus among liberals as well as conservatives, especially in Ulster, that nationhood would entail imposition of a retrogressive régime equally harmful to the religious, social, and economic interests of the Protestant community. The resultant religious polarisation was never complete, and even in 1914 there were far more Protestant nationalists (and Catholic unionists) than is commonly acknowledged.

During the revolutionary period, nationalism was fragmented and then reconstituted on less sectarian principles than those of Devlin's Ancient Order of Hibernians. Yet the new Sinn Féin was not only overwhelmingly Catholic in membership and leadership but also deeply influenced by the Catholic clergy and even by aspects of Catholic doctrine. Especially in Belfast, it proved impossible to avoid sectarian confrontation between 1920 and 1922, in which nationalists and loyalists alike were dragged into an intercommunal conflict demarcated by religious affiliation. Even in southern Ireland, where the small Protestant minority posed no severe threat to the dominant community, there were moments when an ostensibly anti-colonial campaign transmuted into systematic violence against Protestants (often labelled as 'spies' or 'informers'). The predominant response of vulnerable Protestant minorities, as in west Cork, was a combination of short-term panic, communal rebuilding, and eventual acceptance of the legitimacy of the new order despite its faults.

After partition, southern governments of all parties deferred increasingly in moral matters to the episcopacy, confirming the worst fears of Ulster Protestants that the triumph of nationalism would entail something like a theocracy in the Irish Free State. The adoption of 'confessional' politics had few practical implications for individual Protestants, partly because successive governments bent over backwards to display their magnanimity and also to secure much-needed investment of Protestant wealth and expertise. Most southern Protestants who remained at home soon abandoned public exhibitions of their redundant unionism, and a few became actively involved in the various nationalist parties competing for control of the new state. The effect of partition was strikingly different in Northern Ireland, where the equation of religion and politics became sharper than ever. This was reinforced by the exclusion of Catholics from public representation as unionists, as well as the shared belief of all nationalist factions that Northern Ireland was an 'Orange state' governed on rigidly sectarian lines. Many Catholics have always, on economic or social grounds, preferred the retention of Northern Ireland within the United Kingdom; but Northern Ireland offered no political outlet for such views. Likewise, Protestants with nationalist views were often viewed with distrust in 'constitutional' nationalism, though declared Protestant republicans were more conspicuous than overt Catholic loyalists.

This survey suggests that the notorious religious polarisation of Irish politics, far from being an inevitable consequence of tribal or communal solidarity, was mainly the result of Protestant reaction to the increasing identification of nationalism with Catholic values and Catholic leadership. Each new episode of conflict, whether violent or peaceful, reinforced the sectarian alignment of politics despite the qualms of leaders in both camps. Both nationalists and loyalists believed that patriotism required Irishmen and women of all denominations to act as good citizens, disagreeing only about which fatherland or form of government was entitled to claim their allegiance. In principle, neither side could afford to admit that its appeal was limited to one religious community. Yet, in practice, loyalists were more inclined than nationalists to abandon the pursuit of cross-communal support. How should we account for this contrast?

The explanation may lie in the belief of so many Protestants that allegiance to the Crown was an affirmation of 'civil and religious liberty', whereas Catholicism with its rejection of individual conscience tended to subvert liberty. A strong Catholic might readily welcome an advocate of free conscience as a worthy and dutiful citizen of the nation; but an equally strong Protestant would remain wary of loyalty to the Crown as attested by one submitting to a foreign potentate. Certainly, nationalist rhetoric contained far less denunciation of false religious doctrine than its loyalist counterpart, perhaps because nationalist discourse was so deeply indebted to Protestant writers and orators from Henry Grattan and Theobald Wolfe Tone to Thomas Davis, Isaac Butt, and Erskine Childers. For many nationalists, Catholicism signified not so much the post-Tridentine or contemporary church as the entire western Christian tradition, encapsulated in the cult of St Patrick. For loyalists, the Reformation represented a repudiation of past errors just as fundamental as the Glorious Revolution that defined the Orangeman's political creed.

Because Irish loyalism was centred on an abstraction distilled from the distant past, it did not entail submission to the current government or even the prevalent constitution. This concept of 'conditional loyalty', so perplexing for historians as well as contemporaries, left loyalists with considerable room for manoeuvre in practical politics. Loyal subjects of the monarch of Great Britain and Ireland, being Protestant, could adopt many conflicting views. Most advocates of ascendancy opposed the Act of Union and some continued to seek its repeal despite that statute's pretension to permanence. Within a few decades, however, the union was generally accepted as a stronger bulwark against Rome than a restored Irish parliament which might eventually be dominated by Catholics or their liberal allies. As Catholic 'Emancipation' and church disestablishment accelerated the trend towards 'descendancy', a substantial section of the Orange Order contemplated expunging all reference to the union from its constitutions and obligations. Reforms were blamed upon obnoxious governments imposing their 'unconstitutional' innovations on a reluctant but increasingly impotent monarch. Loyalists pinned their hopes not on current governments or living monarchs, but on an idealised conception of the British 'constitution' and monarchy as proclaimed by William III.

Despite a tendency for Irish loyalists to ally themselves with conservative interests rather than the descendants of Williamite Whigs, those confronting 'descendancy' did not universally oppose reform of the franchise, land tenure, or other sites of social inequity. Loyalism, especially as expressed in the Orange Order, was no less affected than nationalism by the pressure to broaden its social base and achieve mass participation in political demonstrations and organisations. In order to mobilise tenant farmers and workers of humble means, populist Orange leaders such as William Johnston of Ballykilbeg did not hesitate to espouse radical causes despite resultant confrontations with the Order's aristocratic leaders. The conversion of many Irish liberals to unionism after 1886 forced the emerging Irish Unionist Party to mitigate its conservative rhetoric, following the example of the equally inclusive Home Rule movement. By concentrating on the constitutional issue, both movements could defuse but not eradicate the social tensions associated with all-embracing populism. Even under Stormont, Craig and his associates did their best to promise all things to all classes, a tendency reinforced by the benefits of applying to Northern Ireland social reforms inspired and indirectly funded by Britain. The attempts of the Orange Order and the Ulster Unionist Party to cater for labour and radical elements of loyalism were never wholly successful, leading to the creation of an Independent Orange Order in 1903 and many unionist splinter groups. Even so, the dominant institutions of loyalism, like nationalism, provided a fairly broad church in matters of social policy and class composition.

Attachment to the union, though seemingly an immutable element of loyalist rhetoric in the century after 1886, was no less conditional than loyalty to the Crown. Many southern loyalists, alarmed by the partitionist implications of Ulster's Solemn League and Covenant and Carson's campaign against Home Rule, found it easier to accept all-Ireland autonomy than a division of authority that was bound, in the absence of 'the North', to leave them even more vulnerable to the Catholic majority. In pursuit of local supremacy, most Ulster unionists were prepared to ditch their southern brethren and subsequently those living in the 'three lost counties', a strategy notably at odds with their long-cherished principle of preserving the United Kingdom intact. Their acceptance of Home Rule for Northern Ireland in 1921 was equally at odds with conventional unionist rhetoric, Home Rule having been fiercely denounced as an innovation bound to unleash further disintegration of the United Kingdom and indeed the empire. Unqualified unionism was useful only so long as it protected the remaining power and security of the 'descendancy': when other constitutional arrangements promised better protection, they were accepted by loyalists with impressive alacrity. More radical options, such as seeking dominion status or even independence for Northern Ireland, were also contemplated by loyalist leaders at times of crisis. Yet the protagonists of all of these strategies continued to describe themselves as 'unionists', just as pragmatic parties in the Irish Free State such as Labour and Fianna Fáil continued to proclaim their adherence to some form of 'republic'. In both cases, the retention of an obsolete label asserted a romantic link with the past more than a hard-headed aspiration for the future.

Like their nationalist adversaries, Irish loyalists were deeply ambivalent in their views about the use of violence, intimidation, and secretive conspiracy in pursuit of their political aims. In both cases, it was commonplace for the same person to veer, according to circumstance, between open, 'constitutional' political activity and the deployment of tactics fundamentally at odds with the Orangeman's obligation to obey and uphold the law. Redmond's respectable if not always sober parliamentary party was mainly composed of former agrarian agitators and secret-society men, whose exotic past only enhanced their authority and electoral appeal. The surviving rebels of 1916 and their revolutionary successors, re-emerging as 'democrats', provided the core leadership for all major political parties in southern Ireland for nearly half a century.

Likewise, the loyalist conspirators and proto-revolutionaries who created the Ulster Covenant and the Ulster Volunteer Force dominated unionist parliamentary politics in Northern Ireland for a similar period. Mainstream loyalism, however, was at most periods more successful than mainstream nationalism in restricting unwanted violent and conspiratorial activity by fringe groups. The greater success of loyalist 'discipline' was partly attributable to the persistent influence of the Orange Order, which long outlasted the Ancient Order of Hibernians as an effective instrument for defusing intracommunal divisions. Another difference was the fact that nationalist rebellions had actually happened, whereas loyalist rebellions had only been threatened. Would-be loyalist paramilitaries could not draw inspiration and hope from the same rich mythology of uprisings and martyrdom that kept the 'republican flame' perpetually flickering, however unpropitious the political conditions for renewed violence. For most of the era of 'descendancy', loyalist violence was a sporadic and largely seasonal phenomenon which seldom threatened to supplant conventional political activity. The relative strength of the republican and loyalist traditions of political violence would be tested in Northern Ireland after 1969. The republicans were always one step ahead.

Part I

Orangeism

2 Orangeism and Irish military history

I

The Loyal Orange Institution, to this day, carries unmistakable traces of the martial culture that gripped and fractured Europe during the revolutionary and 'Napoleonic' wars. Like many fraternities, it adopted and parodied the structures and rituals of army life, reproducing much of its swagger, display, extravagance, and horseplay both within and beyond the lodge-room. On anniversary days such as the celebration of William's victory at the Boyne, first marked by Orange processions on 12 July 1796,[1] the assembled lodges mimicked the military parades that provided such colourful diversion in eighteenth-century garrison towns. From the start, the Orangemen marched in something like military formation, headed by their lodge officers carrying distinctive insignia of rank, and accompanied by flags and bands with fifes and drums. Civilian brethren, initially identifiable only by orange ribands or sprigs of orange lily in their tall hats, were increasingly equipped with brilliant regalia reminiscent of military dress uniform. The martial impression was heightened, in many early processions, by the presence of uniformed Yeomanry or soldiers, military bands, and firearms as well as ceremonial swords. Orange marches, like military parades, were designed not only to intimidate potential rebels, but also to excite and attract well-disposed onlookers. The Twelfth was an occasion for drum-head enlistment as well as a demonstration of strength and cohesion.

Military practice also influenced proceedings in the lodge-room, which until the later nineteenth century was almost invariably in a tavern rather than an Orange or Protestant hall. Curious outsiders were held at bay by tylers, admission being confined to those who knew the secret passwords and signs of 'the system', akin to the responses required of a soldier when challenged by a sentry. The ceremonies of initiation that enlivened lodge

---

[1] [R. M. Sibbett], *Orangeism in Ireland and throughout the Empire, by a Member of the Order*, 2 vols. (London, Thynne, rev. edn. [1939]), vol. i, 331–2.

meetings, particularly in lodges administering the mysterious 'higher degrees', were marked by the crude buffoonery and whiff of sadism associated with similar ordeals in schools and military barracks. Sword-tips pricked the posteriors of blindfolded, half-clad candidates for the 'Royal Arch Purple', projecting them on to a bed of pebbles, or off a Jacob's ladder into a blanket as a prelude to being tossed in the air, and finally dumped on the floor before the throne of the worshipful master. The prayer which closed the lodge also signalled the introduction of whiskey or ale, and dinners on festive nights recreated the atmosphere of the mess with its profusion of loyal toasts, songs, and ribaldry. It is scarcely surprising that the martial public displays and boisterous secret proceedings of Orangeism appealed to many servicemen, particularly to warrant officers and other ranks who would never gain a commission but might well become Purplemen and even worshipful masters. Fraternal parodies of military discipline provided welcome relief from the real thing, without any ostensibly subversive consequences.

The martial ritual of Orangeism was closely modelled on Freemasonry, itself an amalgam of religious, secular, and military elements which had already gained a strong following in the armed services.[2] What distinguished Orangeism from Freemasonry and other convivial fraternities was its practical commitment to the defence of the Protestant Ascendancy in church and state, which for Orangemen was indistinguishable from the pursuit of 'civil and religious liberty'. The language, rhetoric, and civic values of Orangeism were as much a product of the Enlightenment as those of the Freemasons or United Irishmen, yet utterly different in their practical application. Like the French revolutionaries whom they so deplored in other respects, Orangemen considered that those subordinating individual conscience to papal authority had excluded themselves from civil society and threatened its very survival. The Orangeman's 'conditional loyalty' to the monarchy, so long as it remained Protestant, gave his loyal toasts a headier flavour than the more abstract and less sectarian loyalism of contemporary Freemasons. The effect was to strengthen Orangeism's appeal to the threadbare military forces confronting the threats of invasion, sedition, and revolution in Ireland. For many loyal officers and soldiers, the unabashed simplicity of the Order's ideology was even more appealing than its martial ritual and posture. Orangemen viewed themselves as a rock of loyalty in a sea of treachery

---

[2] R. E. Parkinson, *History of the Grand Lodge of Free and Accepted Masons of Ireland*, vol. ii (Dublin, Lodge of Research, 1957), ch. 5; Capt. William Thomas, 'Freemasonry in the British Army', *Journal of the Society for Army Historical Research*, xiv (1935), 24–32.

and duplicity, and in times of crisis this outlook was shared by many servicemen and occasionally also by beleaguered governments.

Certain direct links between early Orangeism and the armed services are already well known. One of the Institution's forerunners, the Loyal and Friendly Society of the Blew and Orange, founded in about 1730 in the King's Own (4th) Regiment of Foot, was the context in which the future monarchs George IV and William IV were reputedly 'made Orangemen'.[3] Several army and Militia officers, having reached the Diamond just too late for the 'battle' of September 1795, are said to have participated in the subsequent meetings that created the first network of Orange lodges in Armagh and Tyrone.[4] The rapid expansion of the Volunteers or 'Yeomanry' in 1798–9 was largely attributable to Castlereagh's decision to exploit the military potential of the Institution by commissioning its leaders to embody Orangemen as a public rather than a private army. Though the Yeomanry was not initially dominated by Orangemen, they were incorporated *en masse* after March 1798 when the foundation of a grand lodge in Dublin gave the Order a much-needed patina of respectability.[5] In addition, as the Order expanded, it enrolled many existing Yeomen who regarded it as a useful tool for 'the Defence of this Kingdom during the present War', the statutory purpose for which the Volunteers had been revived in late 1796.

II

Less familiar is the extent to which Orangeism infiltrated almost every existing branch of the army between 1795 and the Order's nominal dissolution in 1836.[6] Despite the absence of a comprehensive register of lodge warrants, it is possible to assemble a partial but impressive inventory of 'marching' and other military warrants from the surviving registers and

---

[3] 'History of the Loyal and Friendly Society of the "Blew and Orange"', *The Lion and the Rose: The King's Own Royal Lancaster Regimental Gazette*, viii, no. 5 (1913), 365–72; Lt.-Col. J. H. Leslie, 'The Loyal and Friendly Society of the Blew and Orange', *Journal of the Society for Army Historical Research*, vi, no. 26 (1927), 199–214; Edward Rogers, *The Revolution of 1688; and the History of the Orange Associations of England and Ireland, from the Landing of the Prince of Orange* (Armagh, pr. *Armagh Guardian*, 1860), 21: GOLIA.

[4] Those named as initiates by informants of Col. Robert H. Wallace were Capt. Giffard (Dublin Militia), Col. Sheldrake, Capt. Cramp, and Capt. Elson: *The Formation of the Orange Order, 1795–1798*, ed. Cecil Kilpatrick (Belfast, GOLI, 1994), 30.

[5] Allan Blackstock, '"A dangerous species of ally": Orangeism and the Irish Yeomanry', *Irish Historical Studies*, xxx, no. 119 (1997), 393–405; Blackstock, *An Ascendancy Army: The Irish Yeomanry, 1796–1834* (Dublin, Four Courts Press, 1998), esp. chs. 9, 10.

[6] For a brief survey and partial lists of military lodges, see Cecil Kilpatrick and David Cargo, 'The Early Institution and Its Military Connections', in *Battles beyond the Boyne: Orangemen in the Ranks, 1798–2000*, ed. David Hume (Belfast, GOLI, 2005), 6–17.

manuscript minutes of the grand lodge of Ireland, supplemented by evidence presented to the parliamentary inquiries of 1835 which prompted dissolution. The scale of Orange military organisation far exceeded that revealed in 1835; and even the 124 military lodges enumerated after an internal investigation, in 1873, account for scarcely half of the total.[7] My own incomplete survey indicates that at least 267 such lodges had been established or authorised by 1835, of which only a tiny proportion were formed in the Yeomanry.[8] No less than 93 warrants were assigned to Militia regiments, including 24 in British units, 37 in Ulster regiments, and 32 in units originating in the other three Irish provinces. The greatest concentrations of Militia lodges were in Monaghan (11), Armagh (8), Dublin (7), and Fermanagh (6). Orange lodges were formed in at least 26 of the 38 Irish regiments specified in the Act of 1793. Since service in the Militia was a much resented civic duty, with provision for enlistment by ballot, Orange Militiamen were particularly eager to form alliances for mutual protection and surveillance of suspected rebels within the service.

By contrast, only 32 lodges seem to have been created in the multitude of Volunteer (Yeomanry) corps deployed during and after the emergency of 1796–8. These included 13 lodges in British Fencible forces, 6 in other British units ranging from the Duke of York's Highlanders to the Loyal Hampstead Cavalry, and 13 in a miscellany of extempore Irish troops such as Ogle's Royal Wexford Blues, the Beresford Infantry, the Vinegar Hill Rangers, the St Stephen's Green Infantry, the Loyal Dublin Cavalry, and the Baltinglass Yeomanry. In Yeomanry corps instigated and manned by Orangemen, the subsequent creation of an associated Orange lodge would have been superfluous. In the more common case where the officers of a Yeomanry unit joined the Order after receiving their commissions, their introduction to Orangeism was often through the grand lodge or the élite grand master's lodge 176, which provided opportunities for fraternisation among officers from many different corps. Furthermore,

---

[7] Since several warrants were assigned successively to more than one military unit, these 124 lodges bore only 115 separate warrant numbers: William Archer, 'Report on Marching Warrants' (13 Feb. 1873). Unless otherwise stated, all MSS and confidential prints relating to the Orange Order were consulted in GOLIA.

[8] In addition to Archer's list, this inventory is derived from the following sources: GOLI, MSS Minutes of Proceedings, 1798–1819, 1831–6; GOLI Committee, MSS Minutes of Proceedings, 1828–9, 1829–31, 1831–9; GOLI, MSS Registers of Warrants, 1823–4, 1828–9. Military warrants issued by GOLE are listed in *Report from the Select Committee appointed to inquire into the Origin, Nature, Extent and Tendency of Orange Institutions in Great Britain and the Colonies* [Hume Committee], xii–xiv; *Appendix*, 141–4: HCP 1835 (605), xvii, 1. The inventory incorporates warrants granted to servicemen identified by rank, whether or not identified as moveable (marching) warrants. It also includes several warrants without recorded numbers for which approval was granted, as well as lodges with warrant numbers formerly held in other military units (see previous note).

no 'marching warrant' was needed for groups of Volunteers restricted to part-time local service. A few warrants, however, were granted to the permanent sergeants who maintained a skeletal local organisation during the long periods of disembodiment.

Most early marching warrants belonged to the Militia and the emergency forces, which in the virtual absence of the over-stretched regular army were largely responsible for suppressing the rebellion and maintaining what passed for peace thereafter. However, as regular units of infantry and cavalry resumed training and service in Ireland, they too became riddled with Orange lodges. At least 71 lodges were formed in 45 infantry regiments, mostly in the less troubled years after 1815. Several regiments of foot (the 1st, 32nd, 42nd, and 59th) had no less than four lodges apiece. Twenty-six Orange warrants were also assigned to 16 cavalry regiments, about half of the total, with notable concentrations in the 4th, 5th, and 6th Dragoon Guards. Another 35 lodges were created in auxiliary services such as the Royal Artillery (22), Royal Irish Invalids (5), Royal Sappers and Miners (3), and Royal Veterans (2). In short, Orangeism permeated all major branches of the armed services, with the perhaps surprising exception of the Royal Navy. King Neptune was slow to add an orange lily to his crown.

The character and functions of Orange military organisation changed radically as the menace of renewed rebellion faded. Initially, the lodges were a rough but ready source of solidarity for panic-stricken Protestant servicemen, and an engine for generating further enlistment of reliable loyalists. Few senior officers were granted marching warrants, and the early activists were often sergeants with a closer affinity to the rank and file. The majority of those who agreed in March 1798 to construct the first grand lodge of Ireland were NCOs (including nine sergeants), several of the remainder being commissioned officers.[9] The early military lodges were predictably unruly, and even the guarded minutes of the governing body reveal several cases of military behaviour particularly unbecoming an Orangeman. In March 1799 James Maxwell, late ensign in the North Cork Militia, was expelled as 'a notorious Swindler', and his notoriety splashed across 'all the Publick Prints'.[10] Three months later, a Dublin master was reprimanded for trying to establish an impromptu military lodge in a tavern, having 'read the Book of Instructions in a Public tap

---

[9] GOLI, MSS Minutes, 1798–1819, f. 1 (8 Mar. 1798). The participants were a lieutenant-colonel, a major, two captains, a quarter-master sergeant, a sergeant-major, nine sergeants, and only four without specified military title (including William Blacker and Thomas Verner, both of whom commanded Yeomanry corps).

[10] Ibid., f. 65 (5 Mar. 1799): lodge 441.

room to Persons not belonging to the Society and having given the same into the hand of a Soldier not an Orange man'.[11] In March 1801, two members of the Royal Irish Invalids were expelled for 'Dishonesty' and, in the other case, 'on Suspicion of being a Papist, and not proving Himself a Protestant'.[12] Even more than in civilian lodges, military Orangemen were vigilant in exposing dissolute brethren and pretended Protestants who might constitute a fifth column within the loyalist camp.

The enduring problem of indiscipline generated special regulations for military lodges, which after 1800 were formed into regimental districts directly accountable to the grand lodge instead of the largely autonomous county authorities. Successive rule-books published between 1800 and 1824 required regular returns to the grand lodge of the names and ranks of all members of military lodges, and forbade masters to 'make an Orangeman except the Officers, Non Commissioned Officers, and Privates of their respective Regiments'.[13] This attempt to separate military and civilian Orangeism was probably ineffectual, and was successfully challenged at least twice. As a master in the West Yorkshire Regiment of Militia protested, 'his Lodge would in a short time be entirely reduced' if this regulation were to be enforced.[14]

Another factor discouraging military segregation was the expanding function of marching warrants as a source for spreading Orangeism throughout the British Isles and, before long, the Empire. In both England and Scotland, the earliest Orange lodges were formed by servicemen returning from duty in Ireland who had joined military lodges before departure.[15] The simplest mechanism was to enrol British civilians under these marching warrants, though in many cases new civilian warrants were granted to veterans by the Irish grand lodge and later by the English. The appeal of Orangeism was not peculiar to Ireland, and the movement developed autonomously among poor Protestants in the major industrial regions, garrison towns, and ports. Almost a third of all the marching

---

[11] Ibid., ff. 78–9 (12 June 1799): lodge 599. The complainant was deputy master of a military lodge in the Regiment of Invalids (lodge 592): ibid., f. 33.

[12] Ibid., ff. 208–9 (3 Mar. 1801): lodge 592.

[13] *[First] Report from the Select Committee appointed to inquire into the Nature, Character, Extent and Tendency of Orange Lodges, Associations or Societies in Ireland* [Patten Committee], *Appendix*, 2–34: HCP 1835 (377), xv, 1. As revised in 1828 and 1834, the rules omitted all reference to 'regimental lodges'.

[14] Jonathan Hopkinson (lodge 1001), in GOLI, MSS Minutes, f. 184 (1 July 1800). Hopkinson was permitted 'to admit such Persons as He may approve of into the Society', a similar dispensation being given to Sgt P. Henry, Louth Regiment of Militia (lodge 485), on 7 Jan. 1819: ibid., f. 321.

[15] Hereward Senior, *Orangeism in Ireland and Britain, 1795–1836* (London, Routledge, 1966), ch. 8; Elaine McFarland, *Protestants First: Orangeism in Nineteenth-Century Scotland* (Edinburgh University Press, 1990), ch. 4.

warrants in the regular army were assigned by the grand lodge in England,[16] sometimes to units about to depart for service in Canada, New South Wales, India, Malta, Gibraltar, Jamaica, or Barbados. Such lodges in turn spawned Orange organisations throughout the Empire, the influence of soldiers being at least as great as that of emigrants in 'replanting the old Orange tree' (known initially as 'the Tree of Liberty', an outgrowth more commonly associated with the United Irishmen). Exotic stories of the peregrinations and miraculous survival of marching warrants became part of Orange folklore. It was said of one infantry lodge that its members met in a cave in the Crimea, 'and many a time the proceedings have been enlivened by the shrieking shells flying overhead and the rattle of musketry'. The warrant was captured by Turks, who bemusedly handed it to a former member of the Irish Constabulary in the Ambulance Corps, leading to its eventual deposit in the Armagh Orange Hall.[17]

Important though these military lodges were to the spread of Orangeism, it was the Yeomanry which provided the most potent proof of Orange militarism in practice. In the virtual absence of either muster rolls or lodge registers, the best available index of Orange permeation of the Yeomanry is the overlap between the published lists of commissioned officers and the Orange élite. The names of over 900 Orangemen (almost always masters or senior officers) have been extracted from the first grand lodge minute book, embracing all those linkable to a particular lodge and entered between March 1798 and September 1819.[18] The database also includes the members of the élite lodge 176, formed by the first grand master (Thomas Verner).[19] These 1,100 or so names have been checked

---

[16] Of the 142 identified lodges in infantry, cavalry, and auxiliary units, 42 held warrants from GOLE. No less than 11 of the 22 artillery lodges were under English jurisdiction. These English military warrants, however, generally replaced earlier Irish warrants, possibly leading to duplication in the above returns: as a former English DGS observed in 1835: 'most of the lodges formed in the army originated under Irish warrants, and under the Irish Institution; I do not know of any military lodge that originated under an English warrant.' See Hume Committee, *Minutes of Evidence*, 13, q. 276 (evidence of C. E. Chetwode, 13 Aug. 1835).

[17] [William Banks], *The History of the Orange Order* (Toronto, author, [1898]), 29 (lodge 359).

[18] 917 names were extracted from entries in the first GOLI minute book (excluding members of lodges associated with regular or British-based military units, with non-Irish warrants, or without ascertainable location). In addition to two consolidated lists of masters compiled after meetings on 8 March and 18 May 1798 (covering numbers up to 470 and 733 respectively), names were transcribed from signatures of attenders and proceedings of all reported meetings between 8 Mar. 1798 and 2 Sept. 1819. In many cases, names were assigned to lodge numbers or locations by inference from several references.

[19] Lodge 176, Register, 4 June 1797–Nov. 1799: photostats in GOLIA and NLI, MS 5398.

against Yeomanry lists for 1797–9, 1803–5, and 1820. No less than 237 prominent Orangemen may be identified, in most cases with confidence, as Yeomanry officers holding 269 commissions.[20]

A more incisive index of the importance of Orangeism in the Yeomanry is the proportion of Yeomanry officers in each county whose names appear in the Orange database (including, in this case, members of Verner's lodge). The 269 'Orange' commissions account for 8% of the 3,332 officer posts in the Irish establishment on 13 December 1803.[21] This ratio overstates the Orange component in 1803, since some Orange Yeomen had yet to secure a commission or had already relinquished one. However, when applied to the Yeomanry establishment in each Irish county, it provides a useful basis for regional comparison. In Dublin, with 373 Yeomanry officers in 1803, there were no less than 70 Orangemen in the officer cadre (19%). The corresponding ratio was 9% in Ulster, 8% in non-metropolitan Leinster, 4% in Connaught, and 2% in Munster. The regional concentration of Orangemen in the Yeomanry was sharply defined, the highest ratios being recorded in a swathe of religiously 'mixed' counties including Monaghan (26%), Longford (24%), Carlow (19%), Tyrone (14%), Cavan (13%), Wexford (13%), Armagh and Leitrim (12%), and Wicklow (9%). With the exception of Cork (4%), no county to the south and west of the diagonal between Ballina and Waterford exceeded 3%, with equally minor Orange components in Antrim and Londonderry. As an element in the Yeomanry leadership, the influence of Orangemen was highly localised and concentrated in counties with sizeable Protestant minorities or small Protestant majorities. In no county, however, were known Orangemen predominant in the officer cadre.

Since Orangeism had few followers when the Yeomanry was re-established in late 1796, it is not surprising that the great majority of Orange Yeomanry officers were Yeomen before they became Orangemen, rather than Orangemen who had infiltrated the Yeomanry. Since the Yeomanry of 1796 was itself a resuscitation of the Irish Volunteers of 1782, likewise formed to defend the realm against foreign

---

[20] In 183 cases, names and locations within counties are firmly matched, 54 nominal matches being uncertain because of anomalies in address or multiple qualified candidates. Another 29 matches are too tenuous to merit inclusion in my analysis. Of these 237 Orange Yeomen, 69 were associated only with Verner's, 123 with other numbered lodges, 12 with lodges whose numbers can be inferred from other reports, 20 with lodges of known location but not number, and 13 exclusively with higher office at national, county, or district level.

[21] The Yeomanry establishment fluctuated sharply between 1796 and 1820, peaking at 82,682 in Dec. 1803: see county tabulations in Blackstock, *Ascendancy Army*, 117–18 (variant totals for Ireland: 114–16). The establishment was far smaller in 1798–9, but reached similar peaks in 1806 and 1810.

and domestic enemies, it is equally unremarkable (despite the often undeserved radical reputation of the earlier force) that several Orange Yeomanry officers had also served in earlier corps. These included Francis Charles, 1st Earl of Annesley, Jonah Barrington, Henry Vaughan Brooke, and John Giffard. For many Yeomanry officers, there was no patriotic contradiction between upholding the constitution of 1782 and combating sedition by joining a loyal fraternity. In the immediate aftermath of the rebellion, Orange Yeomen found no reason to conceal their dual affiliation which carried no admitted division of allegiance. In May 1799, 'the Masters of the different Lodges in Dublin [were] instructed to desire those Brethren who are yeomen, to wear their proper Colours at the Review' scheduled for the following week.[22] In 1801, the Earl of Annesley, grand master of County Down, looked forward when reviewing his followers on 12 July to observing 'an increase of your Numbers – (Yeomanry in Uniform), steady to support the great cause of our *Origin* with firmness and moderation'.[23]

Soon, however, Orange influence in the Yeomanry became an embarrassment to Dublin Castle as well as an outrage to Catholic opinion. In 1825, Daniel O'Connell denounced the sectarian influence of Orangeism in Tarbert, Co. Kerry, where the Yeomanry was formed by Palatines imported from Co. Limerick. The commanding officer 'was said to have established, an Orange lodge; they played party tunes to church, and that created a very bad feeling among the lower classes, spreading to the upper, in that neighbourhood'.[24] O'Connell, himself a loyal member of the Lawyers' Artillery in 1798 and former grantee of a Masonic warrant in Tralee,[25] was well placed to understand the fraternal appeal exercised upon soldiers by his Orange adversaries. His bitter hostility to Orangeism was crucial in securing its condemnation by successive Whig administrations, and the enforced curtailment of its public activity. Central to the Whig case against Orangeism was the assertion that its influence on both the Yeomanry and the army was malign, being by some insinuations part of a deeper conspiracy to advance the power and possible succession to the

[22] GOLI, MSS Minutes, 1798–1819, f. 73 (7 May 1799).
[23] *BNL*, 2 July 1801. I am grateful to Dr Dominic Bryan of the Institute of Irish Studies, Queen's University of Belfast, for allowing me to consult his collection of photocopied reports relating to processions in that newspaper (1738–1835).
[24] *Minutes of Evidence taken before the Select Committee of the House of Lords, appointed to inquire into the State of Ireland*, 142 (evidence of Daniel O'Connell, 9 Mar. 1825): HCP 1825 (181), ix, 1.
[25] Warrant 886 was granted to O'Connell on 5 June 1800, being cancelled on 6 July 1815: John H. Lepper and Philip Crossle, *History of the Grand Lodge of Free and Accepted Masons of Ireland*, vol. i (Dublin, Lodge of Research, 1925), 311; Philip Crossle, *Irish Masonic Records* ([Dublin], GLI, 1973), 146.

Throne of the Duke of Cumberland, for some years its titular grand master (when also Chancellor of the University of Dublin).

III

Even if the Orange Institution had no ulterior design to manipulate the army for political purposes, its continuing infiltration of the forces posed an obvious challenge to military discipline. Individual officers sometimes took draconian action against military lodges, as in December 1799 when an officer and guard of the 24th Light Dragoons, 'with fixed Bayonets, entered the Room, put the Officers of the Lodge in Confinement, and carried off the Lodge Chest'. After two senior officers in the grand lodge had spoken to Captain Purdon, the unit's 'popish' commanding officer, it was agreed to release the Orangemen and their chest after the master had apologised and promised 'not to hold a Lodge for a short time'. Eight months later, the chest was still in the custody of the Chamberlain in Barrack Street, Dublin.[26] At Chelmsford army base in Essex, Irish Protestant trainees were forbidden to meet in lodge or wear Orange colours; and various English military lodges continued to meet after 1811, despite attempts to suppress them by the grand secretary as well as by army commanders.[27]

By 1823, the campaign against Orange influence in the Yeomanry was powerful enough to induce the Lord Lieutenant to direct that 'every means will be used' to prevent members of the Yeomanry corps from 'appearing either in uniform or with arms, on the 12th July', and from performing party tunes. In Belfast, this order was put into effect by the 2nd Marquess of Donegal as Governor, who himself seized a drummer boy carrying a regimental instrument, and incarcerated the offending object in the Nelson Club.[28] Such strictures reflected the prominent part taken by Yeomen in the disturbances that so often followed the processions, particularly in Belfast, where rioting and shooting commonly disturbed the evening as Orangemen and their opponents drank themselves to a frenzy of conflicting allegiances. In 1831, a concerted effort was made to identify and dismiss Yeomen participating in Orange processions, provoking a storm of Orange outrage without any concerted response from a nervous grand lodge.[29] The partial elimination of Orange influence was soon

---

[26] GOLI, MSS Minutes, ff. 124–5 (3–4 Dec. 1799); f. 185 (1 July 1800): lodge 1000.
[27] M. E. Phelan, 'Early Orange Societies in England, 1798–1836' (typescript, *c*.1990s): GOLIA.
[28] *BNL* (15 July 1823).
[29] GOLI, MSS Minutes, 1831–6, ff. 11–13 (11 Feb. 1831); GOLI Committee, MSS Minutes, 1829–31, ff. 239, 241–3, 249–50 (4, 9 Aug., 22 Sept. 1831).

followed by the decline and disembodiment of the Irish Yeomanry, leaving Orangemen to engross themselves in the Militia, by then also in
practice a force of local volunteers but with a large Catholic component.
Meanwhile, servicemen were welcomed and fêted by many civilian
lodges, such as the Trinity College district lodge, which in February
1831 exempted 'all officers on actual service, in his Majesty's army and
navy', from the usual guinea for admission and annual subscription of 10s.
6d.[30] Secure from prying eyes, servicemen on leave could help themselves
to the comforts of fraternity.

During the century after 1822, a succession of orders and regulations
was directed against the formation of Orange lodges or political meetings
in the army. These mostly seem to have been dead letters, though a
directive from the Horse Guards in 1829 required all regimental com-
mands to identify and suppress extant lodges. Investigating officers were
to reassure the men that this action 'has become necessary on military
grounds, and that they will not be exposed to any reflection or disgrace, on
account of being Orangemen'.[31] Though later claiming ignorance of such
'private and confidential communications', the grand lodge committee
was well aware of the prohibition of military lodges and devised various
strategies of evasion. In 1832 two new warrants were granted free of
expense to the 64th Regiment, those 'under which they hitherto met
having been destroyed by order of the Commanding Officer'.[32] When
faced with possible suppression in 1835, the Irish grand secretary and
treasurer undertook that no warrant bearing their signatures 'shall ever be
applied to the purpose of forming Orange lodges either in Regiments or in
the Police'.[33] Though outraged by the charge that Orangemen were
'dangerous tamperers with the fidelity of the soldier', let alone the insin-
uation that they desired 'to alter the succession' (a thing 'too ridiculous for
sober examination'), the grand lodge agreed to open its books and registers to parliamentary scrutiny while obscuring the scale of its military
enterprise.[34] Few marching warrants were exposed apart from those of
42 lodges subordinate to the English grand lodge. In return for this
profession of transparency, the Irish leadership tried to induce the
adjutant-general in Dublin to return all military warrants hitherto 'delivered up to Commanding Officers, otherwise the Grand Lodge cannot be

---

[30] Trinity College District Lodge, MSS Minutes of Proceedings,1830–9 (15 Feb. 1831).
[31] Circular letters from adjutant-general, Horse Guards, 1 July 1822, 14 Nov. 1829, in
Patten Committee, *Second Report*, *Minutes of Evidence*, 12, q. 13 (evidence of Maj.-Gen.
Sir John Macdonald, 6 Aug. 1835): HCP 1835 (475), xv, 501.
[32] GOLI Committee, MSS Minutes, 1831–9, ff. 21, 33 (23 Feb., 11 Apr. 1832).
[33] Ibid. (12 Aug. 1835).
[34] Grand secretary's report, in GOLI, MSS Minutes (18 Nov. 1835).

responsible for the holders of its warrants'.[35] This bold attempt to save parchment seems to have come to nothing.

The continuing prohibition under the *Queen's Regulations* of attendance at political meetings, and of 'attending countenancing instituting or being connected with Orange lodges' (1844 edition), did not deter the grant of a marching warrant as late as in 1849, when a battalion of the 14th Foot was setting out for Jamaica.[36] During the 1850s, it was repeatedly claimed that the attendance of Militia officers at the grand lodge was gravely affected by these restrictions, and various committees were appointed to draft resolutions of protest or send influential deputations to the commander-in-chief. None of these protests was put into effect, the leadership preferring to await the expected disembodiment of the Militia rather than to invite renewed scrutiny of its continuing military involvement.[37]

In order to evade detection through the printed county reports and central registers, most lodges with military brethren were now headed by civilians and submerged within the general pyramid of county and district organisations. In 1864, the Loyal Schomberg lodge in Limerick, though dominated by 'young men in business', included six army sergeants. The district master reported that these were

all good and devoted men, but Since our commemoration of the Marriage of the Princess of Wales last year these noble fellows have been unable to attend with the rigid punctuality which had previously marked them. A papist Quarter Master named Burke, an upstart from the Ranks watched our poor fellows and reported them all to the adjutant.

Arrest would have followed but for the intervention of a colonel whose wife was from Armagh, 'to which circumstance I have no doubt our brethren owe their Escape'.[38]

The abandonment of marching warrants, and the scarcity of membership returns, make it unfeasible to estimate the prevalence of Orangeism in the later Victorian army. In 1873, however, the numbers of 30 former marching warrants were still listed in Irish county returns, exclusively in Ulster.[39] In the following year, the grand lodge declined to issue a

---

[35] GOLI Committee, MSS Minutes (13 Jan. 1836).
[36] Archer, 'Report of Marching Warrants' (lodge 1594). The *Queen's Regulations* for 1844 were quoted and discussed in GOLI, MSS Minutes, 1848–58 (9 Jan. 1856). This discussion, like those cited in the next two notes, was excluded from the reports printed for the brethren.
[37] Ibid. (9 Jan. 1856, 28–9 May 1856); GOLI Committee, MSS Minutes, 1853–62 (27 Nov. 1855, 27 May 1856, 26 May, 27 Aug. 1857, 21 Sept. 1858).
[38] GOLI, MSS Minutes (11–12 May 1864): lodge 1080.
[39] Of these lodges, six had not been 'working' for several years: Archer, further 'Report on Marching Warrants' (25 June 1873).

warrant to a brother in the 28th Regiment, stationed in Malta, 'stating that it would be irregular and improper to grant a Warrant to a person in military service'. Instead, 'the application could be complied with by issuing the Warrant to a civilian'.[40] Despite all impediments, as the well-informed *Belfast Weekly News* reported in 1899, military Orangeism remained robust and resistant to curtailment, except within Ireland:

It is a curious thing that while there are several military lodges in England, and quite a number in India, China, and the colonies, there is not a single one working in Ireland just now ... Of course, it is not strictly within the Queen's regulations, but some commanding officers of Irish regiments rather liked it. At the present moment there are at the least 5,000 Orangemen, including many officers, in the British army.[41]

By the end of the century, the army seems to have dropped its specific prohibition of Orange lodges, while forbidding attendance at political meetings for those serving in the regular army, the Volunteers, and the Yeomanry Cavalry. King's Regulation 451 (1908) stated that 'an officer or soldier is forbidden to institute, or take part in, any meetings, demonstrations, or processions for party or political purposes, in barracks, quarters, camps, or their vicinity. Under no circumstances whatever will he attend such meetings, wherever held, in uniform.'[42] In addition to allowing military involvement in civilian lodges, this regulation might be construed as permitting military lodges on the assumption that Orange meetings and processions had religious or commemorative functions rather than 'political purposes'. No similar regulation seems to have been imposed on officers or ratings in the Royal Navy.[43] KR 1693 further forbade 'the wearing of any unauthorized ornament or emblem', with the exception of 'a sprig of shamrock in their head-dress on St. Patrick's day' in the case

---

[40] GOLI, *HYR* (3–4 June 1874), 7; *Report of the Proceedings of the County Down Grand Orange Lodge, at General Meetings* (1 May 1874), 6.

[41] *BWN*, 28 Jan. 1899. This weekly offshoot of the *BNL* also served as the main forum for lodge reports and Orange news for both Ireland and Scotland.

[42] Revised editions of the *Queen's* (later *King's*) *Regulations and Orders for the Army*, with variant wording and numbering, were issued every few years by the War Office, separate series being published for the army, the Militia, Yeomanry Cavalry and other auxiliary forces, and the navy. The bewildering range of military regulations is best mastered through the periodic *General Index to the Army Regulations and Instructions* (covering, in 1901, no less than 52 sets of rules).

[43] The only political instruction in *The Queen's Regulations and Admiralty Instructions for the Government of His Majesty's Naval Service* (1893 edn.) was QR 443: 'In all dealings with foreigners, Naval Officers are to show an example of moderation and courtesy. They are to preserve a strict neutrality in all cases of civil dissensions, and are not to interfere directly or indirectly in any political questions which may be in agitation.'

of Irish soldiers. Though later extended to embrace roses, thistles, leeks, and poppies, the list of approved flora never embraced the orange lily.[44]

IV

The military appeal of Orangeism, and the impracticability of suppressing it, were demonstrated anew during the Great War.[45] The immediate response of the grand secretary in England was to propose formation of 'a special Orange Battalion', but this was soon rendered redundant by the creation of the 36th (Ulster) Division.[46] The Irish institution worked hard to promote enlistment, and grand lodge officers commanded at least two of the division's six reserve battalions.[47] Since the Ulster Division was raised from the Ulster Volunteer Force, itself largely an offshoot of the provincial grand lodge of Ulster, it is scarcely surprising that Orange lodges were formed in almost every infantry battalion before departure for the front. Most warrants were granted by Louis Ewart (the English grand secretary) during training at Seaford camp in Sussex, but some battalions had already acquired Irish warrants in Antrim or Down. With a few exceptions such as the Inniskilling True Blues (in the 11th Royal Inniskilling Fusiliers), the Ulster Division's lodges retained the titles of the UVF units from which they had sprung.[48]

The creation of the first five lodges on 29 July 1915 was perfectly open, involving the presentation of 19,000 'beautifully bound' New Testaments, tea for all at the Seaford Church Institute, and mass initiations continuing till midnight. The grand secretary proudly declared that the hierarchy of the lodges mimicked that of the army: 'he was pleased to

---

[44] The *King's Regulations* for 1928 specified these floral emblems (KR 947), but no longer prohibited participation in political meetings. Instead, servicemen were forbidden to stand for various parliaments or actively campaign for political organisations or parties (KR 517).

[45] For a recent study, dubiously alleging that 'well over 100,000 Orangemen fought in the First World War', see Jack Greenald, 'In the Forefront of Duty: Orangemen in World War One', in *Battles beyond the Boyne*, 26–44 (26).

[46] *Orange Standard* (Birmingham), i, no. 9 (Sept. 1914), 131. This invaluable journal was edited by the Revd Louis A. Ewart, GS, GOLE.

[47] In December 1915, all lodges in Antrim were asked to urge 'eligible young Protestant Ulstermen, whether members of the Institution or not', to join the 20th Royal Irish Rifles, a reserve battalion then being raised by Lieut.-Col. T. V. P. McCammon, DGM, Down: printed circular, GOLIA. McCammon and his men contributed enthusiastically to the suppression of the 1916 rebellion.

[48] The printed reports of the GOLs of England, Antrim and Down indicate that eight lodges were granted English warrants (lodges 862–865, 868–871), three others receiving Irish warrants (lodges 881, 1113, Antrim; 1501, Down). No English warrant has been traced for the 9th Royal Irish Rifles (Armagh, Monaghan and Cavan Volunteers), or the 10th Royal Inniskilling Fusiliers (Derry Volunteers).

say that all the lodge officers were officers in the Ulster Division'.[49] The last four such lodges were opened 'for the duration of the war' in September 1915, and the *Orange Standard* trumpeted that a major, three captains, five lieutenants, and one sergeant-major had joined the East Belfast Volunteers lodge 862 (8th Royal Irish Rifles) at a special meeting in the cinema hall.[50] The *Standard* carried enigmatic reports of lodge meetings at unusual sites somewhere at the Front. The lodge-room of the Young Citizen Volunteers lodge 871 (14th Royal Irish Rifles) 'was a little attic in a very much battered house, and the usual regalia was absent'.[51] The last meeting in March 1919 of The Chosen Few lodge 882 (110th Field Ambulance) was held in the college of Notre Dame at Mouscron in western Flanders.[52] Where fitter, than a Jesuit college, for an Orangeman to be raised to the Purple?

With rare exceptions, the proceedings of these lodges remain obscure, though participation in Orange ceremonies clearly reinforced the solidarity of Protestant soldiers and perhaps helped mitigate the demoralising effects of 'wastage', and 'dilution' of the Ulster Division with British reinforcements. On 30 June 1918, however, lodge 862 was reported to have organised a service, 'somewhere in Flanders', to commemorate the first appalling day of battle at the Somme. In addition to senior visiting Orangemen and politicians, 'a large number of those at the service took part in the famous charge'. The *Orange Standard* referred to several resolutions passed by the lodge in support of Carson, condemning attempts at a 'premature peace', demanding that the government 'immediately enforce conscription in Ireland', and sending home good wishes 'for the coming Twelfth'.[53] These resolutions came to the attention of the assistant adjutant-general at 2nd Army Headquarters, who enquired 'whether such a meeting was held, and if so, whether permission was granted for it and if so by whom. If permission was not granted it should be ascertained who was responsible for organising the meeting', and 'what action' should be taken against the organisers.[54] Despite KR 451, the lodge survived and flourished, reaching 250 members before demobilisation, being reorganised in the Rhineland in 1919, and reconstituted after demobilisation as the 36th (Ulster) Division Memorial lodge 977.[55]

[49] *OS*, ii, no. 21 (Sept. 1915), 135, 142.   [50] *OS*, ii, no. 23 (Nov. 1915), 165–6.

[51] *OS*, ii, no. 24 (Dec. 1915), 185.   [52] *OS*, vi, no. 65 (May 1919), 62.

[53] *OS*, v, no. 56 (Aug. 1918), 126–7.

[54] Minute, 19 July 1918 (AG/2092/PS): copy kindly made available by Mr Derek Parkhill.

[55] *OS*, vi, no. 62 (Feb. 1919), 25; vi, no. 68 (Aug. 1919), 101; vii, no. 73 (Jan. 1920), 9. Of 252 members on the roll in March 1918, 112 had been initiated over the previous year, and 116 'belong to Belfast, including 80 new members with no home lodge': ibid., vi, no.

Even today, that lodge remains a focus for Orange commemoration of the Somme on 1 July, having responsibility for an unostentatious but moving ceremony of wreath-laying at Belfast's cenotaph.

The survival of a minute book for lodge 871, covering October 1915 to March 1917, allows insight into the membership and workings of Orangeism in the Ulster Division. The Young Citizen Volunteers, originally an apolitical youth organisation catering mainly for the Belfast middle classes, had long since been sucked into the UVF, the propaganda campaign against Home Rule, and the recruiting drive for the Ulster Division.[56] A consolidated but undated list names 133 members, of whom only five were marked 'killed' and one 'wounded'. The minutes for meetings held in late 1915, during the first phase of training in France, record the ranks of 32 candidates for membership, of whom five were NCOs and the remainder privates. The intake was transformed when meetings resumed a month after the 14th Royal Irish Rifles had been blooded at the Somme: of 39 candidates, 7 were captains or lieutenants, 18 NCOs, and only 14 privates.[57]

Following its first and only meeting in England at the cinema house in Bramshott camp in Hampshire, the lodge followed the battalion from billet to billet in France and Belgium, including Pernois, Ailly-le-Haut-Clocher, Ploegsteert, Romain, St Yves, and Méteren. At its second meeting, the lodge resolved to meet on the Sabbath (unthinkable for a civilian Orangeman) and to order rituals and ribbon for regalia; the lodge had already received 'warrant and bibles for the brethren' from Louis Ewart. To the amusement of brethren, protocol was flouted in December when Thomas Murphy presided over his own election as worshipful master. It was agreed with 'enthusiasm' that the next meeting should be held, if possible, in the cinema hall, to be followed by a 'social evening'. When reconvening in Ploegsteert on 3 August, the lodge resolved to 'reaffirm their loyalty to the crown'. Brethren were clearly worried about the impact of catastrophic recent losses: 'The question of supplies of Officers & men sent out to make up the Ulster division was discussed.' Another meeting considered 'the subject of recruiting in Ulster', after Lieut. W. H. Mayes had offered 'a very elaborate report of how things were at Home in Belfast, & also the way that our wounded were being treated when they were fit for service'. At a social evening a few nights later, glasses were

---

63 (Mar. 1919), 38. An annotated photograph of a banner marked 'LOL Military 862' indicates that this warrant was later granted to a lodge formed before March 1939 at Rawalpindi in north Bengal: GOLIA.

[56] Timothy Bowman, *Carson's Army: The Ulster Volunteer Force, 1910–22* (Manchester University Press, 2007), 25–32.Bowman does not discuss the Orange lodges formed in association with the YCV or other battalions derived from the UVF.

[57] YCV, lodge 871 (GLE), Minutes, 26 Sept. 1915–16 Mar. 1917.

raised to 'The King Institution Visitors Fallen Brethern [*sic*] & the C.O, Officers, also the old Officers of the Battalion & Col [R. Spencer] Chichester' (who had raised the YCV in 1912).[58] Afterwards, songs or recitations were delivered by three officers, three NCOs, and four privates, whose names as usual were recorded in descending order of rank. At the last recorded meeting, the monthly subscription was fixed at only one franc. Despite this egalitarian gesture, the dominance of commissioned and non-commissioned officers as lodge officers, speakers, and singers suggests that lodge 871 mirrored external hierarchies rather than subverting them. Likewise, after meetings of the Inniskilling True Blues lodge 870 in the 11th Royal Inniskilling Fusiliers, officers not belonging to the lodge were invited to join the brethren for the 'social hour'. The visitors included Cyril Falls, an officer in the Ulster Division and its first historian.[59] Orange democracy had its limits, reinforced by unavoidable submission to the authoritarian machinery of war.

The Ulster Division was not the only centre of military Orangeism during the Great War. Dozens of other military and naval lodges warranted by the grand lodge of England were active between 1914 and 1920, 'the queerest place that any of the lodges met' being Siberia.[60] Many of these lodges catered for the Canadian or Australasian contingents, reflecting the success of Orangeism in harnessing Protestant working-class passions throughout the Dominions. In January 1915, 'a huge Orange Lodge' was formed on Salisbury Plain for the Canadians, who were treated to grim reminders of 'Rome's hand in the war' from the English grand secretary, speaking in a 'dimly lighted tent'.[61] Candidates for an Australian military lodge in France and Belgium 'were initiated in woods, gardens, between eight haystacks, and in a judge's court-room'.[62] It was even revealed that 'the Orange tree has been planted in Egypt by our New Zealand brethren', meeting in a tent, who subsequently 'decided to advertise in the "Egyptian Mail", inviting all Orangemen in Egypt to

---

[58] Bowman, *Carson's Army*, 29.

[59] W. J. Canning, *Ballyshannon, Belcoo, Bertincourt: The History of the 11th Battalion The Royal Inniskilling Fusiliers (Donegal and Fermanagh Volunteers) in the First World War* (Antrim, author, 1996), 82; Cyril Falls, *The History of the 36th (Ulster) Division* (London, Constable, 1922).

[60] *OS*, vi, no. 62 (Feb. 1919), 25. Unknown in the earlier nineteenth century, naval as well as military lodges were already working under several English warrants before the outbreak of war. The rather enigmatic official returns suggest that these included lodges 577, 615, 802, 827, and 842 (naval); and 108A, 703, 833, and 839 (military): *Report of the Annual Meeting of the Loyal Orange Institution of England* (July 1914).

[61] *OS*, ii, no. 15 (Mar. 1915), 45 (evidently lodge 859, eloquently entitled the 4th Canadian East Belfast Volunteers).

[62] *OS*, vi, no. 64 (Apr. 1919), 51 (Victoria lodge 234).

give their names to the Secretary. The aim is to get all Orangemen in the Australasian contingent acquainted with one another.'[63] In every theatre, Orangeism contributed to the cultivation of mateship which helped make war bearable.

For many Orangemen of all nationalities, the Twelfth remained a festival even at the front and in spite of the King's Regulations. In 1915, when the Ulster Division was still encamped in England, it was reported that 'long before reveille, and just as day was breaking, drums were beating and the flutes and bugles and other instruments resounded through the camp ... Large numbers of them wore Orange colours in their caps throughout the day, which was observed as a general holiday after the morning parade ... In the early evening a great meeting was held, at which some thousands of soldiers were present.'[64] In France on the same day, as a private in the Canadian Army Service Corps wrote to his mother in Belfast:[65]

We all gathered together with a good many Ulstermen to celebrate the anniversary of the battle of the Boyne. The procession started from 'Shrapnel Square' and was headed by an old scout mounted on a white horse with its mane and tail plaited with Orange and purple ribbon. Next came the fife and drums well decorated with orange lilies, and 'No Surrender' was painted on the flag which we carried.

In Gorenflos five months later, on 'Lundy Day', two effigies of Derry's 'traitor' governor were filled with gunpowder and blown up after a procession with a band playing 'Derry Walls' and 'The Boyne Water', the traditional accompaniment of broken windows being achieved by throwing bombs in jam tins into a pond near the village.[66]

No doubt, as the war dragged on and the decencies of life were displaced by the grim struggle for survival, the ceremonial elements of Orangeism fell into disuse. Yet, as an obituary for John Crumlin of lodge 862 observed, there were some who struggled 'to keep Orangeism in the forefront even in the difficult conditions of the battlefield. In the retreat from St. Quentin he wore his Orange regalia and carried in his pack the warrant of an Orange lodge he had formed in the field.' Having lost

---

[63] *OS*, ii, no. 22 (Oct. 1915), 150.   [64] *OS*, ii, no. 20 (Aug. 1915), 120.
[65] *OS*, ii, no. 21 (Sept. 1915), 139 (Private George Kirkwood, Canadian Army Service Corps). Cpl P. G. Parker, 2nd Battalion, Transport Section, 1st Brigade, Canadian Contingent, also observed the inscription 'No Surrender', along with two bagpipes, two side drums, four bugles and four fifes, and identified King William as Pte. James Beattie of Cobourg, Ontario: *OS*, ii, no. 23 (Nov. 1915), 169.
[66] Extract from Diary, 2nd Lieut. Guy Young (18 Dec. 1915), quoted in Timothy Bowman, *Irish Regiments in the Great War: Discipline and Morale* (Manchester University Press, 2003), 28–9.

possession of the precious box containing warrant 862, he had risked his life by returning behind German lines to recover it.[67] By clinging to such symbols of Orange culture, soldiers could to some extent domesticate the harsh environment of camp or trench.[68] There seems no good reason to doubt that many of the structures and rituals of Orangeism were successfully transplanted to the battlefield; or that Orange soldiers were indeed sustained in combat by the belief that the Great War was but the latest round in that great conflict, between good and evil, which William had fought at the Boyne, and which the Yeomanry had pursued with such lack of scruple in 1798.

Despite the importance of the Great War in Orange history and mythology, it is not possible to quantify the military participation of Orangemen. Unlike the Freemasons, the Order in Ireland never compiled a roll of honour based on lodge returns, perhaps in recognition of the notorious reluctance of lodge secretaries to respond to such demands from superior officers. A roll of honour published by the grand lodge of England in 1915 excluded the new military lodges associated with battalions in the 36th (Ulster) Division.[69] A recent attempt to assemble a list of 'Orange casualties' in the 'Somme Campaign' yielded only 189 names, an implausibly tiny fraction of the dreadful losses of the 36th Division and other units with Ulster servicemen.[70] The vast majority of Orange servicemen have so far escaped the net of commemoration.

Even before the Armistice, the feats of Ulstermen at the Somme, in particular, had become part of the Orange tradition of martial commemoration. In later years, in step with the (Royal) British Legion and public protocols of remembrance, the Orange Order incorporated the Second World War and subsequent campaigns in its elaborate panoply of military

[67] Undated newspaper cuttings (c. July 1947) in Evangelical Protestant Society and National Union of Protestants (Belfast), Scrapbooks, i, ff. 17–18: Linen Hall Library, Belfast. A contemporary report confirmed Crumlin's part in maintaining the lodge up to the Armistice, but states that a Br Postlethwaite had custody of all lodge boxes during the retreat from St Quentin, being instructed to soak correspondence in paraffin, and burn it, if threatened with capture: OS, vii, no. 73 (Jan. 1920), 9.
[68] For some revealing personal accounts of Orangeism in the trenches, collected by Robert H. Stewart, see Philip Orr, The Road to the Somme: Men of the Ulster Division Tell Their Story (Belfast, Blackstaff, 1987), 129–31.
[69] GOLE, Report (July 1915), i–xii. The roll of brethren 'serving with His Majesty's Forces on Land and Sea' listed 1,360 men in 150 lodges, only one of which was military (Pride of Armagh lodge 839, associated with the 1st Royal Irish Rifles). Excluding this lodge and three serving naval ports (as well as fourteen names not linked to male private lodges), the roll recorded 992 men in 146 lodges, compared with the estimated total paid-up membership in 1914 of about 8,020 brethren in 328 lodges (excluding women and juveniles).
[70] Jack Greenald, 'The Somme Remembered: A Listing of Orange Casualties in the Somme Campaign', distributed with Battles beyond the Boyne.

banners, lodge-titles, wreath-laying ceremonies, and commemorative publications.[71] The Orange tradition extends far beyond the involvement of Orangemen in the recognised military forces discussed in this chapter. The Orange Institution has been a major force in Ireland's equally colourful paramilitary history, raising informal militias and armed offshoots in response to every major political crisis (1798, 1848, 1867, 1882, 1886, 1893, 1910, 1913, 1921, and beyond). Its members have also participated in hundreds of violent confrontations with their papist adversaries, providing the matter for innumerable ballads in celebration of victories at Dolly's Brae or Scarva. In the Orange recital of Irish military history, no clear distinction is drawn between campaigns undertaken by regular, irregular, and factional forces: all contributed to the defence of civil and religious liberty, the Orangeman's choice of army depending on the fickleness or stalwartness of the incumbent government.

Some hint of the Orangeman's sense of his military tradition is provided by the treasures which various Orange collectors lent to the organisers of Dublin's Grand Orange Bazaar in November 1901, in response to an appeal for relics of William III.[72] Amidst the predictable engravings, coins, medals, lockets, and scraps of royal clothing, collectors offered an old Yeomanry jacket with grenade, horn and spurs; three pikes; a small engraving of Dolly's Brae; a drawing of a grenade designed to repel Fenian assailants in 1867; and a revolver and 'emergency outfit' used in the anti-boycotting campaign of the 1880s. For Orangemen, as for so many Irish nationalists, the most potent symbol of their shared history remains the gun.

---

[71] See David Hume, '"Faithful Sentinels" who Stood for the Cause of Freedom: The Orange Order and the Second World War', and Greg Hopkins, 'Orangemen in Troubled Times, 1920–2000', in *Battles beyond the Boyne*, 45–67, 68–82.

[72] Correspondence and files relating to Grand Orange Bazaar, 1901.

3   The Orange Order and the border

Relief was the dominant response of northern loyalists and Orangemen to the tripartite agreement of November 1925, which confirmed the border as defined in 1920. A year later, when the prime minister visited Newry to preside over the grand lodge of Co. Down, he and 'Lady Craig were made the recipients of very handsome presents from the Loyalists and Orangemen of Newry and District in recognition of valuable services in connection with the settlement of the Boundary question'.[1] The agreement promised to end fourteen years of uncertainty, during which the frontier of loyal Ireland had contracted to a point where it seemed barely defensible. Under relentless pressure from successive governments as well as nationalists, the opponents of Irish self-government had effectively abandoned hope for the three southern provinces in 1911, and for the three Ulster counties with large Catholic majorities in 1916. The survival of the Free State remained in doubt until 1923, and the ludicrously vague terms for the proposed boundary commission created justifiable fear among loyalists that further attempts would be made to cripple the northern state by massive territorial transfers. Craig's great success, apart from stifling the northern civil war in June 1922, was to hold the line of the six counties until Cosgrave's government acknowledged the *fait accompli*.

For loyalists on the wrong side of the border, however, the pragmatic policy adopted by Carson and Craig constituted both a callous betrayal and a repudiation of the very essence of unionism. Accepting Home Rule for six counties seemed a bizarre outcome to the bitter and protracted struggle to avert Home Rule in all 32 counties. It is easy to gloss over the fact that the betrayal occurred in two distinct phases, with very different results for the future of loyalism in the two regions affected. Long before

---

[1] Co. Down CGL, *AR* (11 Nov. 1926), 16: GOLIA. Unless otherwise stated, all cited manuscript and rare printed sources (including the cited reports of CGLs printed for internal circulation) were consulted there.

loyalists of the three 'Lost Counties' raised their moan against the treachery of their fellow-Covenanters of 1912, they themselves had prepared through that very Covenant to abandon the far more vulnerable loyalist minority in Leinster, Munster, and Connaught. The evasive reference in the Covenant to the disastrous consequences of Home Rule for 'the material well-being of Ulster as well as of the whole of Ireland' could not mask the prospective abandonment of the unionist demand outside Ulster.[2] Many southern loyalists began the tortuous process of seeking a practicable alternative to Carson's strategy, whether through coexistence with nationalists, emigration, or 'diehard' resistance.

Until 1916, however, there was no discernible border separating the Covenanters of Cavan, Donegal, and Monaghan from their northern brethren. When Carson visited Newbliss, Co. Monaghan, in August 1913, his audience was swollen by special trains from Fermanagh as well as Cavan and Louth.[3] When he promised early in the Great War to summon the provisional government at its conclusion, he assured his audience that 'their first Act shall be to repeal the Home Rule Bill as regards Ulster', and to enforce that edict through the Ulster Volunteer Force formed in all nine counties.[4] Enrolment in the UVF had been particularly brisk in Cavan and Monaghan, and even in Donegal (with its lingering reputation for cautious liberalism among Protestants) the ratio of recruits to the Protestant population was higher than in Down, Antrim, or Belfast.[5] When the 36th (Ulster) Division was formed on the framework of the UVF, none of its battalions was identified exclusively with the three counties: the 9th Royal Irish Fusiliers incorporated Armagh, Monaghan, and Cavan, while Donegal and Fermanagh Volunteers spawned the 11th Royal Inniskilling Fusiliers.[6]

The absence of an informal boundary within Ulster is scarcely surprising, since the predicament of Protestants outside the north-east of the province differed only in the degree to which they were outnumbered.

[2] See below, Chapter 7.

[3] *Northern Standard*, 9 Aug. 1913, quoted in Peadar Livingstone, *The Monaghan Story: A Documented History of the County Monaghan from the Earliest Times to 1976* (Enniskillen, Clogher Historical Society, 1980), 366–7.

[4] *OS*, i, no. 11 (Nov. 1914), 171.

[5] For police returns of membership of the UVF on 31 May 1914, see *Chief Secretary's Office: Intelligence Notes, 1913–16*, ed. Breandán Mac Giolla Choille (Dublin, Stationery Office, 1966), 100. By comparison with the non-Catholic population recorded in the Census of Ireland for 1911, the percentage in each county belonging to the UVF is as follows: Cavan, 20.5; Tyrone, 16.1; Londonderry, 12.3; Monaghan, 12.1; Armagh, 11.6; Fermanagh, 11.1; Donegal, 9.0; Down, 8.1; Antrim, 7.8; Belfast, 7.6.

[6] Philip Orr, *The Road to the Somme: Men of the Ulster Division Tell Their Story* (Belfast, Blackstaff Press, 1987), 44.

By 1911, Protestants still accounted for over a fifth of the population of the three counties, the proportion being highest in Monaghan and lowest in Cavan. Protestants were likewise a decided minority in Fermanagh, Tyrone, and Londonderry City, only barely outnumbering Catholics in Armagh.[7] The impulse for defensive alliance was found wherever parallel communities existed, and these long-standing divisions knew no border. The most enduring of all Protestant defensive alliances was the Loyal Orange Institution. The rest of this chapter concerns its sometimes unexpected responses to partition, particularly in the three abandoned counties.

The Order's leaders had played a crucial part in shifting the focus of resistance from all Ireland to Ulster, and from Dublin to Belfast. The creation in December 1911 of a provincial grand lodge of Ulster, with plenary but temporary jurisdiction 'during the present Crisis', provided a forum for Orangemen to organise drilling, raise funds for arms, enlist in the UVF, and prepare for a provisional government in Belfast. Formed on the motion of Captain James Craig, its organiser was Colonel Robert H. Wallace of Myra Castle, a Downpatrick solicitor and Boer War hero who already presided over the Belfast grand lodge.[8] Nothing seems to have come of the proposal for a matching grand lodge 'for Dublin and the South of Ireland'.[9] Orangeism soon fell into terminal decline in most southern counties as the futility of conventional unionism outside Ulster became apparent. Three county grand lodges closed between 1913 and 1918 (in King's, Longford, and Cork), and only a handful of lodges remained operative in Sligo and Leitrim after the Great War, which had hastened the decline in membership.[10] Except in parts of Dublin and Wicklow, the Protestant minority was too small and vulnerable to maintain active resistance to Home Rule without support from Ulster. Southern hearts went out of the Orange after Ulster Day.

When Carson accepted the principle of Home Rule for 26 counties in the aftermath of the 1916 rebellion, one might have predicted a similar collapse of Orange enthusiasm in Cavan, Monaghan, and Donegal. In the words of Sir James Stronge of Tynan Abbey, grand master of Ireland, 'the

---

[7] The non-Catholic percentage of the census population of each Ulster county in 1911 was as follows: Cavan, 18.5; Donegal, 21.1; Monaghan, 25.3; Londonderry (Co.), 43.8; Fermanagh, 43.8; Tyrone, 44.6; Armagh, 54.7; Londonderry (Co. Borough), 58.5; Down, 68.4; Belfast (Co. Borough), 75.9; Antrim, 79.5. See also below, Chapter 6.

[8] GOLI, *HYR* (6 Dec. 1911), 26–7.   [9] Ibid., 27.

[10] The decisions to dissolve the grand lodges of King's Co. (Offaly) and Longford were taken on 11 June 1913 and 15 Dec. 1915, and the last returns for Cork and for the Trinity College District Lodge were approved in Dec. 1915 and Dec. 1921 respectively: ibid. On 12 June 1918, the Cork grand lodge had been suspended indefinitely 'on account of war': GOLI, Central Committee, MSS Minutes of Proceedings, 1884–1927.

three counties have been thrown to the wolves with very little compunction'.[11] When the Order's governing body met in Cavan Protestant Hall in June 1916, a tone of weary resignation marked its response:[12]

That while we reiterate our opposition to Home Rule for any part of Ireland, in view of the recent decision of the Ulster Unionist Council, we request our Grand Master to urge upon Sir Edward Carson and the Ulster Members, the necessity of safeguarding by every possible means the interest and property of the Orange Institution and also our Protestant schools from interference by any legislation which may hereafter be introduced by a Home Rule Parliament.

Six months later, the grand lodge sought to 'reassure their Orange Brethren and Loyalists outside Ulster of their fervent desire in every possible manner to protect them and their interests', through 'assistance both moral and physical'. Though deploring the proposed 'dismemberment of Ireland', the grand master's published address held the government responsible while justifying Carson's compromise on the half-loaf principle.[13]

The hypothetical compromise of 1916 became an irreversible concession in March 1920, when a majority of the UUC endorsed Lloyd George's proposals for the Better Government of Ireland through its partition into two states under Home Rule. The Order's leadership refused to countenance protests from Cavan and Monaghan against acceptance of 'the principal [sic] of a six-county Ulster instead of demanding a nine-county Ulster', and against 'their County being placed under the control of a Dublin Parliament'. In response, the grand lodge declined 'to enter into judgement on the action of the Ulster Unionist Council, believing that it was purely a matter for each individual delegate's conscience'.[14]

Its energies were thereafter devoted to defending the six counties against republican invasion or subversion, first by enrolling Orangemen in the new 'Ulster' Special Constabulary (never organised in the three counties);[15] and then by giving practical backing to Craig's unpredictably successful attempt to create a functioning state amidst civil war and

---

[11] Sir James Stronge, Bt, to Hugh de Fellenburg Montgomery, quoted in John Tunney, 'The Marquis, the Reverend, the Grand Master and the Major: Protestant Politics in Donegal, 1868–1933', in *Donegal, History and Society: Interdisciplinary Essays on the History of an Irish County*, ed. William Nolan, Liam Ronayne and Mairead Dunleavy (Dublin, Geography Press, 1995), 690.

[12] GOLI, *HYR* (14 June 1916), 11. This resolution was moved by Michael Knight, grand master of Monaghan.

[13] GOLI, *HYR* (13 Dec. 1916), 32, 44.

[14] GOLI, *HYR* (9 June 1920), 8; Co. Antrim GOL, *AR* (20 May 1920), 8; (17 Nov. 1920), 13.

[15] The grand lodge adopted a resolution from Armagh, calling 'upon all loyal Orangemen to do everything in their power – both by joining up themselves and urging others to do so – to further the new Special Constabulary Scheme': GOLI, *HYR* (15 Dec. 1920), 23.

without whole-hearted British support. Signature of the Treaty in December 1921 only heightened Orange fears of renewed and expanded conflict, and the grand lodge pronounced 'that if an Irish Free State is set up, Loyalists will be compelled to defend their lives and liberties by force – a result most distasteful to them – but Force is the only argument accepted by His Majesty's Government'.[16] Though the location of the expected conflict was unspecified, the Order had no practical strategy for defending loyalists outside the six counties. The shift northwards took tangible form at the end of 1921, when three senior grand officers resigned and headquarters were moved from Dublin to Belfast – just before occupation of the Dublin premises by Irregular forces, who wittily converted Fowler Hall into accommodation for 'Belfast refugees'.[17]

As sectarian violence intensified in the last months of the Anglo–Irish conflict and during the so-called 'Truce' after July 1921, Orangemen were once again invited to defend their liberties by joining a private army. The Orange, Black, and Loyalist Defence Association of Ireland, formed jointly in May 1921 by the two main Protestant fraternities, sought to exploit and control the paramilitary urge already evident in such bodies as the Ulster Imperial Guards and the Lisburn Association.[18] In its first 'confidential' appeal for support on 30 December 1921, the Belfast-based association requested 'that all members of Orange Lodges and Black Preceptories will not only join up themselves, but will use their influence to have every member and loyalist over 17 years of age enrolled ... After enrolment members will be classified, and thoroughly qualified commanders will be appointed so as to get the military position of our Defence Association properly organised.' Its military function was 'to meet any attack which may be made at any moment to drive us out by force from our British citizenship', evidently promising the defence of the border rather than that of the loyalists who dwelt beyond it.[19]

In practice, the association's military contribution was apparently restricted to feeding recruits into the USC.[20] From the outset, it had sought recognition as a unit within the C Special Reserve, a mobile force designed for deployment throughout the six counties in lieu of the

---

[16] GOLI, *HYR* (14 Dec. 1921), 48.

[17] Ibid., 7, 12, 32. For a report on the occupation of this building, see Diarmuid O'Hegarty (secretary, Provisional Government) to Peter Ennis (Chief of Republican Police), *c.* 12 Apr. 1922: NAD, H 5/63.

[18] OBLDA, MSS Minutes of Proceedings, 1921–4, 1924–9, Executive Committee (11 Nov., 2 Dec., 9 Dec. 1921): GOLIA.

[19] Printed circular in GOLI, Central Committee, Minutes (17 Mar. 1922); GOLI, *HYR* (13 Dec. 1922), 28.

[20] Ibid., 28. This report omitted all reference to military organisation, observing enigmatically that 'there may be some doubts as to the objects of this Association'.

army.[21] The association's overtures were warmly received by the Northern government's new military adviser, Major-General Sir Arthur Solly-Flood, when he met the executive committee in June 1922. Explaining that the C Specials were 'composed largely of ex servicemen', Flood appealed for help in 'getting suitable Officers ... and also for men of military age and fitness with experience if possible'.[22] Once the USC had been securely established, the association seems to have relinquished any paramilitary activity. This shadowy organisation is best seen as an auxiliary to the Northern security forces, not as an independent all-Ireland militia. As for the provincial grand lodge of Ulster, it had long since abandoned its attempt to coordinate active resistance throughout the province, though its nameplate was not detached from the wall of Belfast's Old Town Hall until early 1922.[23]

In areas of mixed religion, each community had long been vulnerable to intermittent hostility or violence from the other. This was amply demonstrated during the civil wars on both sides of the border, which anticipated most of the sectarian horrors practised with even greater effect after 1969. During 1922, loyalists were less concerned about the border than about survival, few being free from the fear of murder, arson, and intimidation. The reiterated destruction of centres of Protestant community, such as churches and Protestant, Orange, and Masonic halls, surely reinforced the very fraternal bonds which such outrages were designed to snap. The conflict created another generation of Protestant martyrs such as the six victims of the Altnaveigh massacre in south Armagh.[24] Unlikely new heroes emerged such as Anketell Moutray, the aged grand master of Tyrone, who survived kidnapping by republican forces to return in triumph to the grand lodge of Ireland in June 1922.[25]

---

[21] OBLDA, Minutes, Executive Committee (9 Dec. 1921).

[22] Ibid. (21 June 1922). Solly-Flood also appealed for information, 'so that he could at least place the leaders in internment camps or ships', and received 'a hearty vote of thanks'.

[23] GOLI, Finance Committee, MSS Minutes of Proceedings, 1922–40 (7 Feb. 1923, 7 Mar. 1923). The Old Town Hall in Victoria Street had also served as headquarters for the UVF.

[24] The murders at Altnaveigh are commemorated in the banner of lodge 37, Newry No. 9 district (Co. Down), which depicts the victims' houses over an inscription 'in memory of our friends who died because of their faith, 17th. June 1922': Neil Jarman, *Displaying Faith: Orange, Green and Trade Union Banners in Northern Ireland* (Belfast, IIS, 1999), 47. For this and other references, I am much indebted to Jane Leonard.

[25] W. H. H. Lyons (grand master of Ireland), telegram to Northern Ireland cabinet, 10 Feb. 1922, in GOLI, Central Committee, Minutes (17 Mar. 1922); GOLI, *HYR* (28 June 1922), 6; Dennis Kennedy, *The Widening Gulf: Northern Attitudes to the Independent Irish State, 1919–49* (Belfast, Blackstaff Press, 1988), 73–5. Lyons was correct in his supposition that the 40 kidnapped unionists were detained with the connivance of 'the so-called Provisional Government of Southern Ireland': Tim Pat Coogan, *Michael Collins: A Biography* (London, Hutchinson, 1990), 344–7.

Though systematic anti-loyalist campaigns occurred even in remote Cork, the Ulster border counties were the site of the most intense sectarian violence outside Belfast. The effect of civil turmoil on Orange organisation was predictably negative, lodges being forced underground or into abeyance with the result that no dues could be collected in most southern counties in either 1922 or 1923.[26] Yet, in the longer run, the widespread Protestant experience of fear, loss, and sectarian persecution helped to preserve and renew the appeal of Orangeism in unpropitious conditions.

II

The creation of an Irish Free State, explicitly deriving its sovereignty from the Irish people rather than the Crown, seemed likely to split the Irish Orange Institution into two jurisdictions requiring different expressions of allegiance. How could southern Orangemen continue to pledge their support for an obsolete union, when they were also bound by their obligations and qualifications to support the civil magistrate in upholding the law of the land? Immediately after the formal creation of the Free State in December 1922, these points were raised by the Monaghan grand lodge, which warned that the current constitution and rituals rendered the institution 'illegal' outside Northern Ireland, and that its membership had already declined almost to the point of collapse. Nothing short of a separate constitution and grand lodge for Monaghan, in association with other counties in the Free State, could arrest that process.[27]

Though approved by the grand lodge without reported discussion, the split was delayed by the refusal of Cavan to follow Monaghan's lead,[28] and then averted by an ingenious alteration of the rubrics of Orangeism throughout Ireland. Instead of upholding 'the Laws of the Realm, the Legislative Union, and the Succession to the Throne . . . being Protestant', the Orangeman's allegiance was to be confined to the monarch and the

---

[26] GOLI, Finance Committee, Minutes (7 Mar. 1923); GOLI, *HYR* (1922–3).

[27] GOLI, *HYR* (13 Dec. 1922), 22.

[28] The grand lodge resolved that 'we recognise that there is no alternative to the proposed Grand Lodge for the Free State', though the proposal had provoked 'considerable discussion' in the Central Committee. In June 1923 Monaghan sought an adjournment of the issue; three months later, Cavan intimated 'that this Grand Lodge would expect to work under Grand Lodge of Ireland as formerly'; and by December, Monaghan 'had decided not to proceed with the formation of a Grand Lodge for the Free State' but to resume its adherence to the grand lodge in Belfast: GOLI, *HYR* (13 Dec. 1922), 22; (12 Dec. 1923), 24; GOLI, Central Committee, Minutes (12 Dec. 1922, 23 June, 3 Oct. 1923, 11 Dec. 1923).

'Realm' – left undefined.[29] Technically at odds with the unique oath incorporated in the Free State's constitution, which required parliamentarians and officials to offer allegiance to the constitution but only to be 'faithful' to the monarch, these tinkerings satisfied all factions that the Orangeman's qualifications were equally consistent with loyal residence in an 'imperial province' and in a dominion-like Free State.

It is worth noting that even the declaration of a 'Republic of Ireland' in 1949 failed to produce any further printed amendment of the laws and rituals of Irish Orangeism. Both the Northern government and John Miller Andrews, formerly only a prime minister but now the incoming grand master, deemed the repeal of the External Relations Act of 1936 to be 'further proof of the unbridgeable gulf between Northern Ireland and Southern Ireland'.[30] The grand lodge of Ireland and the 'Eire Sub-Committee', established in 1939 to coordinate Orangeism beyond the border, could not secure general agreement on any change of wording, this time because of objections from Donegal. Instead, it was agreed that in Donegal, and maybe elsewhere, the printed ritual would be varied in practice to accommodate the Republic.[31] Belatedly adopting Lloyd George's formula of 1921, designed to placate republicans by inviting them to be merely 'faithful' to the monarch, Donegal Orangemen ceased to affirm their 'true allegiance'. Instead of undertaking to uphold 'the Laws and Constitution, as established by William the Third, of glorious memory', they made the less onerous promise to defend 'the Laws and Constitution of the Loyal Orange Institution', while reaffirming their support for the civil magistrate.[32] In public, care was taken to salute the monarch only as defender of the Protestant faith rather than as 'our ruler'.[33] Such apparent sophistries were the product of a century's experience in adapting Orange rubrics to diverse constitutional contexts, the institution having flourished in the overseas Dominions and even in the United States. Reassuring precedents thus existed for combining Orange

[29] GOLI, *HYR* (12 Dec. 1923), 24–5; GOLI, *Laws and Ordinances of the Orange Institution of Ireland* (1913 edn.); *Constitutions, Laws and Ordinances of the Loyal Orange Institution of Ireland* (1924 edn.). Likewise, the Orangeman's 'Particular Qualifications' no longer required maintenance of 'the Laws and Constitution of the United Kingdom', but only of 'the Realm'.

[30] GOLI, *HYR* (8 Sept. 1948), 35–6.

[31] GOLI, *HYR* (13 Dec. 1939), 29; (14 Dec. 1949), 34; (14 June 1950), 15–16; (13 Dec. 1950), 27.

[32] Albert Ellis (grand secretary, Donegal CGL) to Harry Burge (grand secretary, GOLI), 27 Dec. 1962.

[33] The words 'God save the Queen' were used in lodge meetings, but not in public until 1967, when a county referendum approved the latter practice by 106 votes to 81: Alexander Elliott (grand secretary, Donegal CGL) to Walter Williams (grand secretary, GOLI), 15 Nov. 1965, 7 Dec. 1967.

principles with affirmations of loyal citizenship in Southern Ireland, both before and after 1949.

No form of words, however ingenious, could have ensured the survival of southern Orangeism had it failed to cater for Protestant needs and welfare. In fact, most of the benefits of belonging to an Orange lodge were maintained or even enhanced after independence. Many southern Protestants, understandably wary of their Catholic neighbours, relished the relative privacy afforded by exclusive clubs such as Masonic or Orange lodges. If, however, privacy within the lodge were to be preserved, extra care must be taken to prevent interception of confidential letters. In December 1923, a letter from the Newry district urged brethren 'to address communications to those outside the Six Counties personally and not in their Office in the Orange Society'.[34] This theme was reiterated by a Wicklow Orangemen who had been lent £25 by the OBLDA. 'We are looked upon as Enemies of the free State. Now that all the staff in the National Bank at Tinahely are RC I hope your draft wont [*sic*] be like the Heading of the bill' – which had been emblazoned with the association's picturesque letterhead.[35] However well Orangemen might get on with their Catholic neighbours, the sense of division and possible conflict always remained.

This underlying uneasiness is well expressed in an anecdote concerning Cavan, recorded for the Irish Folklore Commission in 1960. A Catholic had 'got very great with a young Orangeman', to the extent that if they had 'only the one fag between them, they'd halve it'. On his deathbed, the Orangeman had 'one bit of advice to give you, before I die. Don't ever be as stiff with an Orangeman again. There were times there and I thought as much about you as a brother and other times I had th' open knife in one pocket, ready to stick in you.' This is one of at least four similar stories, an Englishman being substituted for the Orangeman in one case.[36] Though illuminating Catholic anxieties more than Orange treacherousness, this narrative graphically conveys the brittleness of intercommunal goodwill in the border zone.

As the prospect of partition loomed, Protestant borderers became ever more anxious about the retention of their farms and jobs, and their future economic security. In December 1918, the grand master of Monaghan

---

[34] GOLI, *HYR* (12 Dec. 1923), 23.
[35] George Griffin (Coohor, Tinahely) to W. N. Cross (joint hon. sec., OBLDA), 3 June 1924; OBLDA, Minutes, Executive Committee (16 Jan., 7 Mar., 21 May 1924).
[36] IFA, MS 1574, ff. 522–3 (testimony recorded by James Delaney, *c*. Oct. 1960). Apart from the quoted anecdote, in which a Kilkenny farmer (Michael Moore) described 'Young' Carty's visit to a cousin in Cavan, these tales emanated from Longford.

seconded a motion to 'give financial support to Members of the Orange Institution and Protestants generally for purchase of Lands'.[37] Two years later, the Donegal grand lodge put forward a similar resolution.[38] These early initiatives culminated in a loan scheme administered by the OBLDA, which distributed over £3,300 between 1924 and 1929 to help needy Protestants buy farms or houses which would otherwise have passed to Catholics. Many of the recipients were in border counties such as Tyrone, Cavan, and Monaghan, where economic infiltration was thought to be most severe.[39] By 1927, the defence of Protestant Ulster against this silent invasion had become the main preoccupation of the association:[40]

It is common knowledge that a policy of peaceful penetration by the means of the purchase of small farms is being carried out at present throughout Ulster, with the hope thereby of bringing about an all-Ireland Parliament.

Subsequent experience reinforced such fears, and several similar purchase schemes have since been undertaken under Orange aegis. But these more recent projects, unlike the assistance provided by the OBLDA, seem to have been confined to Northern Ireland.[41]

When first formed, the association was embroiled in a second economic campaign dictated by the border, which created sharp divisions between Orangemen in the two states. In December 1921, the grand lodge appealed 'to every Orangeman under our jurisdiction to help to fight the boycott of Belfast and other towns by ceasing to deal with any merchant or retailer who stocks any commodity from Southern Ireland, and by consistently asking for goods manufactured in the loyal portion of the British Empire'.[42] The association had already applied pressure to four firms in Belfast, Lurgan, and Portadown which had been caught 'dealing with Sinn Feiners in County Cavan'.[43] Its standing committee later offered a 'hearty welcome' to Brigadier-General Cyril Prescott-Decie, the celebrated perpetrator and advocate of systematic 'reprisals' for republican outrages, who 'gave a lengthy report of the work of the

[37] Resolution from Portadown district: GOLI, *HYR* (18 Dec. 1918), 41.
[38] GOLI, *HYR* (15 Dec. 1920), 24.
[39] OBLDA, Minutes, Executive Committee (1928–9), with List of Loans (1924–8). Most applications for grants and loans before 1924 were refused for lack of funds.
[40] GOLI, *HYR* (14 Dec. 1927), 42.
[41] Down CGL, *AR* (11 May 1933), 5–6; GOLI, *HYR* (14 Dec. 1938), 26, 29; (10 Dec. 1941); (10 June 1942), 13.
[42] GOLI, *HYR* (14 Dec. 1921), 30. On 30 Dec. 1921, the OBLDA had specified 'anti-boycotting' as an object for funding: GOLI, Central Committee, Minutes (17 Mar. 1922).
[43] 'If found necessary', a deputation was to wait upon each firm: OBLDA, Minutes, Unemployment and Boycott Committee (15 Nov. 1921).

Anti Boycott and hoped to have the hearty support of every Loyalist'.[44]
For Orangemen outside Northern Ireland, the Anti-Boycott was not
only unenforceable at home, but potentially damaging for southern
Protestant merchants and manufacturers serving the northern market.
After vigorous protest from Dublin City, whose grand lodge deemed 'the
Resolution unworthy of the principles of the Orange Institution', the
iniquitous policy was rescinded in June 1922 (shortly after relaxation of
the rival Belfast Boycott).[45] Though short-lived, this dispute illustrates
the divisive impact of the border among Orangemen, and the persistent
difficulty of reconciling the interests of northern and southern loyalists.

For many Protestants, Orangeism was not only a bulwark against the
papist or republican menace, but also a forum for strengthening communal solidarity by giving substance to the idea of brotherhood. Orange
lodges, in south Ulster as elsewhere, provided opportunities for meat
teas, drinking and singing, easy conversation, evangelical uplifting, theatrical initiations and ceremonies, committee-room conspiracies, and other
such fraternal diversions. Though the more censorious evangelical faction
fought against the demoralising pursuits of alcohol, gambling, and dancing, the brethren of lodge 155 in Monaghan town had no compunction
in holding dancing classes in support of their band in 1924.[46] The rituals
of initiation, especially for degrees more arcane than the plain 'Orange'
or the 'Little Purple', continued to supply melodramatic entertainment
within the lodge, sometimes under the supervision of officers based in
Northern Ireland. In 1930, the same Monaghan lodge thanked its worshipful master, Major Irwin, for 'the valuable assistance he gave at the Arch
Purple meeting by taking his moter [sic] to the Border for the Lecturers &
also bringing them back'.[47]

Ever since 1796, the climax of the Orangeman's theatrical calendar
has been the commemoration of William's victory at the Boyne, and
the associated 'walks', demonstrations, church services, binges, balls,
and dinners or teas. Whenever governments, magistrates, or grand lodges
have attempted to suppress the traditional public procession with its
brilliant regalia, music, flags, and banners, such decrees have provoked
either defiance or demoralisation in the private lodges. No ordinary lodge
meeting or political rally could provide a substitute for the 'Twelfth'

---

[44] OBLDA, Minutes, Standing Committee (29 Dec. 1921). For Prescott-Decie's robust
   defence, following his resignation as a divisional commissioner (RIC), of 'counter-
   reprisals ... done under my directions', see *Armagh Guardian* (23 Sept. 1921).
[45] GOLI, Central Committee, Minutes (17 Mar. 1922); GOLI, *HYR* (28 June 1922), 12.
[46] Cumberland True Blues lodge 155, Minutes of Proceedings, 1924–38 (15 Oct. 1924).
[47] Ibid. (8 Jan. 1930).

experience, in which Orangemen display enigmatic tokens of their shared secrets and ideology before a mixed audience of brethren, friends and neighbours, potential recruits, and hostile or sceptical outsiders. Depending on one's viewpoint, the event might be seen as a joyful reunion, an entertainment, an invitation, or a taunt laden with menace. Such parades are characteristic of fraternities, and the functions of the Twelfth scarcely differed from those of St Patrick's Day and Lady Day for Ribbonmen and Hibernians, or St John's Day for early Freemasons. Yet in 1923, as sectarian violence subsided into mutual distrust, few would have predicted the revival of the Twelfth in the alien and unsettled environment of the post-revolutionary Free State.

The bitterness of southern hostility to the Williamite cult became audible at 3 a.m. on 31 May 1923, when the massive Boyne Obelisk at Oldbridge, Co. Louth, was mined, toppled, fragmented, and scattered over a radius of 200 yards. Its destroyers were apparently not Irregulars frustrated by the recent ceasefire, but members of the National army.[48] Erected in 1736, this monster had long been under threat, and for several decades Orange organisers had been making discreet but fruitless efforts to acquire the site and maintain the neglected monument.[49] Following this setback, only in Monaghan was the grand lodge confident enough to organise its first county demonstration since partition. Ernest Blythe, the Free State's only non-Catholic minister and its expert on Orangeism, advised that 'it would be a good thing if the Civic Guard and the Military took special, but *unostentatious*, precautions, to ensure that no unpleasantness occurred on the occasion of the meeting'. The police reported that 'everything passed off very quietly', necessitating only four prosecutions following the seizure of 'a large quantity of intoxicating liquor' on the public road.[50] Warm relations between Orangemen and Guards had developed during the civil war, when the Orange hall at Glasslough, Co. Monaghan, was offered for police use after destruction of the barracks.[51]

[48]   Information from Jane Leonard and Gordon Lucy.
[49]   Extract from *BNL* (31 May 1923), in GOLI, *HYR* (June 1923), 12–13. When urged by the New South Wales GOL to organise a special appeal to rebuild the obelisk, the central committee resolved that 'it would be useless to think of replacing the monument and to thank the Grand Lodge of New South Wales for the kindly thought': GOLI, Central Committee, Minutes (3 Oct. 1923).
[50]   Earnán de Blaghd (minister for Local Government) to Kevin O'Higgins (minister for Home Affairs), 27 June 1923; Eamon Ó Cugáin (assistant commissioner, Civic Guard) to Éinri Ó Frighil (secretary, department of Home Affairs), 20 July 1923 (enclosing superintendent's report): NAD, H 75/15.
[51]   Conor Brady, *Guardians of the Peace* (Dublin, Gill and Macmillan, 1974), 79–80.

Throughout Cosgrave's presidency, speakers from 'Twelfth' platforms in Monaghan declared their readiness to cooperate with the government in consolidating the new state:[52]

We are not going to be sulky in a corner. We have to live in this country and we are going to make the most of it. [Alexander Haslett, 1923]

We are now citizens of the Irish Free State and now that that Government has been forced upon us against our will . . . we are all determined to do the best we can to support it. [William Martin, 1924]

As far as the civic guards are concerned, they have almost outshone the old RIC and have left nothing to be desired. [Revd T. C. Magee, 1924]

The annual county demonstrations continued without interruption until 1931, with Cavan and Leitrim soon following Monaghan's lead.[53] Reassured by the government's unexpected toleration of Protestant interests and idiosyncrasies, the lodges resumed their traditional cere-monies and displays. In 1928, Cumberland True Blues lodge 155 pur-chased a 'new flag and rope for the pole' on Monaghan Orange hall, though the union flag no longer adorned the Church of Ireland as it had done before the Great War. Next year, the lodge deputed brethren to prepare sandwiches for the band and assigned '3 doz. Cups and 2 Large Jugs to the Field also 1 can if necessary'. Even greater largesse was offered in 1931, when the lodge treated the band to 'a meat tea in the Hall in the evening'.[54]

The price of rapprochement between Orangeism and Cosgrave's gov-ernment was to make the Twelfth a target for republican attack, as para-military violence resumed and intensified. In 1931, after a confrontation fondly recited in the folklore of Newtowngore, Co. Leitrim, that county's last celebration of the Twelfth was aborted by a force of armed 'Catholics' imported from the Ballinamore district, who set up roadblocks and heroically prevented the 50 Orangemen from assembling. At midday, 200 Catholics

marched through the village, and went to the field, where the meeting was to have taken place. They smashed the platform and tore down the colours and flags. They conducted themselves in an orderly and deliberate manner. Many guards were brought in but the Catholics could not be dealt with.

---

[52] *Northern Standard* (Monaghan), 20 July 1923, 18 July 1924: quoted in Livingstone, *The Monaghan Story*, 394, 419, 421. Haslett was the county's deputy grand master, and Martin represented Monaghan on the grand committee of GOLI.

[53] I am informed by Gordon Lucy that Twelfth processions were resumed in Cavan (incor-porating Leitrim brethren) in 1924, followed by Donegal in 1925.

[54] Lodge 155, Minutes (15 June 1928, 3 July 1929, 10 June 1931).

The 'Catholics', in fact members of the proscribed IRA, also saw off two army lorries sent to secure the Orangemen's right to parade, and 'the Orangemen did not dare to try to walk'. In a triumphant conclusion following a familiar pattern in folklore, the narrator declared that 'no walks were since held in Newtowngore. It was the last time that they occurred in Leitrim, and I think Connacht.'[55]

For once, the peroration was factual rather than wishful in its assertion that Orange parading had been well and truly laid to rest by Catholic pugnacity. Though taunted by the erection of a large green arch over their route to Hilden in 1931, the Monaghan lodges had proceeded as usual with banners and bands, returning for their lodge dinners 'in good order and peaceful'.[56] But the confrontation in Leitrim, re-enacted with even greater ruthlessness a month later at Cootehill, Co. Cavan,[57] eventually persuaded the Monaghan grand lodge to make a tactical withdrawal. Initially encouraged by an assurance from the Guards that 'no interference' was expected, they had resolved to hold a county demonstration at Clones rather than joining the northern brethren at Aughnacloy, Co. Tyrone. By late June, however, the grand master of Monaghan

had received secret information from a very reliable source that arms were being distributed by the same party who had caused all the trouble at Cootehill, with the object of interfering with our July demonstration. The attacks which have been made on Roman Catholics recently in the Six Counties would be made an excuse for interfereing [sic] with other Brethren.

The demonstration was abandoned without dissent, members observing that 'there was a very strong element of opposition against the orange institution there', and deploring the effect that any clash 'would have on our Institution'.[58] Private lodges obediently cancelled their demonstrations, 'walks', and dances; but in the Cumberland True Blues, submission was immediately followed by a notice of motion from Major Irwin to consider winding up the lodge and handing in its warrant.[59] Despite many subsequent discussions and murmurs of unrest or despair, it

[55] IFA, MS 1404, ff. 492–4 (testimony of Gus Martin, citing Thomas Kiernan from Newtowngore, recorded by Conall Ó Ceirin, 24 Mar. 1955).
[56] Livingstone, *The Monaghan Story*, 421; Co. Monaghan CGL, MSS Minutes of Proceedings, 1932–42, 1943–60, incorporating extract from minutes of lodge 272 (13 July 1931).
[57] The occasion of this outrage was a demonstration arranged by the GBC for 11 Aug. 1931, in commemoration of Jacobite defeats in Derry and Newtownbutler in 1689: Livingstone, *The Monaghan Story*, 422.
[58] Co. Monaghan CGL, Minutes (17 May, 28 June 1932). The usual church services were to be held, but without processions or regalia.
[59] Lodge 155, Minutes (18 May 1932). The lodge survived.

seems that no further major processions were held in the Free State outside Donegal.

III

The survival of Orangeism in the 'Lost Counties' is best explained by its continuing political importance for Protestant minorities enjoying the benefits of proportional representation in both local and national government. Though well below a quarter in all three excluded counties, the Protestant electorate, if efficiently mobilised, was capable of returning a deputy to the Dáil in each of these multiple-member constituencies.[60] The increasing fragmentation of the Catholic vote, and the frequent convergence of interest between Orangeism and parties representing farmers or ratepayers, encouraged Protestant politicians to use the institution as a basis for fund-raising and campaigning. Their electoral support, by today's standard, seems astonishing. In Donegal, Major James Sproule Myles of the Royal Inniskilling Fusiliers and 36th (Ulster) Division headed the poll at all seven elections between 1923 and 1938, before slipping to defeat in 1943 and 1944. Though not identified as an Orangeman, Myles was a Prince Mason in a chapter well stocked with Orange luminaries.[61] In Cavan, John James Cole of Cloverhill contested every election between 1923 and 1948, being narrowly returned on five occasions. Cole served as grand master of Cavan for two decades, being succeeded for an even longer term by his son Jack.[62] And in Monaghan, Alex Haslett of Mulladuff was successful in three of his six contests between 1927 and 1943, having been a prominent member of the Monaghan grand lodge throughout that period with the exception of a year's 'misunderstanding' over electoral strategy.[63]

Though nominally 'Independents', all three Protestant deputies relied in varying degree on the Orange vote. In Monaghan, the Cumberland

[60] The non-Catholic percentages of the censal population in 1926 (and 1936) were 21.5 (18.9) in Monaghan; 18.1 (16.4) in Donegal; and 15.9 (14.5) in Cavan. The number of deputies elected for each county between 1923 and 1948 was as follows: Monaghan: 3; Cavan: 4; Donegal: 8 (7, for two constituencies, from 1937). See *Parliamentary Election Results in Ireland, 1918–92*, ed. Brian M. Walker (Dublin and Belfast, RIA, 1992), 108–74. Individual electoral records were abstracted from the same work.

[61] *Irish Freemasons' Calendar and Directory for the Year A.D. 1914* (Dublin, GLI, 1914), 177–8. Myles's brethren in the Londonderry Chapter (no. 13) of Prince Masons of Ireland included three members of GOLI: Maj. Charles F. Falls and Maurice C. Hime, headmaster of Foyle College, Londonderry (DGCs), and the bishop of Derry, Dr George Chadwick (GC). Myles was among those kidnapped in February 1922.

[62] The names and addresses of all members of GOLI, including county grand officers, appear annually in GOLI, *HYR*.

[63] Monaghan CGL, Minutes (14 Nov. 1939).

True Blues deputed three brethren to assist Haslett in his first election campaign in 1927. Five years later, another lodge undertook 'to give all assistance possible to help our candidate Bro Haslett', and 'to join with the Protestant Association in making arrangements for election'.[64] Indeed, the two bodies were scarcely distinguishable, sometimes meeting in the same hall on the same day under the same chairman. The 'County Monaghan Protestant Defence Association', as it was first named, had been formed in 1920 to represent 'all Protestant interests' while giving special representation to the Orange Institution.[65] Its instigator was the legendary Michael Elliott Knight of Clones, grand master from 1904 to 1960, whose comfortable adjustment to the Free State was demonstrated in 1936 by his election as president of the Incorporated Law Society.[66] A photograph published in 1915 depicts a dapper, slim figure utterly unlike the obese creature of 1920 portrayed in Darach MacDonald's otherwise evocative novel *The Sons of Levi*.[67] In retrospect, Knight recalled with pride Monaghan's refusal to have 'accepted our fate and allowed our people to disappear as a Party in the County'.[68] Despite subsequent electoral reverses and conflicts over alliances of expediency, both the association and the grand lodge remained active and sometimes effective participants in national and local politics throughout the 1930s.

The ominous victory of Fianna Fáil in 1932 stimulated an attempt to coordinate Protestant political strategy in the three counties. In October 1932, Knight convened an 'informal conference' including Haslett and Sproule, but not Cole from Cavan, which agreed that 'politically we should keep apart' from both major parties without attempting to exclude Protestants from the Irish Farmers' Union. However, the conference concluded that 'there is not any hope of having an effective three County Organization'. Instead, strategy 'must be left to each County to work out for itself'.[69] Meanwhile, southern Orangeism gradually reinvolved itself in the workings of the grand lodge of Ireland, thus securing

---

[64] Lodge 155, Minutes (11 May 1927); Monaghan CGL, Minutes, incorporating extract from minutes of lodge 272 (2 May 1932).

[65] Address on the history of Monaghan Protestantism by Michael Knight, in Monaghan CGL, Minutes (12 Nov. 1940).

[66] Ibid. (19 May 1936). Like Cole in Cavan, he was succeeded as county grand master by his son. Three times a candidate for North Monaghan in the House of Commons, Knight was last defeated, in December 1918, by Ernest Blythe. For Knight's wide-ranging contribution to politics and local administration, see Livingstone, *The Monaghan Story*, 284, 362–4, 377, 406, 546.

[67] *OS*, ii, no. 21 (Sept. 1915), 130. MacDonald's *The Sons of Levi* (Monaghan, Drumlin Press, 1998) graphically depicts the plight of Orangemen in Monaghan during the turmoil of 1920–2, and their ambivalent relationship with brethren north of the border.

[68] Monaghan CGL, Minutes (12 Nov. 1940).   [69] Ibid. (5 Oct. 1932).

moral if not political backing from beyond the border. In November 1932, Haslett attended the world-wide triennial council of Orange delegates in Belfast, taking 'full advantage of all the hospitality provided'. He received ample attention, 'varying from admiration of our determination to carry on under adverse conditions, to pity, for our plight ... Whatever grudge I may bear to the Belfast brethren for throwing us out of Ulster, I must give them credit for the very great difference [*sic*] and kindness shown me as your representative.'[70] Brotherhood straddled the border, but only just.

How successfully did Orangemen of the three counties maintain their organisation, in the teeth of hostility down south and treachery up north? Grand lodge returns suggest striking resilience, despite the disproportionate decline of the Protestant population. In 1921, there were 76 lodges working in Cavan, 57 in Monaghan, and 17 under the Donegal grand lodge.[71] By 1964, the number in Cavan had dropped sharply to 43 lodges; but elsewhere there was little change, with 40 remaining in Monaghan and 16 in Donegal.[72] No precise returns of membership are available for the three counties in earlier years; but in 1935, according to Michael Knight, Monaghan's 48 lodges had at least 1,000 members.[73] The absence of precipitate decline is confirmed by the record of resignations in the three counties, only five resignations being confirmed between 1918 and 1923, and nineteen between 1924 and 1929.[74]

In 1965, both Cavan and Monaghan still had about 700 members, while over 300 were attached to the Donegal grand lodge. It is remarkable that even then, 40 years after confirmation of the border, Orangemen were almost as densely organised in Cavan and Monaghan as in Londonderry, Armagh, or Tyrone. They accounted for well over a tenth of the entire non-Catholic population, and therefore for at least a third of all Protestant adult males. Support for Orangeism in both counties remained far stronger than in Antrim, Down, or Belfast, where Protestants had no immediate incentive to engage in mutual defence.[75] Until the advent of

---

[70] Ibid. (14 Nov. 1932).

[71] These figures are based on county dues returned in GOLI, *HYR* (Dec. 1922).

[72] MSS enumeration of lodges by county, c.1964. About eight East Donegal lodges were affiliated with the City of (London)derry CGL. Their combined membership probably exceeded that of the lodges affiliated with Donegal CGL.

[73] Monaghan CGL, Minutes (21 May 1935).

[74] All county returns of resignations confirmed by GOLI were normally listed in the printed *HYR*s for December. My abstract indicates that recorded resignations from lodges in the three counties amounted to 33 (1851–1917) and 11 (1930–75).

[75] The percentage ratio of brethren returned by CGLs in 1965, to the censal population of non-Catholics in each Ulster county in 1961, was as follows: Fermanagh, 14.9; Tyrone, 12.7; Armagh, 11.5; Cavan, 10.8; Londonderry (Co. and City), 10.6; Monaghan, 10.4; Antrim, 6.5; Down, 5.4; Belfast, 4.7; Donegal, 2.2 (excluding lodges affiliated with the City of Londonderry CGL).

terror and civil conflict in Northern Ireland, Orangemen in south Ulster were left alone to age quietly in undisturbed fraternity. Thereafter, the reinvigoration of sectarian animosity in the Republic contributed to a rapid decline in membership.[76] Thus the overflow of the northern conflict accomplished what southern civil war and independence had failed to achieve. At long last, the Orange Order seemed on the brink of retreating behind the border.

---

[76] Part of that decline is presumably attributable to the ageing profile of the southern Protestant population, which exacerbated the problem of finding younger recruits.

4   The gardener and the stable-boy: Yeats, MacNeice, and the problem of Orangeism

I

When I read Yeats's account of his childhood I find many things which are echoed in my own or in that of other Irish people I know – in particular, the effects of loneliness, or a primitive rural life; the clannish obsession with one's own family; the combination of an anarchic individualism with puritanical taboos and inhibitions; the half-envious contempt for England; the constant desire to show off; a sentimental attitude to Irish history; a callous indifference to those outside the gates; an identification of Ireland with the spirit and of England with crass materialism.[1]

So Louis MacNeice declared his sense of affinity with W. B. Yeats in his perceptive study of Yeats's poetry published in 1941. No sycophant or imitator of Yeats, MacNeice recognised a familiar mentality behind the elaborate façade that he had first encountered in Rathfarnham seven years earlier. Each had been 'brought up in an Irish middle-class Protestant family', as MacNeice acknowledged;[2] each was profoundly affected by family roots in Connaught; both expressed violent and inconsistent responses to Irish political and religious conflicts; both lived mostly in England while preserving their very different Irish identities and accents.

Like so many Irish writers adapting to a cosmopolitan world, Yeats and MacNeice found it expedient to conceal or distort certain awkward elements of their background. Being Irish in England was bad enough, without having to overcome liberal repugnance for the fabled arrogance of Yeats's 'Anglo-Ireland' or, worse still, the bigotry of MacNeice's 'Black North'. Yet, however eloquently they disowned such stereotypes, neither writer could erase the imprint of a Protestant Irish upbringing. As MacNeice expostulated in 'Valediction':

> Cursèd be he that curses his mother. I cannot be
> Anyone else than what this land engendered me:

[1] Louis MacNeice, *The Poetry of W. B. Yeats* (London, Oxford University Press, 1941), 47.
[2] MacNeice, *Yeats*, 44.

> ... I can say Ireland is hooey, Ireland is
> A gallery of fake tapestries,
> But I cannot deny my past to which my self is wed,
> The woven figure cannot undo its thread.[3]

When reviewing an edition of Yeats's correspondence in 1954, MacNeice remarked that 'Yeats too was born and bred Protestant (which in Ireland does imply both violence and arrogance) and ... his motto to the end was "No Surrender".'[4] And so it had been in the beginning: 'In reading Yeats's *Autobiographies* I noticed an odd paradox: Yeats, as a little boy in the west, read Orange songs and fancied himself dying facing the Fenians; I, as a little boy among Orangemen, imagined myself a rebel against England.'[5] Typically, MacNeice left it up to readers to unravel the 'odd paradox'. Hence this chapter.

II

I judged people's social importance mainly by the length of their avenues. This idea may have come from the stable-boy, for he was my principal friend. He had a book of Orange rhymes, and the days when we read them together in the hay-loft gave me the pleasure of rhyme for the first time. Later on I can remember being told, when there was the rumour of a Fenian rising, that rifles had been served out to the Orangemen; and presently, when I had begun to dream of my future life, I thought I would like to die fighting the Fenians.[6]

So Yeats, writing in 1914, conjured up the seven-year-old visitor at Merville, Magheraboy, the big house on the outskirts of Sligo which offered sanctuary to the family for over two years while his father struggled to establish himself as an artist.[7] Yeats left several accounts of his mother's people, the Pollexfens, mythologising Grandfather William, the puritanical corn-miller, his amiable wife Elizabeth, and their more or less

---

[3] 'Valediction' (Jan. 1934), in Louis MacNeice, *Collected Poems*, ed. Peter McDonald (London, Faber, 2007), 8.

[4] Review of *The Letters of W. B. Yeats*, ed. Allan Wade (London, Hart-Davis, 1954), in *New Statesman and Nation*, 2 Oct. 1954, in *Selected Literary Criticism of Louis MacNeice*, ed. Alan Heuser (Oxford University Press, 1987), 191.

[5] MacNeice, *Yeats*, 45.

[6] 'Reveries of Childhood and Youth' (1914), in Yeats, *Autobiographies* (London, Macmillan, 1955), 14.

[7] Suburban Magheraboy makes a veiled appearance in revised versions of 'The Fiddler of Dooney' (1892), in *The Variorum Edition of the Poems of W. B. Yeats*, ed. Peter Allt and Russell K. Alspach (New York, Macmillan, 1956), 178–9: 'My cousin is priest in Kilvarnet, | My brother in Mocharabuiee'. According to Yeats's footnote, it was 'pronounced as if spelt "Mockrabwee"'. See also Sheelah Kirby, *The Yeats Country: A Guide to Places in the West of Ireland Associated with the Life and Writings of William Butler Yeats* (Dublin, Dolmen Press, 1962), 17, 44.

melancholic progeny.[8] As sister Lily's recollections confirm, the children spent their happiest hours with neighbours and servants, who introduced Yeats to the magical Sligo which was to haunt his late masterpieces as much as his early romances. Among those servants was Johnnie Healy, the stable-boy.[9]

Strangely, for the alleged owner of an Orange songbook, Johnnie Healy was almost certainly Roman Catholic. Indeed, all 630 Heal(e)ys enumerated in the county in 1901 were Catholic, including an elderly 'general labourer' named John Healy and his daughter living in Magheraboy.[10] It is of course possible that Catholic lads amused themselves by circulating some chapbook of loyalist ballads, perhaps *The Ulster Harmonist* by Robert Young, originally published in Derry in 1840.[11] If so, they would have particularly reviled 'Croppies Lie Down', the unofficial anthem of the Irish Yeomanry in 1797 and 1798. This ballad was also widely circulated as 'a favourite Irish song' in English comic songbooks, with merry titles such as *Monstrous Good Songs and Sentiments*, *The Myrtle and Vine*, *The Hive*, and *The Jovial Songster*.[12] The tune is jaunty rather than strident, each stanza subsiding into anti-climax as the croppies are gently put down. The version reproduced by Young has been ascribed to Captain Daniel Frederick Ryan of the St Sepulchre's Infantry, a prominent Orangeman who was mortally stabbed by Lord Edward Fitzgerald as he struggled to apprehend the United Irish leader on 19 May 1798:

> WE soldiers of ERIN, so proud of the name,
> Will raise upon *Rebels* and *Frenchmen* our fame,
> We'll fight to the last in the honest old cause,
> And guard our religion, our freedom and laws;

---

[8] See David Fitzpatrick, 'Yeats and Sligo', in *Yeats in Context*, ed. Ben Levitas and David Holdeman (Cambridge University Press, 2009), 69–79.

[9] Various notes and letters by Susan ('Lily') Yeats strongly suggest that Healy was one of the 'servants and men in the stable and gardens' who conveyed 'a good deal of the Catholic side' to the children: R. F. Foster, *W. B. Yeats: A Life*, 2 vols. (Oxford University Press, 1997, 2003), vol. i, 19–21.

[10] Family schedules, Census of Ireland (1901): NAD (accessible on-line).

[11] Robert Young, *The Ulster Harmonist, Consisting of Constitutional Songs, Original and Selected, with Historical and Biographical Notes* (Derry, Sentinel Office, 1840 and Standard Office, 1848). Several other anthologies of similar vintage are listed in Georges-Denis Zimmermann, *Songs of the Irish Rebellion: Political Street Ballads and Rebel Songs, 1780–1900* (Dublin, Allen Figgis, 1967), 327–8.

[12] *Monstrous Good Songs, Toasts and Sentiments* (London, pr. for R. Rusted, 1799); *The Myrtle and Vine: or, Complete Vocal Library; containing a Judicious Collection of the Most Popular and Captivating Songs on Every Subject that can Charm the Ear, or Enliven the Heart; selected from the Harmonic Treasures of the Sister Muses of the Three Kingdoms* (London, pr. for West and Hughes, undated), vol. ii, 105–6; *The Hive: or, the Songster's Miscellany* (4th edn., Southampton, undated; pr. T. Skelton), 92–4; *The Jovial Songster: or, Laugh and be Fat* (Alston, undated; pr. J. Harrop), 2–5.

> We'll fight for our country, our king and his crown,
> And make all the traitors and croppies lie down.
> Down, down, croppies lie down.[13]

Ryan's ballad was restrained by comparison with some of the other sixteen versions published, soon after suppression of the rebellion, by William McKenzie in *A Collection of Loyal Songs, as Sung at all the Orange Lodges in Ireland* (1798). One song grimly foretells the fate of any croppy daring to attack the 'sons' of William of Orange; another mocks the supernatural pretensions of Father John Murphy of Boolavogue, flogged and hanged in the town square of Tullow on 2 July 1798:

> Should croppies attempt for to murder his sons,
> We'll shew them that orange-boys can handle guns;
> We'll treat them as he treated James at the Boyne,
> Nor e'er will be subject to candlestick coin:
> And should they attempt on the Orange to frown,
> We'll cut them down first, then sing croppies you're down.
> Down, down, croppies lie down.

> Priest Murphy declar'd to the fanatic crew,
> (Who believ'd all his words as the gospel were true)
> No bullet could hurt a true son of the Church!
> But the devil soon left the poor saint in the lurch:
> For by some sad mistake, thro' a hole in his skin,
> A heretic bullet just chanc'd to pop in.
> Down, down, croppies lie down.[14]

Orange bogeymen certainly figured in Sligo's popular imagination. In later years, Jack Yeats would regale the family in London with recitations of 'Sligo nonsence [*sic*] rhymes':

> You take the needle & I'll take the thread
> And we'll sow the dogs tail to the Orange man's head.[15]

---

[13] This version appears in *A Collection of Loyal Songs, as Sung at all the Orange Lodges in Ireland*, pts. i–iv (Dublin, W. McKenzie, 1798), 27–8; Young, *The Ulster Harmonist*, 50–2 (with minor amendments); *Auty's Orange and Protestant Melodist: Consisting of Constitutional Songs, Toasts, and Recitations, Original and Select* (Bradford, Squire Auty, 1863), 4–6. Auty tartly observed that the ballad was 'forbidden to be sung in Ireland for fear of hurting the feelings of the poor Roman Catholics, its contents being strictly true'. It is ascribed to 'the late gallant Captain Ryan' in *A Collection of Constitutional Songs* (Cork, A. Edwards, 1799), 28, and Zimmermann, *Songs*, 307.

[14] *Loyal Songs*, 103, 24.

[15] Yeats (Bedford Pk) to 'Miss' Tynan, 10 Oct. 1889, in *The Collected Letters of W. B. Yeats*, vol. i, ed. John Kelly (Oxford University Press, 1986), 190 (original spelling and punctuation). This motif recurs in 'The Tower' (1926), as 'Decrepit age that has been tied to me | As to a dog's tail'.

The most likely source of the songbook, however, was not the stable-boy's Catholic friends, but the Pollexfens themselves. In an earlier version of this anecdote, Yeats drew an interesting connection between the epiphany in the hay-loft and his mother's politics, sliding directly from Orangeism to unionism:

> I remember when I was nine or ten years old walking along Kensington High Road [*recte*, Street] so full of love for the fields and the roads of Sligo that I longed – a strange sentiment for a child – for earth from a road there that I might kiss it. I had no politics; a couple of years before, I had read with delight a volume of Orange verses belonging to my grandmother's stable-boy, and my mother, who loved Sligo where she had been born and bred with the same passion, was, if she had any politics, Unionist.[16]

Yeats, though far more interested in the imprint of his father's rationalism and quirky nationalism, did not deny that his mother came from a family of firm unionists. When expressing 'Remorse for Intemperate Speech' (28 August 1931), Yeats blamed his maternal rather than paternal line (and 'Ireland' in general) for his fanatical disposition:

> I carry from my mother's womb
> A fanatic heart.[17]

Yet nothing in the *Autobiographies* suggested that his Sligo world was also a nest of Orangeism.

III

Unrevealed by Yeats and therefore unknown to most Yeatsians, the poet had an impressive Orange pedigree in both the maternal and paternal lines. His father's uncle Thomas Yeats (1808–72), a land agent, cess-collector, and high constable,[18] belonged to a lodge in the town in 1856.[19] When remembering Thomas and his brother John, John Butler Yeats told Lily: 'You would be proud to have their blood. They were so clever and so innocent. I never knew and never will know any people so attractive.'[20] When John died in 1865, his widow and children came to live at Seaview,

[16] 'Journal' (Jan. 1909), in W. B. Yeats, *Memoirs*, ed. Denis O'Donoghue (London, Macmillan, 1972), 154.

[17] Yeats, *Variorum Poems*, 506.   [18] Obituary, *Sligo Chronicle*, 20 Apr. 1872.

[19] Thomas 'Yeates' was one of twelve members of lodge 235, Sligo, suspended for non-payment of dues in Nov. 1856: *Report of the Commissioners of Inquiry into the Origin and Character of the Riots in Belfast, in July and September, 1857*, 291 (app. 14), in HCP, 1857–8 [2309], xxvi.

[20] John Butler to Lily Yeats, 15 Sept. 1916, quoted in William M. Murphy, *The Yeats Family and the Pollexfens of Sligo* (Dublin, Dolmen Press, 1971), 7.

Ballincar, with Thomas, a lifelong bachelor. The Yeats children were constant visitors to Seaview, but only the beloved great-aunt 'Mickey' appears in the *Autobiographies*. Among John's sons was another John, who was to die in Winnipeg in 1908.[21] In late 1880, this John T. 'Yeates' of Seaview participated in a purge of the Sligo grand lodge, serving as grand secretary for two years at the height of the Orange Order's campaign against the Land League. His own lodge (464) included the new grand chaplain and incumbent of Lissadell, whose church had been built by Sir Robert Gore-Booth in 1841. A third member of the same lodge became county grand master. He was none other than Frederick Pollexfen of Merville.[22]

Frederick Henry Pollexfen (1852–1929) has been widely reviled as a 'black sheep'. When the family business was reorganised after William Middleton's death in 1882, Frederick was deposited on the 'lowest rung of the corporate ladder', and was later ignored in his father's will though once 'his father's favorite'. His sober siblings were offended by Frederick's aggravating manner and extravagance with yachts and horses. When his marriage collapsed, the Pollexfens sided with his wife.[23] Yet, in the early 1880s, the young notary's star was in the ascendant. Just after his year as grand master, he became one of the 50 founding members of the Sligo Constitutional Club amidst a glittering array of his social superiors, such as Sir Henry Gore-Booth of Lissadell.[24] While still grand master of Sligo, he had also married upwards, his bride Henrietta being a sister of the grand master of Cavan, Robert Johnstone. Robert Johnstone later became master of Bawnboy House and a substantial estate, presiding over the Cavan Orangemen for more than 50 years.[25]

Frederick played a brief but conspicuous part in launching the Order's campaign in support of beleaguered landlords, initiated by William Johnston of Ballykilbeg, Co. Down. Johnston, celebrated for his defiance of the Party Processions Act and brief imprisonment in 1867, went on to represent Belfast for a third of a century.[26] With notable success, the

---

[21] William M. Murphy, *Prodigal Father: The Life of John Butler Yeats (1839–1922)* (Ithaca, Cornell University Press, 1978), 642, n. 16.

[22] GOLI, *HYR*, passim.

[23] Murphy, *Prodigal Father*, 150; Murphy, *Family Secrets: William Butler Yeats and His Relatives* (Dublin, Gill and Macmillan, 1995), 25–6, 83.

[24] 'Sligo Constitutional Club, 1882. Original Members': Sligo, County Library.

[25] Robert Henry Johnstone (1849–1934), of Corvilla and later Bawnboy House, JP, DL, successor to an estate of 866 acres with an annual valuation of £686 (in 1873). After a brief spell as deputy grand master of Cavan in the 1870s, he presided over the county grand lodge until death.

[26] In Dec. 1880, Johnston proposed and Pollexfen seconded the appointment of a committee 'for the purpose of Collecting Funds, and generally organizing a Defence for the Brethren throughout Ireland'; the nomination of that committee was seconded by Robert Johnstone: GOLI, *HYR*.

Order raised an Emergency Fund to supply labourers, arms and ammunition, bidders for boycotted farms, and other protection against the dreaded Land League. It may be this episode which Yeats had in mind when he referred to rifles being 'served out to the Orangemen'.[27] Though Frederick is ignored in his memoirs, it seems implausible that the young Yeats, who again visited Merville in summer 1880 and winter 1881, was unaware of his uncle's views and entanglements. Frederick was certainly a childhood presence, as attested by a photograph showing William when a forlorn seven-year-old, standing beside a sedate Uncle Fred, cradling his dog Spot.[28]

IV

The stable-boy, I propose, was a surrogate for Yeats's Orange relatives, craftily suggesting that he encountered Orangeism as a quaint folk practice rather than a system of beliefs and precepts embedded within his own family circle. By writing Frederick Pollexfen and John T. Yeats out of his reminiscences, and also marginalising the role of his unionist mother, he obscured the sectarian strain in his upbringing. Whereas exotic variants of Freemasonry permeated his writings, Orangeism left few clear marks. When mentioned, it was portrayed as something alien and unfamiliar. Thus he wrote to Lily after a visit to Sligo in 1894:

I have just returned from Lissadell where I have been staying first with the Gore Booths & afterwards at the Parsonage. I lectured in the School House on Fairy lore chiefly to an audience of Orangemen. It was a novel experience. I found that the comic tales delighted them but that the poetry of fairy lore was quite lost on them. They held it Catholic superstition I suppose.[29]

Admittedly, his closest friend at the High School in Dublin was a Johnston of Ballykilbeg, which Yeats visited in late July 1891. But Charles Johnston was no Orangeman, having repudiated his father's evangelical Anglicanism and become a Theosophist.[30] Yeats's autobiographical account of the visit made no reference to politics or religion:

---

[27] The only request for assistance from a Sligo applicant to the Orange Emergency Committee occurred, however, as late as 1883–4: GOLI, *HYR*.

[28] Murphy, *Prodigal Father*, 82.

[29] Yeats (Thorn Hill, Sligo) to Lily, 16 Dec. 1894, in *Collected Letters*, vol. i, 418.

[30] Of the five children from William Johnston's third marriage who survived infancy, such was their father's negative influence that three became Theosophists, one a Roman Catholic, and the other an unbeliever: Aiken McClelland, *William Johnston of Ballykilbeg* (Lurgan, Ulster Society, 1990), 104–5, 115.

I left Dublin next day to stay somewhere in Orange Ulster with the brilliant student of my old Dublin school, Charles Johnston, and spent a week or ten days with him and his elder brother, making fire balloons. We made the fire balloons of tissue paper and then chased them over the countryside, our chase becoming longer and longer as our skill in manufacture improved.[31]

His letters to Katharine Tynan from Ballykilbeg also expressed no affinity with 'Orange Ulster': 'I am doing a certain amount of writing . . . but much of my time is spent in helping to make fire ballons [*sic*] & in letting them off & in exploring old castles or in such like country pursuits. I have found no folklore nor heard of any to speak of and am in all ways living a good out-o-door life with little of the mind in it.'[32]

When reporting his visit for an Irish-American journal founded by a Fenian, Yeats firmly dissociated himself from loyalism. Disappointed by the folklore of Down's 'half-Scotch people', he had found compensation by buying nationalist 'ballad sheets' from an itinerant singer in his forties, who implausibly claimed in 1891 that he was a veteran of Waterloo: 'The man when he sold them to me did so timidly, mistaking me, most evidently, for one of the loyal minority. "There is a deal of liberality in them," he said, in quaint apology.'[33] No doubt William Johnston, himself a balladeer, had shown the singer similar liberality in the past.

Yet Yeats's early exposure to Orange influences in Sligo left some traces. It helps to explain the ferocity of his invective against Catholicism in later life, and his apocalyptic anticipation of a final show-down between the cultivated Protestant minority and Catholic philistines. Such attitudes are most obvious in polemical writings such as his two notably ill-judged contributions to the debate on divorce in 1925, and his subsequent campaign against censorship and Catholic puritanism. But hostility to the Catholic Church is also a significant theme in his later poetry. It first emerges in 'September 1913', with its sneering reference to adding: '. . . the halfpence to the pence, | And prayer to shivering prayer, until | You've dried the marrow from the bone'.[34]

'Crazy Jane' (alias 'Cracked Mary') has several rude things to say about the bishop, with his 'skin, God knows, | Wrinkled like the foot of a goose' and his 'holy black':

> I am tired of cursing the Bishop,
> (Said Crazy Jane)

---

[31] Yeats, 'Autobiography' (*c*.1915), in *Memoirs*, 45–6.
[32] Yeats (Ballykilbeg) to 'Katie' Tynan, late July 1891, in *Collected Letters*, vol. i, 260.
[33] 'The Celt in Ireland', *Boston Pilot*, 12 Sept. 1891, in Yeats, *Letters to the New Island*, ed. George Bornstein and Hugh Witemeyer (New York, Macmillan, 1989), 53–6.
[34] Yeats, *Variorum Poems*, 289–90.

> Nine books or nine hats
> Would not make him a man.[35]

Several other late poems include side-swipes at the hierarchy, as in a famous but historically dubious couplet in 'Come Gather Round Me, Parnellites' (August 1936): 'The Bishops and the Party | That tragic story made'. In 'Those Images' (August 1937), Yeats is ecumenically dismissive of Communism and Catholicism as enemies of creativity:

> I never bade you go
> To Moscow or to Rome.
> Renounce that drudgery,
> Call the muses home.[36]

As MacNeice observed: 'Living in the Irish Free State Yeats had come to realize more vividly the drawbacks of Catholic Ireland.' Intermittent 'envy for the believing Roman Catholic' had given place to disgust at the very notion of conversion, fed by resentment that 'Maud Gonne had turned & given me up'.[37] His aversion to the institutional Church was most memorably expressed in 'Church and State' (February 1934): 'What if the Church and the State | Are the mob that howls at the door!'[38]

This was also the period of his infatuation with the Blueshirts, whose strong links with the Catholic Church he forgave, briefly believing that O'Duffy and his followers were sufficiently authoritarian to drive back 'the mob that howls at the door'. The springs of Yeats's growing exultation in violence and conflict cannot be reduced to latent sectarianism or the residue of a faintly Orange upbringing. Yet some wild passages in the marching songs composed for O'Duffy's Blueshirts, 'Three Songs to the One Tune' (February 1934), surely derive from Orange ballads of 1798, especially the thumping refrains in various versions of 'Croppies Lie Down':

> Derry down, down, traitors bow down.
> Down, down, priestcraft bow down.
> Derry down, down, rebels lie down.
> Down, down, croppies lie down.[39]

---

[35] 'Crazy Jane and the Bishop' (spring 1929) and 'Crazy Jane on the Mountain' (July 1938), in Yeats, *Variorum Poems*, 507–9, 628.

[36] Yeats, *Variorum Poems*, 586–7, 600–1.

[37] MacNeice, *Yeats*, 151, 81–2, 147; Foster, *Yeats*, vol. ii, 548.

[38] Yeats, *Variorum Poems*, 553–4 (originally published as an untitled addendum to 'Three Songs to the One Tune').

[39] Seventeen ballads set to 'Croppies Lie Down' appear in McKenzie's *A Collection of Loyal Songs*; see also Zimmermann, *Songs*, pt. 3, 'Songs of the "Loyal" Party', 295–320 (esp. 307–11). Other refrains called on Frenchmen to sink down, and priestcraft,

Listen then to Yeats:

> Down the fanatic, down the clown;
> Down, down, hammer them down.[40]

As Yeats explained, 'I first got my chorus, "Down the fanatic, down the clown," then the rest of the first song'[41] – which recounts the ferocious sentiments expressed by the narrator's 'Grandfather' while he awaits execution as an United Irishman. Yeats's bloodthirsty ballad of '98 had thus been grafted incongruously on to a chorus derived from an equally robust song celebrating Grandfather's enemies, the Irish Yeomanry. Though ostensibly set to 'O'Donnell Abu', the Blueshirts' theme-tune, the chorus wrestles painfully with the scansion of the verses and with the melody. Indeed, it is barely singable:

> Grandfather sang it under the gallows:
> 'Hear, gentlemen, ladies, and all mankind:
> Money is good and a girl might be better,
> But good strong blows are delights to the mind.'
> There, standing on the cart,
> He sang it from his heart.
> *Those fanatics all that we do would undo;*
> *Down the fanatic, down the clown;*
> *Down, down, hammer them down,*
> *Down to the tune of O'Donnell Abu.*
>
> Soldiers take pride in saluting their Captain,
> The devotee proffers a knee to his Lord,
> Some take delight in adorning a woman.
> What's equality? – Muck in the yard:
> Historic Nations grow
> From above to below.
>
> *Those fanatics all that we do would undo;*
> *Down the fanatic, down the clown;*
> *Down, down, hammer them down,*
> *Down to the tune of O'Donnell Abu.*

serpents, and reptiles to bow down. An untraced issue of this collection, which was several times revised and expanded during 1798, included a version substituting 'papists' for 'croppies', whereupon the grand lodge of Ireland expressed its 'strongest disapprobation, being directly contrary to our principles as reflecting on a part of our fellow subjects for their religious persuasion'. The printer, Br. William McKenzie, was chastised, and disavowals were to be sent to four Dublin newspapers: GOLI, Minute Book, 1798–1819 (20 Nov. 1798).

[40] 'Three Songs to the One Tune', in *Variorum Poems*, 543–9. In later versions, this chorus was retained only for the first of the three songs.

[41] Yeats, 'Three Songs to the Same Tune', *Spectator*, no. 5513 (23 Feb. 1934), 276. Foster dismisses the chorus as 'an elephantine attempt at the demotic' without investigating its inspiration: *Yeats*, vol. ii, 477.

Here, for comparison, is the final stanza of Michael Joseph McCann's famous rallying song (1843), in which McCann's dactyls faithfully match the 'old Irish tune':

> Sacred the cause that Clanconnell's defending –
> The altars we kneel at and homes of our sires;
> Ruthless the ruin the foe is extending –
> Midnight is red with the plunderer's fires!
> On with O'Donnell, then,
> Fight the old fight again,
> Sons of Tirconnell all valiant and true!
> Make the false Saxon feel
> Erin's avenging steel!
> Strike for your country! –*O'Donnell-aboo!*[42]

Yeats, no musician himself, was unsure if his ballads could be performed: 'Here are my songs. Anybody may sing them, choosing "clown" and "fanatic" for himself, if they are singable – musicians say they are, but may flatter – and worth singing.'[43] In his note to 'Remorse for Intemperate Speech', Yeats implausibly claimed to 'pronounce "fanatic" in what is, I suppose, the older and more Irish way, so that the last line of each stanza contains but two beats'.[44] But his idiosyncratic pronunciation also appears in an early version of 'Croppies Lie Down', already quoted ('Priest Murphy declar'd to the fanatic crew'). Humming deep in the imagination of Ireland's smiling public man were echoes of Orange songs, which the gauche boy may once have chanted in the hay-loft or the drawing-room at Merville.

V

Louis MacNeice also had something to hide when alluding to his background as a Protestant Irishman. As he reflected at the age of 50:

My father was one of the very few Church of Ireland clergymen to be a Home Ruler. This was another reason for despising Co. Antrim and regarding myself as a

---

[42] The celebrated ballad by Michael Joseph McCann, first published in the *Nation*, 28 Jan. 1843, was originally entitled 'The Clanconnell War-Song – A.D. 1597': *The Spirit of the Nation: By the Writers of the Nation Newspaper* (Dublin, James Duffy, 1843), 68–9.

[43] Yeats in *Spectator* (23 Feb. 1934). MacNeice, an intensely musical poet, perceived that the 'Three Songs', with their 'surprising' refrains comprising 'a little self-contained stanza', were only 'professedly to the tune of *O'Donnell Abu*': MacNeice, *Yeats*, 169.

[44] Yeats, *Variorum Poems*, 544. The first syllable of 'fanatic' is also stressed in John F. Poole's '"No Irish Need Apply": An Original Irish Song', in *Tony Pastor's New Irish Comic Songster* (New York, Dick and Fitzgerald, 1867), 6–7: 'Though fools may flout and bigots rave, and fanatics may cry, | Yet when they want good fighting-men, the Irish may apply'. I am indebted to Peter Brown for a copy of this poem.

displaced person. Sometimes this feeling caused an inner conflict in me. Shortly after World War I, I was sent from Belfast to Dublin in the charge of a dear old gentleman who was pestered on the way by a drunken American soldier, fresh from the Front and full of hatred for kings; they were all, he said, including King George, Germans. The dear old gentleman, being a loyal Orangeman, was outraged, so the American appealed to me and I, as an Irish nationalist, sided with him. 'This little boy,' said the American, 'has more sense than you.' I felt guilty.[45]

MacNeice's account of travelling back to school in Dorset takes pains to distance himself and his father from the dear old Orangeman, counterbalancing betrayal of his guardian with filial endorsement of the Revd Frederick MacNeice's nationalism. This unsettling division of loyalties is even more explicit in an earlier version of the story:

And as for the dear old man, what did he think of Carson? The dear old man drew himself in, his watch-chain sagged on his belly, he said he admired Carson. The American soldier turned to me; 'You're only a kid,' he said, 'but you look like an American kid. What do you think of Carson?' Feelingly shockingly disloyal to the dear old man but remembering my father and Home Rule, I said I thought Carson was a pity.[46]

Why did MacNeice, writing decades after the event, express such guilt at betraying a mere acquaintance, and such loyalty to the political opinions of a father whose moral code he had so outrageously discarded?

The puzzle is compounded by another anecdote, involving the headmaster at Sherborne Preparatory School (Littleton Powys) and his deputy 'Mr. Cameron', in fact Frederick Lindsay from Grange, outside Portadown:[47]

On the Twelfth of July [1921] Powys came into my dormitory and said: 'What is all this they do in your country today? Isn't it all mumbo-jumbo?' Remembering my father and Home Rule and the bony elbows of Miss Craig and the black file of mill-girls and the wickedness of Carson and the dull dank days between sodden haycocks and foghorns, I said Yes it was. And I felt uplifted. To be speaking man to man to Powys and giving the lie to the Red Hand of Ulster was power, was freedom, meant I was nearly grown up. King William is dead and his white horse with him, and Miss Craig will never put her knuckles in my ears again. But Powys went out of the dormitory and Mr. Cameron came in, his underlip

---

[45] 'Landscapes of Childhood and Youth' (c.1957), in MacNeice, *The Strings are False*, ed. E. R. Dodds (London, Faber, 1965), app. A, 223.

[46] MacNeice, *Strings* (drafted c.1941), 71.

[47] Frederick Richard Lindsay (1886–1972), later proprietor and headmaster of the school, was a teacher's son from Grange, between Portadown and Loughgall. While a master at Bishop Foy's school in Waterford, he signed the Ulster Covenant, as did four Lindsays in Grange. See signature sheets, Ulster Covenant: PRONI, D 1327/3/3832 (accessible online); family schedules, Census of Ireland (1901, 1911). I am grateful to Jane Leonard for locating Lindsay in Bishop Foy's school.

jutting and his eyes enraged. 'What were you saying to Mr. Powys?' Oh this division of allegiance! That the Twelfth of July was mumbo-jumbo was true, and my father thought so too, but the moment Mr. Cameron appeared I felt rather guilty and cheap. Because I had been showing off to Powys and because Mr. Cameron being after all Irish I felt I had betrayed him.[48]

Like the dear old Orangeman on the train, Frederick Lindsay represents decency, 'Irish' decency, whereas Frederick MacNeice exhibits fearless dissent from Orange and unionist orthodoxy.

These autobiographical accounts of Louis MacNeice's background are profoundly misleading. In reality, his father was never a Home Ruler, being eloquently apprehensive of Rome Rule and a strong unionist until the retention of all 32 counties within the union ceased to be a practical option. His refusal to sign Ulster's Solemn League and Covenant in 1912 was based primarily on religious scruples, compounded by his detestation of partition.[49] Like many all-Ireland unionists, he regarded all-Ireland Home Rule as preferable to partition, without abandoning his unionist convictions. It was Carson's betrayal of southern Protestants, not his unionism, that the rector of Carrickfergus abhorred. His views evidently failed to alienate Carrickfergus unionists, who annually re-elected him as a vice-president of the local Unionist Association throughout the Great War. In his decency, piety, and evangelical zeal, he was a model for Orangemen. If not a 'dear old gentleman' in 1919, he was an eminently decent middle-aged gentleman expecting, but sometimes not receiving, his son's loyalty.

And there is yet more to be revealed about the supposedly nationalist rector. Like so many evangelical clergymen, even today, he viewed the Orange Order as a useful vehicle for inculcating working-class parishioners with sound religious, moral, and civic values. Distrustful of all political parties, he repeatedly warned Orangemen to support strong Protestant candidates advocating temperance and social reform, regardless of their party affiliations. By becoming an Orange chaplain, he could also gain access to one of the most powerful social networks in Protestant Ireland, win the trust of the brethren, and avoid the ostracism which might otherwise have faced a non-Covenanter and independent thinker in 'Orange Ulster'.

So it was that Frederick MacNeice became not merely an Orangeman, but for nearly two decades an unusually active Orange chaplain and preacher. Even before moving to Ulster at the end of 1898, he had joined the Order in Dublin and become chaplain of Cumberland lodge 440. During his decade in Belfast, he joined three different lodges, acted as

[48] MacNeice, *Strings*, 78–9.   [49] See below, Chapter 7.

chaplain for no less than four districts covering large swathes of the city, and soon became a deputy grand chaplain in the Belfast county grand lodge. Far from abandoning the Order when transferred to Carrickfergus in November 1908, within a few months he became chaplain to Total Abstinence lodge 1537. This affiliation helped him to placate an initially hostile congregation and to mobilise the brethren against sectarian violence in the troubled years to come. The father that Louis MacNeice knew as a child bore little political resemblance to the liberal 'Home Ruler' depicted by the older Louis, and cherished by MacNeicians ever since.[50]

Why did MacNeice, like Yeats, suppress his Orange upbringing and assert his nationalist credentials when recollecting childhood? Despite his childish ignorance of politics, emphasised in autobiographical writings, it is not credible that an avid reader and sharp observer like MacNeice would have been unaware that he had been 'a little boy among Orangemen' at home, as well as beyond the rectory porch. By retrospectively asserting his father's nationalism, MacNeice dissociated himself from the 'Black North', so despised by his friends in Dublin and London. He was also helping to protect the increasingly liberal bishop of Down and Connor and Dromore from unwelcome allusions to his unionist, Orange, and anti-papist past. MacNeice doctored the record as little as possible: the rector was indeed critical of Carson and unenthusiastic about the Twelfth, but his objections were those of a 32-county unionist and temperate Orangeman rather than those of a Home Ruler. Though likewise never directly lying, his father himself implied that he had abandoned his resistance to Home Rule, and his fear of Rome Rule, far earlier than the record indicates. In a period when MacNeice was seeking reconciliation with his father after long estrangement, he preferred to collaborate in such mild deceptions in order to facilitate the bishop's admirable campaign against sectarianism, during and after the Belfast disturbances of 1935.

VI

In MacNeice's early poems, Orange bands and drums connote violence and fear, which he also associated with republicanism and Catholic superstition. 'Belfast' (1931) pronounces a plague on both houses:

> In the porch of the chapel before the garish Virgin
> A shawled factory-woman as if shipwrecked there

---

[50] David Fitzpatrick, 'Solitary and Wild': Frederick MacNeice and the Salvation of Ireland (Dublin, Lilliput Press, 2012).

> Lies a bunch of limbs glimpsed in the cave of gloom
> By us who walk in the street so buoyantly and glib.
>
> Over which country of cowled and haunted faces
> The sun goes down with a banging of Orange drums
> While the male kind murders each its woman
> To whose prayer for oblivion answers no Madonna.[51]

In 'Valediction' (1934), MacNeice rhetorically farewells his country, 'and in perpetuum':

> Good-bye your hens running in and out of the white house
> Your absent-minded goats along the road, your black cows
> Your greyhounds and your hunters beautifully bred
> Your drums and your dolled-up Virgins and your ignorant
>   dead.[52]

His ecumenical rejection of sectarian violence reappears more wordily in *Autumn Journal* (1938):

> And the voodoo of the Orange bands
> Drawing an iron net through darkest Ulster,
> Flailing the limbo lands –
> The linen mills, the long wet grass, the ragged hawthorn.
> And one read black where the other read white, his hope
> The other man's damnation:
> Up the Rebels, To Hell with the Pope,
> And God Save – as you prefer – the King or Ireland.

Once again, drum and chapel are juxtaposed:

> The grocer drunk with the drum,
> The land-owner shot in his bed, the angry voices
> Piercing the broken fanlight in the slum,
> The shawled woman weeping at the garish altar.[53]

MacNeice's negative images of Orangeism were drawn from childhood observation. Sinister echoes of drum-beats, along with hooting sirens, foghorns, and tolling bells, never ceased to disturb his imagination:

We often heard those drums as we were walking through the country; a couple of men might spend a whole day practising. One would walk in front with a great drum the size of a cartwheel strapped on his back and the sweat running down his face and the other would walk behind with the sweat running down his face and flail the drum on each side with a couple of canes ... And sometimes, we explained

---

[51] 'Belfast' (Sept. 1931), in MacNeice, *Collected Poems*, 25.
[52] 'Valediction' (Jan. 1934), in MacNeice, *Collected Poems*, 7–10.
[53] 'Autumn Journal, XVI' (1938), in MacNeice, *Collected Poems*, 138.

to Miss Hewitt, if you did the job properly you cut your wrists on the rim of the drum and the drum got bloody and proved you were a good Orange Protestant.[54]

For a child, such scenes were thrilling as well as frightening. When little Freddie imagined himself as 'a rebel against England', he probably had in mind, not Fenians, but the Orangemen and Ulster Volunteers of pre-war Carrickfergus as they prepared to rise against the imposition of Home Rule.

Other nightmarish images lingered from MacNeice's Orange upbringing. The drummer-sorcerer was no more sinister than the priest-predator, an ogre for MacNeice as for generations of Orangemen and loyalists. 'Cormorants' waited 'to pounce like priests'; 'the pot-boy priests and the birds of prey were still the dominant caste'; 'the black priest' required 'a big black stick' from Master Blackthorn, 'That his ignorant flock may go straight for the fear of you'.[55] Even Yeats might have baulked at such uninhibited anti-clericalism. Significantly, Yeats excluded 'Belfast' and 'Valediction', with their 'garish' and 'dolled-up' Virgins, from the four poems by MacNeice chosen for *The Oxford Book of Modern Verse* (1936).[56] Nor would MacNeice's father have used anti-papist invective, despite his repugnance for 'Rome Rule'. Attitudes formed as a child, walking around Carrickfergus with his nurse or governess, left MacNeice with a bizarre medley of sectarian prejudice, abhorrence of sectarian violence, and empathy with Orangemen. As in the case of Yeats, it would be absurd to suggest that an Orange element in his background was the dominant factor in shaping MacNeice's views on religion, morality, or conflict. Even so, incorporation of this neglected facet of his early life helps to clarify otherwise perplexing passages in his writings.

In later life, MacNeice mellowed in his depiction of the rituals associated with the Twelfth of July. In June 1939, he informed an American muse that: 'In a few weeks, darling, I am going over to Belfast to broadcast & shall be there for the twelfth of July. Haven't seen the processions (one of the most extraordinary sights in the world) since I was a little boy; I

[54] MacNeice, *Strings*, 57.
[55] 'Prologue' (1959) to *The Character of Ireland*, ed. W. R. Rodgers and Louis MacNeice (never published), in MacNeice, *Collected Poems*, 779; MacNeice, *Strings*, 213; 'Tree Party' (1962), in MacNeice, *Collected Poems*, 595.
[56] Yeats selected 'Circe', 'Turf-Stacks', 'An Eclogue for Christmas', and 'The Individualist Speaks' for *The Oxford Book of Modern Verse* (London, Oxford University Press, 1936), praising MacNeice's 'intellectual passion', commending him (by contrast with Day-Lewis) as 'the anti-communist', and giving him more space than either Spender or Auden (419–27, xxxvi). All four poems, like 'Belfast' and 'Valediction', had recently appeared in MacNeice's *Poems* (London, Faber, 1935).

expect they may have trouble this year.'[57] There was no trouble, so MacNeice did not have to act on his promise to 'write an article anti-Orange'.[58] Instead, he adopted a tone of wry detachment:

The Orange procession was crazy – banners depicting Samson fighting with the Lion, Christ giving water to Total Abstainers, The Storming of Jhansi, William III of course ad nauseam, Queen Victoria pretty often, Lord Beaconsfield quite a bit, plenty of local worthies, a number of local churches & also some allegoricals like Justice & Truth. All very gaudy & the bearers staggering under the weight of them.[59]

Five years later, when drafting a booklet for the British Council on 'Northern Ireland and Her People', MacNeice's treatment of the Twelfth was positively warm, as if he had placated the 'voodoo of Orange drums' at last:

To an English spectator these processions, and the speech-makings which follow them, appear not only primitive but sinister, smacking even of fascism. In fact, however, they probably serve for most Orangemen, who in private life are quiet and unemotional, as an emotional safety-valve – a case of what the Greeks called 'catharsis'. It is not to be denied that in moments of political crisis the Orange Order can become a storm-centre but normally its bark is far worse than its bite . . . For the great majority of Orangemen their idea of goodness is summed up in the common phrase: 'a decent wee man'. The Decent Wee Man is unostentatious, sober, industrious, scrupulously honest, and genuinely charitable.[60]

The 'Decent Wee Man' was embodied in one of the most endearing personalities in MacNeice's imagined world: Archie White, the gardener:

Our best antidote to these terrors and depressions was the gardener Archie, in whose presence everything was merry. My father did not think of him in that way, as Archie, whose professional pride was easily wounded, would sometimes absent himself for weeks out of pique . . . The hawthorn sprigs would leap from his shears as he rambled along in a voice that was half singing, going over and over again about the gentlemen's places he had worked on and his wife Maggie and his canary and King William and the Twelfth of July. For Archie, though he could neither read nor write, was a great Orangeman and played a flute in the Twelfth of July procession. Until, that is, his rheumatism made him unable to march. The Orange Lily was his fitting emblem, for he took a childish delight in the gaudy and was naturally histrionic, would sometimes turn up in the morning with a small Union

---

[57] MacNeice to Eleanor Clark, 20 June 1939, in *Letters of Louis MacNeice*, ed. Jonathan Allison (London, Faber, 2010), 343. As Allison notes (idem, n. 1), his diary for 12 July 1917 reported that 'Daddie and I went to North Street and there were flags sticking out of the wall. We went to see Orangemen.'

[58] MacNeice to Eleanor Clark, 17 June 1939, in *Letters*, 346.

[59] MacNeice to Eleanor Clark, 16 July 1939, in *Letters*, 350.

[60] 'Northern Ireland and Her People' (*c.* June 1944), in *Selected Prose of Louis MacNeice*, ed. Alan Heuser (Oxford University Press, 1990), 148–9.

Jack in his cap . . . He had also his moments of moralising, was a good Temperance man as well as an Orangeman, would speak with contempt of the whisky-drinking corner boys with their big stomachs and their great white faces.[61]

Apart from his age and religion, Archie White had a good deal in common with Yeats's mythic mentor at Merville, the stable-boy. As MacNeice recollected in his last broadcast for the BBC in 1963: 'We also had a most remarkable, ancient, very rheumatic gardener, called Archie White, of whom I have very fond recollections. He was regarded very much as a "character", he was illiterate, he was a passionate Orangeman, and he was a great kind of a one for the make-believe. In fact, he was ideal company for someone about the age of 5 or 6 or 7.'[62] The gardener, like the stable-boy, was a servant who was also a playmate, fond of rhymes and chants, embodying a plebeian Orangeism far removed from the exalted fraternal affiliations of Frederick MacNeice, Frederick Pollexfen, or John Yeats. The menace that MacNeice associated with the Twelfth dissipated when filtered through Archie's 'cornflower-blue' eyes, as in an affectionate 'novelette' written in mid-1939:

> And every year he waited for the Twelfth of July,
> Cherishing his sash and his fife
> For the carnival of banners and drums.
> He was always claiming but never
> Obtaining his old age pension,
> For he did not know his age.

As rheumatism and sickness overtook him and he became house-bound, the gardener was left to gaze at 'a framed | Certificate of admission | Into the Orange Order'.[63] Few writers have captured the benign side of popular Orangeism with such fidelity, drawing on reserves of personal knowledge which MacNeice took care to conceal.

Lurking behind the gardener, with his simple decencies, was another more complex but familiar figure, MacNeice's father. Too shrewd and calculating to be a 'Decent Wee Man', too ambivalent towards Orangeism

---

[61] MacNeice, *Strings*, 47–8.
[62] 'Autobiographical Talk: Childhood Memories' (recorded 2 July 1963), in MacNeice, *Selected Prose*, 269.
[63] 'Novelettes, IV: The Gardener' (Summer 1939), in MacNeice, *Collected Poems*, 694–7. According to his family schedule, Census of Ireland (1911), Archibald White (57) from Co. Derry had been married for 15 years to Margaret (40) from Carrickfergus. Though claiming to 'read and rite' in 1911, he was unable to sign the Ulster Covenant in 1912 and so made his mark on the signature sheet. He was relatively consistent in stating his own age, but less so with his wife's age (46 and 37 respectively in 1901). He should therefore have qualified for the old-age pension in about 1925, when MacNeice was a Marlborough College dandy who no longer played fantasy games in the rectory garden.

to leave framed certificates in his archive, Frederick MacNeice nevertheless was a moralist, a total abstainer, and an exemplary Christian.
Increasingly, Louis MacNeice cherished the virtues that he had once
rejected or ridiculed, as in that mysterious late poem, 'The Truisms':

> His father gave him a box of truisms
> Shaped like a coffin, then his father died;
> The truisms remained on the mantelpiece
> As wooden as the playbox they had been packed in
> Or that other his father skulked inside.

After various adventures, 'through disbeliefs he arrived at a house | He
could not remember seeing before':

> And he walked straight in; it was where he had come from
> And something told him the way to behave.
> He raised his hand and blessed his home;
> The truisms flew and perched on his shoulders
> And a tall tree sprouted from his father's grave.[64]

In belatedly accepting his father's 'truisms', MacNeice also embraced the
humane elements of Orangeism that he had absorbed as a child in
Carrickfergus. Whereas the ageing Yeats drew inspiration from the violent
and sectarian strands of Orange tradition, MacNeice rediscovered the
delight of imagining himself, if only fleetingly, as a 'Decent Wee Man'.
The kindly spirit of the gardener had exorcised the demons released by
Yeats's stable-boy.

---

[64] 'The Truisms' (c.1960), in MacNeice, *Collected Poems*, 565.

5   Methodism and the Orange Order

I

The long-standing connection between Methodism and Orangeism in Ireland has become an embarrassment to many Methodists, impatient with the archaic anti-Catholic rhetoric of Orange leaders and anxious to sustain a mild, ecumenical alternative to secularism. Yet the Methodist Church and the Orange Order still have much in common, and even now Methodists are well represented among the brethren in Northern Ireland. A recent survey of 1,376 members of 90 Orange lodges indicated that 6.5% were Methodists, few by comparison with Presbyterians (50%) and Episcopalians (34%) but not far short of the Methodist component in the entire Protestant population.[1] If applicable to the entire Orange Order, this survey would imply a population of 1,500 or 2,000 male Orange Methodists. The 'people called Methodists' and the Orange brethren both belong to close-knit societies of medium size, which nevertheless make an evangelical appeal beyond their own membership and foster cooperation among Protestants of many denominations. At their peak shortly after the Second World War, both the Orange Order and the Methodist Church had over 70,000 adherents in Ireland, though the comparison is distorted by the fact that Orangeism appealed overwhelmingly to adult males.[2] Both organisations had expanded fairly steadily over the preceding century, and both have experienced slow but inexorable

---

[1] The survey by questionnaire was carried out in 2007–8: Jon Tonge et al., 'New Order: Political Change and the Protestant Orange Tradition in Northern Ireland', *The British Journal of Politics and International Relations*, xiii (2011), 400–19 (402). According to the Census of Northern Ireland (1991), declared Methodists constituted 3.8% of the population and 7.5% of those with a religious affiliation other than Roman Catholicism.

[2] The estimate for membership of Orange lodges (ignoring the few that cater for women and juveniles) is derived from returns and reports of the Loyal Orange Institution held in GOLIA. Unless otherwise stated, this archive contains all Orange documents cited below. The Methodist population as returned at the census considerably exceeds the number of registered adult members of the Society throughout Ireland (as returned annually in the published *MCM*), which peaked at over 32,000 in 1954.

numerical decline since the 1960s with an ageing membership and few entrants.

It is also noteworthy that Methodism, like Orangeism, has long been relatively strong in mid-Ulster counties such as Fermanagh and Armagh (see Table 5.1). This may be traced to the fact that the Church of Ireland provided most of the early recruits for both movements, which seldom flourished in regions dominated by Presbyterians of Scottish origin. The presence of a strong Catholic community in mid Ulster also encouraged Orangemen, and probably Methodists, to band together for mutual support. The most striking contrast between the two organisations is in Belfast, long a citadel of Methodism, where the Orange Order has always been relatively weak and where its decline has been most precipitate.

The factors that drew a minority of Methodists into the Orange Order were not specific to any religious denomination. Particularly in rural Ulster, Orange halls and lodges were essential to Protestant culture, providing much-needed venues for social recreation as well as fraternisation. For many evangelical Christians, Orange lodges provided a valuable forum for meeting and working with like-minded adherents of other churches, and for missionary activity designed to rescue the working classes from religious indifference and social degeneration. It also fostered a form of ecumenicism based upon common condemnation of the 'fatal errors of the Church of Rome'. Until recently, the anti-papist stance of the Orange Order was compatible with a wide spectrum of Protestant opinions about Catholicism, ranging from learned arguments against apostolic succession, transubstantiation, or papal intrusion in temporal affairs, to incredulous denunciation of Romish superstition, 'priest-craft', and 'backwardness'. Within the Orange Order, as within most Protestant churches, there were frequent collisions between liberal and die-hard anti-Catholics, often expressed in disputes about 'ritualism' within the Order which were at least as virulent as the battle against Rome. Likewise, Methodism was broad enough to encompass the High Church anti-Catholicism of the Wesleys as well as the more familiar aversion to superstition and vulgar display as a travesty of the Church of Christ. In one respect, however, Methodist and Orange anti-Catholicism were potentially at odds. Whereas Methodist missionaries participated in the campaigns of proselytism that raised such dramatic hopes of Protestant resurgence between the 'Second Reformation' and the 1870s, the Orange Order was extremely suspicious of converted 'papists' who were only admissible by special dispensation of the grand lodge of Ireland.

In addition to its spiritual functions, the Orange Order has been the nucleus for many movements of resistance to 'Home Rule', republicanism, and political subversion, causes which in times of crisis seemed more pressing than any religious crusade. Methodists were no less likely than Episcopalians or Presbyterians to combine against threats to the union, and Orangeism was one of the most efficient instruments for resisting such threats, whether through political and electoral campaigns, propaganda, fund-raising, or paramilitary organisation. This applied not only to recurrent confrontations between 1885 and 1922, but also to the early years of the more recent 'Troubles'. During the intervening half-century of unionist and Orange ascendancy in Northern Ireland, Methodists with political ambitions had just as strong an incentive as other Protestants to join or endorse the Order as a pathway to acceptance by the governing élite.

Whereas Orangeism is objectionable in principle to certain sects such as the Society of Friends, there is nothing obviously incompatible with Methodist teaching in the 'Qualifications of an Orangeman' or the institution's *Laws and Ordinances*. Admittedly, the Methodist conference resolved in 1932 that all candidates for ministry should be informed 'by the President of the Church of the recommendations of the Conference regarding the attitude of Ministers of the Methodist Church in Ireland towards secret societies'.[3] Yet this 'attitude', whatever it may have been, was clearly consistent with active and public advocacy of the Orange cause, especially when the president of the Church was a prominent Orange chaplain (as in 1938). The motion was introduced by Patrick Ernest Donovan (by origin a Skibbereen Catholic), whose career had been devoted mainly to running city missions. Instead of retiring, he had recently become superintendent of the 'colportage' of bibles throughout Ireland, 'not least amongst the Catholic community'. Having married the daughter of a prominent independent nationalist from Portadown and lived and worked in Dublin since 1900, Donovan was probably unsympathetic to the Orange influence in Methodism.[4] The mysterious rubric on secret societies was quietly dropped in June 1952, when the conference coincidentally elected John Montgomery from Florencecourt (until recently an Orange chaplain) as the new president of the Church.[5] Until Orange excoriation of the World Council of Churches became a

---

[3] *MCM* (1932), 34. This stipulation appeared as a resolution or in the regulations for examining candidates in every issue of *MCM* until 1951.

[4] For the eventful career of Patrick Ernest Donovan (1861–1953), see George Jones, 'Who Remembers P. E. Donovan? A Latter Day St. Patrick', *MN* (Oct. 1991), 2 (reference and further information kindly supplied by Revd Robin Roddie, my erudite adviser on all matters Methodist).

[5] The regulations concerning candidates for the ministry and the Board of Examiners were thoroughly revised in that year, but no reference was made to the excision of that concerning 'secret societies': *MCM* (1952), 29.

major obstacle for many Methodists and other ecumenical Protestants in the later 1960s,[6] doctrinal issues did not seriously inhibit Methodist involvement in the Order. Naturally, at all periods, a great many Methodists and other committed Protestants found Orangeism repugnant for a multitude of reasons and had nothing to do with it.

Orange records reveal very little about the scale or character of participation by Methodist laymen, but a good deal about the clergy who took office as chaplains. Many Methodist clergymen, like their Episcopalian and Presbyterian counterparts, used their status as chaplains to promote evangelisation, to make contacts beyond their own church potentially leading to recruitment of new members, to gain respect in the local community as well as in their own congregations, and (in some cases) to restrain the brethren from sectarian violence and criminality as well as intemperance and profanity. Yet Methodist ministers had a stronger incentive than other clergy to join the Order. Whereas senior Episcopalian and Presbyterian clergymen might serve in a single parish for decades, Methodist ministers normally changed circuits at least every fifth year. Having less opportunity for communal assimilation, they were under even greater congregational pressure to prove their eagerness by throwing themselves into populist organisations such as the Orange Order. Once initiated, they would have little difficulty in securing transfer to any Orange lodge in Ireland or beyond, through a system of certificates well attuned to the itinerant habits of the Methodist ministry.

II

Before charting the involvement of Methodist ministers and preachers in the Orange Order, let us look more closely at the lingering dominance of the Church of Ireland in its counsels and membership. Admission to the Order and its chaplaincy was never restricted to Episcopalians, and an early membership register, compiled in 1798–9, included blank columns headed 'Church of England' and 'Dissenter'.[7] The Orange historian Robert H. Wallace maintained in 1899 that some Tyrone lodges formed immediately after the Battle of the Diamond, in 1795, were

---

[6] A divisive campaign against the World Council of Churches was initiated in 1965, despite the grand master's recent warning 'against the Order getting involved in interdenominational strife'. As Sir George Clark perceived: 'We had many good Clerical brethren who were members of the Presbyterian or Methodist Churches, and if we were to become too deeply involved as an Institution, the situation might become rather delicate to handle': GOLI, *HYR* (June 1964), 14–15.

[7] Lodge 176, Register, 4 June 1797–Nov. 1799: photostats in GOLIA and NLI, MS 5398.

predominantly Presbyterian.[8] The first known reference to Methodist involvement occurs in the spiritual autobiography of William Browne, raised as a Methodist near Newtownbutler, Co. Fermanagh. Having found God at the age of eight in 1789, Browne temporarily mislaid Him a few years later when an 'extreme' aversion to disloyalty led Browne into 'the system called Orangeism, which in the hand of God proved a bulwark against the enemies of our holy religion'. Sympathetic to the political and spiritual aims of Orangeism, Browne also became infatuated by the use of music to promote solidarity among loyalists and to ridicule and 'aggravate the opposite party'. Influenced by 'an old professor of religion' who had read him an Orange song, Browne memorised the meretricious text, probably 'Croppies Lie Down', 'Boyne Water', or 'The Protestant Boys':

When insulted by Roman Catholic boys, I would repeat or sing a verse of it before them; I soon by this practice lost my communion with God . . . I remained destitute of the power of godliness in my soul for the period of nearly eight years.

A local revival in 1801 enabled Browne to stop singing and rediscover God, though fifteen years passed before he disposed of his 'chattel property' and became an itinerant preacher for the Primitive Wesleyan Methodists.[9]

Early Methodist involvement in the Order was confirmed in 1835 by Stewart Blacker, grand secretary of Co. Armagh, before the select committee on Orange lodges:

Are there many dissenters in the Orange Institution? – There are a great many.

Of what sects are those dissenters generally composed? – Chiefly composed of the old light Presbyterians, Methodists and Independents.[10]

Admittedly, the rules for a female lodge formed a few months after implementation of the Act of Union required each initiate to declare 'that I never will marry, or encourage any person to marry a Papist, & that I never will suffer my Children to be Baptiz'd or reard [sic] in any Church but the present Established Church of these United Kingdoms'.[11]

---

[8] Col. R. H. Wallace, 'History of the Orange Order', in *The Formation of the Orange Order, 1795–1798*, ed. Cecil Kilpatrick (Belfast, GOLI, 1994), 25–163 (49).

[9] Extracts from memoir by William Browne (1781–1850), ed. John Thompson, in *PWMM*, xxix (1851), 20–6, 99–106 (22–3): reference kindly supplied by Robin Roddie. The chronology is confused, since the Orange Order was founded only six years before 1801; but some songs that became popular among Yeomen and Orangemen antedated 1795.

[10] Evidence of Stewart Blacker, 3 June 1835, 115, q. 1778–9: *[First] Report from the Select Committee appointed to inquire into the Nature, Character, Extent and Tendency of Orange Lodges, Associations or Societies in Ireland* [Patten Committee], *Appendix*, 2–34: HC 1835 (377), xv, 1.

[11] MSS Rules of female Orange lodge 4, Dublin, 8 May 1801.

But this formulation was conveniently ambiguous, since the established church was Presbyterian in Scotland though Episcopalian in England and Ireland.[12] Equally ambiguous was the Orangeman's 'General Declaration' as formulated in each edition of the *Laws* from January 1800 to 1828, which referred to 'the true religion by him [William III] completely established in these kingdoms'. Though some Methodists might have been unhappy with conformity to any version of the established church, many practising Methodist families opted for baptism, marriage, and burial in the Church of Ireland. Furthermore, for 60 years before their disintegration in the wake of disestablishment, the Primitive Wesleyan Methodists acted as an evangelical preaching network within Episcopalianism. After 1828, the *Laws* did not specifically refer to the established church, and in 1846 the Order was ecumenically declared to be 'exclusively an association of those who are attached to the religion of the Reformation'.[13]

Early editions of the 'Qualifications of an Orangeman' concentrated on the positive attributes of 'the Protestant religion', as in 1828: 'He should love rational and improving society, faithfully regard the Protestant religion, and sincerely desire to propagate its precepts.' In 1846, however, this injunction was coupled with explicit condemnation of Rome:

He should love, uphold, and defend the Protestant religion, and sincerely desire and endeavour to propagate its doctrines and precepts. He should strenuously oppose and protest against the errors and dangerous doctrines of the Church of Rome; he should, by all lawful means, resist the ascendancy of that church – its encroachments, and the extension of its power; but he should abstain from all uncharitable words, actions, or feelings towards his Roman Catholic fellow-countrymen.

With a further injunction against 'countenancing (by his presence or otherwise) any act or ceremony of Popish worship', added in 1860, this

---

[12] In articles given statutory force in the Church of Scotland Act, 1921 (11&12 Geo. 5, cap. 30), that church describes itself as 'a national Church' whose head is not the monarch but God, and denies 'the civil authority any right of interference with the proceedings or judgments of the Church within the sphere of its spiritual government and jurisdiction' (including appointments). I am grateful to the Revd John Knox for pointing out (in a letter communicated to me by Robin Roddie) that, in this sense, it is not an 'established' church. Yet the same articles assert 'historical continuity with the Church of Scotland which was reformed in 1560, whose liberties were ratified in 1592, and for whose security provision was made in the Treaty of Union of 1707'. It remains, in short, a somewhat established church.

[13] Slight variants of the quoted rubric included omission of the phrase 'in these kingdoms' (1798, prior to the union), reference to William's encouragement of 'restoration . . . of the pure form of Religion established in these realms' (1823), and endorsement of 'the true religion by law established in this United Kingdom' (1828). Most editions of the *Laws* are held in GOLIA; many early editions were reproduced in Patten Committee, *First Report*.

formula has remained in force ever since.[14] Despite a local requirement just after the Great War that every candidate seeking admission to a Belfast lodge should be 'a member of an Evangelical Protestant Church', the form of proposal specified in the *Laws* from 1924 onwards merely required the candidate to declare that he 'was born of Protestant parents and was educated in the Protestant Faith'. A 'place of worship' had to be specified, and since 1964 the candidate has been required to name his 'religious denomination', attest 'regular' attendance, and declare that he had 'never been in any way connected with the Church of Rome'.[15]

As Methodist involvement in Orangeism intensified, a few lodges began to cater specifically for church members. A celebrated example was lodge 161 in Portadown, Co. Armagh, which adopted the title 'Wesleyan Temperance' when revived with a mainly Methodist membership in 1950. Within a few years, the lodge included no less than seven Methodist ministers simultaneously, and for three decades John Wesley was depicted on its banner.[16] By the mid-twentieth century, at least six Belfast lodges had adopted Methodist titles, including two commemorating Orange chaplains. Of these, two were more or less committed to Temperance, meaning that liquor was not to be consumed during lodge meetings, and four to Total Abstinence. The earliest Methodist titles were adopted in 1903, and the last in 1940.[17] At the unfurling ceremony in 1939 for the John Wesley Memorial Total Abstinence lodge 1209, the lodge's first banner was dedicated by William Eames, still at that period a Methodist minister. It depicted Wesley on one side and William of

---

[14] The expanded rubric appeared in all editions from 1860 to 1967.

[15] Proposal forms were published in the *Laws* from 1924 to 1967, in GOLI, *HYR*, until Dec. 1998, and sporadically in the CGL reports; for the Belfast proposal form, see Belfast CGL, *AR* (1923).

[16] R. David Jones et al., *The Orange Citadel: A History of Orangeism in the Portadown District* (Portadown, Cultural Heritage Committee, 1996), 93–4. Membership of lodge 161 rose from 6 in 1950 to 80 at its peak in 1955, declining steadily from 71 in 1967 to 21 in 2009. I have identified 9 Methodist ministers belonging to the lodge, of whom 3 held higher office (including Henry Holloway and Derek McMeekin) while 4 others served as Portadown district chaplains for various periods between 1953 and 2001 (William Ernest Morley Thompson, Ernest Shaw, John Keys, and John Barnabas Jennings): Armagh CGL, *County Grand Officers and List of Lodges* (Armagh, 1949–2010). Keys, Jennings, Derek Aldred, and Thomas Woods eventually resigned from the lodge.

[17] All new and revised titles of lodges were submitted for approval by GOLI and listed in *HYR* (1866–1975). My survey is based on those returns and Belfast CGL, *AR* (1956). Ostensibly Methodist lodges were Shankill Road Primitive Methodist Temperance lodge 465 (title approved in 1903), Wesleyan Young Men's Christian TA lodge 939 (1903), Falls Road Methodist Church Defenders' Temperance lodge 1433 (1921), Rev. William Maguire Memorial TA lodge 717 (1927), John Wesley Memorial TA lodge 1209 (1938; Temperance from 1973), and Rev. T. J. Allen Memorial TA lodge 1332 (1940).

Orange on the reverse. Lady Allen, wife of the sovereign grand master of the Royal Black Institution, snipped the cord with a pair of silver scissors and assured the brethren that if Wesley's teaching were to be universally followed, 'they would find a union of hearts, a victory over evil'. As for the Prince of Orange: 'Let them remember his leadership and his victories. That was their heritage.'[18]

Most Methodist Orangemen, however, belonged to lodges of mixed religion, particularly those proclaiming either Temperance or Total Abstinence. By 1910, almost half of Belfast's Orangemen belonged to such lodges, evidence of the success of evangelical clergy in imposing stricter moral discipline on a notoriously rowdy and inebriated institution.[19] Admittedly, many brethren failed to keep to their pledges, as revealed in the minute books of a Carrickfergus lodge embracing all major denominations. Ever since its foundation in September 1896, lodge 1537 had done its best to remain totally abstinent. Every member had to take 'a pledge to abstain from all intoxicating liquors or beverages, in or out of Lodge, in public or private'. Brethren were required to report violations (or face a fine of 5s.), and convicted offenders were suspended from the lodge until they had paid a similar fine and renewed their pledge before doubtless sceptical brethren.[20] The outcome of this moral crusade was discouraging. Nearly a quarter of those on the roll between 1911 and 1914 were punished for pledge violations, and a third of offenders repeated the offence and retook the pledge, sometimes two or three times. The atmosphere at lodge meetings must have resembled that of the Confessional, acts of contrition being rapidly followed by further lapses.

III

Clergymen were active in the Orange Order and the grand lodge of Ireland from 1798, but the first reference in the *Laws* to the office of chaplain dates from 1814. By 1846, there was provision for the appointment of chaplains for county, district, and private lodges as well as the governing body. Thereafter, every clergyman admitted to a private lodge was entitled to attend the district lodge, and every district chaplain could

---

[18] Cutting, evidently from *BT*, 23 June 1939, in 'Wesleyana', vol. ii, 331: MHSIA.

[19] Returns for just over 200 Belfast lodges in 1910 reveal that 2,934 brethren belonged to 60 Temperance lodges and 1,474 to 30 TA lodges, together representing 47.9% of total returned membership (9,195): Belfast CGL, *AR* (1910).

[20] LOL 1537, Minutes, 26 Sept. 1896. Unfounded accusations were also to be punished by a fine.

visit any lodge in that district and vote for county officers.[21] A further enticement to impecunious clergymen was a system of preferential fees approved in 1877, which meant that for several decades grand chaplains and deputy grand chaplains were charged only half of the fees imposed on equivalent lay officers.[22] Periodic attempts were made to restrict the number of chaplains at every level, presumably because of inundations by clergy who either threatened lay dominance of the institution, or ignored summonses to meetings and drifted away as swiftly as they had swarmed in. Chaplains were notoriously negligent attenders, as shown by the published attendance returns for meetings of the Belfast county grand lodge between 1876 and 1932. On average, over two-thirds of clerical members failed to attend any of the dozen or so meetings held each year, compared with only 8% of lay officers.[23] The indifference of most chaplains to Orange administration does not, of course, imply indifference to the social and spiritual opportunities that the Order offered.

The Orange chaplaincy remained virtually an Episcopalian fiefdom until the 1860s, despite the long-standing involvement of lay Presbyterians and Dissenters. The Episcopalian monopoly was first broken by John B. McCrea, a 'ranting swaddler'[24] who conducted the Ebenezer chapel in D'Olier Street, Dublin and held offices in the grand lodge of Ireland from 1831 to 1836. He had gained celebrity for his fulminations against Catholic Emancipation and O'Connell, receiving honorary freedom of the City of Dublin in 1829.[25] McCrea is said to have added an orange and purple sash to his vestments when conducting services for his Independent congregation.[26] The first Presbyterian minister to gain office, as a member of the grand lodge committee in 1835–6 rather than as a chaplain, was

---

[21] Under editions of the *Laws* promulgated between 1860 and 1896, every chaplain of a private lodge also became a district chaplain, an office restricted in number at certain periods. Editions between 1924 and 1967 limited the chaplaincy and attendance at district lodges to those who had been raised to the Purple degree.

[22] Half fees were prescribed in editions of the *Laws* promulgated between 1896 and 1933.

[23] Statistics based on attendance lists in Belfast CGL, *AR*s, 1876–1932 (excluding 1877–8, 1894, 1896, 1913–14, 1921–2, 1924, 1926, and 1930). The annual number of meetings varied between about eight and sixteen. The non-attendance ratio for clergy (68.1%) peaked at 76.8% in the 1910s. That for lay officers (7.9%) fell to 0.3% in the 1920s.

[24] This epithet, commonly applied to Methodist preachers in Ireland after 1747, appeared in a scurrilous pamphlet attributed to 'O'Donohoe, a lay Catholic' and sold in the streets of Dublin in 1835: *The Times*, 16 Sept. 1835 (prosecution of Patrick Gannon).

[25] Jacqueline Hill, *From Patriots to Unionists: Dublin Civic Politics and Irish Protestant Patriotism, 1660–1840* (Oxford, Clarendon Press, 1997), 339.

[26] Note in GOLI, Warrant Register (1856), stating that McCrea was the first master of the Constitutional Calvin lodge 1509 (Newcastle district, Co. Dublin), warranted in 1834 and so numbered in celebration of Calvin's year of birth. McCrea is listed as conducting an Independent meeting-house in D'Olier St. in Pettigrew's and Oulton's *Dublin Almanac* for 1836 and 1837, when the chapel was sold to a congregation of the Presbyterian

William Freeland of the Scots' church in Kingstown. Freeland's services
attracted many naval personnel, Fellows of Trinity College, and other
Episcopalians; but in 1838 the Synod of Ulster moved him to Ballygawley,
Co. Tyrone, following 'serious disagreements' between Freeland and
members of his flock.[27] No other Presbyterian minister held recorded
Orange office until 1853, when William White was returned as a deputy
grand chaplain for Monaghan. Both Freeland and White, son of a Cavan
farmer and 'a remarkably strong and active man', had been educated in
Glasgow.[28]

Notwithstanding Episcopalian dominance in the early chaplaincy, various Presbyterian and Dissenting ministers or preachers who may or may
not have been brethren contributed to the chorus of commemorative
rhetoric at services for Orangemen. Among them was H. H. Campbell, a
Primitive Wesleyan Methodist preacher whose sermon to 'a large body of
Orangemen, and others, assembled in a field near Tandragee' in August
1835, was published in Newry with the approval of the Order's grand
chaplain, Holt Waring.[29] Campbell coupled Satan with 'the Popes of
Papal Rome, and their adherents' as 'enemies of the Church of Christ';
recalled 'the bloodshed of Portadown and Wexford-bridge, Vinegar
and Tara hills; and the wretched burning of the Scullabogue barn'; and
likened 'the Papists' to the Amalekites who had been justly dispossessed
by God in favour of the Jews. Despite the setback of Emancipation,
Campbell declared that 'all former concessions avail them nothing, while
an Orange Banner floats in air – while a Protestant drum echoes through
the valleys – while an Orange Association remains embodied'. Execrating
Rome as the Book of Revelation's 'Babylon the Great, the Mother of
Harlots and abomination of the earth', he was equally scathing about
'Nominal Protestants, drunken, Sabbath-breaking, swearing, unconverted

---

Secession Synod: Steven C. Smyrl, *Dictionary of Dublin Dissent: Dublin's Protestant
Dissenting Meeting Houses, 1660–1920* (Dublin, A. & A. Farmar, 2009), 55, 66, 214–15
(where, however, McCrea is not mentioned as a minister).

[27] *A History of Congregations in the Presbyterian Church in Ireland, 1610–1982*, ed.
W. Desmond Bailie et al. (Belfast, PHSI, 1982), 435.

[28] *The Witness*, ii (12 Nov. 1875), 4–5; James S. McConnell et al., *Fasti of the Irish
Presbyterian Church, 1613–1840* (Belfast, PHSI, 1951), 262, 293. Neither Freeland nor
White was named by Brian Kennaway in his useful lecture to the PHSI, 'Orangeism: A
Prebyterian Perspective' (Mar. 2006).

[29] H. H. Campbell, *A Sermon, Preached … on Sunday, 9th August, 1835* (Newry, pr.
Alexander Peacock, 1835): GOLIA. Though identified as a preacher in this pamphlet,
Campbell's name is absent from the returns of stations and missions for 1834–6 in
the *PWMM*, though the return for June 1834 includes a mission at Castlebar and
Turlough, Co. Mayo marked 'One to be sent': *PWMM*, xii, 296. The magazine carried
regular reports from the anonymous 'Agent' at Turlough, either a scripture reader or
schoolmaster.

Orangemen'. Campbell's sermon is indistinguishable in its themes, tropes, and metaphors from innumerable Orange and anti-Catholic philippics delivered throughout the British Empire since 1795. It displays no specifically Wesleyan imprint, either in its contents or tone.

The lingering dominance of Episcopalians in the Orange chaplaincy is evident in Table 5.2, which records the denominations of clergymen in the grand lodge at decennial intervals from 1856 to 1996. Since the table unavoidably excludes district chaplains not returned as members of higher lodges, perhaps half of all Methodist ministers and other clergy who became Orange chaplains have eluded my net.[30] Of ministers securing higher office, the majority belonged to the Church of Ireland in every year except 1986, when Presbyterians temporarily achieved equal representation after a century of fairly constant infiltration of the chaplaincy. No similar trend is apparent in Methodist representation, which was as large in 1876 as in 1976. The fact that only half a dozen Methodist ministers at a time have typically held higher office is unremarkable, since Methodists accounted for barely 7% of Ireland's Protestant clergy in 1861 and 10% in 1901.[31] Though only a small minority of Ireland's 250-odd Methodist clergy held senior Orange office in any particular year, the proportion serving as chaplains at some point in their career was considerably higher. The Methodist contingent consistently exceeded the sprinkling of Congregational or 'Independent' ministers, who account for most of those tabulated as 'other' clergy. Episcopalian clerical ascendancy was still an object of resentment in 1955, when a futile attempt was made to amend the *Laws* to ensure that 'due regard' be paid to ensuring 'a fair representation from the leading Protestant Churches in Ireland' in appointing grand and deputy grand chaplains of Ireland. After reference to 'the difficulties of sectarian basis becoming a guide', the motion was lost by a huge majority (13: 50).[32]

---

[30] The patchy availability of annual county reports listing district chaplains precludes systematic analysis; but, on the basis of available reports, it may be estimated that the number of district chaplains without higher office (123) roughly equalled that of clergy holding grand lodge or county office in about 1920 (127). The number of mere district chaplains remained substantial around 1955 (83: 125), but was insignificant around 1885 (18: 200) and 1995 (22: 89). For Methodist ministers returned in those reports, ten were returned only as district chaplains while twelve attained higher office.

[31] The census for 1861 returned 3,014 Roman Catholic and 3,265 other clergy, of whom 227 were Methodists of all varieties (7.0%), 677 Presbyterians (20.7%), and 2,265 Episcopalians (69.4%). In 1901, the corresponding figures were 3,711 Catholic and 2,726 other clergy, of whom 277 were Methodists (10.2%), 685 Presbyterians of the general synod (25.1%), and 1,617 Episcopalians (59.3%). See Census of Ireland (1861), *General Report*, HCP 1863 [3204–IV], lxi, 508; Census of Ireland (1901), *General Report*, HCP 1902 [Cd. 1190], cxxix, 117.

[32] GOLI, *HYR* (Dec. 1954), 35; (June 1955), 8.

It should be noted that, in quite recent times, clergy belonging to sects such as the Free Presbyterian Church of Ulster have been debarred from taking office. Between 1952 and 1999, the clerical chaplaincy was restricted to authenticated ministers of eight denominations (Church of Ireland, Presbyterian – along with the Non-Subscribing and Reformed synods – Methodist, Baptist, Congregational, and Moravian). This limitation was advocated by Canon Louis Warden Crooks (a former Methodist minister), who told the central committee 'that a man did not become a Clergyman by meeting his collar at the back. There were some scandals of men claiming Clerical status.'[33] He was referring to the recent inauguration of the Free Presbyterian Church of Ulster by Ian Paisley, a district chaplain since about 1948 who eventually resigned from the Order in 1965. Paisley's accusations of heresy against all major Christian churches made nonsense of the Orange Order's pan-Protestant crusade.[34] Yet there was already provision for the appointment of lay chaplains in the absence of sufficient 'clerical brothers', a stipulation that enabled Free Presbyterians and other pariahs access to the chaplaincy and higher lodges through a side entrance.

IV

Who were the Methodist ministers who have served as senior officers in the Orange Order? I have assembled basic information on the careers of 48 Methodist clergy who served on the grand lodges of Ireland or the various counties between 1853 and 1996.[35] As already indicated, it is likely that a similar number of Methodist ministers served as lodge or district chaplains without being elected to higher office. The 48 ministers include no less than nineteen who changed denomination in the course of their clerical careers, whether before, during, or after their service as Orange chaplains. These religious migrants comprised ten Primitive Wesleyans who became Wesleyan Methodists and two who joined the Church of Ireland, along with nine Wesleyan Methodists who moved on

---

[33] GOLI, Central Committee, Minutes, 8 June 1951. The change was unanimously approved on 12 Dec. 1951 and incorporated in the revised edition of the *Laws* published in 1967. All denominational restrictions on the chaplaincy were lifted, after numerous acrimonious debates, in Sept. 1999: GOLI, *HYR, passim*.

[34] Free Presbyterian Church of Ulster, *Celebrating Our Golden Jubilee: A Brief History of Our Churches and Daily Devotions for the Year* (Belfast, FPCU, 2001).

[35] For names and characteristics of these chaplains, see original version of this chapter in *Bulletin of the Methodist Historical Society of Ireland*, xvii, no. 33 (2012), 5–38 (Table 4).

to other churches.[36] It follows that my survey of the 'Methodist' Orange chaplaincy is neither comprehensive nor restricted to 'pure' Methodists.

As Table 5.3 indicates, the typical (median) Methodist chaplain or officer held office over a fairly brief span (a decade), though three ministers have served, at least intermittently, for almost half a century. Most ministers were well advanced in their careers before taking office, the median age on appointment being 47 and the median period as a minister prior to appointment being nineteen years. The practice of moving ministers every few years to a new circuit helps to explain the substantial number who left office before completing their clerical careers. The extreme case was Thomas Rutherford who ceased to be a county chaplain in 1881, retired as a minister in 1912, and died at the age of 81 in 1929. Even more retained their office as chaplains long after retiring from active ministry, notably Francis Herbert Scott Maguire, who retired from the ministry because of ill-health in 1939 yet died in harness as a grand chaplain in 1969 at the age of 83. The longevity of these ministers was remarkable, the median age at death being 78. The record is currently held by John Hart (1902–2001). It is worth noting that the median age at death for more recent ministers was only slightly higher than for those taking office before 1940, despite marked improvement in mortality for the general population. Ministers entering the grand lodge before 1940 were typically more than a decade younger than their successors, with shorter ministerial experience.[37] Comparison with the set of 43 Presbyterian ministers who took Orange office between 1835 and 1922 indicates that the median Presbyterian entrant was slightly younger, with less ministerial experience, and more inclined to relinquish Orange office before retirement. Methodists may also draw satisfaction from the fact that their Presbyterian counterparts tended to die younger.[38]

In most cases, it has also been practicable to ascertain birthplace, county of residence at the time of taking Orange office, and occupational background. No less than 24 of the 48 ministers were born in the Orange and Methodist heartland of mid Ulster, including 12 in Fermanagh and

[36] Apart from six Methodist clergy who joined the Church of Ireland ministry, James Atkinson became a Congregationalist, Derek McMeekin a Presbyterian, and Robert Bradford a minister accredited by the Missouri Conference of the Methodist Protestant Church.
[37] The group includes 25 ministers taking Orange office up to 1938 and 23 thereafter. The median age at death for the two groups was 77 and 80/83 years; the median age on taking office was 43 and 50 years; and the median period between entering the ministry and Orange office was 19 and 26 years.
[38] For the 43 Presbyterian ministers assuming office before 1922, the median age on taking office was 41/42 years, the median period in ministry was 15 years, the median span of Orange office was 8 years, and the median age at death was 69/71 years.

6 in Armagh. Of the remainder, 12 were born in the north-east, 2 in the 'Lost Counties', 7 elsewhere in Southern Ireland, and 3 overseas. Not surprisingly, the territorial focus moves to the populous north-east when we examine the circuits where Methodist chaplains were serving at the time of taking office. Of the 48 ministers, 23 were working in the north-east (including 11 in Belfast), 17 in mid Ulster, 4 in the Lost Counties, and 4 in Dublin or King's Co. Of the 46 ministers whose fathers' occupation is known, half were farmers' sons.[39] Several others were men of humble origin who had discovered Christ while working as apprentices or drapers' assistants: at least 13 had previous employment ranging from farm labour to the civil service. In the course of their careers, most of the group had experience as missionaries or chaplains (28) and in Southern Ireland (38), while 11 ministered overseas at some period. Thus almost all Methodist ministers associated with higher lodges in the Orange Order spent part of their working lives beyond Ulster, and more than a quarter of them were born outside the 'Black North'.

The county returns of resignations from the Orange Order make it possible to identify eleven Methodist chaplains who formally left the organisation, whether because of conflict, infirmity, or migration.[40] This list excludes the much larger group of those who faded out of Orangeism through indifference and non-attendance, almost always without incurring recorded long-term suspension or expulsion. Though biannual returns of resignation (probably incomplete) were published in official reports between 1851 and 1975, the first case involving a Methodist minister was that of Beresford Lyons in 1934, eight years before his election as president of the Methodist Church in Ireland.[41] Resignations of Methodist chaplains became more frequent in the late 1950s, and doubtless continued after the publication of county returns was terminated in 1975. The age at resignation ranged between 35 and 71 (median 60 years). The resigners, only one of whom attained higher office, were even more likely than senior Methodist chaplains to have come from mid Ulster and served in Southern Ireland. No less than four resigned from Wesleyan Temperance lodge 161 in Portadown between 1959 and 1973. These resignations betoken the extraordinary past concentration of Methodist chaplains in Portadown, where four successive circuit

---

[39] In one case, a farmer's nephew.
[40] For details of these resigned ministers, see original version of this chapter, in *Bulletin of the Methodist Historical Society of Ireland*, xvii, no. 33 (2012), 5–38 (Table 5).
[41] Seventy-three returns of clerical resignations have been abstracted from GOLI, *HYR* (1851–1975), of which 15 occurred in the nineteenth century (1865–1900) and 35 from 1955 onwards.

superintendents between 1945 and 1964 were at some period Orange
chaplains, along with at least four of their fellow ministers.[42]

V

It is noteworthy that all but two of the fourteen ministers who took senior
Orange office in the nineteenth century 'entered the work' as Primitive
Wesleyan Methodist preachers, though half of these had already been
ordained in either the Church of Ireland or the Methodist Church
in Ireland before beginning their Orange careers. The predominance of
Primitives among early Orange chaplains reflects the close association
between that branch of Methodism and the Church of Ireland.[43] Though
lay preachers, they were treated as ordained clergy in Orange records and
accorded the honorific 'Reverend'. A lone Primitive Methodist preacher
of the English Connexion, Thomas Routledge Holtby, served as a Belfast
chaplain for a single year (1886).[44] The only 'original' Methodist in the
group was Robert John Ballard, who spent five years as a Methodist
minister (1871–6) before joining the Church of Ireland.[45] While a curate
working for the Irish Church Missions in Connemara in 1878, he
witnessed the violent consequences of proselytism when the Belleek
schoolhouse was burnt down during a concerted campaign against missionary teachers. Though the teacher and her family escaped, Ballard

---

[42] The superintendents were Ernest Shaw (appointed for five successive years from June
1945), William Thompson (1950), John Barnabas Jennings (1955), and Henry Holloway
(1960). Orange chaplains who ministered with Shaw or Thompson on the Portadown
circuit in this period included Thomas Kennedy (1945), Edwin Colvin (1946, for three
years), John Keys (1950), and another reputed member of 161, William John Wesley Gray
(1951). In all, 8 out of 25 ministers serving the circuit during the quarter-century from
1945 are known to have been Orangemen. For a list of ministers (1859–1960), see
William J. Green, *Methodism in Portadown* (Belfast, pr. Nelson and Knox, 1960), 102–3.

[43] Robin P. Roddie, 'Keeping the Faith: Ireland's Primitive Methodism', *Proceedings of the
Wesleyan Historical Society*, lvii, pt. 6 (2010), 225–45.

[44] Though returned in GOLI, *HYR* (Dec. 1885) as 'John' Holtby, Ormeau Rd (DGC,
Belfast), his name appears correctly as 'T. Holtby' in the *AR* of the Belfast CGL (1886)
and as 'T. R. Holtby', district chaplain, of 4 Connaught Ave, in the reports for 1899–1901.
Again elected as a county DGC in 1899 and 1900, during his second spell in Belfast,
Holtby's appointment was among those rejected by GOLI. See also Robin P. Roddie,
'Primitive Methodism's Irish Connection', in *Bulletin of the Wesley Historical Society of
Ireland*, ix (Winter 2003), 3–38 (33).

[45] Among the DGCs for Armagh (1880–6) was Revd 'G. W.' Ballard of Newtownhamilton.
Since Robert John Ballard was rector of that parish (1880–1913), it may be assumed that
his initials were mistranscribed through excusable confusion with John Woods Ballard (a
Methodist minister posted in Munster, 1879–88) and his brother George Gray Ballard
(who left the Methodist Church in the same year as Robert John Ballard to join the Church
of Ireland, but left for an Ontario parish in 1879). No other clerical Ballard with Armagh
associations in the 1880s has been traced.

found 'nothing but the bare walls standing' when he inspected the site next morning.[46] For ministers like Ballard, anti-Catholicism was no mere attitude but a passion fuelled by personal experience. No doubt the passion remained after his translation in 1880 to the 'frontier' parish of Newtownhamilton, south Armagh, where he became rector and a county chaplain in the same year.

The first Methodist deputy grand chaplain of Ireland, Daniel MacAfee, had switched from the Primitives to the Methodist Conference in 1827. According to an obituary, he had already displayed 'great controversial talent, especially in exposing the errors of Romanism', becoming 'an original thinker' who 'did not tread the beaten track of theological thought'. When he published a letter addressed to O'Connell in 1840, 'the vaunting Goliah [sic] of Popery and priestcraft was thoroughly defeated, and completely silenced, for Daniel O'Connell ... never attempted a rejoinder'. Alas, it may be that O'Connell's attention was never drawn to MacAfee's *coup de grâce*. By 1853–4, when MacAfee held office in the grand lodge while stationed in north Belfast, his glory days of polemical celebrity were past, though he fostered 'a large circle of admiring friends' during several stints in the city before retiring to London on medical advice.[47] Sixteen years passed before another Methodist preacher (William Conlin, while still a Primitive Methodist) took office in the grand lodge.

Obituaries indicate that most of the early Primitive chaplains were caught up in the giddy excitement and optimism aroused by religious revival around 1859. William Conlin witnessed 'remarkable revivals of religion' while stationed in Banbridge and Roscrea; John Ker watched the Irvinestown revival erupt in the house of a Mr Jones on his first visit to Tedd, 'the results of which will never die'; James Irwin's 'peculiar delight was in revivals, with many of which he had the happiness of being associated'; and Thomas Rutherford's father was 'deeply influenced' by the revival in Florencecourt, Co. Fermanagh, seat of the 3rd Earl of Enniskillen who was also grand master of Ireland.[48] The experience of revival fortified the hope that Protestants of all sects could share in the quest for salvation and in common defiance of Satan and Rome. Thus Thomas Absalom Jones addressed 'Protestants of all denominations' in

---

[46] *The Banner of the Truth in Ireland* (1 Apr. 1879), 1. For religious disturbances in west Connemara, see David Fitzpatrick, *'Solitary and Wild': Frederick MacNeice and the Salvation of Ireland* (Dublin, Lilliput Press, 2012), ch. 2, 3; Miriam Moffitt, *Soupers and Jumpers: The Protestant Missions in Connemara, 1848–1937* (Dublin, Nonesuch, 2008).

[47] *Irish Evangelist*, xiv (11 Jan. 1873), 13; *MCM* (1873), 5–6; Robin Roddie in *A Dictionary of Methodism in Britain and Ireland*, ed. John A. Vickers (Peterborough, Epworth Press, 2000), 216.

[48] *MCM* (1903), 6–7; *ICA*, 14 Mar. 1890, 123; *MCM* (1888), 8–10; *MCM* (1929), 16.

Dungannon in 1867, at the last of a series of missionary meetings initiated in Lurgan by the rector of Donacloney, who had called on 'all Christians who hold the truth to be united, and stand against the common foe'.[49] James Bradshaw published polemical tracts with fearsome titles such as *Eating the Gods* and *Blood Worship*, denouncing 'Romish' elements in the Book of Common Prayer and the Methodist Hymnal.[50] Yet Bradshaw was reputedly delightful with children, plucking apples from his garden to distribute among expectant 'little boys' and bringing sweets for the children on country visits.[51] John Elliott was 'a staunch Protestant, and popular member of the Orange Order, yet his dealings with his Roman Catholic countrymen were friendly and kind'.[52] As with a host of anti-Catholic evangelicals from 'Roaring Hugh' Hanna to Paisley, ministers like Elliott drew a clear distinction between abstract denunciation of popery and personal courtesy towards papists, precisely as demanded in the 'Qualifications of an Orangeman'.

Thomas Cather Maguire, initially a Primitive preacher, served as an Orange chaplain for twenty years up to his death in 1889. Maguire's parents belonged simultaneously to the established and Methodist churches, his father being a local preacher in Tempo, Co. Fermanagh. While a missionary preacher in Kerry in 1848, Thomas reported that an 'Irish teacher' in Newmarket, Co. Cork, had taken 'from his pocket a Bible, to prove the truth of his observations', whereupon a 'bigoted Romanist' seized the sacred volume and began to burn it in the street. Despite protests from two women, it was taken to a Catholic house 'and there amidst great rejoicing committed to the flames'. Next day, 22 other bibles were collected, smeared with tar, and consigned to a large fire in the street. Half-burnt volumes 'were lifted up on sticks and tossed into the air, the act being accompanied with the shouting of an ungodly multitude' and followed by the illumination of houses, 'as if exulting at the news of a great national victory'.[53] During Maguire's tenure as an Orange officer, he too switched from Primitive preaching to ministering for the Methodist Church. In common with many of his Orange Methodist contemporaries, Thomas Maguire's outlook was shaped by stark and frightening sectarian confrontations, fostering cooperation

---

[49] Account by John Carlisle in *PWMM*, xlvi (1 Jan. 1868), 57–8.

[50] Copies of several of his pamphlets, including *Blood Worship: Christian Idolatry, The Fallacies and Heresies of Our Hymnology; A Paper Read before the Ministers of the Enniskillen District Synod* (Belfast, John Adams, 1916), are in *MHSIA*.

[51] Notes on Bradshaw, IMP; funeral oration by Thomas Walmsley, DGC, Ireland, in *ICA* (13 Aug. 1926), 393.

[52] *ICA* (17 Apr. 1925), 189.

[53] *ICA* (11 July 1890), 351; *PWMM* (May–June 1848), 221–2.

among evangelical Protestants but allowing little exercise of brotherly love for Romanists.

In 1921, William Maguire became the first Methodist grand chaplain of Ireland. Yet another Primitive from Fermanagh, he had already belonged briefly to the Armagh grand lodge before being absorbed into the united Methodist church in 1878. 'Gifted with a magnificent physique and remarkable energy', he 'shared in many gracious revivals of religion' before and after that union. His later career was spent founding, funding, and supervising the North Belfast Mission, where he relentlessly pursued 'the social and moral elevation of the masses' and 'mingled freely with Christians of all denominations'.[54] In 1888, Maguire was rebuked by English Methodists for describing Parnell's party as 'oily-tongued gentlemen, the paid hirelings of Fenians, who would kiss them [Protestants], as Judas did, and shed crocodile tears'; but his defenders ridiculed the suggestion that Methodist ministers were bound to 'non-interference in political questions' by some 'honourable understanding'.[55] Despite his willingness to enlighten ladies against the will of their Catholic husbands, leading to a court action in 1917, there was reportedly 'no man who would go quicker out of his way to help a Roman Catholic family or feed a hungry Roman Catholic child than he'.[56] Maguire's son Francis became a Belfast chaplain shortly after his father's election as a grand chaplain, duly becoming the second Methodist to hold that office three decades later and exercising, in the opinion of a Methodist magazine, 'a helpful influence in the affairs of the Order'.[57] The ecumenical character of the Orange chaplaincy was personified in the fact that two other sons of William Maguire, who joined the Church of Ireland, also became county chaplains within a few years of their ordination.[58]

By the early twentieth century, the main target of the 'Protestant crusade' and its Orange Methodist protagonists had shifted from popery to secularism. John McCaffrey's preparation for the Methodist ministry was open-air preaching with the Skibbereen convert Patrick Donovan, involving visits to the monthly fair at Downpatrick. He took a 'keen interest' in the troops at Ballykinlar and acted as chaplain to the RAF at Bishopscourt, Co. Down. His funeral was attended by clergy of other denominations,

---

[54] *MCM* (1925), 10–12; *ICA* (19 Dec. 1924), 735.
[55] *ICA* (8 Mar., 5, 12 Apr. 1888), 113, 161, 173.
[56] Notes of Maguire, IMP; *ICA* (26 July 1924), 762.   [57] *ICA* (30 Jan. 1969), 5.
[58] Charles Wesley Maguire (1890–1978) and William John Finlay Maguire (d. 1954) were both ordained in 1920. By 1926, Charles was DGC for Belfast and Ireland, posts that he had relinquished within five years. In 1931, William was DGC for Belfast and Down, subsequently holding office in Antrim until his death.

and he was noted for 'reconciling members of families, and of churches, who had become estranged'.[59] Francis Johnston, a policeman's son from Liverpool but reared near Omagh, was taken up by the Orange landlord John Porter of Belleisle, Co. Fermanagh. Porter engaged Johnston as a rent-collector and allegedly bribed him to conform to the Church of Ireland, to no avail. Johnston, a tall homely figure with a powerful if acquired northern brogue and a way with the violin, was remembered as 'a powerful preacher and strong opponent of hard drink and the breaking of the Sabbath'.[60] John Glass was active in the Masonic and the Black as well as the Orange, regarding them as alternative paths to salvation: 'All these were channels through which he could influence men and proclaim the Gospel. He served them with loyalty, devotion and unabated zeal and was a brother beloved.'[61] Another multiple fraternalist, 'highly respected' in all three orders, was the noted carpenter and craftsman David John Allen.[62]

Noah Edward Mulligan was one of several Orange chaplains to tackle unruly congregations of sinners, returning to deal with Crumlin Road prisoners after five years with the forces in Tunisia and Italy from 1941 to 1946. In 'A Padre's Christmas in Italy', he gave a jolly account of fun and games on Christmas Day, recalling the inversion of normal social hierarchies characteristic of Orange or Masonic lodges where the worshipful master might be a tradesman dictating to his social betters: 'The troopers get much pleasure out of the fact that servants and officers are given most of the duties for the day ... Officers bring sergeants a mug of tea, sergeants likewise wait on the men – who delight in telling the sergeants a few home-truths which they accept with a smile.'[63] Other ministers joined the Orange after overseas service as missionaries. Having failed to secure appointment in the West Indies, John Truesdale spent eighteen years in the Gold Coast and Southern Rhodesia, where he displayed 'great integrity and moral courage'.[64] Henry Cooke was stationed in the West Indies for the same period, facing 'problems of gambling, drinking and the increasing attractiveness of the secular side of life' which supplied useful preparation for his eventual return to Ulster.[65] Both missionaries became Orange chaplains several years after returning to Ireland, perhaps in

---

[59] *ICA* (15 Jan. 1960), 4.   [60] Notes on Johnston, IMP.
[61] Funeral address by Revd W. E. M. Thompson of lodge 161, Portadown: *ICA* (2 Nov. 1956), 4–5.
[62] *MN* (Oct. 1994), 6; *MCM* (1995), 10.
[63] *MN* (Sept. 1980), 7; *ICA* (7 Dec. 1945), 9.
[64] *MCM* (1971), 7; *ICA* (15 Apr. 1971), 2.
[65] *MN* (Feb. 1990), 4; 'Harvest of the West Indian Mission Field: An Address Given at Cranagill Harvest Praise Service by Rev. Henry Cooke', *ICA* (28 Oct. 1949), 1–2.

response to pressure from their respective congregations in Catholic-dominated west Fermanagh and Portaferry.

VI

Eight senior Orange chaplains became titular leaders of Irish Methodism, four being elected to presidency of the annual Primitive Wesleyan Methodist Conference and four more to the equivalent post for the Methodist Church in Ireland.[66] During the decade of disintegration of the Primitives between 1869 and 1878, the presidency was assumed in quick succession by Thomas Absalom Jones (1869), James Irwin (1873), Thomas Cather Maguire (1876), and John Ker (1878). As president in the year of reunion with the Methodist majority, Ker visited the United States in search of funds to underwrite the union.[67] Orange leadership in the reunited Church was more spasmodic, with the election of William Maguire (1917), Thomas James Allen (1938), John Montgomery (1952), and finally Robert James Good (1958). Allen was self-educated with a penchant for Victorian novels and the 'instincts of a good business man', his funeral being attended by five brethren from his Total Abstinence lodge in Newry.[68] By contrast, Good had relinquished the chaplaincy over a decade before his election as president in 1958, when he declared his intention 'to enjoy it all and to seek to bring joy and happiness wherever I went'.[69]

In addition to these senior officers, four other presidents of the Church are known to have been Orangemen at some period: Beresford Stuart Lyons (1942), William Ernest Morley Thompson (1948), Ernest Shaw (1954), and Harold Good (2002). Thompson and Shaw remained district chaplains and members of lodge 161 in Portadown during their presidencies, Brother Shaw being congratulated on his elevation by the grand lodge of Ireland, along with the incoming moderator of the Presbyterian general assembly (John Knowles).[70] But Lyons had resigned from the Order eight years before his election, and Harold Good's tenure as chaplain of the Bessbrook district in south Armagh had ended in 1965, 37 years

---

[66] The leader of the Methodist Church in Ireland, elected at the annual conference, was termed vice-president of the conference from 1868 and also president of the Methodist Church in Ireland from 1921.

[67] *ICA* (14 Mar. 1890), 123.   [68] *ICA* (21 July 1939), 4; *ICA* (25 July 1939), 12.

[69] *MN* (July–Aug. 1976). Good had eloquently but vainly proposed 'Spiritual Regeneration as the Basis of National Reconstruction' after the Great War, in his Devers' Prize Essay for Probationers: *ICA* (4 June 1920), 91–2.

[70] GOLI, *HYR* (June 1954), 9. Shaw was returned as a Portadown district chaplain between 1954 and 1960, and Thompson remained a district chaplain in 1955: Armagh CGL, *List of Lodges* (1954–60).

before his election to presidency of the Church.[71] He was one of many young ministers for whom membership of the Orange Order was almost a precondition for winning the trust of his congregation, though in later years, like his father Robert, he no longer wore the sash. Harold Good's subsequent career as negotiator, peacemaker, and protagonist of human rights demonstrates that a liberal and reforming outlook is quite capable of emerging from an Orange background.

Other Orangemen played less conspicuous but influential parts in organising Irish Methodism. Before becoming president of the Primitives, Thomas Maguire had spent a decade as secretary to their conference (1859–69). Thomas John Crabbe, who 'liked order and discipline', particularly 'enjoyed the fact that he was last secretary of the Committee on Committees'.[72] Henry Holloway was one of several Orange ministers to write columns and articles for the press (the *Portadown Times* as well as the *Methodist Recorder*), and acted as 'press and information officer' for the Church. He was remembered as one of the 'Conference watch-dogs' in Eric Gallagher's funeral address: 'He knew his Manual of Laws and he knew where to position himself in the Conference Auditorium.'[73] William Edward Eames, son of a Cork motor dealer and father of the retired archbishop of Armagh, seemed on course for higher office by 1957, having acted as secretary of the Belfast district synod and Methodist council, conference letter-writer, and secretary of the Church Extension committee. Within a single year, his ascent was successively halted by resignation from the Methodist Church, ordination in the Church of Ireland, and death. The Orange connection may have facilitated his appointment to Knockbreda, where the incumbent was the veteran grand master of Belfast and grand chaplain of Ireland, Louis Warden Crooks. Crooks, who had likewise abandoned the Methodist ministry for the Church of Ireland 53 years earlier, would have easily understood the allure of the more settled and comfortable livelihood promised by Anglican orders.[74]

---

[71] George Harold Good, a son of the former Methodist president Robert Good, was first returned as chaplain of Bessbrook district 11, Co. Armagh, in 1958. He was elected in the year of his father's presidency, having joined Bessbrook Star of Hope Temperance lodge 927 during his first ministerial posting at Bessbrook, and although his active membership effectively ended within two years on his appointment to Dublin, he continued to be recorded as chaplain in official records during subsequent postings at Edgehill College, and Waterford, before disappearing from Orange returns soon after his departure for Ohio in 1964: Armagh CGL, *List of Lodges* (1957–66).

[72] *MCM* (2004), 10–11.   [73] *MN* (Jan. 1996), 5; *MCM* (1996), 10.

[74] *ICA* (8 Aug. 1958), 2; Alf McCreary, *Nobody's Fool: The Life of Archbishop Robin Eames* (London, Hodder & Stoughton, 2004), 5–6, 23–5.

In most cases, Orange records reveal little about the contribution of chaplains beyond the bare details of when and where they held office. Equally frustrating are press reports simply listing those present at demonstrations, unfurling banners, or holding anniversary services. Sermons and addresses to Orangemen, when reported, were almost invariably formulaic, an incantation of familiar precepts and commemorative pieties which the brethren had learnt to expect and endure, along with meat teas and damp afternoons with the lodge at the field. Richer documentation survives for the few ministers who became prominent Orange and unionist politicians. Perhaps the most notable recent example was Robert Jonathan Bradford, a dairyman's son born near Limavady, who was murdered by the IRA on 14 November 1981. Bradford had been edged out of the Methodist ministry when elected to the House of Commons for South Belfast seven years earlier, but retained his clerical status through accreditation by the Missouri Conference of the Methodist Protestant Church. His unsuccessful campaign for the Northern Ireland Assembly in 1973 on behalf of Vanguard, during which he sported a clerical collar for want of conventional shirts and ties, had prompted the Methodist conference to require any parliamentary candidate to relinquish his pastoral charge and, if elected, to vacate his manse. Bradford had allegedly flirted with nuns at Aquinas Hall while a student at Edgehill; but when first returned as a county chaplain in December 1973 he was a British Israelite and a confirmed enemy of Romanism and ecumenicism, against which he campaigned with the slogan 'Methodists Awake'.[75]

Among Bradford's most celebrated predecessors as a clerical politician was the former Primitive preacher Richard Rutledge Kane, who had switched to the Church of Ireland before becoming a crusader against Home Rule as grand master of Belfast (1885–98). According to Frederick MacNeice, father of the poet and chaplain to a succession of lodges in Dublin, Belfast, and Carrickfergus, Kane was a charismatic speaker and leader. He admired Kane's 'fine voice', 'commanding presence', and 'entire absence of bitterness'. Writing as an apostle of reconciliation in the 1930s, MacNeice distanced himself from Kane's immersion in unionist party politics, but praised his commitment to 'religious freedom', his refusal to demand privileges for his own people, his 'warm Irish heart', his love for Ireland, and his pride in being an O'Cahan. 'As a young man' he had found 'something very attractive

---

[75] *MCM* (1974), 31; Methodist Conference, *Reports and Agenda* (June 1974), *MHSIA*; Norah Bradford, *A Sword Bathed in Heaven: The Life, Faith and Cruel Death of the Rev. Robert Bradford B.Th. M.P.* (Basingstoke, Marshall Pickering, 1984), esp. 94–106.

about Dr. Kane', whose record confirmed that zealous Orangeism was perfectly compatible with Irishness and personal tolerance.[76]

MacNeice was also associated with a less celebrated but intriguing Methodist Orangeman, James Ritchie from Hyde Park in Co. Antrim. Son of a local preacher and brother of another Methodist minister, Ritchie spent three years in Carrickfergus (1919–22) while MacNeice was rector.[77] Along with a Baptist deacon and three other ministers (two Presbyterian and one Congregational), Ritchie and MacNeice initiated a press campaign for 'justice and peace in Ireland' in July 1920. This was based on mobilisation of 'Christian forces' of all denominations (though no Roman Catholics participated), in order to stem the spread of sectarian rioting emanating from Londonderry. Five months later, the Carrickfergus clergy instigated the League of Prayer for Ireland, which secured few members but much admiration among liberals and nationalists.[78] In addition to pursuing reconciliation in tandem, Ritchie and MacNeice both served as vice-presidents of the Carrickfergus Unionist Club, joined the same Masonic lodge, and acted successively as chaplain of Carrickfergus Total Abstinence lodge 1537.

Unlike MacNeice, ever diplomatic and even canny in his conduct, Ritchie delighted local brethren by displaying his colours without blushing. As the worshipful master remarked at the presentation of a wallet stuffed with banknotes amounting to £35 on his departure from the town, Ritchie had assumed ministerial duty on Eleventh Night in 1919 and 'was practically the first man to be on the streets with a sash on. He felt it was like an earthquake in Carrickfergus to see a clergyman doing that.' Ritchie responded by declaring 'that Ulster to-day was saving the Empire', applauding Sir James Craig, and exclaiming 'No Surrender'.[79] Ritchie's Orange rhetoric was far more pugnacious and formulaic than MacNeice's, as in a speech to the Unionist Club in which he 'proceeded to trace the history of Ulster from the plantation, and showed how at all times the Roman Catholic Church had plotted for domination', before blessing 'the day that Ulster set up its own Parliament'.[80] This address appalled the town's chief liberal, the Presbyterian ship-owner Charles McFerran

---

[76] John Frederick MacNeice, *Some Northern Churchmen and Some Notes on the Church in Belfast* (Belfast, W. Erskine Mayne and Dublin, Church of Ireland Printing and Publishing Co., 1934), 39–40 (sermon at Christ Church, Belfast, 2 July 1933); idem, *Church of Ireland in Belfast* (Belfast, *BNL*, 1931), 17.

[77] *MCM* (1958), 13–14; *ICA* (30 May 1958), 6.

[78] *The Way to Peace for Ireland* (Carrickfergus, James Bell, 1920); *FJ* (11 Dec. 1920); see also Fitzpatrick, *'Solitary and Wild'*, ch. 9 (esp. 162–3).

[79] *Carrickfergus Advertiser* (14 July 1922); lodge 1537, Minutes (27 June, 31 July 1922), in private hands.

[80] Ibid. (18 Mar. 1921).

Legg: 'Can this be the Rev. James Ritchie who recently signed, jointly with his colleagues in the town, an appeal to all men to promote by prayer and action the peace of Ireland?'[81] Ritchie's Orange brethren responded by expressing their 'appreciation of the services he has rendered to the cause of Protestantism', and testifying 'that his speeches have always been characterised by fairness and tolerance towards all law-abiding citizens'.[82] Ritchie personified the duality of so many Ulster clergymen, now fervent apostles of reconciliation, now equally passionate purveyors of sectarian platitudes. For all but the most astute Orange chaplains, the spiritual and social benefits of espousing Orangeism entailed an undeniable intellectual cost. Critics like Legg interpreted this as culpable hypocrisy. Yet verbal inconsistency, often a seasonal phenomenon in Ulster, is perhaps the most venial sin of which a clergyman may stand accused. For anyone trying to win the confidence of an audience as yet unenlightened, the forked tongue is an almost indispensable tool.

VII

The climax of Methodist influence in the Orange Order was surely the election in 1968 of John Bryans as grand master of Ireland. Bryans, from 'farming stock' outside Portadown, was scarcely a dynamic leader in a period of unexampled turmoil in Northern Ireland, unionism, and Orangeism. Having worked as a commercial traveller from 1909 after stints as a boy brick-maker and grocer's assistant, the new grand master was 82 years old, a sprightly purveyor of homely moral maxims in an organisation ever more tarnished by association with violence and sectarian bitterness. He had combined his peripatetic occupation with local preaching and work for the North Belfast Mission under William Maguire, becoming a notable lay committee-man and Northern secretary of the Special Evangelistic Agency. For 55 years, he endeavoured to save souls from sin by preaching from the steps of the Custom House.[83] His predecessor as grand master, Sir George Anthony Clark, had retired after facing increasing rejection of his close alliance with the government, whose clumsy attempts at reform were widely reviled by Orangemen. Though eight other possible candidates (including prominent politicians such as Brian Faulkner) had apparently been considered, Bryans was unanimously approved by the central committee after nomination by

---

[81] Ibid. (25 Mar. 1921).   [82] Ibid. (27 Apr. 1921).
[83] *MN* (Apr. 1988), 4; *MCM* (1959), 57, 87. Bryans was already a member of the Local Preachers' committee in 1928, but had no such involvements by 1974 apart from the Methodist Orphan Society: *MCM* (1928), 155; (1974), 79.

two Presbyterian clergymen, John Brown and William Martin Smyth.[84] His appointment was eventually endorsed by the grand lodge, in the presence of Faulkner and Viscount Brookeborough; but the true locus of power was signified by the election of Smyth and James Molyneaux as deputy grand masters.[85]

Bryans did his best to avert open rupture of the Order, and also became involved in private discussions between grand lodge representatives and leaders of the three major Protestant churches, including George Good (Harold's cousin) as president of the Methodist Church.[86] Bryans was indefatigable in visiting Orange halls, delivering homilies to ordinary brethren, 'emphasising spiritual side of Order', and exhibiting tolerance and goodwill to all and sundry. But his colleagues and many Orangemen became impatient with his passivity and neglect of political 'leadership', which had surrendered responsibility for active resistance to organisations such as Vanguard. By December 1970, Martin Smyth's support for Bryans had become faint indeed: 'There have been folk who saw you, GM, as a caretaker, but of late are we not putting to[o] much on your shoulders. Not one of us would question your faith, etc.' A year later, Smyth and Molyneaux were among those openly pressing for his retirement, leading to Smyth's own resignation as chairman of the central committee when Bryan urged him to devote more time to his family and church. This was soon followed by Bryans's capitulation and Smyth's unanimous election as his successor in December 1972.[87] In his valedictory speech, Bryans acknowledged

the need for the leader of the Institution to answer much of the misrepresentation against the Order. The Press, Television and Radio must be used in future to advance our principles and in this connection, due to advanced years, [I] did not feel up to this great pressure.[88]

The pressure did no lasting damage, for he remained capable of attending the half-yearly meeting shortly after his centenary in 1985. He remarked that 'this may be the last time he would be present at Grand Lodge but appealed to everyone to stand fast in the faith, to regularly attend their place of worship and ... to diligently study the Holy Scriptures'.[89] Bryans

[84] Central Committee, Minutes and Rough Minutes (25 Oct. 1967).
[85] GOLI, *HYR* (Feb. 1968, postponed from Dec. 1967), 10, 17–19.
[86] Revd A. J. Weir (clerk, Presbyterian general assembly) to Walter Williams (GS, GOLI) and reply, 13, 21 Apr. 1970: Grand Secretary's Correspondence.
[87] Central Committee, Rough Minutes and associated documents (4 Dec. 1970, 3 Dec. 1971, 9 June, 13 Dec. 1972); Smyth to Williams, 8 June 1972: Grand Secretary's Correspondence.
[88] GOLI, *HYR* (Dec. 1972), 15–16.   [89] GOLI, *HYR* (June 1985), 15.

went on to outscore all known Methodist Orange chaplains by surviving to the age of 103.

It is apparent that Methodism and the Orange Order have had a long and complex relationship that even today has not been fully severed. Despite its manifest flaws and tumultuous history, Orangeism has incorporated tens of thousands of devout and unassuming evangelical Protestants whose values were indistinguishable from those of traditional Methodism. Confronted by the seeming triumph of secularism and materialism, each organisation continues to preach a version of 'No Surrender'. The difference is that in high season some Orangemen still shout the slogan, which most modern Methodists merely mutter.

Part II

Covenant

6   Ulster's Covenanters

I

> In Ulster it was indeed a wonderful time. Every county had its organisation: every town and district had its own corps. The young manhood of Ulster enlisted and went into training. Men of all ranks and occupations met together, in the evenings, for drill. There resulted a great comradeship. Barriers of class were broken down or forgotten. Protestant Ulster became a fellowship.[1]

'Ulster Day', 28 September 1912, inaugurated almost two years of unexampled Protestant cohesion in a community long fractured by bitter tensions and tussles between members of different classes and rival religious groups. Even those who deplored menacing assertions of solidarity such as Ulster's Solemn League and Covenant, the Women's Declaration, and the Ulster Volunteer Force, were fascinated by the energy and enthusiasm with which Ulster Protestants bonded together. Thus Frederick MacNeice, the courageous rector of Carrickfergus, did not allow his rejection of the Covenant and the Volunteers to blind him to the 'comradeship' and 'fellowship' unleashed by what he considered a dangerous and immoral political strategy. Even today, Ulster Day is celebrated as a spiritual more than a political achievement, evoking a period when 'unionism' and 'loyalism' were visualised by their adherents as sacred callings, rather than as party labels of rapidly receding practical relevance. In nationalist Ireland, a similar state of communal euphoria was generated by the anti-conscription pledge and campaign of 1918.

In both cases, of course, majoritarian solidarity had unpleasant results for dissentients. The stronger the consensus, the less tolerance was offered to those choosing to stay outside the fellowship. As in all great populist movements in modern Ireland, non-participants risked being denounced as renegades or traitors, facing the prospects of violence, abuse, intimidation, and social ostracism. The next chapter examines the motives and

---

[1] John Frederick MacNeice, BD, *Carrickfergus and Its Contacts: Some Chapters in the History of Ulster* (London, Simpkin Marshall, 1928), 76.

fate of that substantial minority of Ulster Protestants who nevertheless failed to conform to the popular will by adding their signatures to the documents presented to them on Ulster Day. The purpose of this chapter is to explain why so many Ultonians and unionists of otherwise diverse outlooks supported the movement, with particular attention to the published views of the clergymen who did so much to legitimise and sanctify a ruthless political strategy. Though there was probably no radical difference between clerical and lay attitudes towards Home Rule, or the rhetoric in which these were framed, the utterances of the clergy were less overtly partisan and more circumscribed by public opinion and parochial pressures than those of Carsonite politicians. The behaviour and views of Ulster's clergy in 1912 deserve close attention, as serious and considered responses to a dire emergency which was largely outside their control.

II

When the number of signatories in Ulster is compared with the Protestant adult population in 1911 (Table 6.1), it appears that about 77% of men signed the Covenant while 72% of women signed the Declaration. The stipulation that the documents should only be signed by unionists (born or domiciled in Ulster) who had reached sixteen years invites a precise match with the population recorded at the census only eighteen months earlier. However, this crude calculation bypasses several problems: errors of enumeration, the suspicion of fraudulent or multiple signings, the fact that many non-residents came home in order to assert their Ulsterity, and the possible participation of Catholic unionists.

A versifier in the liberal *Ulster Guardian*, a major source of information on clerical dissentients and 'Independents' within Orangeism, ridiculed the pretence that Ulster Day was a rigorous and honest expression of democracy:

> A powder-stained soldier had brought us to grief;
> But an eminent lawyer we have as our Chief.
> And when the world gazing expects us to fight,
> He changes our watchword to ULSTER WILL WRITE!
> Our pens are a thousand – our bosoms are one,
> Sign early and often, but down with the gun.[2]

Access to a digital version of the signature sheets, searchable by name, confirms the integrity of the collection and counting of signatures: despite missing sheets and errors of coding, the match between the official figures

---

[2] 'Ulster Will Write', *UG* (14 Sept. 1912).

and those derived from digital searching is fairly close. Furthermore, in the course of many individual searches I have yet to find an unmistakably duplicated signature.[3] There seems no compelling reason to reject the authenticity or accuracy of the available records. Even so, it is noteworthy that Sir Edward Carson, the first and most celebrated signatory at Belfast's city hall, ought to have been disqualified, not being an Ulsterman by birth, descent, residence, or occupation.[4]

The strongest evidence for Catholic participation on Ulster Day is a police report on political activity in Co. Antrim, submitted to Dublin Castle a few weeks later. According to the county inspector: 'It was very largely signed by those who formerly were regarded as Liberals. It was also the subject of remark that in every district of the County it was signed by some Roman Catholics.'[5] My haphazard attempts to identify Catholic signatories, by checking certain 'Irish' surnames against family census returns, have almost invariably proved fruitless. The existence of a significant minority of Catholic signatories, 'convinced' in their 'consciences' that Home Rule would subvert their 'religious freedom', remains implausible.

Though most adult Protestants signed up throughout the province, there was marked regional variation. The county figures are imprecise, being drawn from imperfect digital searches rather than official enumeration of the original signature sheets. Signatures must be sorted by place of signing rather than personal address, and it was commonplace to sign away from home. Though the provincial totals obtained from both sources roughly correspond, it is obvious that various sheets have not been assigned to the correct districts in the course of coding, while others seem to have been lost. The digital total for Antrim (72,580) falls 5% short of the impressively precise figure reported by the police (76,672), probably because of the disappearance of several thousand male signatures from the constituency of South Antrim (especially from the Lisburn district).[6] In the case of Down, the other county for which consolidated police figures exist, the discrepancy is less marked.[7] Table 6.1 strongly suggests that

---

[3] I recall occasional cases in which an erased signature has been wrongly called up, through digital searching, in addition to the confirmed signature inscribed elsewhere.

[4] The relevant signature sheet is reproduced in *The Ulster Covenant: A Pictorial History of the 1912 Home Rule Crisis*, ed. Gordon Lucy (Belfast, Ulster Society, 1989), 29, yet I cannot trace Carson or his fellow-signatories through digital searching.

[5] Antrim MCR (1 Nov. 1912): NAL, CO 904/88 (accessible on-line). The statement evidently refers jointly to both documents.

[6] Antrim MCR (1 Nov. 1912).

[7] The county inspector reported that '34,460 men are reported by local police as having signed Covenant within the County. 32,000 women are believed to have signed the Declaration': Down MCR (1 Nov. 1912). The corresponding figures derived from digital searches for parliamentary constituencies in Down are 32,379 men and 35,495 women.

participation on Ulster Day was much lower in the Belfast region than in mid Ulster, where the signature ratios for Armagh approached 90% by comparison with about 70% in Down. In the three 'Lost Counties' subsequently ditched by the Orange Order and the Ulster Unionist Council, participation was relatively high in Monaghan but much lower in Cavan. Despite these local contrasts, the enrolment of two-thirds of Protestant adults in almost every county was a matchless triumph of Irish political mobilisation.

Table 6.2 compares county participation ratios on Ulster Day with the reported membership of three major unionist bodies (the UVF, the Unionist Clubs, and the Orange Order). In all three cases, enlistment in the Belfast region likewise fell proportionately short of that in mid Ulster, where Catholics were more prevalent. The impetus for Protestant solidarity was doubtless stronger in the presence of powerful Catholic competition, a pattern replicated in the high concentration of Ulster Volunteers in Cavan and Monaghan (though not in Donegal). In no case did the membership of unionist bodies approach the number of Covenanters, even though the criteria for inclusion were strikingly similar.[8] No comprehensive statistics of Orange membership were compiled, but county returns for various years between 1912 and 1923 indicate that the number of brethren in the future Northern Ireland exceeded 50,000, about a fifth of the adult male population of Protestants in 1911. The police recorded less than 85,000 Ulster Volunteers and 56,000 members of Unionist Clubs, compared with about 218,000 Covenanters and 229,000 women who signed the Declaration within the province of Ulster.[9]

III

The term 'Solemn League and Covenant' had been in public circulation ever since the announcement of the sacerdotal arrangements for 'Ulster Day' on 17 August.[10] The chosen terminology created an indelible but misleading connection between the mystery text and its celebrated

---

[8] In the case of the UVF, participation was deliberately restricted by the initial decision to limit enlistment to 110,000 throughout the province.

[9] For precise figures and sources, see Tables 6.1 and 6.2. The published official return (covering 28 Sept.–14 Oct. 1912) recorded 218,206 men and 228,999 women who signed sheets in Ulster, along with 19,162 men and 5,047 women who signed sheets in southern Ireland or Britain (and beyond) or sent individual signatures to the Old Town Hall.

[10] On 9 Aug., the UUC had called for a general holiday on 28 Sept., to be termed 'Ulster Day'. Eight days later, a preliminary programme was advertised in 42 unionist newspapers, stating that signatories would attend 'a solemn religious service' before pledging

eponym of 1643. As the *Northern Whig* remarked when publishing the announcement:

We congratulate the Ulster Unionist Council on adopting this form of protest, which is so closely associated with the history of the race from which we have sprung ... The Solemn League and Covenant still stirs the blood of the Scottish race. It was not an empty formula. These brave men took a solemn oath to resist tyranny, and they gave effect to it in a way familiar to all students of history. We in Ulster mean to emulate their example. It will be a duty and a privilege to make good our solemn vow. It may, if the Government is foolish enough, mean suffering; it may mean death to many.[11]

The 1643 Covenant was indeed more or less familiar to every Ulster Presbyterian as a Scottish-sponsored assertion of civil and religious liberty, forced upon a reluctant English church and parliament, and eventually upon an even more reluctant Charles II as a price for his coronation in Scotland. The very name called to mind a bold mutual attempt by citizens of a peripheral territory, in combination with English allies, to secure 'the extirpation of Popery ... and whatsoever shall be found to be contrary to sound doctrine and the power of godliness', and 'to preserve the rights and privileges of the Parliaments, and the liberties of the kingdoms'. An additional undertaking, 'to preserve and defend the King's Majesty's person and authority, in the preservation and defence of the true religion, and liberties of the kingdoms', carried an implicit threat made manifest in the execution of Charles I six years later.[12] The precedent of 1643 stipulated that 'each one of us for himself, with our hands lifted up to the most High GOD', would be bound to the Covenant by swearing an oath, as 'some of the local Unionist leaders' had advocated after the heady success of the Balmoral rally on 9 April 1912.[13] The invocation in 1912 of an older Covenant also followed an ancient precedent, a procedure for 'renewing the Solemn League and Covenant' having been laid down by the Scottish general assembly in 1648. This included 'an intimation of a solemn publick humiliation and fast the second Sabbath of December, to be kept upon the next Thursday, and the Lord's day thereafter', when the

---

'themselves to a solemn Covenant', the text of which would be submitted to a meeting of the UUC on 23 Sept.: *Witness* (16, 23 Aug. 1912); *NW* (17 Aug.); UUC, UDC Minutes (16 Aug.): PRONI, UUC Papers, D 1327/2/7.

[11] 'Ulster Day' (leader), in *NW* (17 Aug. 1912).

[12] 'The Solemn League and Covenant for Reformation and Defence of Religion, the Honour and Happiness of the King, and the Peace and Safety of the Three Kingdoms of Scotland, England, and Ireland' was widely circulated in modern documentary compendia such as *The Confession of Faith; The Larger and Shorter Catechisms, with the Scripture-Proofs at Large* (Belfast, Graham and Heslip, 1933 edn.), 276–8.

[13] McNeill, *Ulster's Stand*, 101.

Covenant would again be read by the minister 'and then to be sworn by him and all the people'.[14]

Long before publication of the new Covenant, its organisers had set about enlisting clergymen and securing the use of churches, as their predecessors had done in 1643 and 1648. On 17 August, after approaches to 'the Lord Primate, the Moderator of the General Assembly, and the heads of the various other Protestant denominations', the UUC had called for a 'solemn religious service' in each locality to precede the signing ceremony on 28 September.[15] In early September, the five Church of Ireland bishops in Ulster and the Presbyterian moderator instructed their ministers to hold special services of 'humiliation and prayer' six days before Ulster Day.[16] As Bishop D'Arcy explained to the clergy of Down and Connor and Dromore, that Sabbath was to be 'observed as a day of special intercession for our country in this critical time. There can surely be no better preparation for the great decision of the 28th.'[17] In return for endorsing an unpublished document, Presbyterian and Episcopalian leaders had been incorporated in the drafting process, leading to various deletions and obfuscations designed to assuage Christian consciences. This enabled the organisers to imply that the delay in publication was not a cynical attempt to dupe a credulous public, but an exercise in consultative democracy.

In fact, 'the various documents had been finally settled' on 23 August by the Ulster Day Committee, which later rejected a proposal to publish 'the Gist of the Covenant' in favour of a delayed press release on 19 September.[18] Though the wording of the Declaration was not finally sanctioned by the Ulster Women's Unionist Council until 17 September, it too had been drafted by Sinclair and Craig with due deference to the ladies, who were, 'of course, responsible for settling what Declaration they wish to issue, and the men have nothing to say in regard to it beyond offering their help'.[19] The manner in which the public mind was prepared by the UDC exhibited considerable tactical finesse, as one might expect of a body whose honorary secretaries were Richard Dawson Bates (representing the UUC), Major T. V. P. (Pat) McCammon (Orange Order),

[14] *Confession of Faith*, 280.   [15] UDC Minutes (14, 16 Aug. 1912).

[16] *IT* (5 Sept.); *Newtownards Chronicle* (14 Sept. 1912); Andrew Scholes, *The Church of Ireland and the Third Home Rule Bill* (Dublin, Irish Academic Press, 2010), 41. The Presbyterian directive was issued on 6 Sept., two days after the bishops' pastoral; no corresponding statement was issued by the Methodist Church in Ireland.

[17] *CIG*, vol. liv (13 Sept. 1912), 760.   [18] UDC Minutes, 23 Aug., 5 Sept. 1912.

[19] R. Dawson Bates to Mrs Edith Wheeler, 13 Sept. 1912, in reply to her tart letter of the same date, enquiring 'Are we right to assume that the Covenant [*sic*] that the women of Ulster are to sign is prepared by the men, and that we have nothing to do with this matter?': PRONI, UWUC Papers, D 1098/2/3.

and Captain Frank Hall (Unionist Clubs). Within a few years, Bates would reappear as Northern Ireland's first minister of Home Affairs, McCammon as the commandant of an 'Ulster Composite Battalion' that fought the Dublin rebels in 1916, and Hall as the assistant director of the Security Intelligence Service ('MI5').

IV

How successful were the organisers in mobilising Ulster's Protestant clergy? There is no doubt that Episcopalian, Presbyterian, and Methodist leaders were active opponents of Home Rule and protagonists of the protest on Ulster Day, though their ostensible function was typically to seek 'divine guidance and deliverance in the serious crisis through which our country is now passing'.[20] Hundreds of clergymen throughout Ulster participated in the special services proposed by their leaders. Andrew Scholes reports that 368 Ulster Day services were advertised, of which about half were Episcopalian and a third Presbyterian.[21] Many of these services involved several ministers, often of different denominations.

The number who actually signed the document cannot be precisely determined. Census enumerators returned 1,455 clergymen in the province on 2 April 1911 (excluding Roman Catholic priests and monks), of whom 597 were Episcopalians, 577 Presbyterians, 150 Methodists, and 131 ministers of other denominations.[22] Because of deficiencies in both the digital and original records of Covenanters, it is not practicable to match every Protestant minister's name against the database of signatories. A lower-bound figure may be secured by searching for those with obviously clerical addresses such as a rectory or manse, in addition to a few simply identified as 'Reverend'. This group embraces 529 signatories, over a third of the clerical population of Ulster; but many other clergy signed the Covenant without revealing such signs of their calling.[23]

[20] Circular to Methodist ministers in Ireland from Continuation Committee of Methodist Anti-Home Rule Demonstration: *CA* (27 Sept. 1912). Though its chairman, Revd George Wedgwood, was also president of the Methodist Church in Ireland, this appeal was not reinforced by any official directive (as issued by his Episcopalian and Presbyterian counterparts), despite a letter from Wedgwood stating his 'intention to ask all our ministers and people to unite at an early date in supplicating the God of peace to avert the national peril': *The Witness* (30 Aug. 1912).

[21] Scholes, *Church of Ireland*, 64: citing *BNL* (14, 17, 19, 23 Sept. 1912).

[22] These figures include retired clergy, but exclude 139 missionaries, scripture readers, and itinerant preachers, as well as 98 theological students: Census of Ireland (1911), provincial summary for Ulster, Table xx.

[23] Clerical addresses (excluding a few outside Ulster) included rectories (267), manses (196), vicarages (20), parsonages (12), and glebes (1) – 'Glebe' was almost always the townland address of a layman. Of 48 explicitly 'reverend' signatories, 15 had clerical

A useful indicator of active clerical commitment is the digital list of 'principal agents' responsible for administering the Covenant and Declaration throughout the province, often in churches, church porches or halls, or clerical residences. Mostly on the basis of clerical titles, I have identified 130 clerical agents within Ulster, of whom 78 were Episcopalian and 46 Presbyterian, indicating that Church of Ireland ministers were notably over-represented.[24] A much larger group, of whom one in six were also agents,[25] contributed anti-Home Rule statements to a remarkable exercise in unionist propaganda published on Ulster Day. When the *Daily Mail* circularised all known Protestant clergymen in the province with an invitation to express their opinion as to the future of Ireland under Home Rule, negative assessments were submitted by no less than 298 ministers (including 145 Episcopalians and 118 Presbyterians), accounting for about a fifth of the provincial total. Only four ministers favoured some form of Home Rule, while three others gave neutral replies.[26] Almost a quarter of Episcopalian ministers in Ulster answered the *Daily Mail*'s appeal, compared with a fifth of Presbyterians and only a twelfth of other ministers.[27] These statistics suggest that clerical involvement in Ulster Day was massive, yet far from universal.

Table 6.3 reveals that clerical activists were more heavily clustered in mid Ulster than in the north-east, following the pattern already documented for Covenanters and for members of the UVF, the Unionist Clubs, and Orange lodges. The virtual absence of clerical agents in Belfast is partly explained by the predominance of City Hall as a venue, whereas a large proportion of provincial signatories performed the rite in much smaller groups and often in church precincts. Yet, even apart from Belfast, clerical mobilisation in the north-east was notably lower than in

addresses in Ulster. Collation of identified agents with signatories (see below) indicates that many clerical signatories identified themselves as 'Clk.' (Clerk in Holy Orders), an abbreviation invariably omitted or mistranscribed in the digital index.

[24] Known clerical agents accounted for 78 (13%) of Ulster's Episcopalian clergy in 1911, compared with 46 (8%) for Presbyterians and 4 (3%) of Methodists, and 2 (2%) for other clerical agents (Congregational and Remonstrant Presbyterian). A few agents not identified through clerical titles have been matched with clergy contributing their views to the *Daily Mail* (see following note).

[25] Of the 298 *DM* contributors, 49 (16.4%) were also listed as 'principal agents', including 32 of the 145 Episcopalians (22.1%) and 16 of the 118 Presbyterians (13.6%). 37.7% of the 130 Ulster clergymen identified as agents also contributed to the *DM*.

[26] *DM* (28 Sept. 1912); also summarised in *North Down Herald* (4 Oct.). I am indebted to Scholes, *Church of Ireland*, 64, for alerting me to this valuable source.

[27] *DM* contributors accounted for 145 (24%) of Ulster's Episcopalian clergy in 1911, compared with 118 (20%) for Presbyterians, 15 (10%) for Methodists, and 20 (15%) for other denominations (9 Baptists, 8 Reformed Presbyterians, 2 Moravians, and 1 Eastern Reformed Presbyterian). One Episcopalian resident outside Ulster was included in the survey, presumably as a canon of St Patrick's cathedral, Armagh: Robert Moore Peile Freeman of Collon (Louth).

mid Ulster, with even higher levels of mobilisation in the 'Lost Counties'. Variation between counties in the proportion of clergy contributing to the *Daily Mail* were quite small (ranging between 17% in Monaghan and 30% in Cavan), compared with huge disparities in the proportion acting as agents (2% in Belfast, 22% in Donegal). Despite some local anomalies, all the instruments agree that response to Ulster Day was fairly tepid in Belfast and the north-east, normally regarded as the powerhouse of unionist resistance to Home Rule.

One might expect attitudes towards Ulster Day to have been moulded as much by place of origin as by current location. Table 6.4 highlights a potentially divisive difference in nativity between clergy of the two major churches. Virtually all Presbyterian ministers who acted as agents or contributed to the *Daily Mail* were natives of Ulster, with roughly equal numbers from mid Ulster and the north-east. By contrast, little more than two-fifths of either group of Episcopalian clergy came from the province. The majority were southerners, with predictably large contingents from Dublin and Cork but some representation for most southern counties.[28] The most exotic activist was Andrew Asboe, one of two Moravian ministers to publish his views in the *Daily Mail*, who was born in Greenland and married a native of the West Indies.[29] Such examples confirm that the Ulster Day campaign, far from being restricted to the sons of Ulster, sucked in a remarkably diverse range of clergymen whose origins might well have fostered a very different outlook. Especially in the Church of Ireland, Ulster Day imposed a severe test of the extent to which ministers with origins outside Ulster had embraced the values and loyalties of an initially alien culture. Those with shallow Ulster roots may have felt themselves under particular pressure to affirm their Carsonite credentials.

Clergy lists and other nominal records may also be used to construct a collective profile of the age and experience of those taking a conspicuous part in the struggle against Home Rule. Table 6.5 encapsulates the ages,

---

[28] In descending order, the number of clerical agents (of all denominations) born in each county was as follows: Down and Londonderry 13, Donegal 11, Antrim 10, Belfast and Tyrone 8, Armagh 7, Dublin and Cork 6, Fermanagh, Meath, and Galway 5, Kerry 4, Monaghan and Sligo 3, Kildare, Louth, Wicklow, Tipperary, and Roscommon 2, Cavan, Kilkenny, King's, Queen's, Westmeath, and Limerick 1; non-Irish birthplaces were England 4, Wales, Jersey, and India 1. The corresponding figures for *DM* contributors were Londonderry 35, Antrim 34, Down 32, Tyrone and Dublin 27, Armagh 25, Belfast 14, Fermanagh 13, Monaghan 12, Cork 10, Donegal 7, Cavan and Wicklow 6, Galway 5, Meath and Sligo 4, Louth, Waterford, and Roscommon 3, Carlow and King's 2, Kilkenny, Queen's, Wexford, Kerry, Limerick, and Mayo 1; non-Irish birthplaces were England 8, Scotland and India 2, Greenland 1.

[29] *Census of Ireland* (1911), family schedule, Ballinderry (Antrim): NAD (accessible on-line).

periods in ministry, and periods in current cure of almost all clergymen who acted as agents or contributed to the *Daily Mail*. The table shows that Presbyterian activists tended to be slightly older than Episcopalians, as measured by their median age at the end of 1912. Published census returns reveal that just over half of Ulster's Protestant clergymen in 1911 had reached their 45th birthday, almost exactly matching the proportion for clerical covenant agents. Those contributing to the *Daily Mail* were somewhat older, with over 70% of the group aged 45 or more.[30]

Table 6.5 also indicates the clerical experience of activists in 1912 and the period for which they had ministered in their current cure. For agents, the median period since ordination was 18 years, compared with 25 years for contributors. The median agent had ministered in his current congregation for eight years, a quarter being newcomers with experience of three years or less. Being older than the agents, contributors to the *Daily Mail* tended to have more local experience, the median period being fourteen years. A few had only just taken up local duty, including five Methodist 'itinerants' who had been assigned their current circuits at the Methodist conference only three months before Ulster Day. By contrast, five Presbyterian ministers had ministered locally for half a century or more. Aged 86 by 1912, the most venerable contributor (and agent) was Hugh McIntyre Butler, Presbyterian minister at Magilligan (Londonderry) since 1851.[31] Butler did not retire until 1917 and survived to the age of 103. Ranging from novices to seasoned local luminaries, from southerners to Ulstermen 'born and bred', from Episcopalians to Baptist pastors, the clerical activists of Ulster Day spanned the entire profession.

Though many of its organisers and activists were Orangemen, the impact of the 'Ulster movement', particularly in Britain, depended on its enlistment of myriad Ulster Protestants who were neither members nor advocates of the Orange Order. These included former liberals and others who deplored the influence of fraternities in Irish political and social life, but were prepared to enter a *mariage de convenance* in pursuit of their shared aim. Only 41 contributors to the *Daily Mail*, a sixth of the total, held senior Orange office around 1912. Of these two were Methodists and

---

[30] The proportion of Ulster clergymen aged 45 or more in 1911 was 52.0% (51.1% for Episcopalians, 55.3% for Presbyterians). The corresponding proportions for agents were 51.9% (50.0%, 53.3%); for contributors to the *DM* they were 70.6% (72.2%, 69.5%). All three calculations include retired clergy.

[31] Three had been 'called' to their current congregations in 1862: John Davidson of Glennan (Monaghan); Robert Workman of Glastry (Down); and Henry Osborne of Holywood (Down). William Mitchell had become minister of Ballyblack (Down) in 1854. Osborne and Mitchell had resigned in 1890 and 1902 respectively, but the others remained in harness in 1912.

the remainder Episcopalians, accounting for just over a quarter of all contributors from the Church of Ireland.[32] They included three of the six grand chaplains of Ireland in 1915: Archbishop Crozier of Armagh, Bishop Chadwick of Derry and Raphoe, and the incumbent at Ballycastle (Antrim).[33] The proportion of Orange chaplains among clerical agents was higher, exceeding a third of all the Episcopalians.[34]

The Orange contribution to the *Daily Mail*'s survey was counterbalanced by a dozen ministers, mostly Presbyterians, who dissociated themselves from conservative politics on issues other than Home Rule.[35] Their introductory caveats gave added force to what followed: 'Liberal in politics'; 'not a party politician'; 'a Liberal on most questions'; 'writing as a Liberal', or 'as a lifelong Radical in full sympathy with most of the measures of the present Government', or 'as a Liberal driven out of sympathy with the present Liberal Government'. Others referred to the views of a congregation 'mostly of Liberal tendencies', or comprising 'Unionists of sober and even Liberal sentiment'.[36] John Lynd, Reformed Presbyterian minister on the Dublin Road (Belfast), declared that 'my sympathies are not in most things with the Conservatives'. A

[32] Contributors have been matched against the lists of clergy belonging to GOLI, or entitled to vote in its elections, who were listed in *HYR* (Dec. 1910, Dec. 1915). Those matched included 3 GCs of Ireland, 16 DGCs of Ireland, and 23 DGCs of counties (excluding those with higher office). Orange officers accounted for 14.1% of all contributors and 27.6% of Episcopalians. The only non-Episcopalian chaplains were William Maguire and Thomas Walmsley (both Methodists); though the Presbyterian William Witherow had held Orange office from 1904 to 1906, and the Methodist Francis Herbert Scott Maguire was to serve between 1922 and 1969. Some contributors holding junior office, as chaplains of district or private lodges, may have been missed.

[33] Chadwick, Crozier, and Thomas Cox of Ramoan served as GCs of Ireland from 1894–1916, 1894–1920, and 1915–24 respectively. Others subsequently appointed (with period of service) were John McEndoo (1921–2), James MacManaway (1925–47), William Maguire (1921–4), William Shaw Kerr (1930–60), Albert Edward Sixsmith (1933–8), William James Askins (1939–69), and F. H. S. Maguire (1924–69).

[34] The 28 Orange chaplains (including the Methodist Thomas Walmsley) constituted 21.5% of the 130 agents, the proportion for Episcopalians being 34.6%. All were DGCs (7 of Ireland, 21 of counties alone). Three Methodist agents were subsequently listed as Orange chaplains: John George Hamilton (1915–25) and William Alexander Park (1922–9). The Congregational minister John McKee, ordained as a Presbyterian but subsequently suspended, had served previously as a chaplain (1905–9).

[35] The preface indicates that 'a number of ministers' also sent 'private letters' stating 'what a few say out boldly for publication – that in politics they are Liberals in all but Home Rule'.

[36] George Pigot McCay (P) of Fintona (Tyrone); John Orr (P) of Derramore (Londonderry); John Thompson (P) of Clontibret (Monaghan); William Tindale McClelland (P) of Coagh (Londonderry); John Beattie Wylie (P) of Macrory Memorial (Belfast); Samuel Huston (P) of Myroe (Londonderry); Thomas Edmund Hill Jones (P) of Killymurris (Antrim); Lawson Burnett (P) of Donaghmore (Down). In citations of contributors to the *DM*, Episcopalians, Methodists, and Presbyterians are designated by E, M, and P respectively.

Baptist pastor observed that 'many Liberals in this country are Unionists because of the Home Rule question', another affirming that he had 'never taken an active part in politics or been connected with the Orange Institution'.[37] Perhaps the most striking declaration was by Thomas Clugston Stuart, who had ministered at Macosquin (Londonderry) since 1906:

> I am a Liberal, as are also the great bulk of our Presbyterian Church. We have only got time to breathe since our emancipation from ascendancy, and we believe that the granting of Home Rule to Ireland would again place round our necks that same yoke which in the past neither we nor our fathers were able to bear.

Ulster Day encompassed a broad church, indeed.

V

What commitments did the signatories believe they were making as they lined up to sign on Ulster Day? This question is best tackled by examining the documents presented to them. Certificates reproducing both pledges were set in an archaic but legible Gothic fount with decorative initials, mimicking legal and religious texts of the sixteenth and seventeenth centuries.[38] The impact of this antiquated design was accentuated by the decision to present every signatory with a vellum or parchment copy suitable for framing or display. A painter and decorator in Newtownards offered 'Attractive Frames' at prices between 6d. and 3s. 6d., appealing to Covenanters to fulfil their second obligation to posterity: 'You have signed the Covenant ... Your next duty is to have it neatly framed; as this Solemn Document is of permanent historic interest, and should be preserved as an inspiration to future generations.'[39] It is noteworthy that local organisers were informed of the arrangements for parchment certificates on 9 September, ten days

---

[37] Pastors Burt Sharp of Lisnagleer (Tyrone) and Alexander Jardine of the Mountpottinger Tabernacle (Belfast).

[38] One version of the Declaration, evidently intended as a memento, avoided Gothic except in a header and footer closely resembling those for the men's Covenant. This certificate omitted the term 'Declaration', confusingly presenting the 'Text of the Covenant made by the Ulster Women's Unionist Council, and which has been signed by the loyal women of Ulster in token of their unwavering hostility to Home Rule': *The Minutes of the Ulster Women's Unionist Council and Executive Committee, 1911–40*, ed. Diane Urquhart (Dublin, Irish Manuscripts Commission, 2001), frontispiece.

[39] Advertisement by Henry Savage, 20 High St, supported by paraphrase in 'Local and District News', in *Newtownards Chronicle* (5 Oct. 1912).

before the wording of the Covenant was revealed, emphasising the supremacy of form over content.[40]

The precise meaning and wording of the Covenant, when finally published on 19 September, were probably irrelevant to most signatories. It quickly became not a problematic text but a sacred incantation, sanctioned by the prestige of the lay and clerical leaders who had drafted or endorsed it. Its air of authority was by no means diminished by the absence of any specification of the institutions or individuals responsible for determining which particular means might 'be found necessary to defeat the present conspiracy to set up a Home Rule Parliament in Ireland'. When 'humbly relying on the God whom our fathers in days of stress and trial confidently trusted', most signatories would have called to mind Orange Ulster's unofficial anthem, Isaac Watts's famous metrical rendering of the 90th Psalm:

> O God, our help in ages past,
> Our hope for years to come,
> Be Thou our guard while troubles last
> And our eternal home![41]

Unlike its predecessor of 1643, which had fulminated against 'Popery' and 'Prelacy', the new Covenant avoided any reference to doctrine or church government beyond invocation of the Williamite and Orange mantra, 'civil and religious liberty'. Under God, the only allegiances declared in the Covenant were to George V and to those other 'men of Ulster' who undertook to 'mutually pledge' themselves to 'stand by one another'.

The document conspicuously did not express loyalty to the (uncodified) constitution as currently upheld by the King, Lords, and Commons. Instead, it portrayed the unnamed Liberal government as party to a

---

[40] '"Ulster Day." Signing of Solemn League and Covenant', circular from joint secretaries, UDC, Old Town Hall, to hon. secretaries, 'local' UDCs, 9 Sept. 1912: reproduced in Lucy, *Ulster Covenant*, 39. The text of the Covenant was revealed to the press immediately after approval by the Standing Committee of the Ulster Unionist Council on 19 Sept., though not ratified by the full Council until 23 Sept.: Ronald McNeill, *Ulster's Stand for Union* (London, John Murray, 1922), 106.

[41] For an intriguing account of the ubiquity of Hymn 501 in rebel Ulster, see the remarkably prescient novel (prefaced on 12 July 1912) by 'George Birmingham' (Canon Hannay), *The Red Hand of Ulster* (London, Smith, Elder & Co., 1912), 179–83, 212–13, 286. Hannay remarked that in Ireland the hymn was not sung to William Croft's familiar dirge, 'St Ann' (invariably used in modern Twelfth demonstrations), but to the livelier and more demanding mid-eighteenth-century 'Irish' tune included in General Synod of the Church of Ireland, *Church Hymnal with Accompanying Tunes and an Appendix* (Dublin, APCK, 1936 edn.), 676–7. The 'Irish' tune (in triple time) ranged well beyond an octave (b to high e), whereas singers of 'St Ann' had only to span a diminished seventh (e to d).

'conspiracy' to subvert an idealised constitution equated, by most Orangemen and loyalists, with the Williamite revolutionary settlement. The Women's Declaration was more forthright, referring explicitly to 'Parliament' and 'the Constitution', as well as God and the King. It is also noteworthy that the women offered no justification for their protest and were not asked to make a mutually binding pledge, but only 'to associate ourselves with the men of Ulster in their uncompromising opposition to the Home Rule Bill now before Parliament'. Since women could scarcely be deemed full citizens while still excluded from the parliamentary franchise, the Declaration rather limply substituted Ulster's 'cherished place in the Constitution of the United Kingdom' for the Covenant's celebration of the Ulsterman's 'cherished position of equal citizenship in the United Kingdom'. As the feminist poet James Cousins protested, the documents affirmed the 'cherished position of equal citizenship (for men and equal uncitizenship for women: they are prepared to fight against domination by Nationalists, but no hint of sauce for gander being sauce for goose)'.[42]

By avoiding any definition of what means might be used to resist the civil magistrate if God and the King failed to preserve the imagined constitution, the Covenant sought to maximise support by inviting variant interpretations. Optimists could sign in the belief that the threat of communal resistance alone would compel the government to resign; opponents of violence could assume that the leaders would content themselves with 'passive resistance' such as non-payment of taxes; the growing body of armed men spoiling for a fight could look forward to a showdown. The restriction of the pledge to 'this our time of threatened calamity', occasioned by 'the present conspiracy', enabled those contemplating some future political compromise to limit their resistance to Home Rule in the form currently before parliament. These caveats had been added to the draft Covenant following discussions between Presbyterian leaders and Thomas Sinclair, the elderly provision merchant and Liberal Unionist organiser who was primarily responsible for drafting the document.[43] Religious and legal scruples were presumably responsible for requiring a mere 'pledge' rather than the oath administered in 1643 (Orangemen had long since abandoned ritualised oath-taking in order to avoid the Order's suppression as an illegal combination).

All of these ambiguities and omissions were seized upon by the liberal and nationalist press as proof of the duplicity and bluster of Ulster loyalist

[42] 'J. H. C.' to Francis Sheehy Skeffington, 1 Oct. 1912: NLI, probably MS 41177/13 (unsorted when consulted).
[43] McNeill, Ulster's Stand, 105–6.

leaders. Less widely noted at the time, despite the fact that Carson had already dabbled with the possibility of exempting all or part of Ulster from Home Rule, was the astonishing territorial wobble in the Covenant's opening sentence ('Home Rule would be disastrous to the material well-being of Ulster as well as of the whole of Ireland'). The very limitation of the protest to the loyalists of Ulster naturally alarmed many southern unionists and Orangemen, faced with the possibility of being abandoned by their northern allies and left to defend a much more vulnerable position in a truncated Home Rule state with an overwhelming Catholic and nationalist majority. If, as implicitly contemplated in an accompanying resolution approved by the UUC on 23 September, Ulster's resistance led to the formation of a secessionist government at odds with both Dublin and London parliaments, the situation of southern unionists would be even more precarious.[44] Some nevertheless supported the Ulster movement in the belief that Carson's threats, backed by belligerent Conservative support and concerted defiance in the province, would lead to the downfall of the government and the indefinite abandonment of Home Rule.[45]

VI

In order to classify the diverse attitudes of those who publicly opposed Home Rule in 1912, I have analysed the content of all 298 hostile statements by Ulster clergymen, published on Ulster Day in the *Daily Mail*. Two full pages of transcripts or excerpts, arranged by denomination and county, were published under a chilling headline: 'The Protest of Ulster. Uncompromising Opposition of the Protestant Clergy and Ministers. Predictions of Civil War: Fervent Appeals to Great Britain. A Solemn Warning.' The preface presented the survey as 'an impressive protest against the Great Betrayal of Loyalist Ulster, not less significant than the signing of the Solemn Covenant'. The precise wording of the question

---

[44] This resolution, excised from the draft Covenant, declared that 'although the present government . . . may drive us forth from a Constitution which we have ever loyally upheld, they may not deliver us bound into the hands of our enemies', in which case 'our deliverance shall be by our own hands': McNeill, *Ulster's Stand*, 107. The creation of a 'provisional government' in Sept. 1913, though precautionary, demonstrated that secession was considered as a practical option.

[45] At a meeting in Dundrum, Co. Dublin, organised by the junior branch of the Irish Unionist Alliance almost a week after Ulster Day, Henry Hanna, KC, declared their indebtedness to Ulster for a strategy that would lead to the fall of the government before introduction of Home Rule. His future fellow-officer in the 10th (Irish) Division at Gallipoli, Bryan Cooper, had just declared that if Ulstermen 'were forced to take up arms to resist it, he would be with them': *IT* (5 Oct. 1912).

posed to the clergy was not reproduced, but the newspaper denied any
political bias in the conduct of the survey:

The Daily Mail asked them only for an expression of opinion as to the future of
Ireland under the Government's Home Rule Bill. The names of the clergymen
and ministers to whom this request was sent were taken without prejudice from the
standard directories. No information was available and none was sought concerning the political views of those who were addressed. The invitations were sent
broadcast over the whole area of Ulster.

The fact that only seven responses were neutral or favourable to Home
Rule reveals little about the extent of opposition, since unreformed liberals would have been reluctant to contribute to a propagandist exercise in
an implacably unionist publication.[46] As an expression of unionist mentality, however, the survey is unique and invaluable.

By asking ministers to predict the consequences of imposing Home
Rule, the survey invited two sorts of response. Most answers rehearsed
some or all of the familiar arguments against Home Rule, but many also
discussed the civil and religious strife which any attempt at enforcement
was likely to provoke. It would have been perfectly reasonable to deplore
the consequential strife without rejecting Home Rule in principle, yet no
minister spelt out this distinction. Objections in principle ranged between
apocalyptic generalities and detailed minutiae. One response in eight (37)
included general predictions of ruin (17), disaster (11), anarchy, chaos,
and calamity (2 each). Robert Cummings Elliott, Presbyterian minister of
Duneane (Antrim), believed that 'Home Rule will be utterly bad for
Ireland', so much so that, 'given absolute freedom to vote as they chose,
thousands of Nationalists would vote against it'. His colleague Robert
White of Kilkeel (Down) expected that Ireland under Home Rule would
be 'hell upon earth'; John Winter, incumbent of Augher (Tyrone), likewise declared that 'I dread Home Rule as I do Hell'. The oddest objection
came from Alexander Knight, incumbent of Inniskeel (Donegal), who
was either a master of metaphor or an obsessional train-spotter:

Downright ruin. Ireland as an expensive narrow-gauge system must have the
British taxpayer to keep her rolling stock in good running order. Her own resour-
ces under Home Rule would be utterly inadequate.

Predictably, the most common clerical objection was on religious
grounds, expressed in a majority of contributions (160), of which twelve
referred explicitly to 'Rome Rule'. Several referred to papal interference
through decrees such as 'Ne Temere' and 'Motu Proprio', and predicted

---

[46] None of the dissentient clergy discussed in the next chapter contributed to the *DM*.

clerical domination of politics.[47] According to Isaac Player Bell, the Baptist pastor at Foundry St (Belfast), 'the priest controls the Irish peasant vote'. Some feared a new 'Roman ascendancy' or the eventual extinction of Protestantism in Ireland. William Tarrant Browne, incumbent of Killyleagh (Down), anticipated the 'gradual weakening of Protestantism in Ireland, and possibly its almost total disappearance in the course of a generation'. His colleague George Nathaniel Trinder, of Rossnowlagh (Donegal), expected that 'Protestants generally would lose their grit, emigrate, or suffer absorption'. Edmund Francis Vesey Ross, incumbent of Magherahamlet (Down), predicted 'Chaos! The putting back of the clock centuries; the extinguishing of the Protestant candle; the marooning of the Ulsterman on a desolate isle amid savage and implacable enemies.' Six contributors predicted moral consequences such as 'intemperance rampant', 'moral stagnation', or 'Ireland ... degraded, and demoralised'.[48] No less than 40 perceived a threat to liberty or freedom, often adopting the Orange rhetoric of 'civil and religious liberty'.[49] Andrew Leitch, incumbent of Drumclamph (Tyrone), reverted shamelessly to the language of ascendancy when fearing the loss of 'all civil and religious privileges'. His colleague at Kildarton (Armagh), Thomas Kingsborough, voiced the less anachronistic belief that 'our lives, our liberties, and our holy religion would be imperilled'.

Eight clergymen, of whom six were Episcopalians, drew some solace from the prediction that the Irish would eventually turn against Rome Rule, whether for better or worse: 'in Roman Catholic Ireland the inevitable disillusionment could only mean despair and revolution'; 'expansion of Rome's influence – in time revolt against it'; 'ultimate revolt of Nationalists against religion, as in France'; 'after ten or fifteen years there would probably be an anti-clerical movement'; 'after many years, a revolt against Rome's political power, and probably a lapse into infidelity'; 'ultimate reaction against Rome and predominance of infidelity'.[50] The

---

[47] As the *DM* explained to perplexed readers: 'Ne Temere' invalidated mixed marriages unless conducted according to ecclesiastical law, while 'Motu Proprio' forbade the faithful to summon priests before tribunals.

[48] Thomas Miller Benson (E) of Ballymoney (Antrim); Thomas William Davidson (M) of Donegall Sq. (Belfast); John McDowell (P) of Aughentain (Tyrone). The abbreviations E, M, and P denote Episcopalian, Methodist, and Presbyterian ministers.

[49] All contributors with moral objections also voiced religious arguments, but 11 of the 40 fearing loss of freedom or liberty did not refer specifically to religion; the phrase 'civil and religious' was used in 18 cases.

[50] Charles Henry Leslie Buchanan (E) of Kilwaughter (Antrim); Alfred George Elliott, Bishop of Kilmore, Elphin, and Ardagh; Isaac Purcell Barnes (E) of Boyd Church, Ballycastle (Antrim); Frederick Henry Kinch (E) of Ballinderry (Londonderry); William Ryland Rainsford Moore (E) of Drumgoon (Cavan); Robert White (E) of Dundonald (Antrim).

Presbyterian Samuel John Bennett, of Ervey (Cavan), looked forward to 'the ultimate revolt of the laity against the Roman Catholic clergy, resulting in Ireland taking the same course as Continental Roman Catholic countries'. John Ramsey, Reformed Presbyterian minister in Ballymoney, imagined, 'after years of suffering, liberty won by a general revolt against Rome'. Such prophecies reflected the long-cherished but repeatedly frustrated yearning of evangelical Protestants that Irish Catholics would eventually be drawn towards the glorious light, through exposure to the Open Bible and disillusionment with their priests.

Over two-fifths of contributors (125) voiced economic objections, anticipating over-taxation, damage to Ulster's industries, or bankruptcy. These baneful consequences were often attributed to the expected civil turmoil rather than nationalist proposals for the protection of 'native industries', which may not have been taken seriously. John Edward Browne, incumbent of St Stephen's (Belfast), foresaw 'twenty years of anarchy in Ulster, ending in the ruin of every industry'; his colleague Maurice Henry Fitzgerald Collis of Antrim feared 'resistance and civil war, followed by national bankruptcy'. Nine contributors portrayed Home Rule as a threat to recent progress, whereby enlightened Catholics and Protestants had begun to work together for economic and social advance. Presbyterians wrote that Home Rule 'would assuredly arrest the progress we have been making', or 'recreate a spirit of distrust'.[51] Episcopalians predicted that 'religious and racial prejudices, which had almost disappeared, have been resuscitated and must break forth in destructive fury'; 'Home Rule would destroy that spirit of progress and co-operation and those friendly relations that have made their appearance of late'; and 'party feeling – fast dying out in the past – will be engendered'. Others remarked nostalgically that 'the Protestants and Roman Catholics were beginning to understand each other better than before, but now the breach has widened'; 'we were getting along nicely in Ireland. Party feeling was on the decline.'[52]

The most detailed exposition of Paradise Lost under Home Rule was by Charles Edward Quin, incumbent of Derriaghy (Antrim):

Home Rule would intensify religious differences, starve education, and check progressive movements, so marked in recent years, which were rapidly settling Irish problems by providing labourers' cottages, establishing a peasant proprietary, developing trade and industry.

---

[51] Samuel Thompson (P) of Clifton St (Belfast); William Michael (P) of Trenta (Donegal).
[52] Samuel Roberts Anderson (E) of Lack (Fermanagh); Henry Egerton (E) of Donoughmore Upper (Tyrone); James MacManaway (E) of Monaghan; William Robert Perrott (E) of Grange (Armagh); Edward Daniel Crowe (E) of Annagliffe and Urney (Cavan).

James Rodgers Michael, Presbyterian minister of Kilmacrenan (Donegal), preferred loftier phraseology:

Since the Union domestic peace has grown in Ireland by leaps and bounds, and she is now on the road to freedom of thought and action, but the shadow of the same withering hand has crossed her brightening sky again. I see no reason why, under the Union, the memory of old wrongs and old quarrels should not be for ever buried and the three kingdoms become as inseparable as the leaves of the shamrock by which St. Patrick explained to the Irish the mystery of the Unity of the Trinity.

Home Rule, in short, was a reactionary proposal at odds with the spirit of the times and the existing process of reconciliation in Ireland.

Though religious and economic objections predominated, other contributors deplored the likely consequences for education (28), emigration (20), and administrative corruption or incompetence (15). Robert Corkey, Presbyterian minister of 1st Monaghan and later minister of education for Northern Ireland, warned that 'Irish would become a compulsory subject' and 'Protestant inspectors would cease to exist', an unusually specific statement of the consequences for schools and universities. Several writers predicted massive Protestant emigration from southern counties, anticipating recent debates about 'ethnic cleansing' in the aftermath of partition. A few suggested that the outflow would be a voluntary response to unfavourable prospects at home: according to two Episcopalians in mid Ulster, 'Protestants would emigrate in large numbers', while already 'the more intelligent and industrious of the Protestant young men and women are emigrating on account of the threat of Home Rule'.[53] More spoke of an 'exodus' or forced migration. Presbyterian writers, also living in counties with large Catholic populations, predicted 'an exodus of Protestants from the south and of Roman Catholics from Belfast', and 'a serious exodus of a large part of the Protestant population'.[54] Samuel Bennett of Ervey warned of the dire consequences of partition: 'Home Rule for Ireland is impossible for at least a generation. *Provincial* Home Rule would mean in the three provinces the gradual boycott of all Protestants, resulting in their speedy elimination from the community.' George Pigot McCay, Presbyterian minister of Fintona (Tyrone), believed that 'the future of this country will be such that no Protestant could or would live in it'. Likewise, Episcopalians expected 'expulsion of the loyal minority' from 'the south and west', or 'intolerable pressure either to apostatise or go'; 'Protestants would be gradually but

---

[53] John Montgomery Browne (E) of Aghalurcher (Fermanagh); William Glenn (E) of Altedesert (Tyrone).

[54] William Thomas Latimer (P) of Eglish (Tyrone); David Miller (P) of 1st Armagh.

surely squeezed out of the country', or 'marked out for banishment'.[55] Matthew Banks Hogg, of Keady (Armagh), was no less bleak: 'Under Rome Rule there is no possible future for unionists, but despairing servitude or its preferable alternative – annihilation.'

Ten contributors believed that Home Rule would enhance distrust between the 'parties' in Ireland, and the same number warned of resultant Anglophobia on the part of the betrayed unionist population. Distrust of those administering Home Rule would set the conditions for strife and violence. Episcopalians in Tyrone predicted that 'both parties would be suspicious' but 'Roman Catholicism would get the upper hand', imagining 'a Parliament of rebels ... dominated by Hibernians'.[56] Robert Blair of Magheracross (Fermanagh) wrote contemptuously of 'a party whose tendencies are well known and who cannot therefore be trusted'. Presbyterians declared that 'we do not trust the Home Rule leaders'; 'there is a profound distrust of the men who would be our legislators in a Dublin Parliament even more than of their measures'.[57]

In the volatile context of 1912, it is not surprising that several writers expected Irish loyalists to turn against the United Kingdom and the Empire that they had formerly lauded. According to four Episcopalians, the outcome of Home Rule would be 'Unionism alienated'; 'loyalty vanish[ing] entirely among Home Rulers, and seriously weakened in law-abiding north'; 'irreconcilable and undying hatred of Irish Protestants towards England for the great betrayal'; 'deep-rooted hatred towards England among betrayed Irish Protestants'.[58] Thomas Dagg, incumbent of Fivemiletown (Tyrone), predicted that 'the suffering minority, stung by England's base betrayal, would regard her with permanent and contemptuous hate'. James Morrow Patterson, Presbyterian minister of Clougherney (Tyrone), believed that 'if it satisfied the two-thirds of its population it would leave the remaining third – hitherto contented and loyal – permanently discontented and its loyalty severely strained'. Equally impassioned, if less coherent, was the warning by George Alexander Chadwick, bishop of Derry and Raphoe and grand chaplain of Ireland:

[55] James Richardson (E) of Stonyford (Antrim); Kivas Collingwood Brunskill (E) of Donaghendry (Tyrone); Thomas Gibson George Collins (E) of St James's (Belfast); William Alexander Baird Jackson (E) of Drumnakilly (Tyrone).
[56] Thomas Edward Adderley (E) of Killeshill (Tyrone); Thomas Lindsay Fitzgeorge Stack (E) of Langfield (Tyrone); Robert Blair (E) of Magheracross (Fermanagh).
[57] William Corkey (P) of Townsend St (Belfast); Lawson Burnett (P) of Donaghmore (Down).
[58] Frederick William Austin (E) of St Columba's, Knock (Belfast); John Blacker Aikin Hughes (E) of Ballywalter (Down); Robert Crozier (E) of Bovevagh (Londonderry); William Shaw Kerr (E) of St Paul's (Belfast).

My conviction is ... that it will add to the party of revolution tens of thousands of those who are now the most loyal of Irishmen; that it will do this not by way of resentment, but by a deep conviction that if we must be governed by a Roman and an alien majority, at least their mandates must not be enforced upon us by the brute force of the Empire.

As Kipling wrote in 'Ulster' (1912): 'If England drive us forth | We shall not fall alone!'

For true unionists, the menace of Home Rule was not restricted to Ireland: 30 statements anticipated future threats to the United Kingdom or the Empire, while 29 predicted enhanced pressure for full separation once Home Rule had been achieved.[59] Joseph Abbott, incumbent of Muckross (Fermanagh), imagined 'a struggle such as the United Kingdom has not seen for three hundred years' resulting in 'ruin and desolation in Ireland, and England's fall to a third-class Power'. Episcopalians feared betrayal in time of war, raising the uncomfortable options of 'ruin or Germany'; an Ireland 'reconquered by England, or, a colony of Germany'; 'a perpetual menace to England and the Empire, especially in the case of war'; a country that would 'welcome any English enemy into Irish ports'.[60] William Bagot Stack of Magheraculmony (Fermanagh) predicted 'anarchy and bloodshed now and the break up of the Empire later'. James Wilson, Presbyterian minister at Argyle Place (Belfast), pronounced that 'Home Rule would ruin Ireland, endanger England, impoverish Scotland, and taunt Wales'; his colleague Joseph Morrison of Leckpatrick (Tyrone) perceived 'a menace to the stability of our Empire'. Clerical fears of damage to Britain and the Empire were heightened by the justified belief that most nationalists regarded Home Rule merely as a first step towards independence: 'it will result in final separation'; 'complete separation from Britain would be the inevitable result'; 'Irish-American Republicans not satisfied'.[61]

VII

Apart from religious objections, the most common fear was that Home Rule would precipitate strife and even civil war or rebellion. Nearly half of the contributors (144) expressed one or more of these warnings, while only occasionally endorsing whatever violence might ensue. Most seem to

---

[59] Fifty-three statements (17.9%) expressed either or both of these views.
[60] Samuel Stephen Holmes (E) of Groomsport (Down); John Robert Ballard (E) of Newtownhamilton (Armagh); George Samuel Greer (E) of Ballyphilip (Down); Joseph Grundy Burton (E) of Killinchy (Down).
[61] Robert McCready (P) of Dunfanaghy (Donegal); Jackson McFadden (P) of Badoney and Corrick (Tyrone); Frederick William Austin (E) of St Columba's, Knock (Belfast).

have accepted Carson's argument that the only practical strategy for preventing Home Rule was to intimidate the government through demonstrations of communal solidarity, such as Ulster Day, reinforced by the latent menace of violent resistance. Whatever undiscussed advantages Home Rule might have in principle, it was widely accepted that popular resistance in Ulster was inevitable, and that the clergyman's moral duty was to reduce the risk of collision by supporting the Carsonite strategy.

Episcopalian contributors warned of 'fierce riots between non-religious of both parties'; 'endless strife, civil and religious'; 'anarchy and bloodshed'; 'friction between Unionists and Nationalists leading to rioting'; 'years of bloodshed and religious strife'; 'riot and bloodshed'.[62] Others expected 'persecution and disorder, and I fear many lives will be lost'; 'nothing but strife and bloodshed'; 'violence and boycotting'; 'turmoil, discord, and civil strife'; 'unending strife and unrest'; 'scenes of strife and bloodshed'; 'bitter sectarian strife'; and 'widespread violence and bloodshed'.[63] Likewise, Presbyterians expected 'years of internecine strife'; 'bitter and prolonged strife'; 'strife and bloodshed'; 'ever-recurring reprisals and riot'; 'strife and bloodshed throughout the province'; 'very serious trouble'; 'rapine, ruin, bloodshed'.[64] Methodists feared 'complete national upheaval', 'strife, confusion, and blood', and 'religious strife and rancour'.[65] Joseph Moffett of Letterkenny (Donegal), the sole Eastern Reformed Presbyterian contributor, predicted 'further agitation and misery'; and the Moravian Harold James Wilson of Gracehill (Antrim) expected 'long years of disastrous internal ferment'. The prophetic litany uttered by clergy of all denominations could be prolonged indefinitely!

Apart from strife based on religious or 'racial' animosities, several predicted nationalist fragmentation once the common goal had been achieved: 'continual dissension among the Nationalists'; 'strife among

---

[62] John Blacker Aikin Hughes (E) of Ballywalter (Down); Arthur McQuade (E) of Kilteevock (Donegal); William Bagot Stack (E) of Magheraculmony (Fermanagh); John Matthew Young (E) of Kildress (Tyrone); Michael Hamilton Gibson Willis (E) of St Michael's (Belfast); Alfred Wade Johnston (E) of Richhill (Armagh).

[63] William James Askins (E) of Danesfort (Cavan); William Edward Fleming (E) of Kilskeery (Tyrone); Albert Edward Sixsmith (E) of Kilrea (Londonderry); Robert Frederick Graham (E) of Kilmacrenan (Donegal); Arthur Langtry (E) of Kilcoo (Down); Edward Russell Moncrieff (E) of Agherton (Londonderry); Arthur Thomas Webb (E) of Enniskillen (Fermanagh); Thomas Schoales Hall (E) of Upper Falls (Belfast).

[64] Samuel Reid (P) of Cushendall (Antrim); William Alexander Hill (P) of Hamilton Rd, Bangor (Down); William Colvin (P) of Connor (Antrim); Robert Corkey (P) of 1st Monaghan; John Davidson (P) of Glennan (Monaghan); Robert Hastings Smythe (P) of 1st Castleblayney (Monaghan); John Stewart (P) of Seaforde (Down).

[65] Robert Knox (M) of Ardara (Donegal); Alexander Abraham (M) of Bailieborough (Cavan); Thomas William Davidson (M) of Donegall Sq. (Belfast).

the Nationalists'; 'the Nationalists would split up into many hostile parties' and 'the country would soon be in ruin'.[66] Behind such gloomy prognostications lurked the widespread assumption that the Irish, unlike the British, were inherently faction-ridden and quarrelsome. Archibald John McMaster Yair, incumbent of Trory (Fermanagh), envisaged 'two camps bitterly hostile to each other and requiring a British Army Corps to keep the peace between them'. Henry Todd, incumbent of Camlough (Armagh), clarified this point for readers of the *Daily Mail*:

The antipathy between the two parties in Ireland exceeds beyond conception the antipathy between the various English parties. It is therefore better that neither should perpetually govern the other.

Without the union, all hope of reconciliation and mutual tolerance would be lost.

Whereas southern nationalists and British liberals often dismissed the threatening language of Ulster unionists as mere bluff, few Ulster observers shared this opinion. Long before the successive creation of the UVF and a provisional government gave institutional shape to loyalist threats, widespread drilling and procurement of arms had persuaded even Belfast-born Canon Hannay, Home Ruler and sceptic though he was, that the Orangemen and their allies were in earnest. No unionist contributor to the *Daily Mail* cast doubt on the authenticity of those threats of violence if Home Rule were applied; no fewer than 45 predicted civil war rather than mere strife; and 18 anticipated rebellion or conflict with the forces of the Crown.

Predictions of civil war were often apocalyptic in tone. Episcopalian contributors anticipated 'sectarian animosity, issuing in open conflict'; 'a regular battle ground for the first twenty years'; 'riots and bloodshed, if not [to] civil war'; 'strife and civil war'; 'civil war and bloodshed'.[67] Others expected 'serious rioting, issuing in a civil war' if taxes were imposed on Ulster; 'a state of civil war waged with a bitterness that would find few parallels in history'; 'civil war in Ireland, and a repetition of the sad events of 1641'; 'resistance and civil war, followed by national bankruptcy'; and 'nothing but a civil war for us'.[68] Presbyterians

---

[66] William John Gregg (P) of 2nd Dromara (Down); David Marshall (P) of Mountjoy (Tyrone); George Sweetnam (E) of Killelagh (Londonderry).

[67] Francis Medcalf (E) of Dunluce (Antrim); Thomas B. Ward (E) of The Barr (Tyrone); Thomas Cox (E) of Ramoan (Antrim); George Patton Mitchell (E) of Drumbo (Antrim); Samuel Thomas Nesbitt (E) of Ballynure (Antrim).

[68] Henry St George McClenaghan (E) of Killaghtee (Donegal); Joseph Ruddell (E) of Clones (Monaghan); William Dorin Falkiner Wilkinson (E) of Dromara and Garvaghy (Down); Maurice Henry Fitzgerald Collis (E) of Antrim; William Wallace (E) of Billis (Cavan).

imagined 'a period of religious strife, riot, and bloodshed unparalleled in the annals of the country'; 'open conflict in populous centres and secret depredations in the country' involving firearms; 'civil war the normal condition, with the Imperial troops called in to quell loyal disloyalty'; 'disturbances and civil war'; 'civil war, which I shudder to think of as a Christian minister'; or 'bankruptcy, strife, riot, war, and bloodshed'; 'civil war (Ulster offering determined and organised resistance)'; 'an endless civil war'; 'civil war in Ulster' and 'blood-stained desolation'.[69]

The Methodist William Maguire of the North Belfast mission, a prominent Orange chaplain, expected 'a serious conflict between the parties'; his colleague Beresford Stuart Lyons of Coleraine (Londonderry) predicted 'a civil war unparalleled since 1798'. The Presbyterian Hugh Abraham Irvine, minister of Drumlee (Down), predicted that 'simultaneously with the creation of a Dublin Parliament a provisional government will be set up in Belfast. A struggle must ensue.' George Magill, the Presbyterian minister of Cliftonville (Belfast), predicted that 'civil war would ensue, and then – what then? "Wait and see."' Canon Kerr Hamilton Thompson of Convoy (Donegal) had a sharper premonition of what was to come:

A recent conversation: Roman Catholic: 'We'll soon have Home Rule, and then we'll stick you all like pigs.' Protestant: 'And what would we be doing while you did that?' Roman Catholic: 'Oh, we'd do it while you were not looking.'

Small comfort would have been derived from the Catholic protagonist's evident familiarity with the imperial sport of pig-sticking.

Even more alarming to unionists was the prospect of rebellion against the Crown. William Brown Allman, incumbent of Milltown, wrote that 'preparations are being made in this county (Armagh) to resist Home Rule; men's passions are stirred, and no man can foresee anything but ruin, should the present wretched Bill become law'. Other Episcopalian contributors foresaw 'Bloodshed ... Rowdyism. Reprisals. Rebellion', 'open rebellion', or 'dauntless resolve to resist Home Rule by all means', maintaining that 'Ulster's inclusion means revolution', that 'Loyalists ... would sooner die, and glory in the sacrifice, than submit', and that 'Ulster's resistance to Home Rule could only be quelled by military

---

[69] Thomas Doey (P) of Bessbrook (Armagh); Joseph Moorhead (P) of Anaghlone (Down); James McFarland Guy (P) of Ballindrait (Tyrone); George Benaugh (Reformed P) of Knockbracken (Belfast); John McDowell (P) of Aughentain (Tyrone); William Witherow (P) of Westbourne (Belfast); David Aiken (P) of Port Stewart (Londonderry); Thomas Madill (P) of 1st Garvagh (Londonderry); William Bradley Sproule (P) of 1st Lurgan (Armagh).

force'.[70] Presbyterians agreed that 'Home Rule can only be maintained here by force', and that 'disturbances in Ulster would arise, only to be suppressed by martial law'; while two Baptist pastors believed that 'to force this measure on the country will eventually lead to bloodshed', and that 'there will be a serious revolution'.[71]

Only two contributors openly endorsed armed resistance, as distinct from deeming it an inevitable consequence of Home Rule. James Morell, Presbyterian minister of 2nd Ballybay (Monaghan), declared that 'I am determined to resist it to the very uttermost'. Thomas Johnston Bayly, incumbent of Termonaquirke (Tyrone), invoked Thomist doctrine by musing that 'rebellion may become a duty. Ireland under Home Rule is a terrible prospect!' No doubt many other clergymen would have become active participants, rather than mere observers or prophets, if their fearful predictions had been fulfilled.

It is noteworthy that less than a quarter of respondents (66) referred specifically to Ulster or 'the North' of Ireland, despite the fact that the survey was published on Ulster Day. In most cases, therefore, clerical objections to Home Rule were not restricted to the province in which they ministered. The conviction that Protestant Ulster was immovable was shared by clergy of all denominations and all regions of origin. Naturally, some of the firmest declarations of northern implacability came from Ulster Presbyterians. According to James Kennedy Cronne of Portaferry (Down):

No human eye can pierce the clouds that hang over the future of Ireland under Home Rule. It is simply a fact, crucial and vital, that a northern people, brave, industrious, and law abiding, are determined that they will not recognise a Parliament in Dublin, and so Home Rule can only be maintained here by force.

Other Presbyterians concurred: 'she must resist it to the death'; 'we are standing on the brink of a volcano here in Ulster'; 'Home Rule if forced upon Ulster will be resisted'; 'Protestant Ulster will not submit to the nefarious conspiracy'.[72] It is clear that 88-year-old David Mitchel of

[70] Benjamin Finch White (E) of Inch (Down); Henry Egerton (E) of Donoughmore Upper (Tyrone); William Alexander Baird Jackson (E) of Drumnakilly (Tyrone); George Nathaniel Trinder (E) of Rossnowlagh (Donegal); John Thomas Henry Abbott (E) of Mullaghadun (Cavan); John Robert McKim (E) of Desertlyn (Londonderry).
[71] James Kennedy Cronne (P) of Portaferry (Down); David Thompson Macky (P) of Newmills (Tyrone); James Shields (Baptist) of Milltown (Belfast); William James Thomson (Baptist) of Clough (Antrim).
[72] William Witherow (P) of Westbourne (Belfast); Robert Thomas Megaw (P) of College Sq. (Belfast); Robert Barron (P) of Whitehouse (Antrim); James Dick (Reformed P) of Trinity St (Belfast).

Hamilton Road, Warrenpoint (Down), did not share the political views of his late brother, the Confederate John Mitchel:

Home Rule would bring loyalists under the control of the disloyal and rebellious, and certainly lead to the ascendancy of a system always hostile to freedom and toleration. Ulster is resolved to render this irrational scheme unworkable.

In Enniskillen, Samuel Cuthbert Mitchell (moderator of the general assembly in 1911–12) foresaw 'a serious increase of racial bitterness, party strife, religious intolerance, and priestly rule, together with the most determined opposition of half a million Ulster loyalists – a prospect none too pleasant for those who have to live in the country'. David Raphael Moore, who had retired in 1895 from 1st Killinchy (Down), drew a familiar history lesson from the Siege of Derry:

Can Ulster do without the other provinces? I answer Yes, very well. Can the other provinces do without Ulster? I answer No. What may be said in future of to-day's fight we know little, but we do know the results of our Derry siege in the same cause, when our very forefathers for 103 days held the city against fearful odds.

Methodist ministers were no less adamant, affirming that 'Ulster will "resist unto blood"', being 'determined not to submit to the betrayal'.[73] Similar views were expressed by the Ulster-born minority of Church of Ireland contributors: 'I believe it would be as easy to destroy the loyal men of Ulster as to enslave them'; 'Ulster repudiates a parliament of rebels'; 'let no man mistake the temper of Ulster. The storm is only now beginning to gather'; 'I have come across instances repeatedly of the strong determination there is in Ulster to resist Home Rule'.[74] Less predictable was the outlook of Episcopalians born in Southern Ireland, for whom Ulster's intransigence was a matter of observation rather than inbred conviction. None doubted Ulster's resolution, attesting to 'the certainty of Ulster's determined and unalterable opposition', 'Ulster's opposition being irreconcilable'; that 'serious bloodshed in Ulster would be unavoidable'; and that 'Ulster would inevitably remain actively hostile'.[75] Indeed, southern-born Episcopalians were responsible for some of the most ringing declarations of Ulsterity. George Charles O'Keeffe of Garrison (Fermanagh), though a Dubliner, identified himself emphatically with his neighbours:

[73] Richard Edward Sherwood (M) of Banbridge (Down), native of Dublin; John James Hutchinson (M) of Ballyshannon (Donegal).
[74] John McEndoo (E) of Ballymore (Armagh); Thomas Lindsay Fitzgeorge Stack (E) of Langfield (Tyrone); Ernest Aylward Nelson (E) of Drumbanagher (Armagh); Robert Blair (E) of Magheracross (Fermanagh).
[75] William Hardy Holmes (E) of Kilbarron (Donegal); Alfred Wade Johnston (E) of Richhill (Armagh); Frederick Henry Kinch (E) of Ballinderry (Londonderry); George Alexander Stephenson (E) of St Mary Magdalene's (Belfast).

'here in Ulster we will not have it, and we will not give in'. Another Dubliner, William Alexander Roe of Templeport (Cavan), declared that 'Home Rule for the whole of Ireland is impossible. Let the southern half have it, and exempt Belfast and Ulster.'

A particularly interesting case was that of Alexander Roderick Ryder of Drumbeg (Antrim), whose father had left the Roman Catholic priesthood to proselytise in Connemara on behalf of the Irish Church Missions. He was the only contributor to the *Daily Mail* to refer explicitly to any Covenant:

The spirit of the Covenanters is in the blood of Ulstermen, who are cautious in entering in a quarrel, but who, when liberty, religion, and loyalty to persecuted brethren are in question, may be destroyed but can never be subjugated.

Among Carson's clerical defenders in Ulster, some looked with approval and admiration on the determination of their neighbours to defy the government, others with awe or bemusement, while a few sensed romance rather than mere obduracy in the spirit of Ulster Day.

VIII

By publishing almost 300 statements with densely overlapping themes and phraseology, the *Daily Mail* doubtless hoped to create an irresistible impression of unanimity and shared determination, transcending all normal distinctions of place or precept. That impression may well have been reinforced by the almost mesmeric recurrence of certain themes and phrases, reflected in the preceding synthesis of clerical arguments against Home Rule and prophecies of doom. Overall, more than half of the statements in the *Daily Mail* raised religious objections (54%), compared with economics (42%) and fears for the Empire or the United Kingdom (19%). Nearly half (48%) predicted serious strife in the wake of Home Rule, often amounting to civil war (15%). These aggregate figures conceal significant discrepancies associated with location, denomination, and birthplace. Table 6.6 cross-tabulates the occurrence of major themes with various sub-groups of clergy, showing striking variations which reveal the imprint on clerical attitudes of background and neighbourhood. These differences confirm the multiple meanings of Ulster Day for contemporaries, whose preoccupations were deeply affected by their origins and circumstances.

Clergymen in the heavily industrialised north-eastern counties were almost twice as likely to raise economic objections as their counterparts in more rural counties (63% by comparison with 37% in mid Ulster and 33% in the 'Lost Counties'). Those in the three predominantly Catholic counties later included in the Irish Free State were far less preoccupied with religious issues than elsewhere (35% compared with 61% in the north-east and 55% in mid Ulster). They were also much more likely to anticipate civil or religious strife (63% compared with 44% and 47%). It is interesting, if scarcely surprising, that fear of violence and unrest was greater in counties where Protestantism was relatively weak. There was little regional variation, however, in the frequency with which the clergy discussed other major themes, such as threats to the Empire or the United Kingdom and issues relating specifically to Ulster.

When contributors are classified by birthplace, different patterns emerge. Apart from a strong tendency for those born in the north-east to mention economic issues (62%), there was little variation in thematic preoccupations between natives of the various Ulster regions. The most striking finding concerns those born in the southern provinces (over a quarter of all contributors). They too were disproportionately concerned with economic objections (48%), as also with consequences for the Empire beyond Ireland (29% compared with 16% for natives of Ulster). They were also more inclined to anticipate strife (59% compared with 44% for Ultonians) and to refer specifically to issues affecting Ulster or the North of Ireland (27% compared with 21%). In general, perhaps because of their external perspective on the Ulster crisis, southern-born contributors were more probing and wide-ranging as analysts than their Ultonian counterparts.

To some extent, these variations according to locality and nativity are by-products of differences between Presbyterian and Episcopalian contributions. Presbyterians were much more likely to raise religious objections (60% compared with 46% for Episcopalians), less inclined to discuss economics (34% compared with 50%) and consequences reaching beyond Ireland (15% compared with 23%). They were also much less preoccupied with the risk of strife (42% compared with 56%). In all of these respects, the 35 contributors serving other churches (such as Methodists and Baptists) conformed quite closely to the Presbyterian rather than Episcopalian model. Table 6.6 reveals that much of the difference between southerners and Ultonians is accountable to the fact that most southerners belonged to the Church of Ireland, probably the best educated and least parochial of Ulster's clergies. When Episcopalians are sub-divided according to birthplace, the residual differences between themes discussed by Ultonians and others are quite small. Those born outside the province were still more inclined to discuss imperial consequences (27% compared with 19% for natives of Ulster) and to anticipate strife (60% compared with 50%). But both groups of Episcopalian clergy had far more in common with each other than with their Presbyterian counterparts. Religious denomination seems to have been the strongest factor in moulding which arguments and predictions concerning Home Rule would be selected by an Ulster clergyman in 1912.

Finally, let us examine the statements of ministers known to have been active in other aspects of the campaign against Home Rule. Those contributors who also acted as Orange chaplains or Covenant agents were disproportionately inclined to make specific reference to Ulster, and to anticipate strife or civil war should Home Rule be applied. It is worth noting that 8 of the 43 clergy identified as Orange chaplains referred to variants of 'civil and religious liberty', a mantra for orators at the 'field' on the Twelfth of July and in anniversary services for the brethren. This represented 19% of all Orange contributors, compared with 13% of the entire group (40 out of 298).

Ulster's opposition to Home Rule was derived from a multitude of arguments and fears, voiced in different combinations by various sub-groups of clerical spokesmen. Most of these diverse views were compatible with the documents signed on Ulster Day. The Covenant's impressive verbal economy was a source of both strength and weakness. By inviting variant interpretations, it embraced a remarkable range of incompatible outlooks (liberal and reactionary, peace-loving and bellicose, Irish and Ulster-centred) whose only common factor was opposition to Home Rule. Yet the studied ambiguities of the Covenant also alienated some opponents of Home Rule, who feared that the implicit threats might be realised with disastrous consequences. The next chapter explores the diverse and often neglected minority of clerical non-Covenanters, who straddled a political and religious spectrum even broader than that so triumphantly exhibited to the world on Ulster Day.

7   Ulster's non-Covenanters

'Ulster Day', 28 September 1912, is rightly remembered as the most comprehensive demonstration of communal solidarity in the history of Ulster unionism. As noted in the preceding chapter, almost half a million people, about three-quarters of the province's Protestant adults, signed the Ulster Covenant or the Women's Declaration. Admittedly, there were regional variations in the success of Ulster Day, with proportionately few signatories in Cavan, Donegal, and the Belfast region. Mid Ulster was the epicentre for all of these manifestations of fervent unionism. The sacerdotal form and ambiguous wording of the Covenant and Declaration were skilfully designed to embrace a remarkably wide range of political and religious viewpoints, united only by shared opposition to Home Rule. Many signatories held liberal opinions on social issues, abhorred religious intolerance, deplored violence and defiance of the civil magistrate, and were fearful of defending Ulster's interests at the expense of the southern Protestant minority.

At first sight, such views were incompatible with a campaign based on alliances with conservatism and Orangeism, involving the threat of revolutionary violence, and centred on Ulster. Yet, as demonstrated by my analysis of the views of several hundred Ulster clergymen, many supported Carson's strategy in the belief that the only way to avoid a sectarian bloodbath was to intimidate Asquith's government into abandoning Home Rule. Most of them were not so much party politicians as pastors, attempting to reconcile public opinion with moral imperatives. They had not devised the reckless political strategy that they felt obliged to justify, or else to embrace with misgivings as an expression of the popular will. Their views may therefore reveal more about the hidden roots and ambivalences of Ulster unionism than the more familiar harangues of Carson and his Ulster advocates.

For some clerical opponents of Home Rule, as well as for the tiny nationalist minority, Carsonism seemed more likely to precipitate mayhem than to avert it. The precise extent to which Protestant ministers opposed, questioned, or simply failed to sign the Covenant cannot be determined. Yet the persistence of clerical dissent, though mainly muffled or mute, made it hazardous for the churches to propose ringing endorsements of Carsonism, in case existing divisions among both clergy and laity were exposed and deepened as a result. The Church of Ireland was unique in calling a special general synod, in April 1912, to discuss the perils of Home Rule with a view to petitioning both houses of parliament. Only five synodsmen voted against Primate Peacocke's declaration of 'our unswerving attachment to the Legislative Union'.[1] All but two endorsed the denial by the provost of Trinity College (the Ulsterman Anthony Traill) that 'our civil and religious liberty may safely be entrusted to a Parliament in which we should be out-numbered by men who are dominated by traditions and aspirations wholly different from our own'.[2]

In 1912, the Presbyterian and Methodist churches avoided formal denunciations of Home Rule by their all-Ireland governing bodies, instead relying on furious resolutions adopted by unofficial 'conventions' and 'representative conferences' summoned in Belfast. In June 1912, the government committee of the general assembly was induced to drop its withering denunciation of the Home Rule Bill, in favour of a limp statement that previous affirmations made it unnecessary 'to make any pronouncement on the subject at present'.[3] A fortnight later, the Methodist conference adopted an almost identical formula, which was 'passed unanimously amid amens and hallelujahs'.[4] In each case, the compromise was jointly sponsored by a liberal and a diehard unionist, in the hope of conveying the determination of all factions to avoid confrontation. The fragile compromise soon collapsed, leading to fierce but contested denunciations of Home Rule at the next general assembly in 1913 and the Methodist conference in 1914.[5] It is clear that both churches approached Ulster Day with some trepidation, having narrowly escaped serious political embarrassment only three months earlier.

---

[1] Joseph Ferguson Peacocke (1835–1916), from Longford, was archbishop of Dublin and primate of Ireland (1897–1915).
[2] *IT* (17 Apr. 1912); *Weekly IT* (20 Apr.) None of the dissentient speakers (Walter MacMurrough Kavanagh, Revd J. O. Hannay, and Lt.-Col. William Hutcheson Poe) was resident in Ulster.
[3] *IT* (5, 8 June 1912); *Weekly IT* (15 June); PCI, *Minutes of the Proceedings of the General Assembly* (Belfast, 1912), 356.
[4] *CA*, xxx (28 June 1912), 306–8.
[5] PCI, *Minutes* (1913), 635–6; *Daily CA* (19, 20 June 1914). Amendments reaffirming the fudge of 1912 were defeated by 921 votes to 43 in the general assembly (swayed by a memorial demanding a fierce resolution signed by 131,351 'members and adherents of the Church'), and by a much smaller margin (143 votes to 110) in the Methodist conference.

II

Despite the impressive range of special church services heralding Ulster Day, the furtive approach of its organisers generated some disquiet. A minister could open his church or conduct a service without implying personal endorsement of the Covenant, the text of which was not published until long after the local arrangements for Ulster Day had got underway.[6] One clergyman who declined to endorse an unseen pledge was Frederick MacNeice. He was not among the Carrickfergus clergy who discussed the town's Ulster Day arrangements on 2 September. Though agreeing at the next committee meeting to hold a service at St Nicholas's church, held on the eve of the Covenant's publication, he sounded a jarring note: 'The Rev F. J. McNeice briefly stated that in the absence of the text of the Covenant, and to obviate any misconception, it must be understood that the services were quite distinct, and it did not neces-sarily follow that those who attended must sign the Covenant.'[7] The local organisers evidently proceeded, without demur, to make arrangements for signing ceremonies at the town hall and several other sites, and for a joint Nonconformist service at the Joymount Presbyterian church as well as that in the parish church.

Others, presumably, did not share their doubts with the congregation or the press. Those who expressed public dissent were few, despite the spirited attempts of the liberal *Ulster Guardian* to suggest widespread non-compliance. All six reports of non-Covenanting clergy or unavail-ability of churches for Ulster Day services referred to Antrim and Down, few names or details being published by the *Guardian*.[8] An anonymous 'Irish Presbyterian Minister' claimed that less than a fifth of his clerical colleagues had signed the Covenant, and 'that very few of the Episcopal clergy signed it, the younger men almost entirely refusing'.[9] The accuracy and basis of these claims are untestable.

When the *Daily Mail* published its Ulster Day survey of 305 clerical predictions about the consequences of Home Rule, only four contributors

---

[6] See preceding chapter.

[7] *Carrickfergus Advertiser* (6, 20 Sept. 1912). At this period, the rector's surname was still usually spelt 'McNeice'. For a fully documented discussion of his responses to Ulster Day, see Fitzpatrick, *'Solitary and Wild'*, ch. 7.

[8] *UG* (5 Oct. 1912).

[9] 'Irish Presbyterian Minister' to *British Weekly*, reproduced in *UG* (19 Oct. 1912). The writer stated that only 3 of 'nearly' 20 ministers in his presbytery signed, and only 7 among 'over 300 communicants on rolls' of his own congregation. The author may well have been J. B. Armour, whose presbytery of Route had 20 ministers in June 1912, and whose Holy Trinity congregation in Ballymoney returned 240 communicants: PCI, *Minutes* (1912), 486, bound with *Statistics of the Presbyterian Church in Ireland, for the Year ending March 31, 1912*, 10.

supported the measure while three expressed 'neutral' views. Though not prominent among Ulster's dissentient clergy, these alien voices deserve some attention. All four Home Rulers were Presbyterians, if we include Jonathan Townsley of Cullybackey (Antrim), a minister of the United Free Church of Scotland (Presbytery of Ireland) or 'Wee Frees'. The three major churches each provided one 'neutral' contributor. All except Townsley were natives of Ulster, and most were long established in their current congregations (three of the seven had served for more than three decades). Four were in their sixties, the only youthful dissentient being William Rutherford, the 24-year-old curate of Ballymore (Armagh). Rutherford's neutrality was a striking departure for the son of a Primitive Wesleyan Methodist preacher who had served as an Orange chaplain in the 1870s.[10]

None of the dissentients was very enthusiastic about Home Rule in principle. James Dickey Craig Houston, of Hyde Park (Antrim), believed that the measure would scarcely affect Ireland's 'material prosperity':

But Home Rule in some acceptable form would remove a sentimental grievance of long standing by satisfying the reasonable claim of a large majority of the people of Ireland to legislate for themselves in local affairs and thus facilitate and render less costly the administration of the law at home.

James Scott of 2nd Banbridge (Down), having served in Armagh and Antrim, had 'no doubt that Home Rule [with] subordination to the Imperial Parliament will tend to the religious, economic, and social welfare of the Irish people as a whole, and consequently to their peace and prosperity, and also to the unity of the three kingdoms and of the Empire'. Thomas Bartley of Ballycarry (Antrim) was even more sanguine:

Home Rule, by removing Ireland from the game of English party politics and giving to the Catholic and Protestant democracies a common patriotic platform and common interests would in a *comparatively* short time liberate and combine 'Hibernian' and 'Orangeman' and make their common country a prosperous, loyal, and contented unit of the Empire.

Jonathan Townsley likewise predicted that 'with additional safeguards (D.V.) ... a common spirit of patriotism would arise to foster more kindly manifestations of religion', and that 'Ireland would become more educated and enterprising in commerce and agriculture'. All four expressions of dissent were notably earnest, if ponderous, rejecting the apocalyptic ardour of so many clerical opponents of Home Rule.

---

[10] Thomas Rutherford (1848–1929), Methodist minister, entered as Primitive preacher (1873), DGC for Co. Down (1876–81). For background, see above, ch. 5.

The three 'neutral' contributors also did their best to deflate the debate. According to William Rutherford in Ballymore:

There will be riots, but not civil war. If the Nationalists keep their promises things will settle down. Rome will lose, not gain. Unless treated generously Ireland will go bankrupt. Home Rule will not do so much good as its supporters assert, nor so much harm as its opponents imagine.

Robert Warnock, Presbyterian minister of Glenhoy (Tyrone), agreed: 'The Home Rulers will not find it the blessing they expect, and the anti-Home Rulers will not find it the curse that they dread.' Most gnomic of all was the Methodist William Clarke of Glastry (Down), who simply recited Asquith's irritating taunt – 'Wait and see.'

III

The form and content of the Covenant raised numerous theological and political problems for Christian ministers. As Scholes notes, oddly few Episcopalians were bothered by its aggressively Presbyterian genesis, despite the 1643 Covenant's withering attack on 'Prelacy'.[11] Frederick MacNeice, however, made a pointed allusion to this issue when discussing the Covenant ceremony of 1644 in the Carrickfergus parish church:

We know that fair-minded, and very well-informed men, have defended the policy enshrined in the Solemn League and Covenant ... We are not convinced. In our judgment the promoters of the League and Covenant failed to discern the signs and needs of the hour. How men, with any knowledge of the English people, could have hoped by such a covenant to compel their conformity to a Presbyterian polity, and to Presbyterian discipline, passes our comprehension.[12]

The invocation of 1643 in 1912 was even more obnoxious to the committee on Covenant-renovation and witness-bearing of the 'Old Covenanter' synod, representing about 4,000 diehard opponents of all parties and constitutions that countenanced popery or prelacy.[13] Though the Old Covenanters (alias Reformed Presbyterians) were implacable opponents of Home Rule on religious grounds,[14] they were no more enamoured of the existing form of the union. Shortly before publication of the Covenant, the committee issued a fearful admonition: 'There is little doubt that in

---

[11] Scholes, *Church of Ireland*, 48.   [12] MacNeice, *Carrickfergus*, 47.
[13] In June 1912, the Reformed Presbyterian Synod of Ireland returned 33 ministers for about 40 congregations, comprising 1,888 families, 3,868 communicants, and 3,167 attenders ('on average') at public worship: *The Covenanter*, n.s., xxii, nos. 8–9 (Aug.–Sept. 1912), statistical appendix.
[14] A 'most emphatic protest against the Home Rule Bill', being 'in all its main features in flagrant opposition to Christ's law', was adopted by the Synod in June 1912: ibid., 311–15.

this time of great political excitement pressure will be brought to bear on you to induce you to adopt the programme of the Unionist Party, and to join in the swearing and signing of what is called "The Ulster Covenant".' The address warned against 'rashly joining in any Covenant that assumes that allegiance should be sworn to the British Constitution, which is a Covenant-breaking and anti-Christian Constitution'.[15] Though the final document did not entail any specific declaration of allegiance to that constitution, many Reformed Presbyterians probably agreed with one correspondent 'that it is not necessary to ask a Covenanter to be a Covenanter', since their existing pledge against Popery implied opposition to 'Home Rule, which means Rome Rule'.[16] The eight Reformed Presbyterian ministers who denounced Home Rule on Ulster Day in the *Daily Mail* evidently concurred, for none of them is known to have signed the Covenant.[17]

The most common theological objection was to the implied threat that force might be used in defiance of the civil magistrate. Many clerical objectors, particularly outside Ulster, protested that the church of Christ should pursue peace through exclusively peaceful means. Yet all major Christian churches accepted the Thomist doctrine that Christians were entitled, as a last resort, to use force for temporal ends (a doctrine soon afterwards expressed in the almost unanimous endorsement, by Irish Catholic and Protestant clergy alike, of the war against Germany and her allies). As 'A Staunch Churchman and Unionist' informed the *Church of Ireland Gazette*: 'Under certain circumstances, resistance to authority and even revolution are justifiable ... Surely the right to resist cannot reasonably be denied us who are strong Unionists.' The writer cited divine approval of the revolt against Judah by the ten tribes of Israel (1 Kings 12).[18]

Others, like 'John Presbyter' (possibly a pseudonym for Frederick MacNeice), maintained that participation

would be in opposition to all we have ever striven to teach. There are those, clergy and laity, who see things differently. They will be able, with a clear conscience, to take the pledge. We judge them not. Let them not judge us ... We think the policy, which those terms would bind us to, should not be recommended, that it would be an end to Constitutionalism in politics, that, if translated into action, it would involve anarchy and civil war.[19]

---

[15] Old Covenanters were opposed to 'Roman Catholics, Jews, Atheists and Pagans having any share in the government': *UG* (21 Sept. 1912); *The Witness* (27 Sept.).
[16] 'A Covenanter' to *The Witness* (27 Sept. 1912).
[17] Ulster Covenant, signature sheets: PRONI, D 1327 (accessible on-line).
[18] *CIG*, liv (13 Sept. 1912), 772.   [19] *CIG*, liv (30 Aug. 1912), 733.

Some objectors chose the narrower ground of the clergyman's responsibility to God and the congregation, emphasising his duty to preach and practise peace amidst violence. Avoidance of clerical intervention in 'party politics' was conventionally justified by the need to pursue unity within the congregation, though this argument was less convincing in periods of overwhelming public support for a particular party or programme.

Three distinct sources of political objection to the Covenant influenced Ulster clergymen in 1912. A few ministers, mainly north Antrim Presbyterians associated with liberal organisations or the Independent Orange Institution, supported Home Rule in principle. These formed only a small fraction of the minority of clergy of all denominations who had voted against church resolutions condemning Home Rule, usually on the ground that clergymen and synods should not intervene in party politics. A second objection, seldom voiced yet surely often pondered, arose from the very essence of conventional 'unionism' – attachment to a United Kingdom whose constitution was enshrined in King, Lords, and Commons. If Ulster were truly unionist, what justification could there be for exempting any region of the union from the will of parliament exercised according to law? Finally, many southern loyalists, while retaining a personal preference for the union, regarded partition as an even worse constitutional outcome than all-Ireland Home Rule. The prevalence of this view among Protestants outside Ulster encouraged most southern bishops and clergy to avoid overt endorsement of the potentially secessionist movement sanctified on Ulster Day. Even clergy who admired the sheer audacity of 'Carsonism' were loath to divide their congregations by sponsoring demonstrations of solidarity such as the services of humiliation and intercession, which were not systematically organised outside the province. Nevertheless, special Ulster Day services were held in cities with substantial Ulstonian populations such as Waterford and Dublin, where separate Episcopalian and Presbyterian ceremonies were staged.[20]

Why, despite the cogency of religious and political objections to clerical endorsement of the Covenant, did so many ministers join the movement? Some approved in principle; some willingly colluded in what they believed to be an ingenious campaign of bluff; some set aside personal quibbles in order to reinforce congregational and pan-Protestant unity. Others, fearful of insult or ostracism, succumbed to pressure from their

---

[20] Services of intercession were held in Christ Church cathedral (Waterford), and in St Patrick's cathedral, Fowler memorial hall (an Orange foundation), and Sackville hall (where 7 Presbyterian ministers participated). A similar service had been held on the previous day at the Mariners' church [of Ireland], Kingstown, Co. Dublin: *IT* (30, 28 Sept. 1912).

neighbours and congregations. As the *Ulster Guardian* observed more than a month before Ulster Day:

Whether the Nonconforming minister take part or not in the services, he incurs grave injury. If he takes part, he hurts his conscience; if he does not he hurts his pocket and becomes a marked man, and the memories of sad sequels to the pseudo-religious Conventions [presumably those held in 1892 and summer 1912] are still too fresh to let us forget what it means to a Protestant clergyman to incur the displeasure of part of his congregation over his refusal to mix up politics with religion.[21]

The consequences of dissent were set out by the anonymous 'Irish Presbyterian Minister' already mentioned:

Never was there such pressure brought to bear on ministers of all Protestant denominations in Ulster to make them false to their conscience and to Jesus Christ their King and Head ... The Covenant is either unmeaning or has such a meaning that no Christian man, and certainly no Christian minister, could sign it. Yet many of our ministers have been forced to sign, or face persecution and starvation. Many more of them were forced against their wills to open their churches and hold what, by an euphemism, they called 'a Gospel service' for the purpose of aiding and abetting the Covenant, yet refusing to sign it themselves.[22]

The extent to which ministers were free to follow their consciences depended on their seniority, their standing in the community, and the depth of their alliances with colleagues and key elders or vestrymen. Let us examine the experiences of three exemplary non-Covenanters, before returning to the remarkable case of the rector of Carrickfergus.

IV

James Brown Armour, who ministered in Ballymoney from 1869 to 1925, was the most celebrated of all Presbyterian Home Rulers.[23] His public disavowal of liberal unionism in 1892 had aroused strong, sometimes violent antagonism, and he claimed to have been 'thrice stoned' thereafter by outraged unionists. When contributing 'a Presbyterian view' to a manual on *The New Irish Constitution* in 1912, he stated that 'Anti-Home Rulers have been threatening, and are carrying out their threat, to boycott any person who shows signs of scepticism about the infallibility of their

[21] 'A Covenant of Little Grace', *UG* (24 Aug. 1912).
[22] *UG* (19 Oct. 1912); cf. n. 9 above.
[23] James Brown Armour (1841–1928), farmer's son from Kilraughts (Antrim), BA, Queen's College, Cork (1864), lecturer at Magee College, Londonderry, ordained Trinity church, 2nd Ballymoney (1869), resigned 1925.

credo.'[24] As clerk of the Route synod and an inveterate polemicist and church politician, Armour had no qualms in pursuing his long-standing feud with the Unionist Party and the Orange Order, and also with the current Presbyterian moderator and co-draughtsman of the Covenant, Henry Montgomery.

In letters to his sons, he treated the Covenant, Carson, and local Carsonites with contempt:

The Ulster are bent on another explosion and have arranged for a great covenanting day when they are to vow not to acknowledge or pay taxes to a Home Rule parliament … It is a climb down however. They were all to swear with uplifted hand that they would oppose Home Rule by violent methods but now it is only a declaration … The orange tail is wagging the Protestant dog.[25]

Armour's correspondence chronicles his moderately successful attempts to dissuade fellow-ministers in Ballymoney and beyond from opening their churches or endorsing the Covenant, and his disgust at those who subsequently wobbled like 'a reed shaken by the wind'. He expressed satisfaction that 'Carson has not set the Route on fire – a sheer mountebank, the greatest enemy of Protestantism in my opinion existing, inflaming men to violence whom he will probably leave and desert if any difficulty arises.'[26] No Presbyterian church in Ballymoney offered a service on Ulster Day, the only religious ceremony being performed outside the town at Leslie Hill.[27]

Armour's campaign was helped by the residual strength of liberalism in the Ballymoney district and strong support from the Independent Orange Institution, which shared his loathing of Carsonism. Digital analysis of the signature sheets suggests that a third of adult Protestant men and two-fifths of women failed to sign in North Antrim, indicating far more widespread dissent than in the other Antrim constituencies.[28]

---

[24] In *The New Irish Constitution: An Exposition and Some Arguments* (London, Hodder & Stoughton, 1912), ed. J. H. Morgan (for the Eighty Club), 462–71 (463–4). The chronology of his political conversion is discussed in J. R. B. McMinn, *Against the Tide: A Calendar of the Papers of Rev J. B. Armour, Irish Presbyterian Minister and Home Ruler, 1869–1914* (Belfast, PRONI, 1985), xxxiii–viii.

[25] J. B. to W. S. Armour, 5 Sept. 1912, quoted in McMinn, *Against the Tide*, 115.

[26] J. B. to Revd J. B. Max Armour, 24 Sept., 3 Oct. 1912, quoted in McMinn, *Against the Tide*, 116, 118. Armour's correspondence (checked against original letters in PRONI, D 1792/A3/3) refers to a number of ministerial non-Covenanters in his district and beyond, including the Presbyterian minister at Holywood, Co. Down (William John Archer), who was 'getting into hot water over Saturday because he refused the church for a service': J. B. to W. S. Armour, 26 Sept. 1912, in McMinn, *Against the Tide*, 117.

[27] *UG* (5 Oct. 1912. The rector of Ballymoney, Chancellor Benson, was assisted by another rector and two Presbyterian ministers from other localities: *Northern Constitution*, 5 Oct.

[28] The ratio of Covenanters to non-Catholic men in the county's parliamentary constituencies was 67.1% (North), 76.9% (East), and 81.8% (Mid); the corresponding ratio for

Armour's standing in Ballymoney was apparently unaffected by his defiance, partly because his views had some support in the district, but perhaps also because his celebrity as an irascible maverick had become a matter of local entertainment and even pride. In the general assembly, as a member of 'the Committee in Correspondence with Government', he still had sufficient authority in June 1912 to prevent any further pronouncement on Home Rule. Yet the limits of Armour's influence were exposed a year later, when his attempt to replicate this success was dismissed by a huge majority. A proposal by the previous year's high sheriff of Belfast (Crawford McCullagh) to publish the names of all 921 advocates of the anti-Home Rule resolution – and, more menacingly, of the 43 dissentients – was eventually withdrawn. In response to incessant heckling during his rambling address, Armour was goaded into asking 'What is the use of speaking to idiots?' and sneering that the assembly might as well resolve that 'no man that professes to be a Home Ruler can enter the Kingdom of Heaven'.[29]

V

Another prominent liberal and non-Covenanter in the Presbyterian ministry was John Waddell, already notable as an advocate of moderate social reform after a decade's ministry in Bangor.[30] This outlook had led Waddell to urge the general assembly to challenge Unionist Party bosses by demanding 'that candidates selected by the Constitutional Associations should be men of sound Temperance principles'. Waddell's suggestion generated 'a stormy scene', followed eventually by assurances from the official candidate that were deemed 'on the whole satisfactory'. Whereas Armour rejected the Covenant on political grounds, Waddell opposed any ministerial involvement in politics: 'I have never been a politician and have never joined any political party. Like any other citizen I exercise the franchise. But I have always held that Ministers should be kept out of the political fray.'[31]

Waddell did not conduct the service of humiliation on 22 September, at which the preacher was another non-Covenanter, John Young Minford

women was 60.4% (North), 68.6% (Mid), 72.5% (East), and 84.5% (South). The absurdly low male ratio for South Antrim (46.8%) is attributable to the disappearance of many Lisburn signature sheets.

[29] *IT* (7 June 1913; *General Assembly Minutes* (1913), 636.

[30] John Waddell (1878–1949), minister's son from Belfast, ordained 1st Bangor (1902), called to Egremont, Liverpool (1914) and Fisherwick, Belfast (1920; resigned 1945); moderator of general assembly (1937–8).

[31] Harry C. Waddell, *John Waddell, by his Brother* (Belfast, BNL, 1949), 42–4. Harry Waddell succeeded Armour as minister in Trinity church, Ballymoney in 1926.

of Joymount Church in Carrickfergus. Minford unwittingly inspired an unruly exchange between members of the 1st Bangor congregation by allowing a layman (James Black) to announce in church that 'it is most desirable that every member of this congregation, and all adherents over 16 years of age, should rally' to the Ulster Day service.[32] Though a service was indeed held in Waddell's church on that day, the preacher was a visitor on holiday from Glasgow, enlisted at the last moment to avoid the embarrassment of a service conducted by the kirk-session for want of a compliant clergyman. Black again took charge at the end of the service, suggesting that the congregation should undertake 'in definite sections and in orderly fashion the transfer from church to Guild Hall', where the Covenant and Declaration were to be signed.[33]

As his brother and biographer observed, Waddell's dissent alienated some of the congregation, for whom he was still a relative newcomer by comparison with Armour:

The vast majority of the congregation of First Bangor were in entire sympathy with the Carson Movement. John thought things carefully out. He refused to sign the Covenant and to join the Carson Volunteers. This was interpreted as meaning adherence to the policy of Home Rule. Eventually he was persuaded, much against his will, to preach a sermon to the assembled Unionist Clubs. In this sermon he deprecated any resort to armed force. The result was an outburst of criticism and denunciation.[34]

According to the *Ulster Guardian*: 'A few months ago the Bangor Unionist Club invited the Rev. John Waddell to preach a sermon to them. That sermon did not come up to their expectations, and since that time they have subjected him to various indignities, and in fact several members of the congregation have gone so far as to boycott him.'[35]

Waddell's isolation was highlighted by the galling fact that his father, who ministered at Newington Church in Belfast, responded to the *Daily Mail*'s survey of clerical opinion by advising that Ireland under Home Rule 'would speedily lapse into the dark days of the early part of the last century'. His words gained local circulation when extracted by Bangor's weekly newspaper. To make matters worse, the elder John Waddell, who had recently moved house from Belfast to Bangor, expressed solidarity

---

[32] *North Down Herald* (27 Sept. 1912).
[33] 'Patriot', 'Hypocritical Bangor', *UG* (12 Oct. 1912); *Newtownards Chronicle* (5 Oct.). The preacher was James M. Brisby, 'a prominent worker and speaker in the Unionist cause', who delivered a 'thrilling and magnificent sermon': *North Down Herald* (27 Sept., 4 Oct.).
[34] Waddell, *Waddell*, 43–4.   [35] *UG* (12 Oct. 1912).

with his son's restive congregation by putting his signature to the Covenant in the Guild hall.[36]

Waddell recalled that 'I remained in Bangor long enough to overcome a good many of these prejudices, though some hot-heads never forgave me.' He retained enough local support to secure the customary purse of sovereigns and even a grandfather clock on his departure from Bangor.[37] Even so, his removal to Liverpool in November 1914 was probably a relief to minister and people alike. After six years in charge of the huge Egremont congregation, Waddell resumed his contentious career in Ulster, eventually becoming moderator in 1937 during a period of unprecedented cooperation between the Protestant churches in pursuit of inter-communal harmony and reconciliation.

VI

More uncompromising than Waddell and more vulnerable than Armour was Arnold Harvey, who moved from Lissadell (Sligo) to Portrush (Antrim) only a month before Ulster Day.[38] Harvey was a celebrated sportsman, who had represented Ireland in both Rugby football and cricket shortly before his ordination as a curate in 1903. He had appeared in eight Rugby internationals between 1900 and 1903, outshining two brothers who also represented Ireland. Though his record as an international cricketer was less distinguished, he had once dismissed W. L. Murdoch (a former Australian captain) and W. G. Grace (caught and bowled) in successive balls, when playing for Dublin University against a visiting London County XI in June 1903.[39] His achievement at the age of 25 was diminished only slightly by the fact that Murdoch was then aged 48 and Grace 54 (Grace had played his last test match only four years earlier and continued to play first-class cricket until 1908). Such was the intrepid warrior who was instituted at Portrush

---

[36] *North Down Herald*, 4 Oct. 1912, extracted from *DM* (28 Sept.); Ulster Covenant, signature sheets, North Antrim. Waddell, though still ministering in Belfast, was resident in June 1912 in Windsor Avenue, Bangor, a few hundred yards from his son's 23-roomed manse in Maxwell Rd: Census of Ireland (1911), family schedules: NAD (accessible on-line); *General Assembly Minutes* (1912), 473.

[37] Waddell, *Waddell*, 44, 51.

[38] Thomas Arnold Harvey (1878–1966), allegedly born in Marsh's library, his father being curate of St Ann's and warden of St Patrick's grammar school, Dublin; BA, Dublin University (1900), ordained curate, St Stephen's, Dublin (1903), rector, Lissadell, Elphin (1907), Ballywillan, Connor (1912), and Booterstown, Dublin (1916), dean of St Patrick's Cathedral, Dublin (1933), bishop of Cashel (1935, retired 1958).

[39] In a drawn three-day match, Harvey scored 36 and 0, and took 7 wickets: *IT* (12, 13, 15 June 1903).

on 29 August 1912, just in time to participate in planning the town's Ulster Day.

Harvey, though performing the preliminary service of intercession on 22 September, 'said that the political question now agitating the public mind was one on which more than one opinion might be held, and trusted that nothing would be done which might lead to an unconstitutional course of action of which the church might not be able to approve'.[40] He compounded the offence by declining (like his Methodist counterpart and presumably other local clergy) to host a service on Ulster Day, forcing the organisers to sanctify proceedings in the skating rink.[41] As James Armour wrote to his son William, two days before Ulster Day:

The new rector of Portrush is getting it loud and strong for refusing to announce the gathering, and for refusing to allow a flag to be put up on the tower and practically telling them he will take no part in the religious orgy. Portrush is much scandalised and the mad-heads may invoke the aid of the bishop to bring the rector as they would say to his right mind.

A week later, Armour expressed disgust that the recently appointed Presbyterian minister at Portrush, John Stanley Pyper, had behaved like 'a stickley-back'[42] by cancelling the diplomatic holiday proposed by Armour and performing at the skating rink: 'His father and brother got round him and compelled him to come back and hold or take part in the service.' Pyper, like 'practically every person present', went on to sign the Covenant. Popular antagonism to Harvey was growing: 'The Portrush people are seething with wrath and would like to stone him but he stuck to his point like a hero.'[43]

By 10 October, 'the hubbub over the matter [was] loud and almost threatening', and Armour reported sending Harvey a letter of congratulation and sympathy, 'advising him to sit tight, preach his best and make no reference to the current insanity'. Harvey wrote a revealing reply:

I was almost entirely alone here in the position I took up which was based on the belief that 'it is not by might nor by power but by my spirit', the Church of Christ can best face difficulties ... I hope I may live down the bitterness that my action has

[40] *Northern Constitution* (28 Sept. 1912), partly quoted in Scholes, *Church of Ireland*, 60. Harvey also announced that a special service would be held each morning of the following week.
[41] *UG* (5 Oct. 1912). In addition to the Presbyterian John Pyper of Portrush, six visiting clergymen attended the service: *Northern Constitution* (5 Oct.).
[42] A stickleback is a small prickly fish.
[43] James to William Stavely Armour, 26 Sept., 3 Oct. 1912, quoted in McMinn, *Against the Tide*, 117–19; *Northern Constitution* (5 Oct. 1912); signature sheets, North Antrim.

caused but I am told that some will never forgive it but they are mostly of a class, or rather an organisation, from which to differ is an honour.[44]

Harvey's condescending dismissal of Orangeism echoed the principled but perhaps naïve view of Ulster sectarianism exhibited by many liberal southerners when first experiencing the 'Black North'. Without some access to the fraternal networks in which so many Ulstermen were enmeshed, liberal clergymen could scarcely expect to win the trust of their parishioners.

Harvey's defiance delighted other dissentients such as the novelist Canon Hannay in Westport, who congratulated him for refusing 'to prostitute the church to the service of a political party' by subscribing to 'obscene rites of deities more debased than Baal or Ashtaroth'.[45] Within four years, Harvey had followed Waddell's example by leaving Ulster, in his case never to revert. One month after the Dublin rebellion of 1916, he was instituted as rector of leafy Booterstown, subsequently becoming dean of St Patrick's and then bishop of Cashel and Emly and of Waterford and Lismore. Harvey's Ulster adventure had not harmed his ascent in the southern Church of Ireland, and his reputation as a principled man of God survived intact. Portrush remained no less steadfast.

VII

One of the most renowned non-Covenanters was the rector of Carrickfergus. Aged 46 in 1912, Frederick MacNeice was 12 years older than Harvey and Waddell but 35 years younger than Armour. In 1936, his son Louis set the tone for many later celebrations of the rector's dramatic announcement, on Ulster Day, that he would not sign the document:

> I leave my father half my pride of blood
> And also my admiration who has fixed
> His pulpit out of the reach of party slogans
> And all the sordid challenges and the mixed
> Motives of those who bring their drums and dragons
> To silence moderation and free speech
> Bawling from armoured cars and carnival wagons.[46]

[44] James to William Stavely Armour, 10 Oct. 1912 (including transcription of Harvey's letter), quoted in McMinn, *Against the Tide*, 119.

[45] Hannay to Harvey, 30 Sept. 1912, quoted in Scholes, *Church of Ireland*, 60.

[46] 'Auden and MacNeice: Their Last Will and Testament', in Louis MacNeice, *Collected Poems* (ed. Peter McDonald), 732. The immediate context for this tribute was Frederick MacNeice's campaign for reconciliation while bishop of Down and Connor and Dromore in 1936.

In his autobiographical writings, Louis MacNeice recorded his father's repudiation of Carson and inferred that he was a Home Ruler, whose southern origins and liberal social views had set him apart from his neighbours and parishioners. This interpretation was at one with Frederick MacNeice's own historical study of Carrickfergus (1928), in which he had stated that 'the extension of the franchise in 1884 made inevitable some form of Home Rule for Ireland' and that subsequent nationalist electoral triumphs were 'a writing on the wall'. In retrospect, the rector ridiculed the notion that the decision lay with the United Kingdom rather than the Irish people:

> Arguments were reiterated for more than a generation which were a denial of the assumed meaning of democratic government. The true entity, it was urged, is Great Britain and Ireland. It is the majority in that unit that should count ... Such arguments, and they had a very Prussian ring about them, did duty for a time.[47]

On the basis of such writings, supported by the rector's own selective extracts from his sermon on Ulster Day, a multitude of scholars has portrayed Frederick MacNeice as a courageous dissentient who, because of his luminous sincerity, managed to retain the affection of his parishioners despite his personal rejection of Ulster's 'fellowship' against Home Rule. As a conscientious Christian minister, he refused to endorse the threat of force; as a far-seeing citizen, though always loath to intrude his political opinions on others, he perceived the futility of resisting the inevitable.

By this account, MacNeice's stance had strong affinities with those of Armour, Waddell, and Harvey. Like Armour, he was courageous enough to align himself with a small political minority, despite the fact that his standing in Carrickfergus was much shakier than Armour's in Ballymoney (MacNeice had faced concerted local opposition when assigned the parish less than four years earlier). Like Waddell, he kept his presumed nationalism to himself, while not hesitating to assert the minister's right to dissociate himself from policies that might lead to bloodshed. The apparent affinities with Harvey were even stronger. Unlike Armour and Waddell, both were southerners from relatively humble backgrounds, whose theological training at Trinity College had exposed them to mildly liberal influences (admittedly, the same could be said of most Episcopalian clergy in Ulster, including many prominent Covenanters and Orange chaplains).[48] Both Harvey and MacNeice emphasised

---

[47] MacNeice, *Carrickfergus*, 70; see also Fitzpatrick, *'Solitary and Wild'*, ch. 1, 7.
[48] Virtually all clergy of the Church of Ireland in the early twentieth century were graduates of Dublin University, and the majority (if the *Daily Mail*'s survey is representative) were born in Southern Ireland.

theological objections to the involvement of ministers in a potentially violent enterprise, and were fearless in declaring their convictions. MacNeice, as a keen rower and vice-patron of the Carrickfergus Rugby club, was also something of a 'muscular Christian'. Though Harvey, as a new arrival in Portrush, lacked the network of supporters that MacNeice had developed, both survived the political and religious turmoil to become, in succession, bishop of Cashel.[49] The most obvious divergence was MacNeice's return to Ulster in 1935, as bishop of Down, and his extra-ordinary success in mobilising Belfast's churchmen in the cause of peace and reconciliation when the threat of civil war again seemed imminent.

Without the addition of four additional facts, the conventional account fails to explain why Frederick MacNeice (unlike Waddell or Harvey) was tolerated as a non-Covenanter by his emphatically 'loyal' congregation. First, MacNeice was not and never had been a Home Ruler, nor (as Scholes has suggested) should he be deemed a 'quietist' in politics.[50] As the *Ulster Guardian* observed in a leading article, eulogising his repudi-ation of the Covenant as perhaps 'the best display of moral courage' provoked by Ulster Day:

But Mr. McNeice's Unionism is of too staunch a character and has been too often manifested in his parish for him to risk being dubbed a Home Ruler because he is commended in a Home Rule organ. It is, indeed, Unionists of the type of the Carrickfergus rector that Home Rulers have most to fear. Men who can face the angry looks of friends as a matter of principle will never run away from the foe.[51]

MacNeice's unrepentant unionism was explicit in passages from his Ulster Day sermon that were not reproduced in his own or later accounts:

Finally, our ideal for Ireland is an Ireland in which no man shall be molested or insulted because of his political or religious convictions; ... and in which the humblest man in the land shall have the strength of an impartial Government behind him while he keeps within the law ... Let no word be spoken, let nothing be done to wound the feelings of our Roman Catholic neighbours ... Let us treat Protestants who may differ from us on this political question in a similar spirit ... One of the chief reasons we oppose Home Rule is because we believe it would lessen individual liberty ... And because such are our ideals, therefore, we recog-nise the rights of others, whether majorities or minorities, to think their own thoughts and be true to their own convictions.

Tolerance was best assured by retention of the union, but no political loyalty could justify the use of force even in self-preservation:

---

[49] Harvey and MacNeice were unacquainted in 1912: Christopher Fauske, *'Side by side in a small country': Bishop John Frederick MacNeice and Ireland* (Dublin, CIHS, 2004), 6.
[50] Scholes, *Church of Ireland*, 61.
[51] 'A Brave Act', *UG* (5 Oct. 1912); also cited in Scholes, *Church of Ireland*, 60–1.

I wish you to know why though holding as I do that Home Rule would be a betrayal of those whose only crime has been their loyalty, and would be a wrong to the country, and to every class in the country, yet I am not persuaded by anything I have heard or read that the Church of Christ, because faced with difficulty and danger, should, for the maintenance of her life, resort to weapons which the Founder and her Lord did not use.[52]

MacNeice's unionism was exhibited publicly through his repeated election to office in the Carrickfergus Unionist Club and the East Antrim Unionist Association throughout the Great War. His dissenting voice, in and after 1912, was that of a decided unionist who (despite his subsequent denial of this opinion) affirmed that the people of the entire United Kingdom, not of Ulster or Ireland, should determine the constitutional outcome.[53]

Second, MacNeice was not merely a public unionist but an active Orangeman, who had served since the 1890s as a lodge, district, and county chaplain in Dublin, Belfast, and Carrickfergus. This affiliation, like his enduring unionism, was ignored in later writings by both Frederick and his son, probably because such associations would have harmed his growing reputation outside Ulster as a liberal apostle of tolerance and intrepid opponent of sectarianism. Within Ulster, seasoned Orangemen and unionists must have been well aware of his personal history; yet the networks of trust that he had established before 1915, when his recorded Orange involvement ceased, protected him from denunciation as an apostate. Within the parish, his success in overcoming initial opposition and threatened boycott was partly attributable to the cultivation of influential alliances in the town's Orange and Masonic lodges.

These alliances were activated in the cause of peace on several occasions, leading to unexpected outcomes such as the mobilisation of local Orange lodges as special constables to prevent the nocturnal smashing of Catholic windows in July 1912; the refusal of his own lodge to establish any formal connection with the newly formed UVF in 1913; and the creation of a successful pan-Protestant crusade against sectarianism in Carrickfergus between 1920 and 1924. MacNeice, like many liberal-minded Orange chaplains, viewed the Institution as a powerful instrument for encouraging temperance, sobriety, and respect for the civil magistrate among potentially unruly working-class Protestants. Empathy with the

---

[52] *Carrickfergus Advertiser* (4 Oct. 1912).

[53] MacNeice maintained that 'Ireland has self-government just as England and Scotland have. There may be some grievances here as elsewhere. If there are we do not think they could be redressed by an Irish Parliament, and we think they could be redressed by the Imperial Parliament. Irish Parliaments have been tried – Protestant and Roman Catholic – and were ghastly failures': *Carrickfergus Advertiser* (4 Oct. 1912).

brethren was helped by his persistent distrust of the Church of Rome and its link with nationalism:

Is it any wonder that the Irish Roman Catholic has been described as a rebel whose feet are in British fetters and whose head is in a Roman halter? ... Are not the Bishops the patrons of the Party? Are not the Priests, almost as a rule, the chairmen of the local branches of the United Irish League?[54]

He repeatedly declared that Orangeism should be a religious rather than a political institution, whose members ought to support political candidates with suitable views on social and moral issues such as temperance. This view, which had encouraged some like-minded brethren to defect to the 'Independents', entailed rejection of the ever-closer alliance between the Orange élite and the Unionist Party. MacNeice's repudiation of Carsonism therefore emerged, in part, from a long-standing argument within Orangeism.

The third distinctive element of the rector's rejection of the Covenant also emerged from an argument within what might now be termed 'the unionist family'. MacNeice, like many southern Protestants, was an 'all-Ireland unionist' who believed that partition would be an even worse outcome than all-Ireland Home Rule. Though he did not raise this issue in his sermon on Ulster Day, MacNeice retrospectively portrayed the Ulster movement as essentially Nationalist rather than unionist:

They might have to separate themselves for a time, or even permanently, from the Unionists outside Ulster. That possibility was foreshadowed in the Covenant. If all the passengers in the ship – the illustration was favourite one – could not be saved, a determined effort should be made to save some. At first, in all probability, Ulster simply thought that she should continue to be governed from Westminster, retaining her full representation there. What her people denied was the assumed moral authority of even a parliament at Westminster to transfer their allegiance, without their own consent, to some other parliament. But the other idea, the idea of a parliament of their own, with powers of legislation and administration, was presented to their minds by the formation of their Provisional Government. Through the influence of that idea Unionist Ulster began to think along Nationalist lines.[55]

Revulsion against any form of partition was widespread among southern unionists including Orangemen, still numerous in Dublin (home of the grand lodge of Ireland) and counties such as Cork and Leitrim. In his distaste for Carson's policies, MacNeice was not rejecting loyalism, but

---

[54] Ibid. In later years, MacNeice portrayed secularism rather than Rome as the major impediment to the attainment of a truly Christian polity.
[55] MacNeice, *Carrickfergus*, 75.

expressing southern loyalist indignation at Carson's potential betrayal of the brethren beyond Ulster. His congregation in Carrickfergus would have been well aware of these intensifying tensions within unionism, and indulgent (if scarcely approving) of the rector's loyalty to his own community of origin.

Finally, the fact that MacNeice was not a lone voice among the local clergy was critical to the acceptance of his dissent. As he later remarked: 'The ministers of religion in Carrickfergus, in permanent charges, did not sign the Covenant.' He chose his words carefully, for the signatories included his own curate, the 'itinerant' Methodist minister, and the two Presbyterian ministers at Woodburn, just outside the town. Nevertheless, MacNeice's stance was shared by John Minford of Joymount Presbyterian church, and by the town's Congregational and Unitarian ministers.[56] Though his colleagues seem not to have publicly voiced their views, the solidarity shown by the Carrickfergus clergy greatly reduced the vulnerability of each individual minister to denunciation or boycott. Whereas Armour had tried to argue, shame, or bully his fellow clergymen into resisting the Covenant, MacNeice, a much subtler and wilier negotiator, quietly formed an united front impregnable to overt attack from Carrick's Carsonites.

Despite his subsequent reputation as an heroic outsider, Frederick MacNeice's true significance as a non-Covenanter arises from the success of his concerted attempt to become an insider in Protestant Antrim. As an office-bearing unionist and Orangeman, he gained credentials that enabled him to survive the turmoil of proto-revolutionary Ulster unscathed. Though his all-Ireland perspective set him somewhat apart from the Carrickfergus consensus, this was offset by opinions and values that he shared with many local loyalists. These included aversion to violence, acknowledgement of the ultimate authority of Westminster, distrust of party politicians, and commitment to social and moral reform. As a trusted insider, his rejection of the Covenant was not merely tolerated but emulated by a strikingly large minority in the parish. Analysis of the signature sheets for the Carrickfergus district reveals that 29% of Protestant men and 35% of Protestant women failed to conform on Ulster Day, proportions far larger than those for the East Antrim constituency as a whole.[57] In his wide-ranging argument against endorsement of

[56] Ibid., 72; Fitzpatrick, 'Solitary and Wild', 118.
[57] As indicated above (n. 28), the proportion of dissenters in the East Antrim constituency was 23.1% for men and 27.5% for women. Using the same criteria, the proportion in the civil parish of Carrickfergus was 29.3% for men and 34.6% for women (the corresponding figures in Fitzpatrick, 'Solitary and Wild', 358 (n. 18) are obsolete).

the Covenant, the rector of Carrickfergus voiced attitudes that resonated widely in a community unaccustomed to violence, rebellion, and practical intolerance. Though temporarily drowned out by the Covenanting chorus, the less truculent voice of Orange and Protestant Ulster was never fully silenced. If one in four openly dissented, others uncounted were seduced into endorsing a strategy at odds with their deeper sympathies.

Part III

Exodus?

8   Protestant depopulation
and the Irish revolution

I

The late Peter Hart's tentative yet provocative application of the term 'ethnic cleansing' to the Irish revolution, especially as practised in Co. Cork, continues to arouse widespread indignation and incredulity.[1] Admittedly, the implied comparison with far greater and bloodier conflicts in Bosnia or partitioned India carries an emotional charge which tends to inflame rather than inform historical debate. The attribution of shared ethnicity to Irish Protestants of English and Scottish stock is also tendentious, though sectarianism is often blind to fine distinctions. Despite such objections, this offensive term compels us to confront some uncomfortable but important aspects of revolutionary history. Two associated issues have dominated the debate: the influence of sectarian hatred on the conduct of the IRA, and the extent to which Protestants were actually forced out of their homes by intimidation or fear. Though some historians have endorsed Hart's claim that a substantial number of Protestants were murdered or expelled because of their religion,[2] most argue that such attacks were primarily motivated by political or economic rather than sectarian factors.[3] Similar points have been

---

[1] The interminable debate about 'ethnic cleansing' among historians and bloggers was prompted by a passage in Peter Hart, *The I.R.A. at War, 1916–1923* (Oxford University Press, 2003), 237, somewhat at odds with denials of 'ethnic cleansing' at 22–3, 245–6, and 251. This passage first appeared in 'The Protestant Experience in Southern Ireland', in *Unionism in Modern Ireland: New Perspectives on Politics and Culture*, ed. Richard English and Graham Walker (Basingstoke, Macmillan, 1996), 81–98 (92). Hart's analysis was anticipated by another Canadian scholar who cited Cork atrocities in arguing that 'intimidation and violence . . . played a part in prompting the exodus of the minority', going 'a long way to explain the unprecedented flight of the minority during these transitional years': Kurt Bowen, *Protestants in a Catholic State: Ireland's Privileged Minority* (Kingston and Montreal, McGill-Queen's University Press, 1983), 22, 25.

[2] A recent example is Gerard Murphy's *The Year of Disappearances: Political Killings in Cork, 1921–1922* (Dublin, Gill and Macmillan, 2010): see my review in *Dublin Review of Books* (Mar. 2011).

[3] See, for instance, James S. Donnelly, 'Big House Burnings in County Cork during the Irish Revolution, 1921–21', *Éire–Ireland*, xlviii, nos. 3 & 4 (2012), 141–97.

made, from the revolutionary epoch onwards, by liberal Protestants as well as republican sympathisers, whose rejection of the 'ethnic cleansing' hypothesis has sometimes degenerated into vicious *ad hominem* attacks on Hart and his allies.[4] The issue of motivation is notoriously resistant to historical analysis: all motives are mixed, some are deliberately concealed, and others are unconscious. Little would be gained by making yet another attempt to disentangle the often contradictory hopes, fears, resentments, and rationalisations underlying republican conduct in the revolutionary years.

This chapter concerns measurable outcomes rather than imputed motives, concentrating on the extent of Protestant out-migration from Southern Ireland in the revolutionary era. Many attempts have been made to enumerate and explain the abrupt depopulation of southern Protestants between 1911 and 1926, and to assess the importance of 'forced' emigration in generating that decline. The available census statistics allow only a snapshot depiction of intercensal change, inviting more or less wild conjectures about the year-by-year pace of the decline and the 'residual' contribution of excess emigration. It is now widely agreed that most of the net population loss (about a third of the Protestant population in 1911) may be explained by other factors such as the departure of British-born military personnel, 'normal' or 'economic' migration, low or negative natural increase, and a top-heavy age-structure.[5] Yet, in the absence of religious returns of migration, fertility, and mortality, residual calculations of 'forced' migration have little force. To advance the study of Irish 'ethnic cleansing' (and 'ethnic flight') beyond conjecture, we must search for new sources.

II

Few doubt that there was a sectarian element in both republicanism and Ulster unionism, in the sense that many protagonists on both sides identified those of alien religious affiliation as potential collaborators and rebels respectively. It is equally clear that the most influential organisers

---

[4] See David Fitzpatrick, 'Ethnic Cleansing, Ethical Smearing and Irish Historians', *History*, xciii, no. 329 (Jan. 2013), 135–44.

[5] For a pithy and cool-headed discussion, placing revolutionary depopulation in the broader context of long-term Protestant decline, see Enda Delaney, *Demography, State and Society: Irish Migration to Britain, 1921–1971* (Liverpool University Press, 2000), 69–83. Recent contributions include Barry Keane, 'Ethnic Cleansing? Protestant Decline in West Cork between 1911 and 1926', *History Ireland*, xii, no. 2 (2012), 35–41; Andy Bielenberg, 'Exodus: The Emigration of Southern Irish Protestants during the Irish War of Independence and the Civil War', *Past and Present*, no. 218 (Feb. 2013), 199–233.

on both sides construed their struggle as a patriotic rather than a religious enterprise, and asserted the right and (more menacingly) the duty of all natives and residents of Ireland, regardless of religion, to act as citizens (whether of the Republic or of the United Kingdom). Denial of sectarianism was essential to the republican claim to incorporate the entire Irish population, repudiating the Hibernian and clericalist strand in the Home Rule movement. Unionists likewise claimed the allegiance of Catholic as much as Protestant subjects of the Crown.

Admittedly, the verbal restraint shown by most political leaders was not always shared by local organisers and orators, who frequently slipped into sectarian slurs and incitements refined over many generations of mutual abuse. Yet little convincing evidence has emerged of systematic campaigns of murder, arson, violence, or even intimidation based primarily on religious alignments and divisions, with the problematic exceptions of the Belfast 'pogroms' of 1920–2 and the 'Bandon Valley massacre' of April 1922. Religious impulses were invariably entangled with political ideology, economic, factional and personal resentments, or the belief that antagonists were 'traitors'. Perpetrators of violence and intimidation never declared, and presumably seldom believed, that they were motivated by doctrinal differences, let alone bigotry. If 'ethnic cleansing' occurred, it was not so visualised by those responsible.

Yet, regardless of personal attitudes or political qualms, the effect of revolutionary conflict was to polarise the Catholic and Protestant communities in Ireland, simultaneously reinforcing their internal solidarity and mutual antipathy. Ingrained, unarticulated assumptions about the malevolent disposition of Catholics or Protestants might engender violence, discrimination, or abuse directed against the rival community, unrelated to the character or behaviour of individual targets. Hostile acts and gestures expressing deeply embedded attitudes might create communal fear and demoralisation to the extent that the will to remain at home would wither away. It is therefore conceivable that the outcome of a complex intercommunal conflict might amount in practice to the forced 'extermination' of Protestants from the South or Catholics from the North, even if the agents of expulsion did not see it that way.[6] On the other hand, Irish minorities had cultivated remarkable resilience in the face of much more overtly sectarian threats from the 1640s through the 1790s to the 1880s. A panic-driven exodus would have been as out of character

---

[6] The regions of the two states formed through partition are denoted in this chapter by 'the South' and 'the North'. The names of counties and provinces follow pre-partition usage. The term 'extermination', in Irish usage, signifies the eviction or involuntary removal of inhabitants from an estate or, by extension, a region.

for beleaguered southern Protestants as for northern Catholics, however threatening their triumphalist adversaries might appear. Irish minorities had become expert in keeping themselves warm in cold houses.[7]

This chapter is designed to reassess the statistical evidence concerning Protestant population decline and migration over the intercensal period 1911–26, in the hope of establishing whether substantial 'ethnic' migration actually occurred. Regrettably, the available census statistics give little insight into the relative weight of fertility, mortality, and migration in causing the undeniably rapid decline in the Protestant population of the South. It is often forgotten that depopulation is not necessarily the result of abnormally high out-migration or mortality (an aspect of 'ethnic cleansing' of little importance in the Irish case).[8] The success of a population in reproducing itself is crucially determined by its age-structure, largely shaped by the levels of nuptiality and fertility within marriage. In the case of religious groups, a population may be swollen or depleted by conversions and by the frequency with which children are reared in a different religion (usually following a 'mixed marriage'). In the absence of relevant census data, I shall also examine a neglected set of annual returns which did record inward and outward population flows, as well as net changes in membership, for the Methodist Church. Though Methodists were a small minority in Irish Protestantism, their net demographic decline in the Free State region closely matched that of the Church of Ireland. The Methodist experience of population change provides a microcosm, however imperfect, of the broader Protestant experience in the wake of revolution.

III

All major religious groups on the island lost population between 1911 and 1926. The post-Famine trend of gradual depopulation was apparently

---

[7] For a sympathetic yet balanced account of the demographic and social consequences of the revolution, see R. B. McDowell, *Crisis and Decline: The Fate of the Southern Unionists* (Dublin, Lilliput Press, 1997), 163–6. McDowell confirms Kennedy's view that the precipitate decline of the Protestant population between 1911 and 1926 was unrelated to 'direct discriminatory actions against Protestants on the part of the new government' and that Protestant emigration 'was a voluntary movement': Robert E. Kennedy, Jr, *The Irish: Emigration, Marriage, and Fertility* (Berkeley and Los Angeles, University of California Press, 1973), 128–9. This is qualified by Kennedy's belief that 'fear of physical harm . . . accounts for at least part of the decline by a third in the number of Protestants between 1911 and 1926' (136).

[8] The murder of a hundred or so Irish Protestants, often labelled as informers, scarcely altered the aggregate mortality of southern Protestants. Fatalities resulting from service in the Great War would have affected Protestants only slightly more than Catholics, since the majority of Irish wartime servicemen were Catholics.

undisturbed by political convulsions, and the pace of Protestant decline only slightly exceeded that for the Catholic population. For every 100 inhabitants of Ireland in 1911 there were 96 in 1926, that ratio being 98 for Catholics, 97 for Presbyterians and Methodists, and 87 for Episcopalians. If members of the armed forces are excluded from the 1911 population (see below), the disparity is reduced (98 for Methodists, 97 for Presbyterians, 90 for Episcopalians). These aggregate figures mask dramatic contrasts between the regions that became Northern Ireland and the Irish Free State in 1921–2. As Table 8.1 indicates, the southern Catholic population declined by only 2% between 1911 and 1926, compared (after adjustment) with 26% for Presbyterians, 29% for Episcopalians, and 31% for Methodists. Since the Catholic population declined at the same rate (2%) in both states, there is no *prima facie* evidence of a long-term Catholic exodus from the northern counties. Yet the marked growth of the non-Catholic northern population does suggest, at first sight, a major transfer of Protestants across the border. As their southern brethren melted away, the number of northern Episcopalians and Methodists rose by 4% and 8% respectively, while the Presbyterian population scarcely changed. It is tempting to infer that uncounted thousands of southern Protestants fled northwards in the wake of revolution. Yet account must be taken of the long-standing prior decline of southern Protestantism, as Robert McDermott (an otherwise obscure clergyman) and the brilliant botanist David Webb observed in an incisive study published around 1940: 'The troubled times and political changes between 1916 and 1922 helped to accelerate, but certainly did not inaugurate, the decline in the South.'[9]

My exclusion of members of the armed forces from the Protestant population in 1911 is justified by the fact that most Protestant servicemen were temporary residents of British birth, spending brief spells on duty in Ireland, who cannot be regarded as part of the settled Protestant community. Admittedly, Protestants and non-natives remained surprisingly prominent in the Free State's defence forces in 1926; but the number of these outsiders was minuscule by comparison with 1911.[10] 'Defence' was

---

[9] R. P. McDermott and D. A. Webb, *Irish Protestantism To-day and To-morrow: A Demographic Study* (Dublin and Belfast, APCK, undated), 2. See also Kennedy, *The Irish*, 110–38.

[10] In 1926, when Episcopalians, Presbyterians, and Methodists comprised 7.0% of all occupied males in the South, they accounted for 8.3% of those engaged in defence (including 8.6% of army officers, 7.0% of other army ranks, and no less than 63.4% in 'other defence' categories). But the number so involved had plummeted from 19,621 in 1911 (including retired officers) to 1,264 in 1926 (excluding retired officers). The Protestant sub-group in defence in 1926 would have overlapped substantially with those

the only branch of the old Irish administration in which Protestants were grossly over-represented. In both national and local government, the Catholic proportion fell only slightly short of that for the entire occupied male population (75%), while there was actually a Catholic excess in the police and the lower ranks of the civil service.[11] In all branches of the armed services, however, Catholics were in the minority, ranging from 41% of naval seamen to only 14% of army officers.[12] Episcopalians, Presbyterians, and Methodists were all heavily over-represented in the armed services,[13] leading to gross distortion of the religious statistics in 1911 in counties with large military or naval bases. In Kildare, 63% of the entire occupied population of male Protestants were in the armed services. This explains the startling fact that for every 100 male Protestants in Kildare there were but 36 females.[14] The other counties most affected by this distortion were Westmeath (33% in the armed services), Tipperary and Cork (27%), Limerick (23%), Louth (14%), and Dublin (11%). It follows that all studies based on the county statistics tabulated in pre-partition census reports, without adjustment for the inclusion of naval and military personnel, are grotesquely warped.

This distortion may be reduced, though not eliminated, by several alternative procedures.[15] First, the digitalised census schedules can be searched and sorted in order to eliminate Protestant servicemen born outside Ireland along with their dependants. Though problematic and incredibly laborious, this method has been fruitfully applied to each district electoral division in Co. Cork, leading to the conclusion that there was 'a small unexplained protestant movement from County Cork' which

born outside Ireland, of whom 1,461 had been born in Britain, 38 in the United States, and 95 elsewhere (mainly in the Empire). See Census of Saorstát Éireann (1926), vol. iii, pt. i, Table 16 and vol. iii, pt. ii, Table 15; Census of Ireland (1911), county reports.

[11] For each major administrative category in the Census of Ireland (1911), the percentages of Catholics were as follows: civil service messengers, etc. (82), police (78), municipal and district council officers, etc. (69), prison officers (68), and civil service officers and clerks (59).

[12] The percentages of Catholics in other categories of defence were as follows: Royal Marines, officers and men (31), navy officers, effective and retired (25), and soldiers and NCOs (25). Catholics predominated among pensioners who had resettled in Ireland: army pensioners (69), navy pensioners (70).

[13] Among men occupied in defence (except pensioners), the percentages in each denomination were as follows: Catholic (24.4), Episcopalian (63.8), Presbyterian (6.9), Methodist (3.6). The percentages of the entire occupied male population in each of these categories were 74.9, 12.7, 9.8, and 1.3, respectively.

[14] My tabulations exclude the small group (1.3%, incorporating those of unstated or no religion) professing religions 'other' than Catholicism and the three major Protestant denominations.

[15] The problem of accounting for foreign-born Protestants is discussed in Census of Saorstát Éireann (1926), vol. x, General Report, 46–8; Kennedy, The Irish, 119–21; and Bowen, Protestants in a Catholic State, 21–2.

was more pronounced in many western divisions of the county.[16] Second, as in this chapter, one may manipulate the published census reports to remove all males in the armed services, while unavoidably leaving their dependants untouched.[17] Fortunately, those manning the military and naval garrisons in 1911 had rather few dependants. In Dublin City, the only locality for which such data were abstracted, 3,873 men were occupied in defence, while 556 wives and 1,005 unoccupied children lived in the households of servicemen.[18] Though still only approximating the true number of settled Protestants, this adjustment allows far more reliable comparisons between counties than the uncorrected census tabulations. An alternative approach is to confine statistical analysis to the female population. Though the elimination of males raises its own problems, this method is used to rank counties in order of the Protestant component of the population in Table 8.2.

That table demonstrates the uneven distribution of Protestants in the South, ranging from a quarter of the female population in Monaghan to a fiftieth in Clare and much of Connaught. There was a firm positive correlation between the initial Protestant proportion in each county and the retention of Episcopalians between 1911 and 1926.[19] No southern county retained more than four-fifths of its pre-war Protestant population, whereas mid Ulster lost about one in ten and Belfast and Down actually gained Protestants of all three major denominations. The most precipitate decline was in Clare, always the least Protestant of all counties, which lost half of its Episcopalians, two-thirds of its Presbyterians, and over four-fifths of its tiny Methodist community. In general, the pattern of county losses is consistent with the model of 'ethnic cleansing', in that the exodus was far greater in counties with small and presumably vulnerable Protestant minorities. By contrast, the decline was relatively small in Wicklow, Dublin, and the three 'Lost Counties' of Ulster, whose well-established and flourishing Protestant communities were better placed to resist any pressure for expulsion.[20] Yet these bare statistics stop far short

---

[16] Barry Keane, 'Ethnic Cleansing?', abridged from 'The Decline of the Protestant Population in County Cork between 1911 and 1926' (accessible on-line, 2012).

[17] The census classification for 'defence' allows us to distinguish army and naval pensioners, mainly of Irish origin, but not retired officers who likewise belonged to the settled community.

[18] Census of Ireland (1911), *General Report*, Table 71. Servicemen were not necessarily co-resident with those returned as their unoccupied dependants.

[19] r = +.65, accounting for two-fifths of the variance (26 southern counties) derived by correlating the non-Catholic component (1911) with the retention ratio for Episcopalians (1911–26).

[20] The apparently aberrant case of Kildare, which experienced heavy loss despite its substantial Protestant component in 1911 (13%), is probably a by-product of the unavoidable

of demonstrating that any such expulsion occurred. Cork, Hart's prime example, did not experience abnormally heavy Protestant depopulation, and several of the other counties experiencing 'similar campaigns of what might be termed "ethnic cleansing"', such as Queen's, King's, and Leitrim, were even less affected.[21] In order to assess the weight of out-migration as a component of depopulation, we must search beyond the crude index of net intercensal change.

IV

Another tantalising clue is buried in the published tabulations by birth-place, which in 1911 divided the residents of each county according to their county or country of birth. In 1926, alas, the tabulation was confined to those born in the other state rather than individual counties (Table 8.3). Only in a few counties did the cross-border population in 1926 exceed one in twenty (10% in Fermanagh, 8% in Londonderry, 6% in Monaghan, 5% in Belfast, Tyrone, Armagh, and Louth). The number of southerners in Northern Ireland (about 64,000) was almost double that of northerners in the Free State (35,000), superficially suggesting a massive net exodus northwards across the border. Yet comparison with the distribution of birthplaces in 1911 suggests that revolutionary turmoil had limited impact on long-established patterns of inter-county migration.[22] The net increase in the number of southerners in Northern Ireland was 7,744 (14% of the 1911 figure), while the Irish Free State had just 152 more northerners in 1926 than in 1911. Most southern counties actually had fewer northerners at the end of the period, with particularly marked declines in Clare (30%) and King's (40%). Though all northern counties had a larger southern-born population in 1926 than 1911, the proportionate increase outside Antrim and Down was less than a fifth. The sharp increases in Antrim and Down presumably reflected a shift in demand for industrial employment

---

inclusion of soldiers' dependants in its base population. Since 44% of Kildare's Protestants in 1911 were in the armed services, it is likely (on the basis of the returns for Dublin City already cited) that a further 15–20% were their wives or dependants.

[21] Hart, *The I.R.A. at War*, 237–40. In the counties so identified by Hart, the percentage ratios of the Episcopalian population in 1926 to that in 1911 were as follows: Queen's (79%), King's and Leitrim (70%), Cork (67%), Limerick (65%), Westmeath (63%), Louth and Mayo (62%), Tipperary (61%), and Galway (48%). Cork's ratio ranked fourteenth among the 26 southern counties.

[22] For trends and fluctuation in cross-border settlement since 1881, see Cormac Ó Gráda and Brendan Walsh, 'Did (and does) the Border Matter?', draft discussion paper for Mapping Frontiers, Plotting Pathways Study Group, no. 16 (2005), 5–13; modifying R. C. Geary and J. G. Hughes, 'Migration between Northern Ireland and the Republic of Ireland', appendix to Brendan M. Walsh, *Religion and Demographic Behaviour in Ireland* (Dublin, Economic and Social Research Institute, paper no. 55, 1970), 37–50.

from the city to its hinterland. As before, it is likely that most cross-border migration was attributable to marriage (often bringing wives into their husband's parish) and differential demand for employment (favouring women and movement from South to North). Women were even more predominant among cross-border migrants in 1926 than in 1911, whereas a forced exodus of families would have eroded the female excess. For every 100 cross-border male migrants in 1926 there were 141 females, compared with 137 in 1911.

The association between cross-border settlement and 'ethnic cleansing' is further weakened by the likelihood that many of the migratory northerners were Protestants, and many of the migratory southerners Catholics. Digital manipulation of the census returns for 1911 shows that the majority of southerners then resident in the North were Catholics, while only a quarter belonged to the Church of Ireland (see Table 8.4). The Catholic majority was particularly pronounced among migrants from the five counties adjoining the border, which together supplied almost two-thirds of all cross-borderers. Though less marked for Church of Ireland migrants, the female excess applied in every northern county, and about two-fifths of the Episcopalian settlers were married.[23] Thus, well before the revolution, there was substantial settlement of both Catholic and Protestant southerners in the future Northern Ireland.

It is unlikely that the religious balance of internal migration was radically transformed in the wake of revolution. Despite partition and the 'Belfast Boycott' of 1920–2, Ulster settlers did not abandon sectors such as banking, the clergy, teaching, the civil service, textiles, or railway work in the South.[24] Northern unionists remained fearful for decades of 'peaceful penetration' of the province by Catholics, though no breakdown by religion was attempted until 1961. This showed that 44% of residents born in the 26 counties were Catholics, 28% Episcopalians, 18% Presbyterians, 4% Methodists, and 5% of other, unstated or no religious affiliation. Though the Catholic component was somewhat smaller than

---

[23] 44% of male cross-borderers were currently married, the highest proportions being in Antrim and Londonderry. The corresponding figure for women was 39%, with the highest proportions in Fermanagh and Tyrone. The 'Lost Counties' supplied more married settlers than the other provinces, accounting for 50% of males and 41% of females.

[24] Natives of Northern Ireland accounted for only 1.4% of occupied males in 1926, but comprised 11.8% of bank clerks, 8.4% of clergymen, 6.3% of railway clerks, 6.1% of civil service officials and clerks, 4.9% of teachers, 3.4% of textile workers, and 2.8% of railway workers. The high proportions in the army (8.6% of officers, 7.9% of men) and the Civic Guard (4.8%) presumably reflect concentrations of Catholic rather than Protestant Ulstermen: Census of Saorstát Éireann (1926), vol. iii, pt. ii, Tables 14, 15.

in 1911 (down from 53% to 44%), the available figures give no hint of a catastrophic Protestant outflow overwhelming traditional patterns of internal migration. As in 1911, females predominated among Protestant as well as Catholic migrants in 1961, and the majority of cross-borderers still settled around Belfast.[25] It seems clear that most cross-border movement was unrelated to revolutionary terror or sectarian fears, being determined by economic or family factors that encouraged Protestants and Catholics alike to migrate.[26]

V

Census reports illuminate one other element of population change, nowadays referred to euphemistically as 'the demographic factor'. Apart from the effects of out-migration and mortality, religious communities may shrivel as a result of low nuptiality and fertility (leading to a top-heavy age-structure), in addition to net losses through conversions and mixed marriages. The combined effect of these factors is apparent in Table 8.5, which shows the number of children under 20 years for every 100 adult women in 1926.[27] The Catholic female population exhibited a healthy ballast of 132 children for every 100 women, a ratio which in the absence of heavy emigration would have led to sustained population growth. The highest proportion was in Connaught, the province which consistently returned the highest rates of both nuptiality and fertility within marriage. Particularly in Leinster and Munster, there was a remarkable dearth of Protestant children. As with Catholics, the ratio was somewhat higher in Connaught; while in the three 'Lost Counties' of Ulster the continued vitality of the Protestant communities was evident in a ratio approaching that for Catholics.

The relative shortage of Protestant children was probably only slightly attributable to lower fertility within marriage, since various studies based on the 1911 census suggest that the religious differential in marital fertility

---

[25] Census of Northern Ireland (1961), county reports and *General Report*, Table 16. The total southern-born population (53,125, of whom 61% were female) fell about 10,000 short of the figure for 1926.

[26] For each county, the sex ratios in 1911 and 1926 were as follows: Londonderry, 158, 157; Antrim, 143, 160; Down, 142, 148; Armagh, 140, 140; Belfast, 134, 137; Tyrone, 127, 139; Fermanagh, 118, 117.

[27] Fertility is normally estimated for the period immediately preceding a census from a child–woman ratio involving only infants and women of child-bearing age. Since my purpose is to find a proxy for fertility broad enough to incorporate the demographic experience of a prolonged period of social turmoil, it is necessary to include far broader age-bands than is customary.

was quite small.[28] To some extent, it may have resulted from the divisive effects of 'mixed marriages'. The *Ne Temere* decree of 1908 had made it more hazardous for Catholics marrying Protestants to bring up any of their children as Protestants, so tending to reduce the Protestant proportion among the children of mixed marriages.[29] It may also be the case that Protestant women were already abnormally prone to marry late or never, a phenomenon which in subsequent decades posed a major threat to the reproduction of the Irish population in general.[30] The ageing spinster was certainly a familiar figure of fun or pity in the stereotypical Big House of twentieth-century fiction. Unfortunately, the relative weight of these factors in depopulating Protestant Ireland cannot be determined from any official statistics.[31]

The deficiency of Episcopalian children varied markedly between counties, as shown in Table 8.6 (county figures are not available for other Protestant communions or for the North). Whereas the ratio exceeded 100 in Ulster and several counties of Leinster, it fell below 90 in most of Munster and Connaught. The lowest figure of all (68) was in Dublin, partly because of a surfeit of elderly Protestant ladies in the suburbs. It is noteworthy that the relative shortage of Protestant children was much greater in Co. Dublin than in the city, whereas in Cork the contrast was reversed and still more marked.[32] In every county, the child–woman ratio was lower for Episcopalians than Catholics, the proportionate differential ranging between 10% in Cavan and 45% in Dublin. As the table also shows, there was a marked positive correlation between the relative dearth of children and rapid disappearance of the Episcopalian

---

[28] Cormac Ó Gráda, *Ireland: A New Economic History, 1780–1939* (Oxford University Press, 1994), 221–2.

[29] Note that even if the children of mixed marriages were divided equally between Protestantism and Catholicism, the statistical impact would be more negative for the Protestant child–woman ratio, since the number of mixed marriages would constitute a far smaller proportion of all marriages involving Catholics than the proportion for Protestants.

[30] For analysis of religious differentials in fertility in the South from 1926 onwards, see Kennedy, *The Irish*, 117–18; Bowen, *Protestants in a Catholic State*, 29–31; Walsh, *Religion and Demographic Behaviour*.

[31] The civil registers of births and deaths do not record religion. It is conceivable that centralisation and digitalisation of church registers will eventually spawn comparative studies of Protestant and Catholic family formation, fertility, and the religious division of children of mixed marriages. The first census to cross-tabulate age, marital status, and religion was that for Saorstát Éireann in 1937, which revealed that Episcopalian women were more likely to be married, yet far less fertile, than their Catholic counterparts: McDermott and Webb, *Irish Protestantism*, 17, 27.

[32] The ratios were as follows: Co. Dublin, 60; Dublin City, 79; Cork City, 59; Co. Cork, 85. The ratio of adult females to 100 males was 117 in Cork City and no less than 155 in Co. Dublin.

population between 1911 and 1926, confirming the importance of problems with family formation in contributing to the collapse of local Protestant communities.[33]

How novel was the dearth of Protestant children apparent in the Irish Free State in 1926? In the absence of detailed age-breakdowns for 1911, I have constructed a rough proxy. Table 8.7 shows the percentage of females aged under 9 years in 1911 (the only documented age-discriminant) and the proportion under 10 years in 1926 (its nearest counterpart in the published reports). When the proportions for 1926 are compared with the child–woman ratios already discussed, they display very similar contrasts between provinces and between religious groups. The figures for 1911 indicate that, in the North, the Episcopalian female population was actually more youthful (19% being under 9) than that of Catholics (17%). In the 'Lost Counties' of Ulster, as in 1926, the Protestant proportions were not far short of the Catholic standard. Elsewhere, even before the revolution, there was already a marked shortage of Protestant children. Whereas 18% of southern female Catholics were young girls, the proportion was 16% for Presbyterians and only 15% for Episcopalians and Methodists. Yet there is clear evidence that the problem became still worse between 1911 and 1926. In Leinster, Munster, and Connaught, the proportion of under-10s was actually smaller (for all three Protestant denominations) than the proportion of under-9s in 1911. If returns for the same age-group had been available, this disparity would have been much more pronounced.[34] We may conclude that the reproduction of Protestant families in most of the South, already faltering in 1911, became even less efficient over the revolutionary period. Bielenberg's tabulation of registered marriages shows that the brief post-war resurgence of nuptiality was reversed earlier, and more drastically, in the case of marriages not conducted in Catholic churches.[35] We cannot know to what extent the implied underlying disruption of Protestant marriage and social networks was prompted by public events.

[33] r = +.51, accounting for a quarter of the variance (26 southern counties) derived by correlating the retention ratio for Episcopalians (1911–16) with the ratio of Episcopalian to Catholic child–woman ratios in 1926.

[34] One would expect about 10% of the child population under 10 years in 1926 to have been in their tenth year. If so, the proportions under 9 years in the Free State in 1926 would have been 17.7% for Catholics, 12.1% for Episcopalians, 14.0% for Presbyterians, and 11.4% for Methodists. This would imply deficits (compared with 1911) of 2.8% for Episcopalians, 2.2% for Presbyterians, and 5.1% for Methodists, compared with only 0.3% for Catholics.

[35] Non-Catholic marriages registered in Southern Ireland fell from 101 in 1920 to 87, 76, 66, 61, 57, and 60 in succeeding years (1911 = 100). Corresponding index figures for Catholic marriages were 110, 96, 97, 102, 97, 90, and 88: Bielenberg, 'Exodus', 219.

VI

In order to disentangle the various factors causing depopulation, let us examine the unique returns of membership of the (Wesleyan) Methodist Church in Ireland. In both Irish regions, Methodists accounted for only about one Protestant in twenty, though its following had steadily increased since the reabsorption of splinter groups such as the Primitive Wesleyans. Originally an evangelical strand within the established church, Methodism had broadened its appeal through energetic missionary campaigns among nominal Catholics as well as Protestants, paying particular attention to volatile and sin-prone groups such as servicemen, prisoners, and down-and-outs. Relatively weak in the counties of northern Ulster where the Scottish and Presbyterian influence was strongest, Methodism was most deeply rooted in mid Ulster. As Table 8.8 shows, the Methodist proportion of the Protestant (female) population in 1911 varied between 15.5% in Fermanagh and 0.8% in Meath, with intriguingly large components in Munster (except Clare) as well as Sligo and Leitrim. By comparison with other Protestant populations, notably Episcopalians, Irish Methodists comprised something of an occupational and educational élite. In the Irish Free State in 1926, they and the small Jewish population were most over-represented in the professions and shopkeeping, and no less than 9% of male occupied Methodists were clerks.[36] A third worked in agriculture, the majority as farmers occupying relatively large holdings, with a mere handful of Methodist labourers and farm servants.[37]

The Church's official returns, methodically compiled by circuit and district secretaries and published annually for the Methodist conference, allow us to plot, from year to year, the changing membership for more than 120 circuits throughout Ireland.[38] Though most returns are limited to 'full members' who had submitted themselves to Methodist discipline (thus agreeing to attend services, avoid 'spirituous liquors', and subscribe

---

[36] The percentages of male occupied Methodists, Jews, Episcopalians, Presbyterians, and Catholics in each broad category in 1926 were as follows: agriculture, 34, 0.3, 45, 58, 58; producers, 14, 27, 15, 13, 17; commerce, finance, and insurance, 23, 53, 11, 12, 5; public services, 3.7, 0.5, 4.4, 1.8, 3.4; professional, 7.5, 11.5, 6.6, 5.2, 2.4; personal service, 0.6, 0.8, 1.9, 0.8, 1.9; clerks, 9.2, 2.8, 7.2, 4.4, 1.4. See Census of Saorstát Éireann (1926), vol. iii, pt. i, Table 16. Religious differentials in the occupational spectrum (ignoring minor Protestant denominations) are analysed in Kennedy, *The Irish*, 125–7, 131–4; Bowen, *Protestants in a Catholic State*, 78–103.

[37] Within agriculture (excluding the few Jews), the respective percentages for Methodists, Episcopalians, Presbyterians, and Catholics were as follows: farmers, 57, 49, 50, 39; assisting relatives, 37, 33, 34, 35; paid workers, 6.1, 17.7, 15.9, 25.5. Among farmers, the percentages occupying less than 1–30 acres were as follows: 25, 33, 37, 57. See Census of Saorstát Éireann (1926), vol. iii, pt. i, Table 17.

[38] Methodist Church in Ireland, *MCM* (Dublin, annual).

to church funds), the trend over time is reassuringly close to that shown in census returns. As Table 8.9 shows, the census population of Methodists in the South declined by 31% between 1911 and 1926, precisely the same proportion as that for members of the Society enrolled in circuits centred south of the border. The match was less close for the North, where membership increased by 20% compared with only 8% according to census returns. Table 8.8 reveals some marked discrepancies between the figures for census and membership decline by county, most notably in Belfast and Waterford. Such anomalies are partly attributable to the fact that many circuits crossed county borders, while some counties had no Methodist circuits at all. Even so, the overall correlation between the two series is exceptionally strong.[39] Less reliance should be placed on the Church's returns of adherence, based on estimated attendance at Sabbath services; yet the reported number of adherents corresponded fairly closely with the census population in both years. The high degree of convergence between returns of separate provenance gives added credibility to both census and religious sources.

The limited impact of revolutionary events is reflected in Chart 8.1, which traces Church membership for both regions in March of each year between 1911 and 1926. After a slight decline during the Great War, northern membership rose consistently after 1918, the sharpest increase

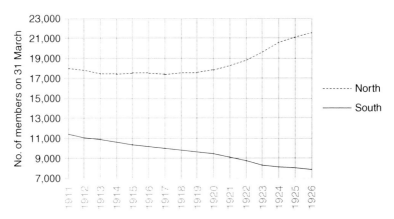

8.1 Methodist membership, 1911–26 (South and North)

[39] r = +.90, accounting for four-fifths of the variance (26 counties, excluding Belfast, Waterford, and 5 for which no circuits existed in 1926); or r = +.85, accounting for nearly three-quarters of the variance (including Belfast and Waterford).

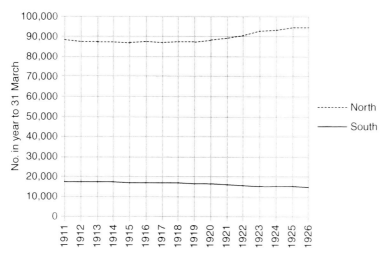

8.2 Presbyterian communicants, 1911–26 (South and North)

being recorded between 1921 and 1924. By contrast, southern membership declined continuously throughout the intercensal period, the linear
trend being only slightly intensified between 1920 and 1923 (see also
Table 8.11). For both regions, annual statistics for communicants of the
Presbyterian Church in Ireland show almost identical trends, with accentuated growth in the North and accentuated decline in the South during
the revolutionary period (see Chart 8.2).[40]

At county level, the number of full members increased throughout the
North apart from Tyrone and Fermanagh, and also in Dublin and
Waterford. Between 1911 and 1926, membership was roughly halved in
Leitrim, Limerick, Kerry, Cavan, King's, Longford, and Westmeath, with
even more precipitate decline in Mayo and Galway. In addition, five
counties were without Methodist circuits by the end of the period
(Kildare, Roscommon, Clare, Kilkenny, and Meath). Rapid decline
affected not only the tiny Methodist communities of southern
Connaught and parts of Leinster, but also counties such as Leitrim and
Cavan where Methodism had once flourished. In Cork, Church returns
confirm census evidence that Methodism did not disintegrate in face of
revolution, retaining two-thirds of its pre-war membership in 1926.

---

[40] Annual statistics have been computed for all congregations centred in each region, using
figures published annually in PCI, *Minutes of the Proceedings of the General Assembly*.

To test the contribution of revolutionary turmoil to these patterns of southern decline and northern growth, triennial membership figures for each church district are presented in Table 8.10. These suggest that both trends were already apparent long before the tumultuous triennium from March 1920 to March 1923. With the exception of Dublin in 1923–6, every southern-centred district lost membership in every triennium. Though all southern districts except Waterford experienced unusually heavy proportionate losses between 1920 and 1923, the discrepancy was negligible in the border zone of Sligo and Clones. Despite Hart's suggestion to the contrary, membership in the Cork district fell in every year between 1911 and 1925, with only moderate acceleration in the revolutionary period.[41] The course of Methodist membership in the North was more convoluted, with the Belfast district alone displaying consistent growth from 1914–17 onwards. Enniskillen and Londonderry fared worse than Dublin overall, and the convulsions of 1920–3 left no clear imprint on northern Methodism. It is also notable that membership had been in decline in most northern districts both before and during the Great War. This table strongly suggests that factors other than revolutionary sectarianism dominated the continuing decline of Methodism in many parts of the North as well as the South.

Local variations in the impact of revolution are best grasped by comparing the membership of each southern circuit in March 1923 with that three years earlier, a triennium encompassing almost all of the lethal violence and much of the arson engendered by revolution and civil war. In the Dublin district, substantial decline in outlying circuits of Leinster was offset by growth of membership in Bray, Kingstown, and the southern suburbs, and even in the Dublin Central Mission (though other central city circuits declined). In the Waterford district, all circuits except Waterford itself fell away, with particularly sharp losses in Abbeyleix and Clonmel. In the Cork district, membership was well sustained in western circuits and the city, but almost halved in Queenstown and Fermoy. It is striking that Bandon, the reputed epicentre of 'ethnic cleansing', lost only one in twenty, while troubled Dunmanway lost less than one in five. The heaviest losses in the Limerick and Sligo districts affected small circuits such as Ballinasloe and Ballina, whereas less than a tenth of the pre-war membership disappeared in Roscrea, Adare, Manorhamilton, and

---

[41] In a passage citing *MCM* (1911–26), Hart claimed that 'Methodist membership [in Cork district] was higher in 1918, 1919, and 1920 than in 1914, but fell precipitately thereafter. Once again, 1921–3 were the crucial years, accounting for seventy-four per cent of the lost population': Hart, *The I.R.A. at War*, 226. Though it is true that 74% of the loss *between 1920 and 1926* occurred in 1921–3, this period accounted for only 30% of the total decline from 1,825 in March 1911 to 1,146 in March 1926.

Drumshambo. Losses were also small in the southern circuits of Enniskillen, Clones, and Londonderry districts, though the northern circuits of those districts almost invariably fared still better. Seven circuits in the South, including Waterford and Donegal as well as five in Dublin, expanded over the revolutionary triennium. Dundalk was the only southern border circuit to suffer heavy loss (exceeding two-fifths), compared with a decline of a ninth in neighbouring Newry. It is noteworthy that the only circuits discontinued over that period were the Curragh Camp and Fermoy–Mallow, both catering mainly for the army and last returned in 1922.[42] Kilkenny and Ballinasloe survived for another year.[43] With these exceptions, the Methodist circuits of the South remained intact, if shaken, throughout the turmoil of revolution.

VII

The statistics collected by the Methodist Church in Ireland go far beyond mere enumeration of members of the Society in March of each year. For each of the ten districts, they also give the number of 'new members now fully received', 'members received from other circuits', 'members removed to other circuits', 'emigrations', 'deaths', and those who 'ceased to be members'. 'New members' excluded juniors under 16 years, but presumably incorporated those rejoining the Society after lapse or expulsion, Methodists from outside Ireland who were admitted to Irish membership, and former juniors. Statistics of both 'receptions' and 'removals' were derived from quarterly returns submitted by the superintendents of each circuit. Care was taken to register removals between Irish circuits in order to prevent multiple membership and to operate a system of certificates and 'notes of removal', designed to facilitate assimilation in the new circuit and also to exclude unworthy migrants.[44] The volume of removals,

---

[42] The closure of military and naval stations deprived Irish Methodism of a couple of thousand 'declared Wesleyans', but few full members. The last return, for Jan. 1916, enumerated 1,900 Wesleyans in the army (including 587 at the 'Curragh, etc.', 388 in Dublin, 122 in Queenstown–Berehaven, 117 in Limerick, and 116 in Cork–Ballincollig), along with 350 in the navy (almost all in Queenstown–Berehaven). *None* of these was returned as a member of the Methodist Church in Ireland. The return for Jan. 1911 gave 962 in Wesleyans in the army and 923 in the navy, including 77 and 28 Church members respectively: *MCM* (1916), 149; (1911), 163.

[43] Three circuits listed separately in 1920 were absorbed by neighbours before 1923 (Ballyshannon, New Ross, and Blackhall Place, Dublin). The only other southern circuits discontinued between 1911 and 1926, all before 1915, were Mullingar, Killarney (united with Tralee), the Clare mission (no longer returned under Limerick), and Mohill (united with Ballinamore).

[44] *Manual of the Laws and Discipline of the Methodist Church in Ireland* (Belfast, MCI, 1934 edn.); Arthur Page Grubb, *A Popular Handbook of Methodist Law and Usage* (London, Charles H. Kelly, 1913).

most of which doubtless involved adjacent circuits or districts, was immense. The statistics relevant to this study refer to *net* removals between districts and between regions, a remarkably precise index of net internal migration.[45] Members removing to circuits outside Ireland were returned separately as 'emigrants', a category designed to exclude those leaving Ireland without seeking to renew church membership abroad. These and other drop-outs, along with offenders against church discipline, were returned as 'ceased', deaths being separately recorded. Despite the composite character of some of these categories, the Methodist church returns provide a uniquely detailed and systematic record of the relative impact on membership of internal and overseas migration as well as mortality. The returns of admission and cessation further illuminate the degree to which the Church sustained and regenerated its Irish following.

The components of membership change for each region, in each triennium, are set out in Table 8.12. These figures highlight the inadequacy of models of depopulation based purely on net intercensal change, as though the Protestants remaining in 1926 were the depleted residue of those enumerated in 1911. In fact, a large part of any human population 'turns over' in the course of a decade and a half, generating considerable movement among those *not* belonging to the original population. In the South, about 11,500 Methodists returned in 1911 were augmented by over 5,000 new members, and the combined body of about 16,500 original and incoming members was depleted by no less than 8,000 removals, deaths, and cessations between 1911 and 1926. If the Methodist population had remained steady, the numbers moving in and out would each have amounted to nearly half of the initial membership. Turnover in the North was even greater, with 17,000 members joining the Church between 1911 and 1926 compared with an initial membership of 18,000, and outward movement of 14,000 members.[46] The Methodist population was far more volatile and unstable than a casual student of census returns might imagine.

---

[45] No returns of 'removals' or other components of membership change, with the exception of emigrations and deaths up to Mar. 1919, were published for individual circuits. The number 'on trial' was also returned until Mar. 1920, and the number of junior members in each circuit was published throughout the period. In the North, four circuits returned in 1911 were discontinued or absorbed over the next triennium, and six new circuits were opened in Belfast between 1911 and 1926.

[46] Note that the true 'flow' was even faster, since the statistics of 'removals' measure *net* movement between North and South, concealing thousands of removals within circuits and between circuits within each region, including multiple removals by individual members. Because the published statistics of inward and outward removals do not specify destination, it is not possible to compute *gross* movement between North and South.

Because of marked changes in the population 'at risk', the most revealing figures are those showing the annual rate of flow. In both regions, the
war years were marked by reductions in most elements of membership
flow, affecting intake of new members, cessations, and especially emigration out of Ireland. Mortality remained steady, with little difference
between North and South, while the rate of cross-border migration
slightly increased. The main contrast between regions arose from emigration, which in general affected the South far more than the North. No
significant changes occurred between 1914–17 and 1917–20, despite the
restoration of peace and the return of ex-servicemen to Ireland. It was the
revolutionary triennium of 1920–3 which transformed the patterns of
flow, leading to a widening gulf between the demography of southern
and northern Methodism. The contrast between North and South is
highlighted by Chart 8.3, which traces the annual number of Methodist
emigrants in each region. Whereas northern emigration levels soon recovered from their wartime slump to a plateau after 1920, the heavy southern
emigration between 1920 and 1923 was not sustained thereafter. The rate

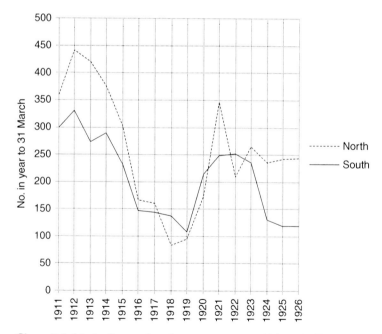

Chart 8.3 Methodist emigration per annum, 1911–26 (South and
North)

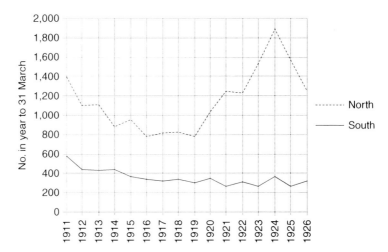

Chart 8.4 New Methodist members per annum, 1911–26 (South and North)

of intake of new members, nearly static in the South, rose dramatically in the North between 1919 and 1924, as shown in Chart 8.4. These factors, compounded by less frequent cessations and deaths in the North and increased movement across the border, account for the simultaneous shrinkage of southern Methodism and expansion of its northern counterpart. The factors generating southern depletion subsided notably in 1923–6, mainly through reduced emigration, whereas northern expansion was only slightly abated. The key contrast remained the rapidity with which northern districts enrolled new members, while southern intake ossified.

The top section of Table 8.13 highlights the relative weight of the various components of change in each district between 1911 and 1926. In most northern districts, cessation was a more important element of depletion than emigration. In-migration from the South contributed about 500 entrants, but this factor was dwarfed by the vast intake of new members, overwhelmingly in the Belfast district. In the South, emigration outweighed cessation as the main source of depletion in most districts, most notably in Cork. Net out-migration within Ireland was an insignificant factor in Cork and Waterford, while Dublin was the only district apart from Belfast to attract more removals than it lost. In Clones, however, internal out-migration amounted to three-fifths of emigration, and in Sligo all four factors made similar contributions to depopulation.

By comparison with the northern districts, the intake of new members was very sluggish in the South, falling short of the combined total of cessations and deaths in Waterford, Limerick, Sligo, and Clones (as also in Enniskillen).

The district patterns of membership change are most clearly exhibited in Table 8.14, which expresses each component as an annual rate of flow, adjusted for the population at risk. The death rate for the entire intercensal period varied little between districts, while the rate of cessations was abnormally high in Belfast and Dublin but markedly low in Enniskillen. The emigration rate was typically lower in northern districts (apart from Londonderry), with an exceptional exodus from Cork. Internal migration (measured by net 'removals') was a major factor only in Sligo, where annual net out-migration amounted to 17 per thousand. The most significant differential applied to new admissions, which ranged from 77 per thousand in Belfast to Limerick, with very slow enlistment in Enniskillen as well as Waterford, Clones, and Sligo. Dublin's enlistment rate was second only to that of Belfast, and Cork's rate of intake exceeded that for Londonderry.

The abnormality of the revolutionary triennium (1920–3) almost disappears when comparison is made with 1911–14. The pre-war southern deficit in the rate of intake of new members was relatively small, the main regional contrast arising from emigration (abnormally high in Cork and Dublin). Except for Waterford, Cork, and Limerick, every district experienced heavier rates of emigration in 1911–14 than in 1920–3. As with the Irish population in general, emigration had resumed in late 1920 after negligible movement during the Great War, without surpassing the pre-war level. In the revolutionary triennium, for the first time, internal removals became a significant source of depopulation in Cork, Sligo, and especially Limerick. In each district except Dublin, Limerick, and Sligo, cessations of membership were less frequent in 1920–3 than in 1911–14, while rates of death changed little.

The only dramatic contrast concerned the rate of intake of new members, which declined by a fifth in the South while rising by a quarter in the North. Far more than before, southern districts such as Waterford and especially Limerick suffered severely from the lack of new members. While Belfast attracted 85 new members per thousand annually between 1920 and 1923, the rate for Limerick was only 12. This analysis strongly suggests that the decline in southern Methodism in the revolutionary triennium was largely due to sluggish enlistment, compounded by heavy emigration which nevertheless scarcely surpassed the pre-war emigration rate. Out-migration, though more marked from western districts, was still a relatively minor source of depopulation.

VIII

If we assume that southern Protestants in general conformed to the Methodist model, the components of adult population flow between 1920 and 1923 may be estimated by multiplying the figures in Table 8.12 by 20.[47] This would imply that an adult population of about 190,000 southern Protestants in 1920 was depleted by 15,000 emigrants over the triennium, well below the loss for 1911–14; 8,000 deaths, somewhat below the pre-war level; and 10,000 cessations of active membership, far below the number recorded in 1911–14. The sole revolutionary aberration was 4,000 net internal removals from the South to the North, almost seven times the pre-war figure. With only 17,000 entrants to compensate for 37,000 losses during the revolutionary triennium, the long-term decline in the South's Protestant community had accelerated significantly. Though the uniquely detailed Methodist record offers only a rough guide to the broader Protestant experience, it would be surprising if the components of population flow for Episcopalians differed radically from those for their Methodist neighbours.

This study indicates that the main source of the Protestant malaise in the nascent Irish Free State was not excess migration but failure to enrol new members, presumably as a consequence of already low fertility and nuptiality, exacerbated by losses through mixed marriages and conversion. If any campaign of 'ethnic cleansing' was attempted, its demographic impact was fairly minor. Statistical analysis therefore suggests that the spectre of Protestant extermination has distracted debate about revolutionary Ireland for too long, and should be laid to rest. It would seem that the inexorable numerical decline of southern Protestantism was mainly self-inflicted. Yet statistics of human movement, however intricate, reveal little about the mentality or emotions of the people lurking behind the numbers. The personal experience of West Cork Methodists during the revolutionary period, and the extent to which they left the region in response to threats or fears, is explored in the final chapter.

---

[47] This multiplier assumes that the numerical components of population flow for all Methodist adults approximated those for full members of the Church, and that the same rates of flow applied to the entire non-Catholic adult population. Methodists comprised 5.1% of the entire non-Catholic female population in 1911 and 4.9% in 1926 (the same ratio applied to women aged 20 or more). The ratio of Church members to the Methodist census population was 74% in 1911 and 73% in 1926, while the proportion of females aged 20 or more in 1926 was 71% for Methodists (as for all non-Catholics). Note that these estimates cannot be extended to children, since the rate of intake of new adult members would only faintly have reflected much earlier patterns of fertility, while mortality, cessation, and emigration rates would normally have been much lower for children than adults.

9   The spectre of 'ethnic cleansing' in revolutionary Ireland

I

Let us begin by inspecting an inconspicuous Irish community now widely forgotten: the Methodists of west Cork. Numerically, they were a tiny minority twice over. In 1911, 8% of the female population of the county were returned as non-Catholics, and 8% of the non-Catholics were Methodists.[1] The census figures are broadly compatible with the Church's own annual returns for 1911, which enumerated 1,825 'full members' in the Cork district (incorporating Kerry), of whom 918 belonged to the six west Cork circuits (centred in Bandon, Bantry, Clonakilty, Dunmanway, Kinsale, and Skibbereen). Church members were adults who had agreed to accept a fairly rigorous régime of church attendance, financial commitment, temperance, and other proofs of self-denial. Methodist ministers also catered in various ways for 'juniors', Protestants of other denominations with an appetite for evangelical enthusiasm, and a medley of sin-prone souls such as military and naval personnel and down-and-outs. This accounts for the fact that, for every full member there was an additional 'adherent' who regularly attended services.[2]

Unlike the sometimes tepid Church of Ireland, the predominant Protestant denomination throughout Southern Ireland, the Methodist community was remarkably well organised and active, permeating many aspects of life beyond church attendance. Methodists in the Cork district were served by networks of small local Sunday schools, temperance associations, and Christian Endeavour societies. In addition to 29 chapels catering for less than two thousand members, there were 151 halls and homes where occasional services were held by the minister who, if he was

---

[1] Figures relate to the combined population of the city and county. The corresponding figures for males (inflated by servicemen, as discussed below) were 10% and 7%; those for the entire population were 9% and 7%.

[2] The total number of members and adherents in the Cork district was 3,722 in 1911. See statistical appendix for each district and circuit published annually in MCI, *MCM*.

lucky, might be offered tea and perhaps a bed.[3] The majority of these places of prayer were in remote townlands in west Cork. The highly dispersed geography of west Cork Methodism reflected its progressive diffusion from Bandon 'to Kinsale, Clonakilty, Ballineeen, Dunmanway, Skibbereen, Bantry, Ballydehob, and Schull', an 'at times romantic' story according to one local history.[4] Methodist ministers, unlike their Episcopalian and Presbyterian counterparts, were still ill-paid 'itinerants' who normally remained for only three years before moving circuit, though occasionally the rule was relaxed to five years (longer in the case of retired 'supernumeraries'). Their status as visiting outsiders ensured that the administration and tone of Methodism were largely controlled by lay members, acting as local preachers, superintendents of schools and societies, class leaders, trustees of Methodist property, secretaries and treasurers, and as representatives to district synods and the annual Irish conference.

All of these offices and activities, especially those involving fund-raising and expenditure, were more or less meticulously documented by the superintendent minister in the prescribed books of each circuit, for perusal and abstraction by district secretaries. As mentioned in the preceding chapter, these books also incorporated quarterly returns of membership and movements in and out of each circuit, recording the names and number of new members, emigrations, 'removals' to and from other classes or circuits within Ireland, deaths, and 'cessations' (often attributable to 'mixed' marriages). Every member, junior, and mover was listed, generating an impressively comprehensive record of the Methodists of west Cork and their migrations. Without such documents, and their preservation in many cases in a central archive, this study could scarcely have been attempted.[5]

The core of west Cork Methodism was a fairly small group of long-established families sharing a much smaller number of surnames. Though seldom 'Irish' in origin, many Methodist surnames were shared not only with Episcopalian neighbours and relatives, but also with Roman Catholics. The diffusion of surnames such as Buttimer, Bradfield, Good, Hosford, Kingston, Willis, and Wolfe reflected two essentials of Methodism: its genesis as an evangelical strand within the established

---

[3] In west Cork alone (excluding Bantry), circuit books record 15 chapels and 86 preaching places in 1911.

[4] *Souvenirs of the Centenary of the Opening of the Methodist Church, Bandon, 1822–1922* (Dublin, pr. R. T. White, 1922), 13.

[5] See Circuit Schedule Books, Membership Registers and Quarterly Class Rolls, and other records of west Cork circuits in MHSIA (kindly made available by the archivist, Revd Robin Roddie).

church, and its early ardour in proselytising nominal Catholics (themselves perhaps descended from Protestant planters). Apart from descendants of colonists, Methodism was regularly reinforced by more or less temporary immigrants. These included naval veterans serving as coastguards, notably in Kinsale, who were far more attentive to religion than the ever-changing population of nominally Methodist servicemen in barracks (for whom the temperance requirement was particularly uncongenial). The development of barytes mines near Schull and Ballydehob (Skibbereen circuit) had attracted numerous Cornish Protestants in the late nineteenth century, and Methodist families with West Country names such as Jagoe and Copithorne remained in west Cork in 1911 despite the recent collapse of the mining industry.[6]

Methodists formed something of an occupational élite in pre-war Cork. Of 620 occupied male Methodists in Co. Cork (excluding the city), 27% were merchants, dealers, or manufacturers, and 26% were farmers or their assisting relatives. Though an even larger group were occupied in defence (29%), most of these were only nominal adherents and played little or no part in Methodist communal life. Methodist naval and military chaplains in the Cork district catered for 1,313 'declared Wesleyans' in January 1912, but just 13 of these were returned as full members. It is instructive to identify the occupations in which Methodist men were over-represented by comparison with Episcopalians, the denomination of the former 'Ascendancy' which, by 1911, was in an advanced stage of disintegration and demoralisation. In descending order, the occupational groups in which Methodists were over-represented included drapers, grocers, tailors, chemists, shopkeepers, merchants, food dealers, medical men, clergy, farmers, shoemakers, and merchant seamen. By contrast, Methodists were under-represented in building, teaching, defence, local government, debt enforcement (a single bailiff), agricultural labour and service, and, most emphatically, national government and law (one solicitor).[7] Many Methodists prospered in trade or agriculture, but few could claim 'Ascendancy' qualifications as landlords, officials, and army officers.

[6] Revd James D. Foster, 'Skibbereen and West Cork', *CA* (Christmas no., 9 Dec.1922).
[7] In Co. Cork (excluding the county borough), the percentage ratio of Methodists to Episcopalians for all occupied males was 7.7. Methodists were represented as follows: drapers and mercers 55, grocers 52, tailors 40, chemists 31, general shopkeepers 18, merchants and agents 15, miscellaneous food dealers 14, medicine 13, clergy 12, farmers and graziers 10, boot and shoemakers 9, merchant seamen 9, farmers' relatives 8, general labourers 7, building and houses 7, teachers 7, defence 5, local government 3, bailiffs 3, agricultural labour and service 3, national government 2, and law 2. See Census of Ireland (1911), report for Co. Cork.

By 1911, west Cork's small, close-knit, prosperous, and highly respectable Methodist population was seldom troubled by overtly sectarian tensions, and prided itself on maintaining good social and economic relations with Episcopalian and Catholic neighbours. Despite doctrinal and stylistic differences between Methodism and the Church of Ireland, there were close congregational and family links between those two churches, whose members routinely attended each other's missions, services, and societies. Many Methodists were baptised, married, or buried in the Church of Ireland, marrying across the denominational divide, changing affiliation in the course of their lives, and rearing children in both churches. An account of Bandon Methodism at the turn of the century notes cooperation in organising harvest services, school children's parties, and choral festivals, and reports that several west Cork families produced ministers serving both churches.[8] Apart from the occasional attendance of Methodists at Catholic schools, no such intimate links united Methodist and Catholic families, intermarriage being abhorred by both communities; yet religious separation was perfectly consistent with good neighbourliness.

Inter-denominational harmony was a fairly recent achievement, early Wesleyanism having generated many bruising collisions with both Catholics and Episcopalians as a result of aggressive proselytism. For six decades from 1816, there had also been an open rift between 'Wesleyan Methodists', who comprised a separate denomination, and 'Primitive Wesleyan Methodists' who maintained the Wesleys' own insistence on remaining, however tenuously, within the episcopal Church.[9] By 1904, however, intra-Protestant tensions had been cooled by the reabsorption of Methodist factions and a directive against missionary poaching:

It is our direction to all agents of our Church that they shall adopt every reasonable method to make known upon such occasions that the first duty of converts is to settle down in their own Churches, if these be evangelical, and to work in their own sphere for the salvation of those in whom they are interested.[10]

There were still occasional disputes provoked by open-air preaching, and colporteurs were not always welcomed as they roamed around rural Munster, distributing free bibles in the hope of leading deluded or indifferent countrymen towards the marvellous light. Another source of

---

[8] George Ferguson, *Ballineen to Belfast: The Life of Rev. Dr. W. L. Northridge* (Dublin, Pericles Publications, 2004), 6.

[9] Ireland also had a few 'Primitive Methodist' and 'Methodist New Connexion' congregations during the periods 1832–1910 and 1798–1905, respectively.

[10] The conference resolution on 'the evangelistic work of our Church', first approved in June 1904, was still being published without alteration as a conference resolution in 1926.

potential conflict was the fact that in Ireland, unlike Wales or England, the great majority of Methodists remained loyal to the union and averse to any form of Home Rule. Even so, most Cork Methodists in 1911 must have imagined that their tempestuous history had yielded a more comfortable phase of peaceful coexistence.

The transition from aggressive evangelicalism to harmonious prosperity was not without cost. As converts lapsed without being replaced, the southern Methodist population had dropped sharply, exaggerating the general process of depopulation in post-Famine Ireland. The number of Methodists in Bandon had fallen from 616 in 1839 to 190 in 1911 (70%), and from 476 to 244 in Skibbereen (48%). Yet Methodist membership, in Cork as in the Dublin district, had recovered steadily between about 1880 and 1905, and the subsequent shrinkage had been gradual.[11] Though ministers might worry that Methodism had lost some of its energy and begun to ossify, there seemed no imminent risk of its collapse in Munster. Cork remained one of the three cities hosting the annual conference in rotation (though conferences were held more frequently in Dublin and Belfast). The early successes in the county of the Wesleys, Ouseley's 'cavalry preachers', and other Methodist celebrities were widely celebrated as a proof that the truth would prevail in the most inauspicious surroundings. Sober, quiet, canny, and clannish, Methodists in 1911 could look forward to a settled life in west Cork and a sure salvation thereafter.

Fifteen years later, it appeared that Methodism had suffered a statistical collapse, in Cork as in most of Southern Ireland. The Irish Free State's first census revealed that the county's Methodist population had fallen by 33% since 1911, and the Church's membership returns indicated an even greater loss (36%). Other indicators of religious activity were even more depressing: the number of preaching places in the Cork district had declined by 53%, and that of attenders at services by 46%. Returns of Sunday scholars for four west Cork circuits showed a loss of 51% since 1911, though temperance associations had fared better with a decline of only 34%.[12] To what extent was the sharp decline in Methodist activity in west Cork a consequence of revolutionary turmoil, or even of a concerted sectarian campaign against Methodists in this remote region?[13] By reconstructing the experience of a small but thoroughly documented

[11] W. H. Massey, 'Methodism and Rural Work', in *Irish Methodism in the Twentieth Century: A Symposium*, ed. Alexander McCrea (Belfast, Irish Methodist Pub. Co., 1931), 25–40 (33–5).

[12] These figures from circuit books relate to calendar years.

[13] According to Gerard Murphy, *The Year of Disappearances: Political Killings in Cork, 1921–1922* (Dublin, Gill and Macmillan, 2010), the campaign of 1922 was particularly

Protestant community, we may identify some of the personal and local mechanisms that shaped 'Protestant depopulation'.

II

The decline of Methodism in the Cork district was unexceptional, despite the unsurpassed ferocity and frequency of attacks against Cork Protestants.[14] The proportionate decline in membership between 1911 and 1926 was close to that for Southern Ireland as a whole, as analysed in the preceding chapter. It was much less severe than in Limerick, Sligo, or even Clones (Table 8.10). The decline was also continuous, though accelerated during the revolutionary years. The downward trend is graphically depicted in Chart 9.1, which compares Cork with the Sligo district

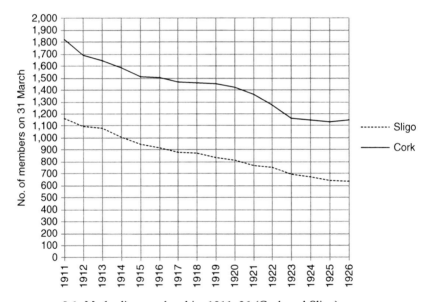

9.1 Methodist membership, 1911–26 (Cork and Sligo)

directed against Methodists, perhaps because of their involvement in youth movements such as the Boy Scouts: 'You have almost what amounts to a pogrom on Methodists in [Co.] Cork' (236). For balanced discussions of such issues, see Barry Keane, 'Ethnic Cleansing? Protestant Decline in West Cork between 1911 and 1926', *History Ireland*, xii, no. 2 (2012), 35–41 (amplified on his website), and Jasper Ungoed-Thomas, 'I.R.A. Sectarianism in Skibbereen?', *Skibbereen and District Historical Society Journal*, vi (2010), 97–115.

[14]   See preceding chapter.

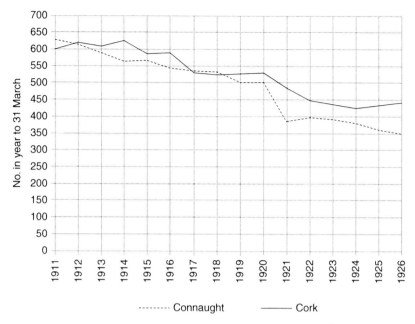

9.2 Presbyterian communicants, 1911–26 (Cork and Connaught)

(incorporating circuits in Mayo, Leitrim, and Roscommon). Though Cork's decline was less severe, it was also less linear with signs of recovery after 1923.[15] The tenacity of Cork Protestants is confirmed by Chart 9.2, which offers a similar comparison between Presbyterian communicants in the Cork and Connaught presbyteries.[16] Once again, the decline in Cork was slower than in Connaught, with some recovery after a pronounced setback between 1920 and 1923.

When the various components of population flow are compared with other southern districts, Cork is noteworthy only for an unusually high rate of emigration beyond Ireland, especially in the revolutionary triennium. The annual rate of emigration from Cork district in that period was 60 for every thousand members, compared with 36 from Limerick, 24

---

[15] See previous chapter, p. 174.
[16] Returns of communicants for every presbytery and congregation, for each year ending 31 Mar., were published annually as an appendix to PCI, *Minutes of the Proceedings of the General Assembly*.

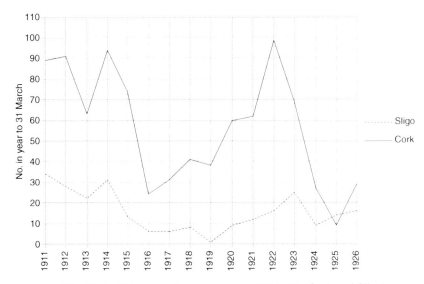

9.3 Methodist emigration per annum, 1911–26 (Cork and Sligo)

from Sligo, and 19 from Clones.[17] Yet even this possible hint of 'ethnic cleansing' is quite faint, since only 230 of the 811 members who emigrated from the Cork district between 1911 and 1926 left during the revolutionary years. Heavy emigration of both Protestants and Catholics was a long-established practice in Cork, and the revolutionary exodus had actually been exceeded by the 248 members who left between 1911 and 1914. Moreover, heavy emigration was counterbalanced by unusually intense intake of new members in the Cork district, even in the revolutionary triennium (Table 8.13). Annual fluctuations in emigration and recruitment are traced in Charts 9.3 and 9.4, which again contrast the Cork experience with that of the Sligo district. Both emigration and enrolment of new members increased sharply after the Great War, with pronounced peaks in the year ending March 1922 followed by a downward trend until 1925. Though almost equally volatile, the fluctuations in Sligo were at a lower level, with relatively few emigrants and recruits by comparison with the Methodist population.

Within west Cork, there was little variation between circuits in the proportionate decline in membership (1911–26), ranging from 30% in

---

[17] For rates of population flow in all districts, see preceding chapter, Table 8.14. Though Cork had the largest number of net outward removals within Ireland from any district (1920–3), the annual rate per thousand (19) was lower than in Sligo (23) and Limerick (27).

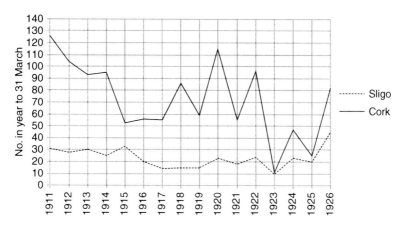

9.4 New Methodist members per annum, 1911–26 (Cork and Sligo)

Clonakilty and Kinsale to 33% in Dunmanway, 35% in Bandon and Skibbereen, and 39% in Bantry (Table 9.1).[18] Elsewhere in the Cork district the decline was greater (41%), reflecting the general tendency for heavier Protestant depopulation in cities and in garrison towns such as Mallow and Fermoy.[19] Triennial membership fell almost continuously in all circuits, apart from minor post-war recoveries in three circuits (1917–20) and likewise in the final triennium (1923–6). There were, however, marked contrasts in the impact of emigration during the revolutionary period, with relatively heavy emigration from Kinsale but little from Dunmanway (Table 9.2). It is notable, however, that all circuits lost more members through emigration in 1920–3 than in 1911–14, reversing the general pattern in Southern Ireland. Comparison with the total figures for Cork district (Table 8.13) shows that the turnover of membership in west Cork was sluggish by comparison with the residue of the district (dominated by the city). Though almost half of the members belonged to west Cork circuits (excluding Bantry), these accounted for only about a quarter of the district's new members, emigrants, and cessations.[20] The

[18] The decline in Bantry may have been inflated by the mistaken inclusion of juniors in 1911, contributing to a reduction from 106 to 86 recorded members by 1912.
[19] Following the discontinuance of the Fermoy–Mallow circuit in 1922, in response to the evacuation of military barracks in those towns, the remaining circuits outside west Cork were Cork City (405 members in 1926), Tralee and Killarney (77), Queenstown and Berehaven (29), and Youghal (27).
[20] Returns of membership flow are not available for Bantry, for Kinsale (1923–6), or for the circuits outside west Cork. For the period 1911–26, the west Cork circuits accounted for 27% of the district's new members, 24% of emigrants, 26% of cessations, and 48% of

records for Cork confirm my general finding that the statistical imprint of revolutionary disruption was perceptible but fairly minor.[21]

Yet there is more to be said.

III

To what extent did southern Methodists feel themselves under threat, even if most endured and survived the revolutionary ordeal? Before returning to the revolution's personal and organisational impact in west Cork, let us examine some contemporary public responses by leading Irish Methodists. In June 1920, at a time of accelerating carnage and destruction, the Irish conference expressed 'its profound sorrow for the present condition of Ireland, and its abhorrence of those acts of violence and bloodshed which are being committed'. There was no suggestion that Methodists had been a particular target of 'terrorism and murder'. While noting 'the surge of world-wide restlessness and unsatisfied desire', the conference secretary (James M. Alley, superintendent of the Cork circuit) declared in his pastoral address that the Irish Methodist Church remained 'ordered amid its uncertainties. We have gone in and out among its circuits in unmolested quietness.'[22] Alley's sanguine tone belied the fact that in February 1920 he himself had been stoned in Blackpool, outside Cork City, his right eye being damaged and almost blinded.[23]

By contrast, Alley's next address was almost apocalyptic in tone, reflecting horror at the brutal killing of dozens of alleged 'informers' and 'collaborators', including several Cork Methodists, in early 1921:

The storm that rolled across Europe has struck our shores, and with it the added bitterness of domestic strife. As it rages everything that can be shaken is falling, and much has fallen already. Institutions which were regarded as bulwarks of the community are gone. The majesty of the law and the value of well-ordered society are outraged and despised. We cannot but think of homes from which some of our most Christlike members were callously done to death, of others from which our people's goods have been unlawfully distrained, and of others from which our people have had to fly to seek a home beyond the seas, and the cry ascends: 'How long, O Lord, wilt Thou hide Thyself for ever?'

Though he celebrated the 'magnificent courage, patience and fidelity of their people in the midst of tremendous difficulties' and the unexpected

---

deaths. Corresponding percentages for 1911–14 were 28, 21, 19, and 56; those for 1920–3 were 31, 33, 39, and 49. Note that such calculations are invalid in the case of net outward removals.
[21] See preceding chapter.   [22] *MCM* (1920), 114, 125, 123.
[23] R. Lee Cole, *History of Methodism in Ireland, 1860–1960* (Belfast, Irish Methodist Pub. Co., 1960), 110.

success of 'their colporteurs in remote parts of Ireland' in distributing more bibles than in any previous year, Alley admitted in his annual address to the British conference that 'the political unrest that prevails has challenged the faith of our people'. He expressed sympathy for 'those who live in lonely isolated parts of the country, whose lives and property are in continual danger'.[24]

Another minister familiar with Cork, Dr John O. Park, expressed optimism when interviewed by an English Methodist journal in early January 1922:

In my long experience of South and West Ireland I have never known either priests or people to interfere seriously with our Methodist people except on political grounds ... I admit that some of my brethren in the Irish ministry would bear a different testimony ... Undoubtedly there have been cases in which grave injustice has been done to our people. Some have been boycotted and driven out of the country. But I believe in most cases of this kind the motive has been covetousness on the part of rivals, who have used political prejudice to promote their private ends, to obtain a farm or a shop which was prospering in the hands of its Methodist proprietors.[25]

Like many Methodist observers and the republicans themselves, he shied away from sectarianism as an explanation for intimidation and violence, though his alternative analysis was equally unflattering to the perpetrators.

As the Methodist historian Richard Lee Cole remarked, the advent of partition had created 'a certain amount of difficulty' for the Methodist conference, bound to recognise both new governments while maintaining 'the solidarity of the Church both North and South'. Cole concluded that there 'can be no reflection on the Conference that the resolutions on Irish affairs were soft-pedalled during this whole period'.[26] A message of hope, touched by exhilaration, was sent by the Methodist conference in Dublin to their British brethren on 12 June, a fortnight before the outbreak of open civil war:

We are greatly concerned about the public affairs of our country. Our deliberations have been carried on at a time when our people, North and South, are subjected to unusual strain and suffering. There is widespread anxiety regarding the future, yet we abide in hope ... A wonderful work of revival has taken place in several large cities like Belfast, Portadown, Londonderry, and Cork. The work has spread to the more remote parts of the land, and hundreds of souls have been born into the

---

[24] *MCM* (1921), 105–6; *CA* (21 Jan. 1921); *Minutes of Several Conversations at the ... Yearly Conference of the People Called Methodists* (London, Wesleyan Conference Office, 1921), 337.
[25] Interview in *Methodist Recorder* (12 Jan. 1922), as reproduced in *CA* (20 Jan.).
[26] Cole, *Methodism in Ireland*, 108.

Kingdom. Our Evangelists and Colporteurs, braving all dangers, have won victories of grace remarkable in the annals of the Church's history.[27]

The pastoral address for the conference of 1922 drew a revealing comparison with the aftermath of another bloody episode in the history of Irish Protestantism:

The moment is strikingly opportune for recalling an heroic chapter in our history. In 1799, when revolution had convulsed the land, our fathers sitting in Conference ... instead of exhibiting trepidation or despondency, displayed a splendid spirit of holy audacity and unexpected progressiveness ... They inaugurated one of the most courageous and successful of Irish missionary campaigns, setting apart James McQuigg, Charles Graham and Gideon Ouseley as missionaries to their fellow-countrymen, with the four provinces for their circuit ... These days are ripe for such missionary effort: nay, more, they are crying out for it. With profoundest thankfulness we have heard and seen the unmistakable signs of spiritual revival in our midst.[28]

The providential reading of suffering as an agent for salvation, like earlier interpretations of the Great Famine and the Great War, offered valuable consolation to the faithful, however tenuous the evidence that evil had somehow brought forth good.

The recent dumping of arms by most republican insurgents gave further encouragement to the Belfast conference of June 1923: 'Abnormal conditions have interfered with services; but the interrupted services are being resumed, as the disturbed areas come under the control of the constituted authorities. Southern congregations have been depleted by removals and emigrations ... This inevitable contraction has been more than counterbalanced by expansion elsewhere.'[29] At the next conference, belatedly held in Cork after relocation to safer cities in the three preceding years, the annual rumination about the condition of Southern Ireland was displaced by more familiar preoccupations such as the drink traffic and primary education.[30]

In a book of essays published in 1931, several ministers offered perceptive and revealing assessments of the impact of revolutionary turmoil on southern Irish Methodism. In his chapter on 'Irish Methodism and the War' (broadly defined), Robert H. Foster lamented the effect of violence on a community that had 'no sympathy with violence, or the

---

[27] *Minutes of Wesleyan Conference* (1922), 353.
[28] *MCM* (1922), 102. For context, see F. J. Cole's address to the Dublin Methodist council on 5 Oct. 1944, published as *The Cavalry Preachers: Some Glimpses of the Work and Romance of Early Irish Methodism* (copy, without cover or imprint, in Edgehill College Library).
[29] Pastoral Address in *MCM* (1923), 95–6.   [30] Pastoral Address in *MCM* (1924), 111.

achievement of any political status by non-constitutional methods'. Methodists thus became 'passive sufferers in the disorders and struggles' of the early 1920s:

Many Southern and Western families left our shores as a direct result of those criminal activities, and are now settled in the South of England, and elsewhere … On the changes of 1923, our people almost without exception stood for loyalty to the newly-constituted Governments of Ireland … Non-conformist troops quartered in Ireland during 'the troubles,' and when British soldiers were shot down at our church door in Fermoy[31] it was the Minister's wife who first tended them, when every other door in the street was closed in terror. We want to forget those days. Would that we could wipe out 1914 and the years that followed.

But Foster expressed pride that, like Tommy Atkins, 'We did our bit.'[32]

The most incisive assessment came from James Alley, chairman of the Cork district when elected as president of the Methodist Church in Ireland in June 1922. Alley maintained that 'not two per cent. of the Methodists of Ireland desired Home Rule', though, 'as the fight grew fiercer', sharp political divisions had developed over the wisdom of continuing 'a policy of blank resistance'. Alley interpreted the attacks on southern Methodists as political rather than sectarian acts:

Some of them who, on conscientious grounds, felt compelled to inform the British authorities of things that were being done in their district, were foully murdered … Some were entrapped into giving information to members of the Republican forces, who came wearing the uniform of British military officers, and then were shot for their simplicity, and their homes burned. Not a few were compelled to fly the country in order to save their lives. Others had their property destroyed, and some, growing hopeless of settled conditions in their lifetime, sought in Northern Ireland, in England, or in lands beyond the seas, a happier home. For the most part, however, with indomitable courage, and a faith that refused to despair, Irish Methodists, in common with their co-religionists of other denominations, held their ground, carrying on their business as best they could; convinced that Ireland in those dark and trying days needed, as never before, the evangelical witness.[33]

Alley recalled 'innumerable illustrations … of the respect and confidence in the Methodist people shown by their Roman Catholic fellow-countrymen', and rejoiced in a 'remarkable change': 'There is a spirit of tolerance in the land to-day which few a decade ago hoped to live to see.'

---

[31] See n. 34.
[32] R. H. Foster, 'Irish Methodism and the War', in McCrea, *Irish Methodism*, 68–84 (83–4).
[33] James Alley, 'Irish Methodism and Political Changes', in McCrea, *Irish Methodism*, 9–24 (18–19).

IV

Reports from the Cork district confirm the resilience of Methodist congregations, despite mounting fear and alarm engendered by republican violence and intimidation. The devastating attack on 7 September 1919 against Wesleyan members of the King's Shropshire Light Infantry, as they assembled for a parade service in the Fermoy Methodist church, could be explained away as an act of 'war' or rebellion without sectarian implications.[34] Methodists were naturally reluctant to view themselves as targets for religious persecution, and took comfort in signs of solidarity with their Catholic neighbours. In January 1921, a few days after the first murder of a Methodist 'informer', James Alley delivered a lecture on 'The Holy Land' to an audience exceeding 300 at Haulbowline, where the civil administrator of the naval dockyard was also a 'well-known Methodist Local Preacher':

The audience included naval officers, members of the civil staff of the dockyard, mariners, patients and nurses from the Naval Hospital, members of the R.I.C., as well as such dockyard workers as reside on the Island, the majority of those present being Roman Catholics.[35]

Further west, congregations maintained the appearance of normality in the midst of mayhem. The *Christian Advocate* reported in April 1921 that 'notwithstanding the conditions which obtain in west Cork, the Skibbereen Circuit has not allowed its finances to suffer'. Juvenile collections had actually increased, 'much credit' being due to William Wolfe of the Corner House, a prosperous draper who superintended the Sunday school in addition to acting as a local preacher.[36]

Though a truce was agreed between the IRA and the British army in July 1921, Methodists could not yet lie easy in their beds. A minister conducting a Home Mission in west Cork, just before signature of the Anglo-Irish Treaty, published a wry account of his experiences:

There was a blockade caused by a railway strike, and motoring ... was the only solution of travelling: even this was complicated by impassably entrenched roads, and trenches only sufficiently filled enough to strain the springs of the stoutest lorries ... In spite of the truce a boycott is still evident. Bodies of armed men keep the beds in good Methodist houses well aired by an unsolicited occupation. And all the while, slowly but unmistakably, many of our people are evacuating the

---

[34] One soldier was shot dead through the heart, another seriously wounded in the thigh, and 'others of the party were bludgeoned and stunned': Cole, *Methodism in Ireland*, 94. Earlier in 1919, Richard Lee Cole had been replaced by James Alley as chairman of the Cork district.

[35] *CA* (4 Feb. 1921).   [36] *CA* (22 Apr. 1921).

territory, and looking for more favourable situations in this and other lands; but the remnant hold strongly and magnificently on.

The same report revealed that Skibbereen had raised more money for the Home Mission fund than any other country district.[37]

Methodist confidence was fortified by the Dáil's endorsement of the Treaty on 7 January 1922, which aroused misplaced expectations of domestic peace. In Skibbereen, William Wolfe was again on hand to 'manipulate' the magic lantern for James H. Munro, a former military chaplain who had assembled 'a very fine set of lantern slides' as a result of his service in Egypt and Palestine, as well as 'a fine set of curios'. The *Advocate* reported that 'our loyal Methodists in Skibbereen are bravely making good the gaps in their membership – gaps which have enriched other circuits and countries', as well as 'courageously' putting on a 'missionary and manse sale of work'.[38] Over the next few months, however, divisions within the IRA and Sinn Féin erupted into unbridled lawlessness and violence in the absence of any effective government, army, judiciary, or police. Though the growing civil conflict was ostensibly a political dispute, many of its victims were Crown servants, loyalists, landlords, or owners of property or businesses coveted by armed men freed from any central discipline. One manifestation of civic breakdown was the 'Bandon Valley massacre' of late April 1922, widely regarded by contemporary observers as a sectarian campaign by what might now be termed 'dissident' republicans.

Despite initial panic and some hasty departures from home, many west Cork Protestants refused to believe that their Catholic neighbours would sustain or tolerate a prolonged sectarian vendetta. A special correspondent of the *Irish Independent* testified on 2 May to the rapid restoration of morale:

The Protestants of South and West Cork are living in a state of most abject terror because of the shooting of members of their creed. There is a substantial Protestant population in this county. Farmers of the well-to-do class, scores of them, are now remaining out in the fields at night, afraid to remain in their homes ... [One] knew no reason for the assassinations, and added that his co-religionists had always been on the best of terms with their Catholic neighbours, and now, in their hours of trial and dismay, they had the whole-hearted sympathy and goodwill of Catholics. The plight of Protestant women and children is pitiable. They remain at home, but most of the elder folks remain up in turns to keep watch. A belief obtains that the worst has passed and that this mad crime wave will stop at once. The outspoken condemnation of the clergy and the Republican force is welcome, and the optimism of the people is based on it. Many

Protestant shopkeepers have left Bandon, Dunmanway, and Clonakilty, and have gone to other parts, some in England.[39]

According to a brief press report on 'The Exodus' from Bantry, also submitted on 2 May to the ex-unionist *Cork County Eagle*, the worst was already over:

Now that things appear to have quieted down and look likely taking [*sic*] an immediate turn for the better in a more stable and lasting manner than for some time back, and it is thought that many, if not all, of these refugees will return to their homes and businesses and matters proceed normally as heretofore.[40]

On the previous day, naval intelligence in Queenstown had dismissed as 'exaggerated' an English 'press report that large number of refugees [had been] entering this country from Co. Cork'. Though 'on good authority some 200 left Dunmanway district', none had left the county from Queenstown and only 'normal numbers' had taken the steamer from Cork.[41]

The Cork district synod, held on 2–3 May, offered anonymous condolences for 'those so cruelly murdered in West Cork', but also passed an optimistic resolution calling on Methodists to perform every 'duty of good citizenship' under the new (provisional) government.[42] Since the attacks were widely interpreted as reprisals for a recent 'pogrom' against Catholics in Belfast, optimism must have been particularly encouraged by a resolution from the Belfast comhairle ceanntair of Sinn Féin, published in a Cork unionist newspaper: 'That we record our horror at the brutal extermination of our Protestant fellow-countrymen in Cork, and hope the efforts of Dáil Éireann to bring the murderers to justice will be successful; and we tender our sincere sympathy to the relatives of the victims.'[43]

The rejection of despair by Church leaders was particularly telling when voiced by Alfred Harbinson, a chaplain to the forces in France and Belgium before ministering in Dunmanway (1919–22). As he wrote to the *Irish Times* a few days after several of his congregation had been killed or put to flight:

During the disturbances reported the Methodist Manse was neither visited nor attacked, and there is no truth whatever in the statement that I had to seek refuge in

---

[39] 'In Abject Terror', in *II* (2 May 1922) and *CC* (3 May).   [40] *CCE* (6 May 1922).

[41] Copies of telegrams, Admiralty to Admiral Queenstown and reply, 1 May 1922: NAL, ADM 116/2135. In paraphrasing the report from Queenstown, Murphy mentions the exodus from Dunmanway but not the absence of emigration by sea from the county: *Disappearances*, 326.

[42] *CA* (12 May 1922; *CC* (6 May). A similar resolution was approved by the Limerick district synod: *CC* (4 May).

[43] *CC* (4 May 1922).

the fields or elsewhere. Never, at any time, have I been molested or interfered with in any way. I have always received the utmost courtesy from the people of this town and surrounding country.[44]

When asked later about his 'term in Dunmanway', Harbinson made no reference to 'disturbances'; but praised 'the spirit of the people, they were kind, affectionate and loyal'.[45] His potential successors in Dunmanway were evidently less sanguine. John Woodrow, who had been invited to replace him a month before the 'massacre', subsequently 'changed his mind about coming to Dunmanway' (the only allusion to these events in the minutes of quarterly meetings of church officers).[46] Two other ministers were put forward for Dunmanway but withdrawn before the conference of June 1922, which eventually appointed another former military chaplain accustomed to dangerous situations (Henry George Martin, previously in Fermoy).[47]

Though only one Methodist in the county was killed during the civil war (William Levingstone Cooke of Blackrock Road, Cork), ministers continued to face formidable challenges, as hinted in a report of a Home Mission in Bandon in November 1922 by William Corrigan: 'The deputation [Corrigan] captivated the children, and more besides, by recounting some of the thrilling experiences during this tour of his Methodist diocese ... Did ever deputation have such adventures and hairbreadth escapes?'[48] Corrigan published a longer but reticent report of his 'journey totalling 260 miles, at a cost of 6s 6d to the Home Mission Fund', for which his 'last two years in Belfast' had provided 'a useful preparatory course'. Loath to hire or borrow transport, he had hitched lifts on numerous cars and lorries whose owners (including 'two ministers of other denominations') were thanked by name. Travelling by night without headlights to Clonakilty after a visit to the Cork district synod, one car had been left 'in ruins' after crashing into a 'broken bridge'. Corrigan and his companions had to walk thirteen miles back to Cork, 'our only sustenance being stories and expletives'. Traffic diversions caused by 'the Battle of Ballineen' had not disrupted the mission schedule, even though

---

[44] *IT* (1 May 1922). The report that Harbinson and the rector 'had to take refuge in the fields' had also appeared, only to be retracted, in *CA* (5, 12 May 1922).

[45] Ian D. Henderson, *Dunmanway Methodist Church: 150 Years, 1836–1986* (no imprint, 2003; 1st edn. 1986), 9.

[46] Dunmanway circuit, Minutes of Quarterly Leaders' Meetings, 1900–31 (27 Mar., 6 Sept. 1922).

[47] Bertram C. Moran and William Buchanan had also been named in draft lists showing 'changes of stations': *CA* (9, 12, 16 June 1922). Two other former military chaplains also served in revolutionary west Cork: James Henry Munro in Bandon (1920–3) and Ernest Clarence Gimblett in Kinsale (1919–22).

[48] Report by Revd James H. Munro (Bandon) in *CA* (17 Nov. 1922).

eight machine-gun bullets were pumped into the car behind, 'on the edge of the chief danger zone'.

Seventeen meetings and services had been held, some in 'places which would have been closed when their principal supporters were driven away, but for the heart-moving pathos of the appeals made by some who had found their spiritual life and sustenance within their walls'. He praised the 'patient heroism' of those sustaining 'causes which must perish in the not distant future if the present migration continues'. Beleaguered Methodists should 'remain in their place' despite 'the untold agony, loss, and suspense which is the lot of many', and 'their poor return for services to neighbours who esteemed and respected them, but were, doubtless, for the most part afraid to assist them'. Surrender would be a disaster for Ireland as well as themselves: 'their departure from the country would be as serious for it as was the expulsion of the Huguenots from France'. Like a true Methodist minister, Corrigan advised that 'much must be left unsaid'. But he offered his congregations 'close and constant companionship in these days and nights of terror', and called on Irish Methodists in calmer regions to give 'unprecedented support' to the Home Mission Fund to sustain 'small causes'. He concluded ominously that 'if the light of Methodism be extinguished it will never be rekindled'.[49]

Other 'thrilling experiences' while ministering in west Cork were recalled by William Buchanan, who was sent to Bantry just after Collins's death in August 1922. To reach Bantry, Buchanan had to sail from Liverpool to Cork, hang around the city before securing a car to share with his family and other ministers, endure check-points by men in uniform demanding a permit, and bypass broken bridges and trenched roads. He recollected Corrigan, when conducting the Home Mission, 'walking miles, thumbing lifts on farm carts or any other vehicle'. Corrigan had travelled from Bantry towards Skibbereen 'on one of Warner's bread vans':

When he got to Ballineen he was arrested and taken to Headquarters for interrogation, as he resembled Mr De Valera in appearance. The local Methodist minister [Edward Bennett of Clonakilty] was called to Headquarters and succeeded in satisfying the authorities that Mr Corrigan was indeed a Methodist minister.[50]

---

[49] William Corrigan, 'A Home Mission Tour in the South', in *CA* (8 Dec. 1922). I am grateful to Robin Roddie for supplying me with a copy of this article.
[50] William Buchanan, 'The Road to Bantry', *Bulletin of the MHSI*, xvi (2011), 91–6 (96), first published in *Carbery Methodist*, i, nos 2, 3 (1961). Matching photographs (95) suggest that Corrigan, despite a cranium, spectacles, and intense expression not unlike de Valera's, was distinctly better looking.

Circuit records confirm Buchanan's difficulties in Bantry and his determination to overcome them. On 27 September 1922, circuit officers
decided, 'if possible', to hold the annual Harvest Thanksgiving service
in the following month, but the intended Home Missionary meeting
lapsed 'owing to the disturbed condition of the country'. The next quarterly meeting, held three weeks after the inauguration of the Irish Free
State, learned that 'the Work of God was considered satisfactory; the
members attend the services very well considering the disturbed state of
the times, the difficulty in travelling owing to roads being cut, bridges
broken, some having long distances to come etc.'. Likewise, on 28 March
1923, 'the state of the work of God on the circuit was considered satisfactory considering the unsettled state of the times'. Even in March 1924, 'it
was considered advisable' not to invite a minister to conduct a mission in
Bantry, 'as there may be a danger of some disturbance, there may be also a
difficulty in getting a place for him to stay in'. A year later, it was deemed
necessary 'to put in glass in windows broken in church and also to get
screens for the protection of the windows in back of church', suggesting
sectarian vandalism.[51] Throughout the revolutionary period, the Bantry
circuit suffered marked loss of income, leading to largely futile pleading
for small central grants and loans.

In Skibbereen, the Harvest service in 1922 was deemed 'very success
ful', with a slightly increased collection and a musical performance by
Mrs Jasper Travers Wolfe. The *Advocate* reported that 'the lure of the
West has acted wonderfully in depleting the membership of this circuit,
but the loyalty and generosity of those remaining in the old land are
wonderful'. The secretary of the Home Mission Fund in Dublin commended Skibbereen, along with the Kinsale, Bandon, and Dunmanway
circuits, for their success in raising money: 'It must be remembered that in
all these southern circuits the offerings are given by diminished numbers,
as many have left the country during the past year, and given in circumstances that would dispirit folk whose hearts were not full of love and
holy faith.' The minister in Skibbereen contributed a sober feature to the
Advocate's Christmas number:

No part of Ireland has suffered more from recent agitation than Co. Cork.
Pressure direct and indirect has been very severe. Consequently some of the
most promising families have felt compelled to leave the country, and others are
seriously considering it ... The quiet heroism of our people is marvellous.[52]

[51] Bantry Circuit, Minutes of Quarterly Leaders' Meetings, 1904–32 (27 Sept., 27 Dec.
1922, 28 Mar. 1923, 26 Mar. 1924, 25 Mar. 1925).
[52] *CA* (7 Oct., 24 Nov., 9 Dec. 1922).

According to a centennial pamphlet on Methodism in Dunmanway, published in 1936:

> Like many southern churches, Dunmanway has suffered much as the result of the troublesome times in Ireland; some families were compelled to leave, others feeling a sense of insecurity, left of their own accord. Notwithstanding this, there is still a congregation of loyal and faithful people, capable of facing big things.

The author recalled 'two successful missions' conducted by Alfred Harbinson in two Kingston households in Kilbarry and Drimoleague, showing that renewal of faith remained possible amidst revolution.[53] A later historian has questioned its demographic impact on Dunmanway Methodism, citing circuit returns that showed substantial intake of new members as well as departures between 1919 and 1923: 'It is hard to judge accurately what effect the troubles had on the membership.'[54]

Methodist ministers in west Cork had shown considerable fortitude in helping to maintain congregational activity and morale, despite the fact that most were strangers to the region. Of the 22 ministers who served in the six circuits between 1919 and 1923, only one (Edward Bennett, stationed in Clonakilty between 1922 and 1925) was a Corkonian. Three-fifths were Ulstermen, the residue being natives of Leinster, Munster, England, and India.[55] Nearly three-quarters of ministers (16) were married when they took up duty in west Cork, but the group was relatively junior. Their median age in June 1921 was 38, and the median ministerial experience before arrival in west Cork was only nine years.[56] The youngest minister was William James Ewart, stationed in Ballineen (Clonakilty) from 1921 to 1923, a 20-year-old postman's son from Keady, Co. Armagh. He led an ecumenical life, serving as a Presbyterian colporteur before entering the Methodist Church and ending his career in 1969 as archdeacon of Killala. The oldest minister was William Clarke, a farmer's son from Muckross, Co. Donegal, who was 72 when he completed his second year in Skibbereen in 1922. About a third of the group were sons of

---

[53] *Centenary of Dunmanway Methodism* (no imprint), 6, 9.
[54] Henderson, *Dunmanway Methodist Church*, 16–17.
[55] The Ulster counties of origin were Belfast (3) Antrim, Down, and Fermanagh (2 each), Armagh, Donegal, Monaghan, and Tyrone (1 each). Other ministers were born in Dublin and England (2 each), and Cork, Kerry, Tipperary, Westmeath, and India (1 each). Biographical information is derived from the invaluable database of Irish Methodist clergy kindly made available by Robin Roddie, and family returns for the Census of Ireland (1901, 1911).
[56] Ages in June 1921 ranged between 20 and 71 years, and the period between candidature for the ministry and appointment to west Cork ranged between 1 and 40 years.

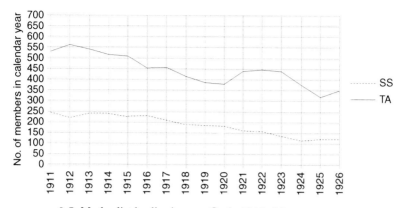

9.5 Methodist bodies in west Cork, 1911–26

farmers, a useful background for those serving in west Cork.[57] An even more useful qualification was service as a wartime chaplain to the forces, an experience shared by four of those ministering in the region between 1919 and 1923.[58] Three west Cork ministers went on to lead the Methodist Church in Ireland,[59] as did every chairman of the Cork district between 1918 and 1925.[60] These credentials suggest that Methodist leaders channelled some of the Church's best and most active ministers to Cork during the revolutionary years.

Further insight into the impact of revolution on west Cork Methodism is supplied by Chart 9.5, which shows the number enrolled in Sunday schools and belonging to temperance associations in four circuits for which returns survive.[61] As already stated, the net loss between 1911 and 1926 was much greater in the case of Sunday schools (51%) than

---

[57] Father's occupation is known in 18 cases, comprising farmers (6, including one father also a linen weaver), clergy, doctors, and postal workers (2 each), and farm labourer, merchant, grocer, basket maker, compositor, and ordnance foreman (1 each).

[58] See n. 47.

[59] William Moore (stationed in Bandon, 1923–5), George Arthur Joynt (Bandon, 1917–19), and Frederick Ernest Hill (Ballydehob, Skibbereen, 1919) were elected as president at the conferences held in 1930, 1943, and 1963 respectively. The dates of service refer to the years beginning in June, when ministers were assigned their stations for the following year at the annual conference.

[60] Richard Lee Cole (chairman, 1918), James Murdock Alley (1919, 1921), Henry Shire (1920), and William Corrigan (1922–4) were elected as president at the conferences of 1933, 1922, 1920, and 1924 respectively.

[61] Annual returns of enrolled Sunday scholars and members of temperance associations: Circuit Schedule Books, excluding Bantry (unavailable for 1911–21) and Kinsale (unavailable for 1922–6).

temperance associations (34%). The decline in Sunday school enrolments was almost linear throughout the decade after 1914, with a slight recovery in 1925–6. The most striking finding is the temporary but marked surge in temperance activity in 1921–3, notably in Clonakilty and troubled Skibbereen. Not only did west Cork Methodism recover rapidly after the civil war, but there is clear if patchy evidence of religious and moral revival during the most violent phase of revolutionary unrest.

What spiritual revival entailed for a Methodist farmer's son in post-revolutionary west Cork is indicated by the recollections of John Wesley Kingston, from Gurteenihir near Drimoleague. Kingston was the eldest of ten children of pious and strictly Sabbatarian parents. Born auspiciously on 5 November 1911 and appointed a local preacher in Skibbereen aged 18, he was soon to become a peripatetic evangelist regaling audiences in Ulster, England, and America with tales of his experiences as an 'Irish Free State Evangelist'.[62] In 1911 his townland contained five households, four occupied by Methodist Kingstons and the fifth by a Catholic family. Jeremiah and Hanora O'Connell must have felt out of place in a townland where three Kingston families were still offering their homes in rotation for services in 1934.[63] Ignoring the predominance of Methodists in the immediate vicinity, Kingston recalled that 'our neighbours were Roman Catholics and, of course, there was a diversity of opinion; but apart from that the spirit of neighbourliness was prevalent'. Even so, fifteen acres farmed by his father had been 'maliciously set on fire' during one dry summer.[64] Distaste for Catholicism was evident in Kingston's tributes to the unshakable faith of his mother ('my heroine', 'of unimpeachable character', 'a shrewd business woman'). She had been raised in the Church of Ireland with Catholic forebears, but was brought to the light upon marrying a convinced Methodist: 'The Roman Catholics who lived in the district indulged in evil practices, but their amusements had no attractions for her.'[65] Reliance on virtue and piety were all the more potent, and necessary, for members of an embattled minority.

Kingston's narratives of personal salvation are obviously self-serving, sentimental, and risibly conventional in their language, structure, and

---

[62] Anon, *A Methodist Evangelist's Reminiscences* (Belfast, pr. John Adams, 1933) and John W. Kingston, *These Miracles did Jesus in Ireland* (London and Edinburgh, Marshall, Morgan, and Scott, [1935]): both in MHSIA. The British Library holds a third instalment, *Great Wonders and Miracles in England: Reminscences of a Travelling Evangelist* (Edinburgh, Marshall, Morgan, and Scott, [1937]). A visit to Watkins Glen, New York State, where this 'gifted speaker' conducted a 16-day mission in the Wayne Methodist church in Nov. 1938, is reported in *Watkins Express* (2 Nov., accessible on-line).
[63] Dunmanway circuit, Schedule Book (1923–38).
[64] Kingston, *Reminiscences*, 16–17.   [65] Kingston, *These Miracles*, 23.

themes, which conform closely to the venerable genre of ecstatic religious testimony. Yet they are redeemed by touches of local colour which evoke the landscape of Kingston's 'conversion'. As a 12-year-old farm boy just out of school in 1924, he 'had to labour under the dark cloud of financial distress which hung over our country during the period of the rebellion'; when the call came, 'opportunity for evangelistic work was hard to find, for you cannot preach in the open air in west Cork, you would be thrown into the river'.[66] The setting of each stage of Kingston's salvation was lovingly depicted: first, an epiphany in the harvest field, followed by frenzied candle-lit reading of mother's 'well-thumbed Bible' in 'a cold, dark room'; then a message from God to his 'chosen vessel' during a service at Drimoleague, culminating in surrender at Meenie Bridge when excitement forced him off his bicycle to 'kneel down on the road'.[67] Equally crucial was a special mission in his 'parents' cottage', with its 'five small bedrooms', conducted by the superintendent minister at Skibbereen and members of Christian Endeavour:

The atmosphere was electric; strong Irishmen were in tears. They did not move, they were transfixed. A Roman Catholic came in and was converted ... I had the joy of pointing two of my sisters to Christ during that mission.[68]

Kingston's accounts of his upbringing clearly attest that revolution, civil war, and sectarian tension had failed to extinguish Methodist enthusiasm in west Cork.

V

The first Methodist victim of lethal violence in west Cork was Thomas Bradfield of Knockmacool in the parish of Desertserges, six miles west of Bandon.[69] He was abducted and shot on 1 February 1921, his body being

---

[66] Kingston, *Reminiscences*, 10; *These Miracles*, 35.   [67] Kingston, *These Miracles*, 33, 39.

[68] Kingston, *These Miracles*, 27, 35.

[69] In the absence of any consolidated list of injuries to property and the person classified by religion, it is likely that some victims have been omitted. In identifying Methodist victims, I was greatly assisted by published and on-line studies of west Cork, especially those by Jasper Ungoed-Thomas, Gerard Murphy, and Barry Keane as well as Peter Hart, and by a list of Protestant fatalities in Cork up to 1921 compiled for *The Dead of the Irish Revolution*, ed. Eunan O'Halpin and Daithí Ó Corráin (New Haven, Yale University Press, forthcoming) and kindly made available by Eunan O'Halpin. All of these names were checked against Methodist circuit and census records, indicating that several victims identified as Methodists by Murphy were Episcopalians. These victims, along with the 'displaced families' identified from Methodist circuit records for west Cork, were checked against the index of claimants to the IGC, and genealogical background sought through various websites for family history. In the course of research, especially in newspapers, a few additional victims were revealed and likewise contextualised.

recovered next day, three miles from his home, bearing bullet wounds and a label marked 'Convicted Spy'.[70] Bradfield, a farmer of 67 acres aged 55, lived in a 'first-class' house with 11 rooms and 14 out-offices in 1911. He had left Kinsale for Desertserges by 1905, shortly after his second marriage to Lizzie Good of nearby Barryshall. Bradfield's only child (by his first wife) married another Cork Methodist only a few weeks before his murder.[71] Like many west Cork victims of terror, Bradfield had a Catholic servant; his father had spoken Irish.[72] Lizzie's parents were also Irish speakers with Catholic servants, but the entire Good family was Episcopalian in 1901. The close link between the two churches is borne out by the fact that Thomas was buried and his daughter married in the Church of Ireland. Though the three Bradfields were regularly returned as members of the Ballineen class of Clonakilty Methodists, they do not appear as lay officers in circuit records. At their quarterly meeting in March 1921, the class leaders decided to send Mrs Bradfield a letter of sympathy, but no reference was made to the circumstances of her husband's death.

Those circumstances were recalled in chirpy detail by James (Spud) Murphy, a section leader in Tom Barry's 'flying column' who had visited Bradfield's house with Barry and Dan Corcoran. Bradfield was in the fields, but returned when told by his maid that 'the officer wanted him':

We were all wearing Sam Browne belts outside our trench coats and Bradfield assumed that we were members of the British forces. When Bradfield came in he welcomed us and invited us into the sitting-room where he gave us some refreshments. He sat down and began to talk to Tom Barry about the activities of the I.R.A. in the area, giving a number of names of prominent officers. At this stage I had taken up position at the front door and Dan Corcoran was likewise at the back door. When Bradfield had given sufficient information, Tom Barry disclosed his identity and Bradfield was certainly shocked. We immediately placed him under arrest and removed him on foot to Ahiohill area. He was tried that night and when we were moving from Ahiohill to Burgatia House on the night of 1st Feb. 1921, Bradfield was executed. His body was labelled as that of a spy and was left on the roadside.[73]

A peculiar aspect of this narrative is its similarity to several accounts of the abduction and murder, ten days earlier, of another Thomas Bradfield, an

[70] SS (25 June 1921).
[71] Elizabeth Mary Susan Bradfield and Joseph Alexander Stoakes, both returned as Methodists in the census of 1911, were nevertheless married on 11 Jan. 1921 in the Desertserges parish church.
[72] Such personal details are normally taken from family schedules of the Census of Ireland (1911 and if necessary 1901): NAD (accessible on-line).
[73] James (Spud) Murphy, WS 1684 (4 Oct. 1957), 12–13; see also Denis Lordan, WS 470 (18 Dec. 1950), 146: Bureau of Military History files (accessible on-line), Military Archives, Dublin.

unmarried farmer aged 65 living in Carhue (Carhoon West), a few miles towards Bandon off the same road. Bradfield of Carhue, an Episcopalian living with his sister and Catholic servant, had likewise been duped by the military paraphernalia of Barry and his men into giving information, and his body too had been dumped outside in the (vain) hope of luring the Crown forces into an ambush as they tried to retrieve it.[74] Odd though it might seem that a second loyalist would have fallen for the same trick, already recounted in the press, contemporary reports confirm the veracity of republican reminiscences.[75] Both were labelled as 'spies' on the ground that they might have become so.[76]

Thomas Bradfield's murder was part of a broader campaign of violence and intimidation that engulfed several of his Protestant neighbours and relatives in spring 1921. A fortnight later, the campaign was refuelled by a reprisal in which two Catholic boys named James and Timothy Coffey of Breaghna, Desertserges, were shot and killed, one body being labelled 'convicted of murder' and the other 'vice Bradfield. Anti-Sinn Fein'. When their father sought compensation in mid April, he gallantly exonerated Bradfield from posthumous blame, declaring that 'Mr. Bradfield was one of the best neighbours witness had'. When Elizabeth advertised the farm for auction of 10 March, the sale was abandoned after posting of a notice warning that 'any person or persons having any dealings or communications with spies or the relatives of spies do so at their own risk'.[77] She had retreated to 'a hiding place', leaving the house 'in the charge of servants, but those servants had been hunted out of the place, and all movable property was then taken away'. In June, Elizabeth and her married daughter were awarded a total of £6,000, though like all pre-Truce awards to civilians, the award remained unpaid until the new Irish and British governments agreed on their respective liabilities for compensation in 1922.[78]

---

[74] Lordan, WS 470, 14; Mrs Anna Hurley-O'Mahony, WS 540 (20 June 1951), 4.

[75] According to *II* (4 Feb. 1921): 'Both were taken from their houses by men who stated they were Crown forces', and both bodies carried notes condemning them for 'communicating information to the enemy'. On 27 Jan. 1921, *IT* had reported that 'John' Bradfield (of Carhue) was visited by six men in 'military uniform' whom he mistook for army officers.

[76] Several historians have recounted the two killings: Peter Hart, *The I.R.A. and its Enemies: Violence and Community in Cork, 1916–1923* (Oxford University Press, 1998), 300, 305; Murphy, *Disappearances*, 73; Thomas Earls FitzGerald, 'The Execution of "Spies and Informers" in West Cork, 1921', in Trinity History Workshop, *Terror in Ireland, 1916–1923*, ed. David Fitzpatrick (Dublin, Lilliput Press, 2012), 181–93 (186).

[77] *II* (13 Apr. 1921).

[78] *SS* (25 June 1921). Following the court award of £4,000 arising from Thomas's death (along with £2,000 for her daughter), which the local authority refused as a matter of principle to pay, liability in the case of Thomas Bradfield, as a 'British supporter', was

The aftermath of the murder is further documented in Elizabeth's claim for post-Truce compensation amounting to £2,109 from the Irish Grants Committee, which eventually awarded her £1,370 in 1929.[79] Having managed to sell some 'removeable [sic] farm effects' in Cork, she had 'come to England, the country then becoming increasingly dangerous to loyalists'. With assistance from her daughter and son-in-law, Joseph Stoakes, she had bought 'High Chimney Farm' near Twyford in Berkshire, but found 'conditions of living very difficult'. During 1922 and 1923 Stoakes had several times visited the farm in the hope of selling it, but found it occupied by 'graziers'. It was finally sold for £800, less than a third of its estimated market value in 1921. The rector of Kilbrogan (Bandon), J. C. Lord,[80] attested that 'he knew Tom Bradfield and had a great regard for him', attributing the murder entirely to his 'extreme loyalty'. Though writing in 1929, Lord's tone was understandably bitter:

His farm was taken by the I.R.A. and let by them for grazing & the meadows were sold and no one allowed into the place unless by their orders – the residence & out offices were absolutely gutted. Nothing moveable was left on the place – It was a regular no mans land [sic] except I.R.A. for years – Mr Bradfield was trapped by I.R.A. dressed as the military to speak his mind about the condition of the country and then murdered.[81]

According to Cornelius Crowley of Knockmacool, a Catholic teacher who had rented a house from Bradfield, the farm was not seized until almost a year after the murder: 'In the month of December 1921 the I.R.A. stated that they had confiscated the farm of the late Mr Thomas Bradfield and in pursuance of such confiscation they announced by public poster the letting of the grazing & tillage of the lands.' The teacher was among those who benefited from the farm's division, redirecting his rent for the house and an additional garden in June 1922 to 'D. O'Donovan Officer of Confiscated Farms 3rd Cork Brigade'. Crowley claimed that he was acting in good faith, under the impression that O'Donovan was exercising 'proper authority'.[82] When Crowley submitted a disingenuous

accepted by the British government and the award paid by instalments during 1922: Return of private persons injured, etc., 1919–22, in NAL, CO 905/15 (copy kindly supplied by Jane Leonard).

[79] Elizabeth Bradfield had previously sought £2,453, arising from post-Truce injuries to property, of which £1,060 was eventually awarded by the Free State authorities. See application by Elizabeth Bradfield to IGC: NAL, CO 762/152/3.

[80] Like several Methodist claimants, Elizabeth Bradfield sought support from the Episcopalian rather than the Methodist minister, partly because most Methodist ministers of the revolutionary period had long since left Cork when loyalists were finally enabled to secure adequate compensation for their post-Truce losses.

[81] Application, Sept. 1927: CO 762/152/3.

[82] James H. Powell (solicitor, Dunmanway) to ministry of Home Affairs, 26 May 1923: NAD, H 5/800. Crowley sought repayment of a fine of £5 allegedly imposed by an army

compensation claim to the Ministry for Home Affairs, the Civic Guard reported that O'Donovan had since been 'killed while engaged in the destruction of a bridge in this area, to impede the advance of the National Army', and that Crowley himself 'was by no means bona fide'.[83] The fact that it eventually proved possible to remove the graziers and enable Bradfield's farm to be sold reflects the political alignment of those who had seized and occupied it. As indicated by the experience of another Methodist victim (William Bryan, below), the new government was more reluctant to interfere with confiscations carried out by its own supporters. Despite the family's gruesome experiences, Elizabeth Bradfield eventually returned to the county, dying in Bandon in 1954.[84]

Several relatives and neighbours of the Bradfields were also punished. These included a 'stone blind' Methodist farmer, 50-year-old Joseph Hosford of Gaggin, a couple of miles east of Knockmacool. He attested to the IGC that he was 'known to the I.R.A. as a supporter of the British Government being always a loyalist and a protestant and suspected of "spying" by reason of his intimate friendship with his neighbour Bradfield shot as a spy'.[85] Blindness must have somewhat diminished his potential value as a spy. Having been at Bradfield's house when he was abducted, Hosford received a letter 'purporting to come from the I.R.A. ordering him to leave the country within 10 days or he would be shot, that no one of his class was to interfere and that nothing was to be removed off the farm or out of the house'. He 'at once cleared out' with his wife to Laxey in the Isle of Man, returning after eight months to find his home had been appropriated as 'dancing rooms' for exclusive use by the IRA, which had rifled the house and broken the furnishings. The Hosfords returned to the Isle of Man 'in April 1922 when the shooting of adherents of the British Government broke out again with more intensity', but resumed life in Gaggin four months later, when 'things quietened down somewhat through the coming of the National Army'. Hosford's post-Truce losses were modest, £183 being claimed for damage to items such as a mahogany

officer who had confiscated his pony 'while still grazing on this field' on 24 May 1923, presumably in the course of repossession of the farm immediately after the cessation of hostilities.

[83] E. O Dubtaig (superintendent, Bandon) to chief commissioner, Civic Guard, 21 June 1923: H 5/800.

[84] Letter from Donald Wood, 6 Oct. 2013, citing report of her will in SS (15 May 1954). I am grateful to Mr Wood for his detailed comments on the first published version of this chapter, which led me to drop a misinformed reference to family connections of Rebecca Chinnery (cf. below, p. 229).

[85] Though Hosford's farm was closer to Carhue than to Knockmacool, a Bandon solicitor informed the IGC that the Coffeys of Desertserges were rumoured to have been killed in reprisal for that of the Hosfords' 'great friend Bradfield' (implying Bradfield of Knockmacool). See John H. Deane to secretary, IGC, 7 Apr. 1927: CO 762/106/4.

table, ten pictures, a candlestick, a gramophone, and thirty records (the final award was £15). Yet the blind farmer had been understandably terrified by the fate of his 'great friend Bradfield' and other neighbours, not daring to seek redress from the courts of the new Irish state.[86]

At 2 a.m. on 7 February 1921, armed men had visited another house at Gaggin, demanding that Gilbert Fenton and his son Frederick 'open up for the military', which Frederick refused to do: 'His father went to the window and cried out "murder." He was fired at and shot through the lung.' Frederick had barricaded the door and rushed at the raiders with a hatchet as they tried to enter through a window. Though Frederick was shot in the groin, he and his father survived the attack, sharing a judicial award for personal injuries of £5,500 in June 1921. In 1911, Gilbert Fenton was returned as an insurance inspector aged 67, a native of Leitrim then resident in Blackrock near Cork City with his wife Emily, son Frederick William (a 44-year-old unmarried insurance agent born in Galway), and two daughters. All were Methodists, though only Emily has been traced in church records (for the Bandon circuit).[87] After the raid, Frederick Fenton 'had to fly to England, and the place at Gaggin was closed down. They were raided on previous occasions too.'[88] When the award was eventually paid to the Fentons, only half of the liability was accepted by the British government, suggesting that the Fentons had not actively collaborated with the Crown forces.[89]

John Good, Elizabeth Bradfield's elder brother, was mortally wounded at the door of his house at Barryshall, Timoleague, on 10 March 1921. This attack was followed on 29 March by the kidnap and murder of his son William, an ex-officer studying engineering at Trinity College, Dublin, who had rashly returned to Bandon after his father's killing.[90] Though John and William Good had not followed Elizabeth's example by entering the Methodist Church, their fate undoubtedly alarmed Protestants of both denominations in a county where there was no sharp division between Methodists and Episcopalians. Elsewhere in the county, the Methodist community had been shaken by the killings of Alfred Charles Reilly in Cork City on 10 February 1921 and John Cathcart in Youghal on

---

[86] Application of Joseph Hosford: CO 762/106/4. Joseph and Barbara Hosford remained on the Bandon class roll in 1928.

[87] Emily Fenton of Gaggin was admitted to the Bandon class in 1914 and died in the last quarter of 1920.

[88] SS (25 June 1921); II (8 Feb.); Murphy, Disappearances, 236 (wrongly referring to Gilbert's 'assassination').

[89] Return in CO 905/15. The same 50/50 division was applied to Elizabeth Good's award of £7,000 for the loss of her husband William.

[90] II (13 Apr. 1921); SS (25 June); IGC, John and William Good: CO 762/152/1.

25 March. Various explanations have been proposed for the murder of Reilly, a 58-year-old confectionery manager, magistrate, and prominent Methodist layman, though the *Christian Advocate* stated enigmatically that 'the motive of the appalling crime is still shrouded in impenetrable mystery'.[91] Cathcart, the 52-year-old manager of a Youghal provision business, was shot at his home after refusing a demand for arms. His body was found in the bathroom by his 14-year-old daughter, with an envelope inscribed 'Convicted spy. Spies and informers beware. – I.R.A.'[92] Catholic clergy and townspeople attended both funerals and were prominent in deploring both killings. All told, Methodists accounted for three of the 22 Protestant civilians known to have died in Cork, as a result of political violence, by July 1921.[93]

Other Methodists experienced violence or intimidation but survived to tell the tale, notably when applying for compensation through the IGC. William Kingston, a 43-year-old farmer at Roughgrove, Bandon,[94] who considered himself 'a Protestant and a Loyalist', initially defied threats directed against him:

From the end of 1920 I was the victim of a succession of outrages to my person and property by the I.R.A. On 31st January 1921 I was shot at and ordered to leave the country. This was on the night of the murder of Thomas Bradfield, a neighbour of mine.[95] I refused.

Three weeks later, Kingston was slightly wounded under the eyebrow during a fusillade of a dozen shots, before 'being captured, taken before an army of about 300, beaten by six men and kicked 4 teeth knocked out'. His 20-year-old son John was also beaten and 'never recovered from the shock'. On 4 March, Kingston was given notice of three weeks to leave the country, leading to a 'hasty clearance sale' entailing a loss of £600 by comparison with the alleged market value of the farm. On 23 March 1921, he left for England with his horses, cattle, wife, and thirteen children, eventually settling on a farm near Ashford in Kent. Since his 'injuries' antedated the Truce, Kingston's claim for £2,631 was dismissed, his sole redress being an award of £25 from the Compensation (Ireland)

[91] *CA* (18 Feb. 1921); Murphy, *Disappearances*, 95–6, 116–18; Hart, *The I.R.A. and its Enemies*, 299.
[92] *CC* (29 Mar. 1921); *II* (28, 30 Mar.); Murphy, *Disappearances*, 234.
[93] The remaining 'Protestants', when matched against census returns, were Episcopalians in 1911. I am grateful to my colleague Eunan O'Halpin for extracting relevant entries from the database underpinning *The Dead* (see n. 69).
[94] Though returned as 33 in his census schedule (1911), the same William Kingston gave his age as 65 when applying to the IGC on 31 Jan. 1927: CO 762/147/4.
[95] Despite the slight error of dating, his neighbour was presumably Bradfield of Knockmacool.

Commission for the shooting of a pony.[96] The Kingstons of Roughgrove, members of the Bandon circuit, were by far the largest Methodist family group uprooted from west Cork during the revolutionary triennium.

William Bernard Roycroft, a 53-year-old Methodist auctioneer and motor and cycle factor in Main Street, Bantry, also left west Cork with his wife and four children in spring 1921. In his hopelessly confused application to the IGC, he reported local boycotts of his businesses, commandeering of goods, confiscation of cash, and '4 motor cars ruined'. Though estimating his losses at £3,000, he applied for only £100 to cover pressing debts arising from his new auctioneering business in Swansea, being awarded nothing as his injuries antedated the Truce. He had 'never received a Brass farthing' from other sources: 'Through Sheer Terror I didn't apply to the Courts, and hoped that the Justice of my case would somehow be recognised and met.' The proof of his allegiance was that he and his two sons had refused to seek a licence from the IRA, instead securing permits from the police and providing their cars for use by the police, 'Auxaliries', and the military. After two ponderously worded warnings from the local battalion commandant, he had closed his business at the beginning of March, disposed of his lease interest and household effects for £500, and settled in Swansea. His application included transcripts of IRA orders warning him not to remove parts from his cars at night, as they must be available for republican use, and promising the 'FULL PENALTY' if he provided petrol or vehicles for 'Enemy forces' after 1 February 1921. Writing from Swansea six years later, he still used his Bantry letterhead decorated with a sturdy bicycle.[97]

Another unsuccessful Methodist claimant was John Willis, a 65-year-old magistrate and farmer from Ballinphelic, eight miles south-west of Cork. Though Willis was reared on a farm near Schull in west Cork and some of his neighbours belonged to the Kinsale circuit, he subscribed to the Cork City circuit.[98] When his life was threatened by five armed men on 31 March 1921, Willis was allowed 24 hours 'to clear out of the country and warned ... never to again return', having supplied a 'substantial sum

---

[96] On 10 Oct. 1922, Kingston had sought compensation of £2,000 through the Provisional Government, attesting that on 23 Mar. *1922* 'I was expelled from my residence at Roughgrove West, Bandon, Co. Cork in Ireland and compelled to leave my Country by Forces of the enemy acting in opposition to the Provisional Government of Ireland': NAD, FIN 1/1076. His application to the IGC made no reference to a second expulsion on the anniversary of the first.
[97] Application and associated papers: CO 762/69/2.
[98] Obituary, *ICA* (2 July 1937): copy kindly supplied by Robin Roddie. His married daughters, Mrs Mary Bateman of Ballinphelic and Mrs Martha Jane Nicholson of Hoddersfield House, Clonakilty, both became stalwarts of the Wesley chapel and regularly hosted 'cottage services' in their houses.

of money' in return for his life. He had left his property, worth over £10,000, in the hands of his recently acquired second wife and a married daughter,[99] borrowing £1,500 from his daughter to enable him to buy a small farmhouse and eleven acres (along with a few cattle and furniture) at Swanmore, Hampshire. Willis found it 'almost impossible for me to define actual and consequential loss', rashly leaving this 'to the judgment of the Committee' and seeking no compensation from other agencies. Despite many aggrieved letters and support from a unionist MP, he duly received nothing, his claim being for injuries prior to the Truce.[100]

Willis attributed his troubles to his 'loyalty to the crown': 'I was the only farmer in the locality who continued to give supplies to the Royal Irish Constabulary. Three of these men were shot by the rebels while taking supplies from my farm. I informed the military of all I knew which was going on by the rebels in the locality.' He alone among eight local magistrates had helped a local solicitor to prepare criminal injury claims. Having refused to resign the magistracy when called upon to do so by the IRA and the Dáil, he believed himself 'entitled to protection which I did not receive, having placed my reliance on a government which failed me'. Willis had been an executive member of the Irish Unionist Alliance and a 'regular attender' at its meetings, being one of the few southerners to address a Methodist demonstration against Home Rule in Belfast on 15 March 1912. He offered several proofs of discrimination against Protestants in Cork, including his own attempt in 1895 to acquire an evicted farm bordering his newly acquired home near Cork City. He had withdrawn after being 'threatened with all sorts of pains and penalties if he took the farm', only to be told a week later that a Catholic had secured possession without application of a boycott because 'the priest gave him liberty to take the farm'.[101] Willis also made an interesting declaration of national identity, stating that 'he had no patience with a Methodist minister who was a Home Ruler. He (the speaker) was an Englishman living in Ireland. The Israelites were 400 years in Egypt, and they were not Egyptians afterwards.'[102]

Yet his family had to some extent gone 'native': their census return for 1901 reveals that Willis and both of his parents were natives of Cork who spoke Irish as well as English. By 1911, Willis no longer admitted to

---

[99] Following the death of his first wife (Martha Frances Moore) in Nov. 1919, Willis had married Sarah Maria Kingston at the Union Hall Methodist church in Sept. 1920: information kindly supplied by Robin Roddie. The younger daughter of his first marriage, Mrs Mary Bateman, remained in Ballinphelic.

[100] John Willis: CO 762/9/8.   [101] *BNL* (15 Mar. 1918).

[102] *UG* (23 Mar. 1912), paraphrased in Jasper Ungoed-Thomas, *Jasper Wolfe of Skibbereen* (Cork, Collins Press, 2008), 72.

speaking Irish, but one of his three servants in 1911 was Catholic.[103] His loyalism was all the more noteworthy because of his deep roots in the county. After the death of his second wife in February 1937, Willis returned to Cork to spend the last few months of his life with his elder daughter and her family near Crosshaven.[104] He was judiciously remembered as 'a man of deep convictions and if to some he appeared narrow and intolerant, it was because of his unshaken beliefs in certain Christian truths he had put into use in his own life'.[105]

VI

In addition to those subjected to physical attacks, several Methodist farmers sought redress for property losses attributable to their political or religious allegiances. It is noteworthy that almost half of those claiming compensation from the IGC, when invited to prove that their losses were attributable to 'your allegiance to the Government of the United Kingdom', used the term 'Protestant' as well as 'loyalist' in explaining the attacks. Only one declared that he had been a 'unionist', and none invoked Methodism as a source of hostility.[106] A rare claimant who used neither 'Protestant' nor 'loyalist' when proving his allegiance was another Joseph Hosford, a 66-year-old farmer at Shanaway East, who belonged to the Ballineen class of the Clonakilty Methodist circuit. He and his son Joseph had acted successively as the Ballineen society stewards from 1895 to 1921.[107] Having put up his farm for sale in March 1921 at a reserve price of £4,000, he was confronted by a notice 'posted on the local

---

[103] Murphy, *Disappearances*, 212, describes Willis as 'an Englishman' and a 'devious individual', charges that are respectively inaccurate and unfair for a man who refused to make a specific monetary claim and made no secret of his loyal views.

[104] Willis's daughter Martha Jane had married Ben Nicholson of Hoddersfield House, also a Methodist, in 1912: information kindly supplied by Robin Roddie.

[105] *ICA* (2 July 1937), quoting eulogy by superintendent minister, Cork district.

[106] Of 13 applications from west Cork relating to known Methodists, 6 (by Elizabeth Bradfield, William Bryan, William Hosford Bryan, Clarina Buttimer, Joseph Hosford of Bandon, and William Kingston) used the terms 'Protestant' and 'Loyalist' (or 'loyal'). William Jagoe and William Roycroft referred only to their loyalism; John Chinnery's Episcopalian mother misidentified him as a member of the Church of Ireland (and a 'supporter of the Government'); John Willis referred only to his former office in the Irish Unionist Alliance; Jasper Travers Wolfe attributed the attacks solely to his having been a 'servant of the British Government'; Wesley Bateman cited his opposition to Sinn Féin and the Irish Republic in the Clonakilty urban district council; and Joseph Hosford of Clonakilty circuit mentioned only his having entertained soldiers. The question (no. 5 on the application form) made no reference to religion.

[107] Thomas J. Bennett, 'Records of the Clonakilty Circuit, Collected between the Years 1938–1945' (typed transcription, with additions, kindly made available by Robin Roddie), 39.

R.C. Chapel by the I.R.A. prohibiting the sale of farms in that district hence our sale was abortive'.[108] A few days later, the fair-minded IRA withdrew its objection, since Hosford's advertisement had been published before the notice. He then received an attractive offer from Cornelius O'Mahony, a Catholic, Irish-speaking farmer from the Macroom district.[109] As the purchaser approached Ballineen to inspect the farm a few months later, he was threatened by an armed gang 'telling him that Mr. Hosford's son was a marked man', inducing him to withdraw from the sale.[110] An auction was announced for February 1922, and the farm and stock sold to a private buyer at a loss of £2,000, subject to payment of 10% (reduced after negotiation to £50) for a 'permit' demanded by an IRA officer who visited Hosford's home. Though the auctioneer confirmed that his claim for £2,050 was genuine, Hosford was awarded only £1,000 after a lengthy correspondence necessitated by his comical reluctance to divulge essential details such as his address.[111]

Hosford maintained that he had been forced to sell 'our property at a great loss as our life was unbearable and very unsafe', the family being 'threatened to be burned out one night' after 'entertaining parties of British soldiers'. His anxiety was deepened by attacks on neighbours and kin:

All during the year 1921 and untill [sic] we left in 1922 life in West Cork was considered to be of little value. My nephew a loyalist was one day brought quite close to our place and shot dead without any apparent reason.[112] Another friend was shot in his own house in the village within a mile of us [Ballineen].[113] Those events together with daily and nightly visits from the rebels for food money and beds produced in my family such a state of nerves and dread that when we heard our dogs bark at night there was no more sleep that night and expecting any minute the worst to happen. Such events made us descide [sic] that life was not worth living ... [After the collapse of the first sale] the political atmosphere and local murder list grew steadily worse. My son's life was threatened so I attempted again to sell my farm.[114]

---

[108] Application of Joseph Hosford, 20 Oct. 1926, and supporting documents: CO 762/7/12.
[109] O'Mahony offered £4,750 for the farm and £1,900 for stock and implements; his home farm was at Toames West, Macroom: Census of Ireland (1911), family schedule.
[110] Daniel T. Lordan (auctioneer, Ballineen) to IGC, 11 Nov. 1926: CO 762/7/12. According to Hosford himself, O'Mahony withdrew following receipt of 'an intimiading [sic] letter': Hosford to secretary, IGC, 25 Oct. 1926.
[111] Application of Joseph Hosford, 20 Oct. 1926, and supporting documents: CO 762/7/12.
[112] The unidentified nephew was presumably the son of a sister of Louisa Hosford. The index to civil marriages indicates that Joseph Hosford and Louisa Busteed were married in the second quarter of 1884, their first child being born about two years later.
[113] This was probably Alfred James Cotter, a 34-year-old baker in Ballineen shot on 25 Feb. 1921.
[114] Hosford to IGC, 25 Oct. [1926]: CO 762/7/12.

Hosford was right to be nervous. In February 1922, his son Joseph was one of only three West Cork Methodists to be returned by intelligence officers of the 1st Southern Division as 'guilty of offenses [*sic*] against the Nation and the Army during hostilities and to date', or else 'suspected of having assisted the enemy during the same period'.[115] Affectionately describing Joseph the younger as a 'stout easy-going' farmer, the Ballineen battalion's intelligence officer reported that 'he seems uneasy in himself & Frightened since Coffey Bros were shot. His father sold large farm his son is likely to leave any day for Canada.' The only evidence of his disloyalty to the Nation was that he was 'friendly' with two local farmers, John Jennings and George Stanley, who were accused of involvement in the killing of George and Thomas Coffey in reprisal for that of Thomas Bradfield of Knockmacool.[116] Methodist circuit records indicate that Joseph and Louisa Hosford, with their children Joseph and Josephine, left Clonakilty circuit in the second quarter of 1922. Hosford eventually 'purchased a small farm of thirty four acres near Exeter and by economy can make ends meet'.[117]

William Hosford Bryan (1865–1940), whose farm at Maryville, Enniskeane, was only a mile or so from Joseph Hosford's, weathered a similar campaign without abandoning west Cork. In November 1921, 'two fat bullocks, ready for butcher, were taken by the I.R.A.' from his home farm. Over a year later, on the day that the Irish Free State was inaugurated, 'four springing heifers, which had been specially bred for milk', were taken from his outside farm on the eve of the Bandon fair 'with the object of disposing of them there'. When Bryan tried in the same month to sell the outside farm, an agreed sale fell through when 'the sale was objected to by members of the I.R.A.', and the farm remained unsold when Bryan approached the IGC in 1926. He ascribed these punishments to the fact that 'as a loyalist & protestant [he] would not pay money for support of the I.R.A.' in its quest for arms, despite several demands and the production of revolvers.[118] When supporting Bryan's application, the rector of Kilbrogan remarked that 'there are very few farmers of his class who escaped loss & great discomfort'.[119] The IGC was unconvinced by his claim for £750, qualified by Bryan's candid admission in 1926 that he was in a 'fairly good financial position', and he was awarded only £100 for

[115] Order quoted in Hart, *The I.R.A. and its Enemies*, 297.
[116] 1st Southern Division, reports by intelligence officers, *c*. Feb. 1922: Military Archives, Dublin, A/0897. This revealing file was recently restored to public access after a prolonged disappearance.
[117] Application, 20 Oct. 1926: CO 762/7/12.
[118] Application of William Hosford Bryan, 22 Nov. 1926: CO 762/45/8.
[119] Revd J. C. Lord to IGC, 10 Jan. 1927: CO 762/45/8.

the stolen cattle. No reference to the family's subsequent emigration has been found in the circuit books, and both Bryan and his wife Fanny died in Ireland.[120] William became the Rushfield poor steward in 1917, a trustee of the Ballineen church in May 1921, and the circuit's junior steward in 1925. His son John Hosford Bryan succeeded Joseph Hosford, Jr, as the Ballineen steward in 1922, becoming a local preacher five years later.[121]

A declaration by the Ballineen auctioneer who had tried to sell Bryan's outside farm in December 1922 suggests that the boycott weapon had not lost its force even at that late stage in the civil war. Having rejected a private bid falling £200 below the reserve of £1,600, Daniel Lordan visited the farm on the eve of the intended auction:

I attended on the lands to inspect the same to point out the lands to an intending purchaser and was met by people who hunted me off the lands and told [me] they would not allow the lands to be sold, and by their attitude I felt I was lucky in escaping injury. There were notices posted up over the farm, signed by the I.R.A. stating that any person who would bid for the farm would be shot. Afterwards on consulting with Mr Bryan we decided that there was no use in the circumstances in holding the auction on the following day, and it was abandoned. The following Sunday at the Church door and on other occasions at my house and elsewhere I was attacked and threats were made against me for having advertised the farm for Mr Bryan, who was unpopular in the neighbourhood by reason of his being a Loyalist and a Protestant and not in sympathy with the I.R.A. movement.[122]

Though Lordan was a Catholic farmer's son from the locality, he thus implied that antipathy to Bryan's Protestantism was a factor in arousing antagonism towards himself.[123]

VII

The most celebrated Methodist target of intimidation in west Cork was Jasper Travers Wolfe (1872–1952), a prosperous middle-aged lawyer in Skibbereen who acted as Crown solicitor for Cork City and west Cork

---

[120] Bryan, his wife Fanny (née Frances Sweetnam, 1868–1946), and their five children were all returned as Cork-born Methodists living at Teadies Lower, Bandon district, in Census of Ireland (1911), family schedule. A thorough family tree is available on-line through ancestrylibrary.com.

[121] Bennett, 'Clonakilty Circuit', 34, 39, 44, 52.

[122] Daniel Thomas Lordan, statutory declaration in support of Bryan's application, 21 Jan. 1927: CO 762/45/8.

[123] The 1911 family census schedule for Timothy Lordan, a Catholic farmer in Lissarourke, Bengour district (three miles north of Ballineen), includes his son Daniel (19), identified as a future auctioneer in notes on the family by Barbara Bouchey, St Louis, Missouri, 22 Mar. 2011 (ancestrylibrary.com).

throughout the revolutionary period. Though undoubtedly loyal to the Crown, Wolfe was no supporter of the Unionist Party. In December 1912, when addressing a meeting of Protestant nationalists in London, he had offered 'testimony to the tolerant treatment that was meted out to Protestants by their Catholic neighbours. He had personally experienced it on local governing bodies, both rural and urban, both as a private citizen, and in his profession as a solicitor.' Wolfe contemptuously repudiated John Willis's assertion at the Belfast Methodist meeting, nine months earlier, 'that the Protestants in the South and South West were being persecuted by their Catholic neighbours. ("Shame.") That gentleman had been dragged from Cork to Belfast to traduce and malign his fellow-countrymen.'[124]

Wolfe did not live in a Protestant bubble: not only were many of his clients Catholics, but so were three of the five servants who in 1911 maintained his first-class house ('Norton') with its 16 rooms and 12 front windows. His religious observance was as unconventional as his politics. Along with his wife Minnie, a regular singer and organist at Methodist events, he was an active member of the Skibbereen circuit (and its solicitor and poor steward) before, during, and after the troubled times. Yet he became a somewhat less 'strict Methodist' in later years, holding 'all-male, all-night sessions of whiskey-drinking, talking and card-playing'.[125] His cousin Willie Kingston recalled a narrow escape with Wolfe in 1920, when republicans looked into their car before waving it on: 'Jasper was too sleepy with drink to realise what was happening.'[126]

For five years after 1919, Wolfe's notoriety as an unusually zealous Crown solicitor obliged him to leave his family in Norton and reside in his office near the military barracks. In early 1921, he was sentenced to death *in absentia* and compelled to stay out of the country 'for some weeks', whereas two others so sentenced were murdered. He was kidnapped near the Eldon Hotel in Skibbereen on 5 October 1921, but released after three days following the reported intervention of his fellow solicitor Edmund Duggan, the IRA's Chief Truce Liaison Officer.[127] According to

[124] *UG* (14 Dec. 1912), also quoted and fully contextualised in Ungoed-Thomas, *Jasper Wolfe*, 175–6. This lively and well-documented biography is also a valuable guide to the interconnections of west Cork Protestants and their experiences in the revolutionary period.

[125] Ungoed-Thomas, *Jasper Wolfe*, 19, 82.

[126] Willie Kingston, 'From Victorian Boyhood to the Troubles: A Skibbereen Memoir', *Skibbereen and District Historical Society Journal*, ed. Jasper Ungoed-Thomas, i (2005), 4–36 (30).

[127] *CA* (14 Oct. 1921); *CC* (7 Oct.); *IT* (7 Oct.); Murphy, *Disappearances*, 236; Ungoed-Thomas, *Jasper Wolfe*, 166 (referring to 'James' Duggan, presumably in fact Éamonn (Edmund John) Duggan).

the outraged *Cork County Eagle and Munster Advertiser*, reportedly owned by Wolfe in later years,[128] he was 'the most popular man in the town' – 'popular because he never neglected to do a good turn for another when it was in his power [and] because of his association with every movement for improvement of Skibbereen or the advancement of its citizens'.[129]

In his application to the IGC, Wolfe confirmed contemporary reports that his 'loss was entirely caused by his being a servant of the British Government', leading to 'frequent attempts' to force his resignation as Crown solicitor.[130] His abduction allegedly caused 'serious injury to his health', and the IGC was advised in 1926 that 'his health may have been affected though he does not give that appearance'. Wolfe testified that, 'following the massacre of Protestants which occurred towards the end of April 1922', he found it impossible to return from Cork to Skibbereen and had to spend further weeks in England. He was again warned that he would be shot and was then kidnapped for one night on 3 July 1922, just after the outbreak of civil war. Having stayed out of the country until the end of August, he returned to Ireland in a schooner from Cardiff. He retrieved Norton from National army occupation, but it was again commandeered and this time his family was also 'expelled therefrom for over two years'.

Wolfe's rollicking narrative is noteworthy for several reasons. First, his social status and wide clientele protected him from murder despite many threats, accounting for his almost cheeky insouciance and enduring professional success: by 1926, he had 'entirely regained his business'. Second, perhaps helped by his prominence as a pre-war Home Ruler, he was able to adjust to the new order so effectively that he was thrice elected as an independent member of the Dáil, representing West Cork between June 1927 and January 1933. According to a priest who met him in 1916 in connection with his prosecution of Gearóid O'Sullivan:

Wolfe was an exceedingly able lawyer with a very big practice. He was a man with a high sense of duty according to his lights; and hence his zeal as Crown Prosecutor. When the national Government was set up he showed himself equally determined to manifest his loyalty to that Government. Many of the men who were prosecuted by him became friends of his.[131]

Third, despite his legendary geniality and wry amusement at the vagaries of political and legal life, he remained bitter in his condemnation of 'the massacre of Protestants', for several of whom he supplied references to the

---

[128] He was identified as the *CCE*'s owner by Thomas Johnson, leader of the Labour Party: Dáil Éireann, *Debates*, xix, no. 22 (11 May 1927).
[129] *CCE* (8, 15 Oct. 1921).   [130] Jasper Travers Wolfe, CO 762/54/17.
[131] Very Revd Patrick J. Doyle, WS 807 (28 Oct. 1952), 9–10.

IGC. Fourth, for all his resilience and professional acumen, he managed to persuade the IGC that he himself deserved redress, eventually receiving £3,000 towards his claim of £7,670 for injury to his business and loss of income upon the abolition of his public office.

Many of Jasper Wolfe's relatives and associates were also affected by republican hostility. His elder brother Willie Wolfe (1871–1960), a merchant and justice of the peace, had flouted family practice by becoming 'agnostic',[132] marrying a Catholic described by his mother as a 'low wretched barmaid',[133] and representing William O'Brien's All-For-Ireland League on the rural district council. He too received IRA threats when he ignored demands to 'withdraw your allegiance' as a magistrate just before the Truce of July 1921.[134] Willie Wolfe remained in Skibbereen; whereas William John Kingston, Jasper's 37-year-old cousin, 'decided to clear off to Dublin' at the end of April 1922, immediately after the murder of Frank Fitzmaurice, who had recently offered him a half-share in his legal practice in Skibbereen. After a nervous night, lying ready to jump into the water tank and breathe through a copper pipe if disturbed, he caught a train 'packed with Protestants, fleeing like myself to Dublin, and some to England', conscious that they were 'sitting on a volcano about to erupt'. Kingston, who worked in Jasper Wolfe's firm for most of his life, was a perennial migrant and traveller. Following the murder of two local Protestants (William Connell and Matt Sweetnam) in February 1921, Willie Kingston had left for Rhodesia in April 1921, returning a year later before his precipitate departure for Dublin and later Durban. After another two years in South Africa, he returned to Ireland via Australasia and Canada, spent a few months in Skibbereen, left again, and finally settled back into Jasper Wolfe's law practice in 1926. Though a member of the Church, he was almost as unorthodox as Willie Wolfe. He was returned as a 'Protestant no particular denomination' in his mother's census form in 1911; signed the pledge against conscription in 1918; and acted for clients in the republican courts. Though he 'abhorred

---

[132]   The term 'Agnostic' as a religious profession was returned for 159 men (including William Wood) and 44 women in the Census of 1911 (along with 1 male 'Agnostic Christian', 44 male and 13 female 'Atheists'): Census of Ireland, 1911, *General Report*, 38–40 (Table 29), in HCP, 1912–13 [Cd. 6663], cxviii, 1.

[133]   Rachel Wood Wolfe, 'The Diaries: Review of 1911', ed. Jasper Ungoed-Thomas (typescript, 2005: kindly supplied by Robin Roddie), 21. Rachel Wolfe was already worried about the spiritual welfare of her adolescent sons William and Jasper on 13 Apr. 1888 (8): 'Got the tea and went to the Missionary Meeting. I tried hard to get Jasper and Will to come but could not induce them – I felt very sad to see how utterly careless they are about the means of grace or the means of improving themselves in any way. I fear the old sceptical spirit is seizing hold of Will again.'

[134]   Ungoed-Thomas, *Jasper Wolfe*, 78–80, 121–2; Murphy, *Disappearances*, 236.

the brutalities committed by both sides', he was never personally molested. His memoir reveals the fear experienced even by liberal Protestants in revolutionary Cork, and also the reluctance to succumb to fear by abandoning home.[135]

Edwin Angus Swanton, managing director of the *Cork County Eagle* and Jasper Wolfe's close friend, was kidnapped on the eve of the Truce and held for ten weeks.[136] Though the Swantons were Episcopalian, the surname was common among Skibbereen and Bandon Methodists.[137] According to the adjutant of the Skibbereen IRA, he belonged to a nebulous entity termed the 'murder gang':

> Edwin Swanton, a loyalist friend of Jasper Wolfe, always carried a small automatic. He was a draper in Skibbereen and though a civilian was one of the enemy's murder gang. He was kidnapped by three section commanders of the Skibbereen Company though when he saw himself in danger he threw his automatic away into a clump of briars instead of using it but it was got afterwards. He was taken around from house to house in the County area but finally escaped during the Truce period.[138]

His 'liberation' on or before 7 October was linked by the *Eagle* with that of Jasper Wolfe, leaving it unclear whether Swanton had been released or retrospectively pardoned after escaping: 'We are also delighted to learn that Mr. E. Angus Swanton's liberation has been sanctioned by the I.R.A., and that he is free to return to Skibbereen when he pleases.'[139] He had fled to England with Jasper's assistance, but returned to live in Skibbereen despite a damaging boycott of the drapery that he operated with his father.[140]

Another republican target was Jasper's Episcopalian cousin William G. Wood, a Skibbereen auctioneer and clerk of petty sessions who offended the local IRA by selling army surplus goods and felling trees on the Castlefreke estate, which he and Jasper had acquired when the 10th Baron Carbery emigrated to South Africa in 1919. In April 1921, Wood claimed £1,000 damages for criminal injuries, of which £700 was awarded by the county court and belatedly paid over in 1922–3.[141] Like Jasper, he fled to England in late April 1922 after escaping an armed gang through the back door, still in slippers, and he too was soon joined there

---

[135] Kingston, 'From Victorian Boyhood to the Troubles', 30–6; Ungoed-Thomas, *Jasper Wolfe*, 50, 90, 142–3, 129; Murphy, *Disappearances*, 245–6.
[136] Ungoed-Thomas, *Jasper Wolfe*, 116, 122.
[137] Swanton is incorrectly included among Methodist victims listed in Murphy, *Disappearances*, 234; no members of his immediate family appear in the circuit books for Skibbereen.
[138] Stephen O'Brien, WS 603 (30 Oct. 1951), 3.   [139] *CC* (8 Oct. 1921).
[140] Ungoed-Thomas, *Jasper Wolfe*, 122, 160, 164, 245.   [141] Return in CO 905/15.

by his wife before returning to Skibbereen in July 1923.[142] He was among the 'victimised loyalists' who sought extravagant compensation at the height of the civil war, claiming £5,000 through his solicitor, Jasper Wolfe, for expulsion from his home by 'forces of the enemy acting in opposition to the Provisional Government of Ireland', and £350 for a commandeered motor car.[143] As in so many cases of violence against Protestants, the ostensible motives were economic and political rather than religious, though most claimants for compensation cited their religion as well as their assets and loyalty when explaining these attacks. Many of those under threat, like the Wolfes and the Woods, believed that their communal connections were strong enough in normal times to neutralise the menaces posed by greed, partisan politics, and sectarianism. A brief tactical withdrawal was therefore sufficient, just as Belfast Catholics would clear out of the city during the recurrent craziness of the 'marching season'. Latent resentment only exploded into violence intermittently, when passions were inflamed by external events or released by breakdown of civic controls.

Even so, the menace of republican vengeance against Jasper Wolfe and his circle was undeniable. IRA intelligence officers were vitriolic when denouncing them as informers or collaborators in February 1922. William G. Wood, with his grey moustache and 'slight stoop', was 'always very bitter against us. Though never in a way of getting any information, any he had he would willingly hand over.' Despite the absence of any 'evidence of guilt', he was deemed guilty of murder in the 'second degree'. Edwin Swanton was guilty in the 'first degree': 'Never gave up his J.P.ship in spite of several warnings. Is confidently supposed to be the instigator of several autonomous [sic] letters to several of our men here. Was a constant companion of Jasper Wolfe's & as guilty as he was of giving information to the enemy.' Equally guilty was the Catholic solicitor Patrick Sheehy, editor of Swanton's *Eagle* (with his 'turned-up nose', 'foxy beard', and bowler hat), who had been awarded £500 'for the tarring of his whiskers'. Sheehy had conducted a 'newspaper campaign against the movement at instigation of Jasper Wolfe', describing Volunteers as 'murderers' and doing 'an immense amount of damage by enemy propaganda despite several warnings'. The evidence of his guilt was 'the back files of the "Eagle"'.

William Wood Wolfe, a 'second degree' man ('Small. Bald-headed. Grey. Wears glasses') was condemned as 'a brother of Jasper T. Wolfe. He always carried & still carries a loaded revolver. Allowed his wife to

[142] Ungoed-Thomas, *Jasper Wolfe*, 135–44.
[143] Wood and Wolfe to secretary, Provisional Government, 30 Aug. 1922: NAD, FIN 1/1066.

entertain enemy officers in her house. He would be quite capable of imparting any information he had to enemy. There is no evidence to prove that he did.' Worst of all was Jasper himself, with his 'hard sharp features' and 'raspy voice':

Was always both in his official capacity & otherwise a bitter enemy of ours. He prosecuted for the enemy in such cases as the trial of Tadg Barry and others. He acted for the Crown at the inquest on late Lord Mayor MacCurtain. On his own admission he was the chief adviser to both the R.I.C. and military. It is a well known fact that the enemy always consulted him in such matters as arrests and acts of aggression. From his minute knowledge of the locality & population he was in a position to do a great deal of damage to us. He always carried a loaded revolver. Very little evidence is required in this case. His own admissions in public & private all prove his guilt as a prominent spy & informer. I would consider him guilty in the first degree.[144]

Such were the rules of evidence governing republican justice. Its limited effectiveness is displayed by the fact that Jasper and all his associates survived to thrive once more in west Cork.

VIII

When the forces of the Crown and the Republic agreed to a ceasefire in early July 1921, southern Protestants had reason to believe that the worst was over. Lethal violence virtually ceased outside Belfast, 'public opinion' seemed overwhelmingly against the resumption of hostilities, and the stuttering movement towards an Anglo–Irish Treaty raised hopes of civic calm and communal harmony. Even the republican 'split' following the Dáil's closely contested approval of the Treaty failed to shake public optimism. This was fostered by the almost universal support of the Treaty terms by the press, local authorities, and church leaders, and the obvious desire of most republican groups to settle their differences by circumventing emotive elements of the agreement such as the oath of allegiance. Though the collapse of effective administrative, judicial, and military authority encouraged civic disorder and contempt for any legal code, few observers expected local squabbles to consolidate into civil war. West Cork's Protestants were therefore unpleasantly surprised when a second wave of lethal violence erupted in April 1922, barely a year after the grim campaign examined above.

The killing of four Protestants in Dunmanway on the night of 26–27 April initiated the infamous 'Bandon Valley massacre', entailing a dozen Protestant fatalities and several attempted murders by bands of armed

---

[144] Military Archives, Dublin, A/0897.

men who have yet to be firmly identified. The immediate motive for this brief but indiscriminately brutal campaign, which was rapidly denounced by all major republican factions and church spokesmen, remains in dispute. Though several other explanations have been proposed, the massacre was probably, as Hart believed, prompted by the local killing of an anti-Treaty IRA officer.[145] Whatever its genesis, the massacre undoubtedly created a short-lived but intense panic among west Cork Protestants, testing their communal resilience and ability to coexist with their Catholic neighbours. As Lee Cole remarked, 'one of the wildest spots in Ireland in 1922 was West Cork'.[146]

The first Methodist to die was James Buttimer, aged 81, who had retired as a draper just before the Great War and was severely afflicted with rheumatism.[147] According to his widow Clara (Clarina), who was seventeen years younger, they had been awakened by a 'rifle firing in the street' and 'heard loud knocking and banging at the hall door and shouts that if we did not open at once the door would be burst in'. While they were coming down the stairs in night attire, James in his slippers, 'a shot was fired through the key hole sending the key halfway into hall. We were quaking with terror and nearly demented.' As the clock chimed 1.15, Clara opened the door amidst further shouting:

'Come out here, Buttimer.' I said, 'What do you want him for?' as I thought they may want to kidnap him, but they shouted, 'You go to bed, we don't want you' (said same several times). My dear husband was holding my hand at the time, as he was so frightened. He said 'Surely boys, you would not harm an old man like me?' Then by light of the candle behind us I saw several faces turn from each side of the door and aim at him and he fell down by my side and was soon lying in pools of blood. His teeth were scattered all over the place as his jaw was smashed in and he was riddled with bullets.

Feelings of helplessness and isolation overwhelmed her:

I stood at the door and screamed and screamed with all my strength, I was heard up in the town, but no one came to my aid ... I dressed partly and waited till the dawn came and then went round by the back of the house to my next door neighbour, only to find her and her children in the same condition, as her husband

---

[145] Hart, *The I.R.A. and its Enemies*, 273–91 (esp. 278). Others have ascribed the killings to outrage at the concurrent campaign against Catholics in the Belfast region, to revelations allegedly made by an intelligence officer kidnapped and murdered by the IRA, or to a delayed reprisal for the killing in Dec. 1920 of Canon Magner, parish priest of Dunmanway: John M. Regan, 'The "Bandon Valley Massacre" as a Historical Problem', *History*, xcviii (2012), 70–98; William Jagoe, application to IGC, 7 Apr. 1927: CO 762/4/1.

[146] Cole, *Methodism in Ireland*, 112.

[147] Notice of auction on 9–10 July 1914: *SS* (4 July). Buttimer's killing is also documented in Hart, *The I.R.A. and its Enemies*, 273, 284–6.

had been butchered before they came to us.[148] To my dying day the awful scenes will be with me, and I am thinking and dreaming of them for ever ... My husband was one of the quietest and gentlest of men, never harmed [any]one and never meddled in politics.[149]

Though composed like a Gothic horror story and well rehearsed,[150] Clara Buttimer's narrative is an irrefutable testament to the fearful consequences of revolutionary violence for the bereaved as well as the immediate victims.

After the murder of James Buttimer, the family's terror persisted:

I wired my two sons in Dublin who arrived soon after. They too were naturally terrified at the events which had taken place and ran the gravest risk in even attending their father's funeral as we heard privately that they were going to be done for too by the same gang. After darkness had fallen they left the house and remained out for the night, as it was strongly rumoured there would be more shootings. You can imagine the mental agony of these hours while my boys were in danger, and this following the earlier shock. Early in the morning my boys had to go a roundabout way to the train, through fields, etc, to return to Dublin and I did not know but they would be done for before reaching their destination. I remained in D'way [*sic*] until the furniture was removed to Dublin and then came on also.[151]

In seeking compensation of over £6,500 from the IGC (including £5,000 for the loss of her husband, £1,000 for 'shock and terror', and £400 arising from property losses), Clara attested that she had 'had to leave Dunmanway hurriedly and to make a forced sale of her house property, at less than half its value and to remove furniture to Dublin and store it there, and there was also some furniture and clothes destroyed'. The Buttimers had lived comfortably. Among the ruined furnishings were linoleum, carpets, and three pictures.[152] According to the auction notice, their house was 'large, substantially built, and in excellent repair', with 'a nice entrance hall' and four bedrooms 'approached by a nice stairs'. The property included stables for two horses, a coach house, and a quarter-acre garden 'well stocked with fruit and vegetables'. 'Immediate possession' was promised on completion of purchase. Also on sale were five

---

[148] David Gray, an Episcopalian chemist, lived with his wife Alice at 6, Main St, next door to the Buttimers at no. 5: Canon Arthur Wilson, reference for William Jagoe, 16 May 1927: CO 762/4/1.
[149] Clara Buttimer, letter to solicitor, 19 Apr. 1927: CO 762/142/17.
[150] Slightly variant exchanges with the killers ('We want you – We want to talk to you'; 'Go to bed; we don't want you') appear in Clara's evidence at her husband's inquest: *CE, CC* (29 Apr. 1922).
[151] Clara Buttimer, letter to solicitor, 19 Apr. 1927: CO 762/142/17.
[152] Application to IGC, 31 Jan. 1927: CO 762/142/17.

small houses on Castle Street which the Buttimers had rented out at a modest profit.[153]

It is noteworthy that Clara Buttimer, unlike many Protestant victims in west Cork, was able to sell her property (albeit at a loss) by public auction. This suggests that James Buttimer's killers lacked sufficient local support to enforce the usual boycott. Clara Buttimer's departure was not quite so precipitate as her own account indicates. Her property was auctioned on 8 June, and she did not move to Dublin until the last quarter of 1922, residing at 14, Tritonville Road in Sandymount as a member of the St Stephen's Green circuit. Clara's claim for compensation for personal injuries was refused by the 'Irish Free State Authorities', evidently because her husband no longer earned income, but the IGC eventually awarded almost half of her claim (£2,800) in recognition of the 'astonishing brutality' exhibited by the murderers of James Buttimer.

In affirming the Buttimers' allegiance, Clara declared that three of her four sons had served in the British army and 'were known to have been absolutely loyal to the British Crown. Also I and my family are of the Protestant religion.' Her four sons had all left Dunmanway for Dublin or Skibbereen between 1910 and 1918, James Clarence being the first to leave home aged 17. He was killed in action at Mons on the very eve of the Armistice.[154] The entire family were active Methodists in Dunmanway from 1900 onwards. Clara was a prayer leader of long standing. Her third son Willie, before his departure for Dublin in early 1918, acted as secretary to the quarterly circuit meeting. James himself, a native of Kilmore, Co. Cork, had seen the Methodist light while an apprentice in Bandon, and 'became at once an active Christian worker, conducting cottage prayer meetings in his father's home'. After 'some years' in Australia he had settled in Dunmanway: 'For 50 years he was a loyal and devoted Methodist, and a generous supporter of our church in Dunmanway.'[155]

Reports of his killing in the Dublin nationalist press approvingly identified Buttimer as a Home Ruler: 'In the Land League days he took an active part in local affairs, and always voted as a Nationalist in

---

[153] SS (2 May 1922). According to documents presented to the IGC, the Buttimers' home was worth £680 but sold for £330, and the five rented houses were worth £100 but sold for £50: CO 762/142/17.

[154] Commonwealth War Graves Commission, on-line record for Private J. C. Buttimer, 19th Battalion, Canadian Infantry, died 10 Nov. 1918, buried in communal cemetery at Mons (Bergen); Dunmanway circuit, Schedule Books; 'silent vote of sympathy' with the Buttimers: Minutes of Quarterly Leaders' Meetings, 1900–31 (5 Dec. 1918); Henderson, Dunmanway Methodist Church, 16–17.

[155] CA (2 June 1922).

Parliamentary and other elections.'[156] It is possible that these surprising claims arose from confusion with John Buttimer, a Catholic farmer re-elected to the Dunmanway rural district council in 1918, who had shown mildly ecumenical tendencies during the Home Rule crisis in 1912.[157] James Buttimer was buried in the Methodist graveyard (having been refused a plot in the parish church) in the presence of a 'large gathering of relatives and friends'. The circuit books recorded his death with a unique annotation: 'Shot by I.R.A.'[158]

Next door to the Buttimers in Sackville Street lived William Jagoe, a 45-year-old Methodist draper, with his wife Lizzie (Elizabeth Margaret) and several teenage children.[159] In August 1921, Jagoe had been warned by Denis Barry, a Catholic tailor claiming to be an IRA intelligence officer, that his name was among seven listed for execution in Dunmanway. He had disregarded the hint since Barry was 'under the influence of drink'.[160] The fullest account of Jagoe's victimisation and narrow escape on 27 April 1922 was given by the Methodist minister in Dunmanway, Alfred Harbinson, who knew the family 'very intimately':

Mr. Jagoe was a staunch loyal subject of King George … His business was boycotted & he himself persecuted because he refused to subscribe to the funds of the Republican party. On one occasion a notice was nailed to the door of his business premises denouncing him as a spy & an informer and more than once threats were made against his life. From my residence which was opposite his private residence I was eye witness of a desperate attempt upon his life in April 1922. During the night an attack was made on five loyalist families one of which was the Jagoe family. The heads of three of these families were murdered. Believing that Mr. Jagoe was behind & about to open his front door, a volley was fired through it destroying the furniture & tearing the walls, floor and ceiling. By the Providence of God, he escaped through his back garden but had to spend the remainder of the night clad only in his pyjamas, in the church-yard. Two days later he escaped from town and country and has since resided in England.

---

[156] *FJ* (28 Apr. 1922). According to that day's *II*, 'he was understood to have voted in the Nationalist interest at the recent elections'. These reports were accepted by Hart, *The I.R.A. and its Enemies*, 286, echoed in subsequent studies.

[157] *SS* (6 June 1918, 2 Nov. 1912; Census of Ireland (1911), family schedule for John Buttimer of Ahakeera, Aultagh DED.

[158] *CA* (2 June 1922); Dunmanway Circuit, Minutes of Quarterly Leaders' Meetings, 1900–31 (3 Oct. 1919); Schedule Book (27 Apr. 1922).

[159] For the Jagoe case, see Hart, *The I.R.A. and its Enemies*, 273–4, 286.

[160] Those named included Patrick Joseph Cronin, a former sailor accused of helping the police, who was indeed shot in August 1921 immediately after Barry's warning to Jagoe: William Jagoe, application to IGC, 7 Apr. 1927: CO 762/4/1; Niall Meehan, 'Distorting Irish History, 2: The Road from Dunmanway: Peter Hart's Treatment of the 1922 "April Killings" in West Cork' (spinwatch website, 24 May 2011), 18.

Jagoe had been the 'proprietor of the most flourishing & up to date drapery establishment in Dunmanway', with at least four assistants and a 'very comfortable income'. But 'after his flight the business had to be wound up at considerable loss', following several attacks in which goods in transit to the shop were 'looted or destroyed', and one in which his wife was 'held up by armed men in his shop while goods were taken'.[161] The unusually generous terms of Jagoe's summer sale in 1922 suggest that closure was imminent, though not yet publicly declared.[162]

Harbinson's account was corroborated by his Episcopalian counterpart, whose rectory was two doors' distant from Jagoe's home:

They called on him to come out & fired several shots through the Hall door (the bullet marks can be seen still). Mrs Jagoe appeared at the window & told the men that he (Mr Jagoe) "could not go now" & they probably thought that the bullets had hit & killed him & went on to Mr. Gray's house.[163]

Jagoe's application to the IGC stated that 'the real reason for the attempted murder was because he had always been an outspoken loyal supporter of the Crown'. As such, he had organised 'a Boy Scout troop, which excited the wrath of the local Sinn Feiners'; found a notice on his house reading 'Spies Beware'; entertained military men stationed in the town; accepted a police request 'to convey the news of the attack [on the Dunmanway barracks] when it took place to the nearest Station'; and received a visit from an Auxiliary intelligence officer 'asking for information'. He believed that 'all this was reported to the Republican Headquarters by spies in applicant's employ'.[164] He offered further proof of his loyalty when rather cheekily writing to the prime minister, Stanley Baldwin: 'On one occasion I was a party to the conveying of certain information to the military. Within half an hour the rebels had heard, through the military, of the information having been given!' A 'leading solicitor who was with me, concerned in the information referred to', was murdered on the same night as James Buttimer.[165] It is noteworthy that Jagoe, unlike the unfortunate Frank Fitzmaurice, was not denounced as an informer or collaborator when the IRA's 1st Southern division prepared its hit-list (based almost

---

[161] Alfred Harbinson to IGC, 25 June 1928: CO 762/4/1. Goods worth £25 (out of £70 demanded) were taken from his wife at gunpoint in July 1922: application, 7 Apr. 1927.

[162] SS (26 Aug. 1922) (cf. sale advertisements in SS (3 Sept. 1921, 18 Mar. 1922)).

[163] Canon Arthur Wilson to IGC, 16 May 1927: CO 762/4/1.

[164] Application, 7 Apr. 1927: CO 762/4/1. Jagoe's family census schedule for 1911 lists two resident employees, both Methodist girls from Tyrone.

[165] Jagoe to Stanley Baldwin, 31 Jan. 1929: CO 762/4/1. His fellow-informer was Frank Fitzmaurice, a 72-year-old Episcopalian solicitor and land agent who lived 200 yards away in Chapel St: Census of Ireland (1911), family schedule.

entirely on hearsay and innuendo) in February 1922.[166] Nobody else killed
in the 'Bandon Valley massacre' appeared on that list, confirming Hart's
argument that vengeance against alleged informers was not the inspiration
for that campaign.

Despite claims to the contrary, Jagoe's loyal credentials were impec-
cable. On 6 June, six weeks after his escape, Jagoe wrote to the nationalist
Southern Star to refute 'various "reasons" that have been put forward in
explaining the attempt on my life', such as membership of the Freemasons
and contributions to funds for 'Orange propaganda'. In denying both
claims, Jagoe added that 'I have never, for many years, given a subscription to political funds, other than to the Free State Election Fund, and,
if these can be styled political, to the White Cross Fund, and to the
Belfast Distress Fund – the latter through one of the local R.C. clergy.'
Contributions to the relief of distress are perfectly consistent with both
loyalist politics and Methodist morality. Jagoe's contribution to the 'Free
State Election Fund', likewise consistent with Methodist support for the
newly established government, hinted that his loyalty to the new rather
than the old order might have prompted the attack.[167]

Jasper Wolfe, on Jagoe's behalf, had sought compensation through the
local courts, 'but the case was turned down without a hearing'.[168] His claim
to the IGC amounted to £3,125, including £1,200 for loss of business
over two years, £1,225 for loss on stock through 'forced clearance', and
£500 for his lease. Jagoe did not prosper in Hampshire, procuring a dairy
farm with stock worth £288 at Highcliffe-on-Sea before 'endeavouring to
make a livelihood on a 2 acre poultry farm' near Ringwood. Jagoe was
eventually awarded £1,900, taking account of the fact that the erosion of
his net profits had long antedated the Truce and his attempted murder.[169]

---

[166] Fitzmaurice, according to the intelligence officer of the Dunmanway battalion writing a
few months before his murder, was 'openly hostile'; in 1916, he had given 'his Motor car
to the Police when they were going arresting some Volunteers, and all through the
struggle was in close touch with the Barracks': Military Archives, Dublin, A/0897.

[167] Meehan, in 'Distorting Irish History, 2', 18, cites this letter to call into question Jagoe's
loyal credentials by suggesting that he was a covert republican sympathiser. Jagoe's
declaration was fully endorsed by a Treatyite county councillor from Dunmanway,
Daniel McCarthy, in a letter of 13 June regretting 'the upset he has got', praising him
as 'an honest and up-to-date trader', and attributing 'all this trouble to the accumulation
of lies, invented by jealous people': *SS* (10, 17 June).

[168] This claim, relating to 'injuries to health having to leave the country and being deprived
of your means of livelihood' was eventually turned down by the Free State's
Compensation (Personal Injuries) Committee. See J. Travers Wolfe to William Jagoe,
18 Feb. 1927: CO 762/4/1.

[169] Application, 7 Apr. 1927; William Jagoe to Stanley Baldwin, 31 Jan. 1929: CO 762/4/1. Jagoe
returned the turnover of his drapery as £5,037 in 1918, rising to £6,510 (1919), £8,119
(1920), and £7,826 (1921); but net profits of £681 (1918) and £868 (1919) gave place to a
loss of £190 ascribed to the trade slump (1920) and a modest profit of £466 (1921).

William Jagoe had been an exceptionally zealous member of the Dunmanway circuit, acting at various times as secretary to the quarterly meetings, representative to the biannual district synod and the annual national conference, Sunday school superintendent, local preacher, and trustee of Church property. One month before his flight, he had been asked to resume secretarial duties and again act as substitute representative for the district synod. No reference was made to his departure in the minutes of quarterly meetings, which merely referred in December 1922 to 'the removal of Protestants & to the unsettled condition of the country'.[170] The circuit books indicate that William and his children Ethel Martha and William Sidney (still a junior) emigrated in the third quarter of 1922, suggesting a delay of some months after the graveyard escape; his wife Lizzie remained in the Dunmanway circuit for a further year. Jagoe's children were already used to migration, three of them having previously moved for various periods to the University Road circuit, Belfast, before returning temporarily to Dunmanway.[171]

During the protracted proceedings of the IGC, Jagoe corresponded first with its secretary (Major Jamieson), and then with the prime minister, repeatedly expressing his gratitude for loans and grants already awarded and his hope for more to come. These letters indicate that reduced circumstances did not prevent him from helping his children to continue their migrations in search of prosperity far beyond Cork. He informed Jamieson that the first compensation payment had enabled him to provide an outfit for his daughter Ethel, when a former patrol leader in his Scout group had expressed a wish 'to marry my daughter and take her out with him' upon securing a well-paid post in Calcutta. Ethel's father-in-law was Dunmanway's clerk of petty sessions, an Episcopalian in 1911 whose family had become active Methodists by 1917.[172]

William Jagoe's bank account was already overdrawn as a result of 'fitting out and sending our younger son to Canada', where he (William Sidney) soon found a position in the Canadian Bank of Commerce.[173] Jagoe, drawing a connection with Baldwin's recent visit to Canada,

---

[170] Dunmanway circuit, Minutes of Quarterly Leaders' Meetings, 1900–31 (*passim*).

[171] Dunmanway circuit, Membership Registers and Quarterly Class Rolls (1899–1928).

[172] Ethel M. Jagoe married James W. Atkins in Hampshire in 1927: Index to Civil Marriages, England and Wales (ancestrylibrary.com). James Walter Atkins (aged 11) lived with his 'Irish Church' family at 2, Bridge St in 1911, but removed to Skibbereen in 1917; his sister Georgina Marion, along with William Sidney Jagoe, collected money for the Methodist Juvenile Associations in 1922–3: Census of Ireland (1911), family schedule for Alfred Atkins; return of connexional funds in Dunmanway circuit, Schedule Book.

[173] Jagoe had two other sons: Leslie Barrett, an executive officer in Northern Ireland's Ministry of Labour, and John Robert, also 'employed, though not very happily, as yet'. See Jagoe to Jamieson, 4 Oct. 1927: CO 762/4/1. William Sidney Jagoe (1908–88), listed

confided to the prime minister that his son 'had been doing exceptionally well at College, but when disaster overtook us in '22, he had to turn to manual toil', before 'making good' after emigrating in July 1927. Encouraged by Baldwin's reply, he wrote again to report a conversation in Alberta between his son and a former serviceman in the Dunmanway district. He had 'confirmed, in detail, the excesses by which the populace were enraged, to wreak on us Loyalists, after the withdrawal of the troops, their vengeance'.[174] Unlike many loyal victims of republican violence, William Jagoe recognised that both parties shared responsibility for the brutality of the conflict in west Cork.

Apart from James Buttimer, the only fatality in the 'Bandon Valley massacre' identified as a Methodist was John Albert Chinnery of Castletown, in the Ballineen class (Clonakilty circuit). Chinnery, an unmarried farmer aged 32, received a visit on the second night (27–28 April) by persons demanding his horse and cart 'in the name of the I.R.A.' He accompanied them 'into the yard and was tackling the horse when, without the slightest warning, he was shot dead' (through the back).[175] The local press reported that 'locally he had the reputation of being a fine athlete, and he was physically very strong'.[176] Though the family was returned as Episcopalian in the census of 1911,[177] John and his brother George became local preachers in 1913, sometimes conducting services at Rushfield in the absence of the minister. Among his effects were the notes of the sermon he had intended to deliver on the following Sunday, taking as his text 'Prepare to meet thy God' (Amos 4:12).[178] George was confirmed as a 'fully accredited Local Preacher' a few months after John's death, and remained on the circuit roll five years later along with an elderly maiden aunt.[179]

In her unsuccessful application for compensation from the IGC for the loss of her son's services as farm manager, John's widowed mother Rebecca alleged that he had done 'all the farming and marketing', as

as a draper in 1927 and a bank teller in 1937, made numerous journeys between Canada and England and died in Delta, British Columbia: Index to Deaths, British Columbia and various passenger lists (ancestrylibrary.com).

[174] Jagoe to Baldwin, 25 June 1928, 31 Jan. 1929.
[175] Bennett, 'Clonakilty Circuit', 73.   [176] *CC* (29 Apr. 1922).
[177] The household was headed in 1911 by Henry Chinnery (75) and his wife Rebecca (51), who was widowed in 1917 and outlived John by a decade: family tree accessed on westcorkgenealogy.com.
[178] Bennett, 'Clonakilty Circuit', 34, 73; see also Hart, *The I.R.A. and its Enemies*, 274, and identical snippets in *FJ* and *SS* (29 Apr. 1922).
[179] Clonakilty circuit, Minutes of Quarterly Leaders' Meetings, Sept. 1922; Membership Roll (1921–7), recording J. A. Chinnery's death without comment. George Chinnery was still on the roll in early 1927, but his mother Rebecca was not listed and presumably remained an Episcopalian.

George had no training as a farmer and was 'studying for the Church'.[180] This claim was undermined by George's own admission, when renewing the family's search for compensation in 1928, that he had been 'helping my brother on the farm. After his death I had to take over responsibility for the work, and a workman had to be hired after a time.'[181] Rebecca had also declared that 'the deceased was a member of the Church of Ireland and a supporter of the Government of the United Kingdom', naming four near neighbours and four others living within six miles, all with the same credentials, who had been murdered at the same period. Her surprising reference to the Church of Ireland reflects the fact that she and her daughters, unlike John and George, had not become Methodists.[182]

The last Methodist known to have been threatened with murder in west Cork was William Bryan of Knocknacurra, within the Bandon circuit, a 49-year-old farmer of 121 acres occupying a 'substantial residence' leased from the Earl of Bandon.[183] The farm was valued by Bandon's agent at £3,500 in 1922. As Bryan informed the IGC in 1926:

On 25th July 1922 men came to my house and under penalty of death ordered me to give up possession of my holding, lands, stock and furniture alternative to being shot. I was offered £100 for everything and to clear out. A Clergyman was in my house at the time, and advised me to sign the paper giving over everything, so as to escape. I did so and escaped to England and lost everything I possessed. Amongst the men who seized the stock was a member of the Dail, and I dare not return.

He explained that 'I was well known as a Protestant loyalist. Several loyalists were shot in their houses in Bandon at that time.' After escaping Bandon in July 1922, 'our children were sent to a place of safety with friends who took charge of them and my wife and I lived in lodgings in England from place to place until May 1923, when money was advanced by the Irish Grants [Distress] Committee on the security of the Farm in Ireland to help to buy the farm in Kent.' Bryan paid £2,650 for the farm near Ashford (close to that of another Methodist claimant from Bandon,

---

[180] Application to IGC, 30 Oct. 1926: CO 762/31/3. Rebecca Chinnery had originally sought compensation of £5,000 from the Free State's Personal Injuries Committee, being awarded only £550; she vainly hoped to secure the rest from the IGC.

[181] In seeking to renew the claim on behalf of his mother ('as she is unwell'), Chinnery enviously drew attention to awards made to neighbours in similar circumstances. See George Chinnery to Miss Murray (secretary, Southern Irish Loyalists' Relief Association), 12, 18 June 1928: PRONI, D 989/B/3/8. The Association advised that 'there would be nothing to be gained by trying to reopen your claim': Murray to Chinnery, 19 July 1928.

[182] Application: CO 762/31/3.

[183] William Bryan should not be confused with William Hosford Bryan of Enniskeane, another Methodist claimant for compensation discussed above.

William Kingston), with the help of a bank loan of £1,500 which had yet to be repaid three years later.[184]

In a preliminary letter, he had explained his situation more graphically: 'I have been Hunted down since 1922, and all my goods & chattels including Cattle, Horses, implements, crops, were seized & disposed of by the Rebels. My house & farm yard are now laid in Ruins & a lot of valuable Timber cut & sold.' Having received no redress, despite a court award for £600, he portrayed himself as 'living here in great privation from want of capital'.[185] He sought compensation of £6,078 for his lost farm, furnishings, stock, and profits, and £1,000 for the 'shock of expulsion'. Apart from 13 milch cows and an impressive range of livestock and farm machinery, he had lost a newly laid parlour carpet, twelve feet square, with linoleum bordering, six leather-covered mahogany chairs, a mahogany mohair-covered lounge, a what-not, and a bamboo table (sure signs of gentility). Worse still was the psychological loss: 'The shock to myself and wife thrown out of home and lands with no hope of returning to Ireland and separated from our children, made us both nearly demented. We had no means of supporting ourselves and had we not received assistance from the Irish Grants [Distress] Committee we should certainly have become demented.'[186]

Bryan's case had political significance because of the involvement of Seán Hales of Knocknacurra House, the pro-Treaty T.D. who had organised the seizure of the farm before himself being murdered by 'Irregulars' on 7 December 1922 (the day after the inauguration of the Irish Free State). After reaching England on 28 July 1922 with assistance from Jasper Wolfe, Bryan (with Wolfe) had persuaded the IGC to provide interim grants of £750 and a loan of £1,500 secured on the property at Knocknacurra. The committee understood 'that repeated efforts have been made to sell the property in Ireland but without success'. According to Bryan's application, 'the largest offer for the Farm was £600 on behalf of the man who had seized the lands – no one else would buy'. When the case was brought before the new government in January 1923, 'they replied that it was likely there would be further trouble if Mr. Bryan returned to the farm to take it over'. The IGC was advised that Bryan seemed 'a thoroughly honest individual' who was 'one of, what we might term the "successes" of the refugees inasmuch as he took immediate steps on arrival in this country to become self-supporting'. Nevertheless, elements of the application were clearly inflated, and the IGC was reminded that Bryan had taken

---

[184] Application of William Bryan, 27 Oct. [1926]: CO 762/15/3.
[185] Bryan to IGC, 21 Oct. 1926: CO 762/15/3.   [186] Application: CO 762/15/3.

'possession of a larger and better farm in this country'.[187] The amount eventually paid was £3,000, in keeping with the IGC's customary and prudent practice of rejecting about half of each claim.

Local animosity to Bryan was sharpened by the fact, ignored by the IGC, that he was regarded as a land-grabber. This was revealed in police reports following a futile attempt by the colonial office to induce the Free State government to facilitate the sale of the farm and hence redemption of the mortgage of £1,500. In 1884, Bryan's father had taken possession after a rent strike leading to the eviction of the Flynns, who were subsequently housed in a hut on lands belonging to the Hales family. Though William could scarcely have grabbed the farm at the age of 11, and though the entire Flynn household had left the county by 1922, Bryan could not escape the ancestral smear. According to Assistant Commissioner Coogan:

It appears that the Volunteers were anxious to reinstate the Flynns on this farm, and as none of them were available, they decided to settle thereon, another family named Flynn relatives of the occupiers. About June 1922, the late Brigadier S. Hales accompanied the Flynns to Bryan's house and told him that he should evacuate the farm, Bryan agreed to do so and, as he had a considerable amount of farm implements etc. it was arranged that he would accept £100 for the lot. When Bryan cleared out he refused to cash the cheque as he considered the amount inadequate. The Flynn family occupied this farm until the Special Infantry commenced operations in this area, and thinking they were on the programme for attention they abandoned the farm which since remains unoccupied ... It is my opinion, that if the farm was put up for sale, there is every possibility that no buyer will be forthcoming as it is still looked upon locally as a 'grabbed farm'.[188]

To enforce the sale of a farm claimed by allies of Hales, formerly a key supporter of the Free State, might have seriously eroded popular support for the government in west Cork. Officials in the Department of Finance therefore devised a disingenuous strategy for avoiding further intervention. The assistant secretary (J. J. McElligott) was advised that 'we should keep out of this matter entirely if we can manage to do so. Why could not Bryan put the sale of the farm in the hands of an Estate Agent here in the Saorstat? I do not see why we should be expected to conduct the sale, and I certainly think that in view of the circumstances of the case, we should avoid having anything to do with it.'[189] Setting aside the police warnings that no purchaser would be found, Tim Healy as governor-general informed the colonial secretary that, 'as a result of our enquiries,

[187] Undated brief for IGC: CO 762/15/3.
[188] Report by Eamonn O Cughain, 13 July 1923: NAD, FIN 1/2375.
[189] G. F. [Fagan?] to McElligott, 19 July 1923: FIN 1/2375.

my Ministers are now in a position to state that the farm is, and has been for some months, unoccupied, and there would appear, therefore, to be no reason why Mr. William Bryan should not now take steps for its sale'.[190] As Bryan's experience confirms, sectarian animosity was compounded by festering agrarian or political resentments, which often outweighed issues of religious affiliation.

No other attempts to murder west Cork Methodists are known to have occurred during 1922, though several farmers continued to suffer from attacks on their property initiated before the Truce. Thomas Wesley Bateman (1871–1959), a farmer in the Clonakilty circuit, informed the IGC that 'in April 1921 Cattle valued for £80 were taken at the pit of a revolver by the I.R.A.' When sheep and lambs worth £34 were stolen one year later, 'at the time of the West Cork murders', Bateman was away from home: 'I was in England at time animals were taken as I feared my life was in danger here.' As his expenses while in England amounted to only £20, he must soon have returned, and by 1926 was 'living on a good farm and in comfortable circumstances' at Barryshall near Timoleague.[191] Exceptionally for a west Cork Methodist, Wesley Bateman was politically active, having followed his father's example by winning election to the local council in January 1920, when he came third in the poll as an Independent candidate. As proof of his allegiance, he informed the IGC that 'during the trouble I was a member of the Cloankilty Urban Council & always refused to acknowledge the S.F. I was always in a minority of one in refusing allegiance to Irish Republic.'[192] As in the case of Jasper Wolfe, his political prominence made him less vulnerable than most Methodists to communal sanctions, except in moments of crisis when invisibility offered surer protection than popularity. Bateman remained an active Methodist layman, as secretary to the Clonakilty quarterly meetings (1922–39) and subsequently as society steward.[193] He and his wife Ethel (1900–80), a niece of Edward Bennett who ministered in the circuit from 1922 to 1925, were both buried at advanced ages in Timoleague's Church of Ireland graveyard.[194]

Many incidents, though well remembered by neighbours and relatives, were doubtless unreported by victims anxious to avoid further attacks. Lee

[190] Healy to Devonshire, 19 July 1923: FIN 1/2375.
[191] Application of Wesley Bateman, 1 Nov. 1926: CO 762/50/13. Bateman was awarded £50 of his modest claim to the IGC for £84, in addition to £50 from the Free State authorities for his pre-Truce losses.
[192] Bateman did not seek re-election after moving from Clonakilty town to Barryshall: Bennett, 'Clonakilty Circuit', 80; CO 762/15/3.
[193] Bennett, 'Clonakilty Circuit', 39, 45.
[194] Transcription of gravestone inscription: Bandon.genealogy.com.

Cole reports that those who fled from their homes in April 1922 included not only William Jagoe and John Willis, but also George Young of Lisnagat near Scariff (Bandon circuit).[195] The need for discretion in the face of local hostility was illustrated by this anecdote of another prominent Methodist household:

> The Kingston family at Drimoleague was raided and their horses and many of their garments were taken. While no one was injured, they were sworn solemnly to secrecy. They were not the only Methodists so attacked, and it was noticed on the following Sunday that all the men in the Drimoleague Church had lost their overcoats.[196]

The violent campaigns of early 1921 and spring 1922 left an enduring imprint on the outlook of the broader Protestant and Methodist communities, engendering defiance as well as fear and strengthening communal solidarity for those who stayed at home. As already shown, revolutionary turmoil did not lead to a massive exodus of Methodists from west Cork. Yet there was indeed a significant increase in the movement of Methodist families out of the district, which requires further investigation using Church records in combination with census returns and other personal documents. Even if southern Protestants as a community were not subjected to 'ethnic cleansing', is it not credible to apply such a term to the Methodist families actually displaced from revolutionary west Cork?

IX

In order to identify the Methodist families displaced from west Cork, the quarterly membership rolls for all six circuits were examined for four calendar years (1920–3). Methodist ministers, coastguards, and military or naval personnel (where known) were discarded, along with their dependants, as their displacement was determined by their employers.[197] Families known to have moved to other circuits within the Cork district were also omitted, on the assumption that their migration was prompted

---

[195] Cole, *Methodism in Ireland*, 112. According to the family census return for 1911, George Young was an unmarried farmer aged 33, living with his parents William (an Irish speaker) and Hester and a 21-year-old sister, Elizabeth Catherine. William died in late 1911, but the membership roll for the Scariff class indicates only the removal to an unstated destination of George and his mother in spring 1915, followed by Lily (to the Bandon class) in summer 1916. Lily remained in the Bandon class until her marriage to Arthur Perrott in June 1922.

[196] Cole, *Methodism in Ireand*, 111.

[197] These categories accounted for 16 emigrants and 26 removals (including a minister's family of 3 who moved within the Cork district). Ministers themselves were omitted from the membership registers.

by economic factors.[198] Apart from these excluded groups, the rolls revealed 162 members and juniors who had departed as a result of either emigration (112) or removal to other districts in Ireland (50). The majority of those who left were female (54%), the proportion being slightly higher for internal migrants (56%) than for emigrants (54%). The median age of emigrants at the time of departure (24) was a decade lower than that of internal migrants (34), and in both categories females tended to be older.[199] No less than 88% of those who left west Cork were natives of the county.[200]

Since members were listed by household, giving addresses, it was possible to aggregate the migrants into family groups. 'Displaced families' were defined as households of two or more,[201] in which no family member remained on the roll thereafter. As usual, many Methodist households remained intact in west Cork despite the departure of individual or multiple family members. In such cases, it seems likely that migration was attributable to economic motives rather than intimidation or panic generated by revolutionary turmoil. Yet nearly three-quarters of emigrants and half of the internal migrants belonged to 'displaced families', exceptionally high proportions in a country notable for the predominance of individual and serial migration.[202]

After filtering, 26 displaced families with 105 members remain (see Table 9.3). Of these families, 17 emigrated and 9 moved within Ireland.[203] Migration was concentrated in the most turbulent years, with 13 families leaving in 1921 and 11 in 1922, but only 1 family in 1920 and in 1923.

---

[198] Excluding the discarded categories, at least 35 members, including 5 family groups, removed to circuits in Ireland outside the Cork district. Since destination was returned for only 29 of the remaining 50 removals, it is likely that part of the residue (21) moved within the Cork district. Removals between classes within circuits were not abstracted.

[199] The ages of 103 of the 112 emigrants and 41 of the 50 removals were ascertained from census returns supplemented by membership rolls and genealogical sources. These figures incorporate 15 juniors under 16 years, whose precise age is unknown. The median age of emigrants was 27 for females and 24 for males, corresponding figures for removals being 45 (due to a surfeit of widows) and 23/24.

[200] The birthplaces of 148 emigrants and removals were ascertained, comprising Cork (130), other Munster (3), Leinster (3), Ulster (5), Britain (4), and overseas (3).

[201] The families of Thomas Bradfield and James Buttimer have been included, despite the fact that only their widows migrated as their children had already left home. The murdered heads have been enumerated as members of the migratory family group.

[202] Displaced families accounted for 79 of 112 emigrants (75.4%) and 25 of 50 removals beyond the Cork district (50%). Of the remaining emigrants, 19 left alone whereas 14 belonged to families with other migratory members. For the remaining removals, the corresponding numbers were 22 and 3.

[203] In 4 of the 10 cases of removal within Ireland, the family's destination is unknown and may have been within the Cork district. In a few cases, the family did not depart as a group, moving serially or to different destinations.

Members of every displaced family have been located in census schedules for 1911 (or 1901). It has therefore been practicable to compile a collective profile of those who departed, enriched by reference to compensation claims and genealogical sources.[204]

The census reveals that fourteen (54%) of the displaced families were headed by farmers, along with nine merchants or dealers (including three drapers and two grocers), a commercial traveller, a merchant's clerk, and an accountant. Thirteen households (50%) had servants in 1911, of which nine employed only Catholics, two only Methodists, and two a combination of Catholics and Episcopalians. Nineteen heads (73%) were natives of Cork, along with three from Ulster and two each from Leinster and England. The median size of the displaced families was four, and the median age of heads at the time of migration was in the upper 50s (far above the normal age at migration from Ireland). These families had occupied quite substantial homes in 1911, the median number of rooms being eight, with five or six front windows. In short, the displaced families were quite atypical of Irish migration, long dominated by the young and the poor, usually migrating without parents or siblings. By contrast, most of these Methodist migrants were mature family groups with considerable assets and social status.

None of those moving within Ireland is known to have taken immediate refuge in Northern Ireland: three chose Dublin and two Wicklow. Of those who left Ireland for known destinations, ten settled in Britain, three in Canada, and one in Philadelphia, confirming contemporary press reports and statements by leading Methodists. The profile of those emigrating beyond Ireland differed notably from those moving within the country, the emigrant heads tending to be younger, their homes roomier and brighter, and the number of those accompanying them greater.[205] The major origin of these contrasts is the fact that widows were far more likely to resettle elsewhere in Ireland than in Britain or overseas. Whereas fourteen of the seventeen emigrant heads were men, six of the nine families moving within Ireland were headed by women. The reputation of south Dublin and Wicklow as a sanctuary for Protestant widows fits this pattern of resettlement.

As already shown, several of the seven emigrant families who approached the IGC lingered in west Cork rather than making a precipitate exit. The two widows of murdered Methodists remained in their homes for some

---

[204] Seven displaced families have been matched with applications to the IGC.

[205] The respective median figures for emigrants and those moving circuit within Ireland are as follows: head's age at migration, 53 and 64; rooms, 9 and 6; front windows, 5 and 6; dependants, 3 (range 1–13) and 1 (range 1–4).

months as they tried to dispose of their property. In eight other cases where no claim was lodged, genealogical documents confirm the impression that violence and intimidation did not necessarily lead to a panic-driven, unplanned, terminal, and irreversible exodus.[206] The destination noted on Methodist records was sometimes a temporary halting point, as for Charles Henry Swanton (1877–1953), a 43-year-old grocer from South Main Street, Bandon, who left for the Isle of Man in early 1921 with his wife Mary Starkey (May) Swanton (1878–1947) and their four children. May died in England, but Charles was buried in Kamloops, British Columbia.[207] For John Howard Henry, a 45-year-old commercial traveller who left Skibbereen with his wife and two children in the second quarter of 1921, the movement to England represented one stage in a migratory life. He and his new wife had both already visited the United States when they travelled to New York and Pittsburgh in 1904, and they voyaged with a daughter from Chile to Liverpool in 1925.[208] Their departure from west Cork in 1921 may have been on business unrelated to political turmoil.

Other emigrants returned to west Cork once the turmoil had subsided. Even the widow of Thomas Bradfield of Knockmacool spent her last years in Bandon after enduring about a decade's exile in Berkshire. Consider also the family of James Good of Ardbrack House, east of Kinsale, a 76-year-old farmer who left with his wife Elizabeth and two very mature spinster daughters in late 1922, after nearly a decade as members of the Kinsale circuit. The entire family returned to Summercove (adjacent to Ardbrack) in spring 1925, Elizabeth being buried in the Killowen parish graveyard in 1930 and joined by 91-year-old James in 1937.[209]

Another who returned was Herbert Gallagher of the Mills, Kinsale, who departed with his wife Hessie or Hester Levis Gallagher (1886–1943), and two of their young sons, in late 1922.[210] They had been living with or near Hessie's father William Jagoe (1856–1944), a corn miller whose

---

[206] I am deeply grateful to Jane Leonard for her advice and assistance in tracing Methodist careers through websites such as ancestrylibrary.com. This applies particularly to sources cited in nn. 208, 215, 218, and 219.

[207] Index to deaths, British Columbia, and records of Eagle Bay Community Church (ancestrylibrary.com).

[208] Henry, a commercial traveller according to the census return for 1911, was listed as a clerk in 1904 and an engineer in 1925: passenger lists (ancestrylibrary.com).

[209] Elizabeth's final address was given as Summercove, Kinsale, while James died at Scilly, Kinsale: gravestone inscriptions, Killowen (accessible on-line through bandon-genealogy). The family was farming in Cloghane, north of Kinsale, in 1901; but only Elizabeth could be traced (at Coolbane, between Millstreet and Mallow) in 1911, when a married son was occupying the farm in Cloghane.

[210] Ernest William Gallagher followed his brothers Herbert and David John out of Ireland in the second quarter of 1923.

home remained a Methodist preaching place in June 1922.[211] Son of a Methodist farmer from Moy, Co. Tyrone, Herbert Gallagher had immigrated to Canada in 1910 and claimed Canadian nationality.[212] Hessie Jagoe had left Kinsale in spring 1913, presumably meeting and marrying Herbert in Canada before returning to Jagoe's Mills with their son Herbert Henry Asquith Gallagher in early 1916. The boy's provocatively liberal name was one that few Methodist parents confined to Ireland would have chosen. Herbert the elder followed them to Kinsale a few months later, having been listed in the census of Manitoba for 1916 as a married insurance accountant aged 30, of Irish 'racial or tribal origin', lodging in Winnipeg. He immediately became active on the Kinsale circuit, succeeding Robert Jagoe as the Sunday school superintendent (1917–20).[213] The family's departure would have been a severe blow for the small congregation in Kinsale. The Gallaghers returned to Jagoe's Mills in spring 1925, but their migrations continued. Herbert, Hessie, and David embarked from Southampton for the Cape in October 1926, leaving the other two boys behind.[214] Hessie returned alone in late 1928 and remained in Kinsale with Herbert and Ernest William throughout the 1930s, until Ernest's removal to Belfast to become a theological student at Edgehill College in 1940. Ernest (1918–84) spent much of his career in South India before returning in 1967 to minister in Dublin, becoming principal of Edgehill College for two years before his death. Herbert the younger went on to become an architect in London before serving as a lieutenant in the wartime army.

Careful planning on a tight budget was evident in the Canadian settlement of John Sweetnam, a 60-year-old farmer from Union Hall, Skibbereen, with his wife Sarah (aged 51) and their children Samuel Earnest (24) and Esther Olive (22). In June 1921, Samuel was the first to reach Quebec, on his way to Montreal to stay with a Sweetnam cousin and 'earn a living'. Then came Esther, who left in November 1921 with the intention to 'housekeep for

[211] The marriage of Herbert Gallagher to Hester Jagoe in 1913, and information on her genealogy, is recorded in the Davis–Jagoe family tree (ancestrylibrary.com). William Jagoe and his wife Eva Maria (*née* Bateman) remained in the Kinsale circuit throughout the revolutionary years, though many of their children emigrated at different dates. Three sons joined the army, including 2nd Lieut. Charles Bateman Jagoe, 16th Battalion, Royal Irish Rifles, killed in action in France on 26 July 1917: Kinsale circuit, schedule book and membership rolls.

[212] Census of Ireland (1901), as Fred. H. Gallagher (scholar, 14); Census of Manitoba (1916), as Herbert Gallagher (ancestrylibrary.com).

[213] Kinsale circuit, Schedule Book (1910–29).

[214] The outward passenger list for the *Windsor Castle* (ancestrylibrary.com) listed the passengers as Mr F. H. Gallagher (an accountant aged 40), Mrs H. R. Gallagher (40), and Master J. D. Gallagher (5).

brother'. Their parents reached Quebec in May 1922 and proceeded to Edmonton, Alberta, to join Samuel and 'make a living'. All four passages were paid for by John Sweetnam, and all members of the family carried small amounts of money ranging from Samuel's $15 to John's $200. The only hint of an intention to return home was expressed by Sarah, who (unlike her husband and children) answered 'No' to the question 'Do you intend to reside permanently in Canada?'[215] The Sweetnams were rather confused about their citizenship, Samuel being returned as 'British', John and Sarah 'Irish', and Esther 'Cork'. Samuel and Esther considered their 'race or people' to be 'Irish', whereas their parents answered 'British'. These dualities were doubtless of less significance in Alberta than in west Cork.

Like the Sweetnams, the family of 71-year-old Mary Anne Buttimer from Sovereign Street, Clonakilty, had the advantage of joining a fore-runner (a married daughter) when they emigrated to Philadelphia on 11 September 1921. Mary Ann was a widowed farmer and shopkeeper, variously returned as a native of Sussex or Co. Limerick, whose daughter Lizzie had been born in the gold-mining town of Ballarat, Victoria, in the 1870s.[216] Her late husband had lent and later sold teapots and crockery for use at tea meetings, but these festivities were abandoned in about 1920.[217] Another elderly emigrant was Louisa Copithorne, a 75-year-old draper's widow who left 'Snugville' in Townsend Street, Skibbereen, for Castletown in the Isle of Man in early 1921. She migrated with her 40-year-old daughter Charlotte Ava or Lottie (1879–1965), whose brother George paid for her passage to Victoria, British Columbia, in 1925. Louisa had clearly died before 1925, as Lottie's nearest relative in Ireland was an unidentified Mr Copithorne of Dundrum, Co. Dublin.[218] Once again, the disruption caused by displacement was eased by previous migration, ensuring that the new arrivals had some prior knowledge of their destina-tion and friends to support them. Even so, migration posed severe chal-lenges for parents in their 60s and 70s like the Sweetnams, Mary Ann Buttimer, and Louisa Copithorne.

Of all the displaced families whose subsequent peregrinations have been traced, only one appears to have settled down abroad without further migratory complications. In summer 1921, John Copithorne, a

---

[215] Canadian passenger arrivals, individual manifests (ancestrylibrary.com).
[216] Elizabeth Buttimer's age was returned as 37 in 1911 but only 40 in 1922, though her hair was grey like her mother's: Census of Ireland (1911), family schedule; immigration manifest of alien passengers, Philadelphia (ancestrylibrary.com).
[217] Bennett, 'Clonakilty Circuit', 89.
[218] Index to deaths, England; index to administration papers, Watford district; various medical and naval records (ancestrylibrary.com).

55-year-old pharmaceutical chemist, vacated the Medical Hall in Main Street, Skibbereen, and settled in England with his wife Edith Watson Copithorne and their two young children. Edith died in Abbots, Hertfordshire, in 1935, being survived by John (by then a 'retired chemist'). Their son Richard Ernest (Rex) Copithorne (1908–81) qualified as a surgeon in 1933, becoming a naval surgeon four years later and rising to Surgeon Lieutenant-Commander on HMS *Jamaica* in 1943.[219] Despite some intervening adventures, his life's transit from Skibbereen to Waveney in Sussex might seem relatively straightforward – but for the fact that all studies of migratory trajectories are based on limited and patchy documentation, so that every undiscovered lurking fact threatens to subvert the historian's tidy classifications.

This study of the demographic fate of west Cork's Methodists suggests that revolutionary turmoil had limited impact on long-established patterns of heavy emigration and inadequate recruitment. Though the murderous sprees of early 1921 and spring 1922 caused temporary panic, most Methodist families either resisted the pressure to leave home or subsequently returned. Even the permanent emigrants seldom abandoned their properties without strenuous efforts to secure a fair price for their assets. Many were more or less familiar with the places in Ireland, England, or America where they settled, being able to draw on assistance and advice from kin or neighbours who had left west Cork in pursuit of a better livelihood before the revolution. For some families with previous experience of international migration, their departure was probably unrelated to revolutionary events, the timing being dictated by the post-war resumption of passenger shipping in 1920. The 'spectre' of extermination was real, in the sense that many feared for short periods that vulnerable southern Protestant communities would be expropriated and uprooted. Yet fear typically succumbed to hope, and panic to common sense. The outcome was not 'ethnic cleansing', but a concerted attempt to rebuild Protestant communities and establish a satisfactory *modus vivendi* in the Irish Free State. Republican terror – venomous, cruel, and brutal though it was – lacked the power to break the spirit of minorities such as the Methodists of west Cork.

---

[219] Documents accessed via ancestrylibrary.com.

Statistical appendix

Table 5.1 *Orangemen, Methodists, and Episcopalians as a percentage of non-Catholics in Ireland, 1926 and 1961/5*

County	1926:OO	1926:Me.	Ep.	RC	1965:OO	1961:Me.	Ep.	RC
Fermanagh	n.a.	14.3	76.3	56.0	14.9	14.4	71.1	53.2
Armagh	9.3	8.1	58.7	45.4	11.5	9.6	51.9	47.3
Tyrone	10.0	4.5	50.4	55.5	12.7	5.0	47.0	54.8
Londonderry	7.6	2.6	35.2	47.5	10.6	2.8	39.2	50.6
Mid-Ulster	*n.a.*	*6.0*	*50.6*	*50.5*	*11.8*	*6.4*	*48.1*	*51.2*
Antrim	5.3	3.3	28.1	20.1	6.5	5.8	29.7	24.4
Belfast	5.8	8.0	41.7	23.0	4.7	11.0	37.2	27.5
Down	6.0	3.9	34.6	30.4	5.4	6.3	32.1	28.6
North-East	*5.7*	*5.9*	*36.6*	*24.3*	*5.5*	*8.2*	*33.6*	*26.9*
Northern Ireland	*n.a.*	*5.9*	*40.5*	*33.5*	*7.0*	*7.7*	*37.2*	*34.9*
Cavan	n.a.	3.6	77.3	84.1	10.8	3.3	77.7	88.3
Donegal	n.a.	4.4	50.0	81.9	2.2	4.7	47.1	86.3
Monaghan	n.a.	2.1	45.8	78.5	10.4	1.5	41.4	85.8
Lost Counties	*n.a.*	*3.6*	*55.4*	*81.8*	*6.1*	*3.6*	*52.8*	*86.7*
Province of Ulster	*n.a.*	*5.8*	*41.4*	*42.8*	*6.9*	*7.6*	*37.6*	*41.8*
Other Provinces	*n.a.*	*5.2*	*86.0*	*93.7*	*0.1*	*4.8*	*76.5*	*95.5*
Ireland	*n.a.*	*5.7*	*47.6*	*75.0*	*6.3*	*7.3*	*41.9*	*74.7*

Note: Statistics of religious denomination were calculated from Census abstracts for 1926 and 1961 in *Irish Historical Statistics: Population, 1821–1971*, ed. W. E. Vaughan and A. J. Fitzpatrick (Dublin, Royal Irish Academy, 1978). With the exception of the columns headed 'RC', showing (Roman) Catholics as a percentage of the total population, the denominator for all columns is the total non-Catholic population. Membership figures for the Orange Order (OO) are derived from returns of members of private lodges submitted to GOLI by county secretaries, many of which appear in the printed annual reports of CGLs. No returns for 1926 have been traced for Fermanagh, Londonderry City, or the three 'Lost Counties' of Ulster, and figures for Belfast, Tyrone, and Londonderry Co. relate to 1923, 1927, and 1927 respectively. The low ratio for Donegal in 1965 is partly attributable to the enrolment of many Donegal Orangemen in lodges under the jurisdiction of Londonderry City.

Table 5.2 *Denominations of clergymen holding office in GOLI, 1856–1996*

Year	Ep.	Pr.	Me.	O.	Total	Year	Ep.	Pr.	Me.	O.	Total
1856	89	1	0	0	90	1936	102	18	4	2	126
1866	75	2	0	1	78	1946	89	28	7	2	126
1876	128	9	6	0	143	1956	80	39	4	2	125
1886	188	6	3	3	200	1966	98	37	6	2	143
1896	161	1	2	1	165	1976	58	43	6	4	111
1906	138	10	2	2	152	1986	51	51	8	5	115
1916	116	6	4	0	126	1996	46	37	4	2	89
1926	99	17	5	2	123						

Note: Figures refer to current denominations of ordained clergymen elected to any office in GOLI for the stated calendar year, or whose election to CGLs was confirmed by GOLI at the end of the preceding year: *HYR*, Nov./Dec. 1852–1995. Denominations have been verified from clergy lists and *Thom's Directory*, except in a few cases included under 'O.' (Other). 'Ep.' refers to Episcopalians, including Church of England; 'Pr.' refers to clergy under the general assembly; 'Me.' refers to Methodists including Primitive Wesleyan Methodists and Primitive Methodists.

Table 5.3 *Careers of 48 Methodist clergymen holding office in GOLI, 1853–1996*

Characteristic (Years)	Number	Min.	LQ	Median	UQ	Max.
Age at death	41	39	67	78	84	99
Period in GOLI	44	1	5	9/11	19	49
Age when entered GOLI	48	23	36	47	53	70
Yrs in min. when ent. GOLI	48	0	10	19	30	44
Yrs in min. after left GOLI	19	2	3/4	14	20/23	37
Yrs in GOLI after left min.	15	1	3/4	6	15/17	30
Yrs of life after left GOLI	22	3	9	24/26	34	47

Note: For records of service of Methodist clergymen in GOLI, see note to Table 5.2. Information on clerical careers is derived from MCI, *Minutes of Conference* (annual), supplemented by published records of service, biographical dictionaries, obituaries in church periodicals, annual clergy lists in *Thom's Directory*, and biographical data kindly made available by Robert Roddie. The group includes all clergy ordained as Methodist ministers, regardless of their denomination when serving as Orange chaplains. For each characteristic, the data were arranged in rank order, the median being the mid-way value, and the lower quartile (LQ) and upper quartile (UQ) figures being mid-way between the median and the minimum and maximum figures respectively. The last three rows exclude those whose term in GOLI ceased upon retirement from the ministry (9) or death (18).

Table 6.1 *Percentage of non-Catholic adults signing Covenant and Declaration*

County	Men	Percentage	Women	Percentage
Armagh	18,754	88.6	20,331	86.6
Tyrone	19,653	87.9	18,532	82.9
Fermanagh	8,219	84.6	6,884	73.8
Londonderry	20,282	81.4	20,403	74.3
Mid Ulster	*66,908*	*85.6*	*66,150*	*80.1*
Belfast	67,316	76.2	61,648	58.9
Down	32,379	72.6	35,495	69.7
Antrim	33,185	68.4	39,395	71.9
North-East	*132,880*	*73.2*	*136,538*	*64.9*
Monaghan	5,397	83.2	5,082	80.0
Donegal	9,007	73.7	8,347	68.7
Cavan	4,423	71.3	3,722	65.4
'Lost Counties'	*18,827*	*75.6*	*17,151*	*70.9*
Ulster	*218,615*	*76.9*	*219,339*	*69.3*
Ulster (official)	218,206	76.7	228,999	72.2

Note: The number of signatories of Ulster's Solemn League and Covenant and the Women's Declaration for each county is based on a digital search of the signature sheets for each parliamentary constituency (certain folders of signature sheets have been lost or omitted): PRONI, accessible on-line. All county totals are approximate because of technical flaws in coding. For the official ('authoritative') return of 218,206 male and 228,999 female signatories aged over 16 years, recorded throughout Ulster (28 Sept.–14 Oct. 1912), excluding 19,162 men and 5,047 women who signed sheets in southern Ireland and Britain and some individual signatures received at the Belfast office, see *BNL* (23 Nov. 1912).

Percentages show the ratio of signatories in each county to the estimated census population of non-Catholic men or women aged over 16 years on 2 Apr. 1911. These estimates give the recorded percentage of non-Catholics in the population aged over 9 years (the only available age-breakdown by religion), multiplied by the total population aged over 16 years: Census of Ireland (1911), county and provincial reports.

Table 6.2 *Participation in Covenant and unionist organisations*

County	Covenant	UVF	UC	OO
Armagh	88.6	36.0	21.7	26.3
Tyrone	87.9	45.9	34.3	31.9
Fermanagh	84.6	30.9	14.6	33.5
Londonderry	81.4	37.5	14.2	29.1
Mid Ulster	*85.6*	*38.7*	*22.0*	*29.7*
Belfast	76.2	25.4	17.7	14.6
Down	72.6	25.3	22.5	22.3
Antrim	68.4	24.9	19.7	19.1
North-East	*73.2*	*25.2*	*19.5*	*17.7*
Monaghan	83.2	33.7	20.2	
Donegal	73.7	26.1	3.0	
Cavan	71.3	55.8	23.0	
'Lost Counties'	*75.6*	*35.5*	*12.5*	
Ulster	*76.9*	*29.8*	*19.5*	

Note: Participation in each group is given as a percentage of the estimated number of non-Catholic males aged over 16 years in 1911. Membership figures for the Ulster Volunteer Force (UVF) on 31 May 1914 and the Unionist Clubs (UC) in Nov. 1912 are derived from RIC returns transcribed in *Intelligence Notes, 1913–16*, ed. Breandán Mac Giolla Choille (Dublin, Stationery Office, 1966), 37, 19. Figures for Orange lodges are derived from the following CGL reports: Antrim (1923), Armagh (1913), Belfast (1912), Down (1913), and Tyrone (1912). Figures for Fermanagh and Londonderry were returned with the MCRs of RIC county inspectors for Jan. 1919: NAL, CO 904/108.

Table 6.3 *Location of clerical opponents of Home Rule*

County	Covenant agents	% of local clergy	*Daily Mail*	% of local clergy
Armagh	8	7	29	24
Tyrone	21	13	36	22
Fermanagh	11	17	12	19
Londonderry	15	10	29	19
Mid Ulster	*55*	*11.1*	*106*	*21.4*
Belfast	5	2	42	17
Down	17	6	51	19
Antrim	18	8	44	19
North-East	*40*	*5.4*	*137*	*18.6*
Monaghan	3	5	12	20
Donegal	24	22	25	23
Cavan	8	14	17	30
'Lost Counties'	*35*	*15.8*	*54*	*24.3*
Ulster	*130*	*8.9*	*297*	*20.4*

Table 6.3 *(cont.)*

Note: Many clergymen listed as agents for administering the Ulster Covenant (or Women's Declaration) may be traced through inclusion of clerical titles in the digital index of 'principal agents'; a few have been identified by other means, and others have presumably been missed. One agent who ministered and acted in England is excluded. Their location refers to the constituency in which they acted as agents, occasionally outside the county where they ministered. The location of clergymen contributing statements abstracted in the *Daily Mail*, 28 Sept. 1912, is that of the county in which they ministered, occasionally outside that in which they resided. One contributor who ministered in Louth is excluded from this table, along with the seven contributors whose opinions were neutral or favourable to Home Rule. Almost all clergy named in the *Daily Mail* or in Covenant records have been definitively matched with published clergy lists for each denomination or with the annual returns in *Thom's Official Directory*. The number of clergymen in each county (excluding Roman Catholics) is given in the published county reports of the Census of Ireland (1911). These returns also record the number of Protestant Episcopalian, Presbyterian, Methodist, and other non-Catholic clergy, with an age-breakdown for each group.

Table 6.4 *Nativity of clerical opponents of Home Rule*

Denomination	Number	NE	MU	LC	South	Other	% Ulster
Covenant agents							
Episcopalian	78	15	11	6	42	4	41.0
Presbyterian	46	15	21	9	0	1	97.8
Other	6	1	1	0	2	2	33.3
Total	*130*	*31*	*33*	*15*	*44*	*7*	*60.8*
Daily Mail contributors							
Episcopalian	145	16	33	15	74	7	44.1
Presbyterian	118	57	50	9	1	1	98.3
Other	34	7	17	1	4	5	73.5
Total	*297*	*80*	*100*	*25*	*79*	*13*	*69.0*

Note: Native counties in Ulster are divided into three regions, as in Tables 6.1–6.3 (NE: Antrim, Belfast, Down; MU: Armagh, Fermanagh, Londonderry, Tyrone; LC: Cavan, Donegal, Monaghan). Irish counties of birth outside Ulster are grouped under 'South'; 'Other' refers to clergy born in Britain or beyond.

Table 6.5 *Careers and characteristics of clerical opponents of Home Rule*

Characteristic (Years)	Number	Min.	Lr. Qu.	Median	Ur. Qu.	Max.
Covenant agents						
Age in 1912	129	25	38	46	56	86
Episcopalian	78	26	38	45	58	72
Presbyterian	45	25	38	46	53	86
Years in ministry in 1912	128	1	10	18	28	61
Years in cure in 1912	128	0	3	8	18	61
Age at death	124	44	68	74	82	103
Daily Mail contributors						
Age in 1912	295	27	43	51	64	92
Episcopalian	144	29	43	50	60	84
Presbyterian	118	28	43	54	66	92
Years in ministry in 1912	286	1	16	25	37	64
Years in cure in 1912	286	0	5	14	26	61
Age at death	282	38	68	75	82	103

Note: For each characteristic, the data were arranged in rank order, the median being the mid-way value, and the lower and upper quartile figures being mid-way between the median and the minimum and maximum figures respectively. Data for 1912 relate to ages and periods (in completed years) at the end of that year; some returns of age are approximate, being based on birth years inferred from age at death or from census returns. Information on clerical careers and characteristics is derived primarily from published clergy lists and reference works for each denomination, supplemented by digital searches of the family returns of the Census of Ireland (1911), giving place of residence and birth and age on 2 Apr. 1911 (in a few cases, data relate to the census of 31 Mar. 1901). In cases of conflict, the census returns have usually been preferred to the clergy lists.

Table 6.6 *Themes in clerical contributions to* Daily Mail

Theme	Number	% of cont.: Rel.	Econ.	Emp.	Ulster	CW	Strife
		Total					
All contributions	298	53.5	42.1	18.9	22.2	15.2	48.5
		Location					
North-east	137	61	63	19	23	16	44
Mid Ulster	107	55	37	19	24	14	47
Lost Counties	54	35	33	19	19	15	63
		Nativity					
North-east	80	58	62	14	24	16	45
Mid Ulster	100	49	40	18	21	15	45
Lost Counties	25	56	14	16	16	12	40
Ulster	*205*	*53*	*35*	*16*	*21*	*15*	*44*
South	79	54	48	29	27	15	59
Other	13	54	46	0	8	15	46
		Denomination					
Episcopalian	145	46	50	23	24	15	56
Born Ulster	64	42	50	19	22	14	50
Other	81	49	49	27	26	16	60
Presbyterian	118	60	34	15	23	14	42
Other	35	63	37	11	11	17	40
		Affiliations					
Orange chaplains	43	44	44	12	33	23	56
Covenant agents	49	47	37	24	24	20	61

Note: Each contribution hostile to Home Rule has been analysed by themes, of which the most common were religious objections (Rel.), economic objections (Econ.), fears of future separation or harm to the Empire (Emp.), specific references to the North of Ireland (Ulster), predictions of civil war (CW), and predictions of civil or religious strife including civil war or rebellion (Strife). The table shows the percentage of contributions expressing each theme, sub-divided by the location, nativity, denomination, and affiliations (as Orange chaplains or Covenant agents) of contributing clergy. Percentages exceeding the corresponding figures for 'All Contributions' are italicised.

Table 8.1 *Change in Protestant and Methodist population by region, 1911–26*

Region	South			North		
Denomination	1911	1926	Ratio	1911	1926	Ratio
Census population (thousands)						
Roman Catholic	2812.5	2751.3	97.8	430.2	420.4	97.7
Episcopalian	249.5	164.2	65.8	327.1	338.7	103.6
Presbyterian	45.5	32.4	71.3	395.0	393.4	99.6
Methodist	16.4	10.7	64.9	45.9	49.6	107.9
Total population	*3139.7*	*2972.0*	*94.7*	*1250.5*	*1256.6*	*100.5*
Census population excluding armed forces in 1911 (thousands)						
Episcopalian	232.3	164.2	70.7	325.2	338.7	104.2
Presbyterian	44.1	32.4	73.6	394.4	393.4	99.7
Methodist	15.5	10.7	69.0	45.8	49.6	108.1

Note: Returns by 'religious profession' are abstracted from the published reports of the Census of Ireland (1911), Saorstát Éireann (1926), and Northern Ireland (1926). 'Episcopalians' include adherents of the 'Irish Church' or Church of Ireland, the Church of England, the Episcopal Church of Scotland, and 'Primitive Church Methodists'; 'Presbyterians' exclude groups such as 'Reformed' and 'Non-Subscribing' Presbyterians and Unitarians; 'Methodists' include 'Wesleyan Methodists', 'Primitive Wesleyan Methodists', and 'Methodist New Connexion'. Figures for 'Total population' include those returned for other religious professions or none. The deduction of those in the 'armed forces' in 1911 is based on returns of occupied males in each county report, tabulated by religious profession, minus those engaged in 'defence' (with the exception of pensioners but unavoidably incorporating retired officers; police and prison officers were returned under other categories). The final column gives the percentage ratio of each figure for 1926 to that for 1911.

Table 8.2 *Change in female population of counties by religious denomination, 1911–26*

County	% FNRC	Ep.	Pr.	Me.	County	% FNRC	Ep.	Pr.	Me.
Antrim	79.4	97	98	133	Leitrim	8.4	70	48	55
Belfast	75.1	107	105	108	Cork	8.3	67	54	67
Down	68.4	100	101	128	Louth	8.1	62	62	70
Armagh	55.0	88	89	97	Longford	7.9	66	55	69
Londonderry	53.8	96	94	99	Wexford	7.9	73	59	66
Tyrone	44.5	89	93	93	Westmeath	7.7	63	47	44
Fermanagh	44.0	90	119	91	Meath	7.2	74	52	31
North	*65.6*	*98*	*100*	*108*	Waterford	5.3	62	63	57
					Kilkenny	5.1	72	54	91
Monaghan	25.4	74	81	74	Tipperary	4.9	61	46	60
Wicklow	22.6	80	75	84	Limerick	4.3	65	41	66
Dublin	21.0	72	74	79	Kerry	2.8	56	40	39
Donegal	21.0	77	81	71	Galway	2.4	48	41	43
Cavan	18.7	78	77	60	Roscommon	2.4	61	56	29
Kildare	13.2	54	46	39	Mayo	2.1	62	53	47
Queen's	11.9	79	51	58	Clare	2.0	50	33	18
Carlow	11.5	76	80	68	*South*	*10.3*	*71*	*74*	*69*
King's	10.6	70	56	76					
Sligo	8.9	77	45	69	*Ireland*	*26.6*	*87*	*97*	*98*

Note: Counties are arranged in descending order by the percentage of *females* who were not returned as Roman Catholics (FNRC) in the Census of Ireland (1911). The remaining columns show the percentage ratio of the population of Episcopalians, Presbyterians, and Methodists in 1926 to the corresponding populations in 1911, excluding male members of the armed forces in 1911 (see note to Table 8.1). Since county tabulations for 'Episcopalians' in Northern Ireland (1926) exclude those returned as 'Church of England' (18,682) and 'Episcopal Church of Scotland' (41), the column headed 'Ep.' understates the true percentage ratios for the seven northern counties, and the cumulative figures for the North and Ireland. The percentage ratios for adherents of the Church of Ireland or 'Irish Church' alone, using slightly inaccurate county returns in the *Preliminary Report* (1911), are 109 (Antrim, Belfast, and Down combined), 104 (Londonderry), 95 (Tyrone), 92 (Fermanagh), 90 (Armagh), and 104 (Northern Ireland).

Table 8.3 Change in cross-border population of Northern and Southern Ireland, 1911–26

County	CBP 1926	% Popn.	Change	Ratio	County	CBP 1926	% Popn.	Change	Ratio
Down	7998	3.8	+2346	142	Donegal	5384	3.5	−78	99
Antrim	4445	2.3	+1248	139	Roscommon	293	0.4	−5	98
Fermanagh	5900	10.2	+938	119	Carlow	182	0.5	−7	96
Tyrone	6665	5.0	+706	112	Cavan	1692	2.1	−88	95
Londonderry	10 993	7.9	+667	106	Sligo	552	0.8	−59	90
Armagh	5312	4.8	+150	103	Cork	1177	0.3	−131	90
Belfast	22 606	5.4	−4531	83	Wexford	305	0.3	−49	86
North	*63 919*	*5.1*	*+1524*	*102*	Waterford	332	0.4	−55	86
					Westmeath	425	0.7	−74	85
Meath	622	1.0	+70	113	Tipperary	367	0.3	−64	85
Kildare	812	1.4	+86	112	Queen's	266	0.5	−48	85
Louth	2982	4.8	+306	111	Galway	461	0.3	−93	83
Monaghan	4115	6.3	+303	108	Wicklow	715	1.2	−198	78
Kilkenny	260	0.4	+19	108	Kerry	166	0.1	−53	76
Limerick	403	0.3	+27	107	Longford	211	0.5	−71	75
Dublin	12 082	2.4	+612	105	Clare	118	0.1	−51	70
Mayo	428	0.2	+1	100	King's	209	0.4	−141	60
Leitrim	573	1.0	−7	99	*South*	*35 132*	*1.2*	*+152*	*100*

Note: The cross-border population (CBP) of each county in Northern Ireland refers to those born in Southern Ireland, and vice versa, according to the published census reports for Ireland (1911), and for Saorstát Éireann and Northern Ireland (1926). The columns show CBP in 1926; CBP as a percentage of county population in 1926; the numerical change in CBP (1911–26); and the percentage ratio of CBP (1926) to CBP (1911). The counties are arranged in descending order of that percentage ratio.

Table 8.4 *Characteristics of cross-border population of the North by province of birth, 1911*

Birthplace	Thousands	% RC	% Ep.	Sex ratio (Ep.)
Leinster	16.1	52	31	120
Munster	4.8	50	31	120
Connaught	5.6	54	30	122
Ulster (3 cos.)	29.6	55	21	128
South	*56.2*	*53*	*26*	*124*
Border counties	*35.6*	*57*	*21*	*128*

Note: The percentages of Roman Catholics and Episcopalians (excluding adherents of the Church of England) were derived from a digital search of the census on-line. The sex ratio gives the percentage ratio of Church of Ireland females to Church of Ireland males. The figure for 'Border counties' aggregates those for Donegal, Leitrim, Cavan, Monaghan, and Louth. The total calculated from the published census reports (56,175) exceeds that derived from digital searches (55,147) by 1.8%, presumably as a result of faulty transcription or standardisation in the digital version.

Table 8.5 *Ratio of children to women by religious denomination by province, Irish Free State, 1926*

Province	RC	Ep.	Pr.	Me.
Leinster	128	77	67	77
Munster	131	80	75	81
Connaught	143	97	81	65
Ulster (3 cos.)	137	114	118	116
South	*132*	*84*	*99*	*83*

Note: The table shows the ratio of all children under 20 years to 100 women aged 20 years or more.

Table 8.6 *Ratio of children to women by religious denomination by county, Irish Free State, 1926*

County	Ep.	RC	Ep.: RC	County	Ep.	RC	Ep.: RC
Cavan	120	133	90	Roscommon	88	130	67
Donegal	117	141	83	Wexford	86	124	69
Kildare	111	148	75	Longford	85	135	63
Leitrim	110	135	82	Meath	85	132	64
Queen's	103	134	76	Galway	83	147	57
Carlow	101	126	80	Wicklow	81	135	60
Monaghan	100	133	75	Tipperary	80	128	63
Sligo	98	131	75	Cork	80	124	64
Kilkenny	96	132	73	Limerick	76	137	55
Westmeath	96	128	75	Clare	75	128	58
Mayo	93	150	62	Waterford	74	124	60
Kerry	91	154	59	Dublin	68	122	55
Louth	90	131	69				
King's	89	133	67	*South*	*84*	*132*	*64*

Note: Counties are arranged in descending order of the percentage ratio of Episcopalian children under 20 to every 100 women aged 20 or more. The other columns show the equivalent ratio for Roman Catholics, and the percentage ratio of the Episcopalian ratio to the Roman Catholic ratio.

Table 8.7 *Juvenile percentage of females by religious denomination, 1911 and 1926*

1911 (under 9)	RC	Ep.	Pr.	Me.	1926 (under 10)	RC	Ep.	Pr.	Me.
Leinster	17.6	14.2	14.3	14.7	Leinster	20.0	12.1	11.0	11.5
Munster	18.1	14.9	18.5	15.8	Munster	19.3	13.3	13.6	13.4
Connaught	18.6	15.6	15.6	16.2	Connaught	19.6	14.8	13.5	11.0
Ulster (3 cos.)	17.8	16.9	16.8	16.5	Ulster (3 cos.)	19.8	17.2	17.9	16.3
South	*18.0*	*14.9*	*16.2*	*15.5*	*South*	*19.7*	*13.4*	*15.6*	*12.7*
North	*17.3*	*18.8*	*17.3*	*16.8*					
Ireland	*17.9*	*17.1*	*17.2*	*16.5*					

Note: For each province and region, and for each major religious denomination, the table shows the percentage of females aged less than 9 years in 1911 (the only available age-breakdown by religion). The nearest equivalent figures for 1926 relate to those under 10 years (not available for Northern Ireland).

Table 8.8 *Change in Methodist female population of each county, 1911–26*

County	% FNRC	Census	Members	County	% FNRC	Census	Members
Fermanagh	15.5	91	82	Wexford	4.3	66	67
Leitrim	9.7	55	48	Kildare	4.3	39	C
Belfast	8.2	108	149	Louth	4.1	70	75
Limerick	8.2	66	56	Carlow	4.0	68	80
Armagh	8.1	97	101	Mayo	3.9	47	41
Cork	8.1	67	64	Galway	3.6	43	12
Sligo	6.7	69	67	Westmeath	3.6	44	52
Queen's	6.4	58	75	Down	3.3	128	126
Kerry	5.7	39	50	Roscommon	2.9	29	N
Waterford	5.2	57	103	Londonderry	2.6	99	105
Tipperary	5.1	60	75	Antrim	2.5	133	153
Donegal	4.9	71	61	Monaghan	2.4	74	65
Cavan	4.9	60	56	Clare	2.2	18	N
Dublin	4.9	79	101	Kilkenny	1.8	91	C
King's	4.8	76	49	Meath	0.8	31	N
Wicklow	4.7	84	86	*North*	*5.8*	*108*	*120*
Tyrone	4.7	93	85	*South*	*5.1*	*69*	*69*
Longford	4.6	69	56	*Ireland*	*5.6*	*98*	*100*

Note: Counties are arranged in descending order by the percentage of *females* who were not returned as Roman Catholics (FNRC) in the Census of Ireland (1911). The remaining columns show the percentage ratio of the census population of Methodists in 1926 to that in 1911 (excluding members of the armed forces); and the corresponding ratio for the number of full members of the Society returned for circuits centred in each county (*MCM*, 1911, 1926). N indicates counties without Methodist circuits in either year; C indicates counties in which circuits existed in Mar. 1911 but not Mar. 1926.

Table 8.9 *Change in Methodist population by region, 1911–26*

Region	South			North		
Criterion	1911	1926	% Ratio	1911	1926	% Ratio
Adherents (Districts)	17 051	12 810	75.1	42 779	49 360	115.4
Full members (Districts)	9784	6837	69.9	19 577	22 485	114.9
Full members (Circuits)	11 388	7827	68.7	17 973	21 495	119.6
Census returns	15 457	10 663	69.0	45 849	49 554	108.1

Note: Census returns exclude males occupied in the armed forces (1911). Returns of membership of the Methodist Church in Ireland are abstracted from *MCM* (1911, 1926), distinguishing between full members received into the Society (excluding juniors and those on trial) and an aggregate estimate of 'members and adherents'. This category (used in 1926) evidently corresponds to the figures (returned in 1911) for 'total not average attendance at public worship on Sabbath', excluding 'additional week night hearers'. Local anomalies suggest that these estimates of adherence were far less methodical and reliable than those of membership, reflecting vague criteria inconsistently applied. The division into the 'South' and 'North' is imprecise, since three of the ten Church districts straddled the border established in 1921–2. Membership data for circuits not within the jurisdiction in which their district was centred have therefore been used to compute membership of all circuits with centres respectively south and north of the border. Even this estimate is imprecise, since membership of many individual circuits also straddled the border.

Table 8.10 *Membership of the Methodist Church in Ireland by district and triennium, 1911–26*

March	Du.	Wa.	Co.	Li.	Sl.	Cl.	En.	Lo.	Be.	Po.	Total
	Number of full members and decrease over period										
1911	3222	861	1825	950	1162	1764	3985	2731	8908	3953	29 361
1914	3145	857	1584	883	1008	1574	3702	2686	8855	3713	28 007
1917	3108	780	1464	802	882	1466	3507	2568	9209	3580	27 366
1920	3080	713	1422	728	815	1283	3397	2440	9726	3641	27 247
1923	2882	651	1160	575	692	1127	3272	2464	11 276	3768	27 867
1926	2959	588	1146	492	636	1016	3184	2386	13 008	3907	29 322
1911–26	*263*	*273*	*679*	*458*	*1128*	*748*	*801*	*345*	*+4100*	*46*	*39*
	Percentage ratio of final to initial membership in each specified period										
1911–14	98	100	87	93	87	89	93	98	99	94	95
1914–17	99	91	92	91	87	93	95	96	104	96	98
1917–20	99	91	97	91	92	88	97	95	106	102	100
1920–23	94	91	82	79	85	88	96	101	116	103	102
1923–26	103	90	99	86	92	90	97	97	115	104	105
1911–26	*92*	*68*	*63*	*52*	*55*	*58*	*80*	*87*	*146*	*99*	*100*

Note: The districts of Belfast, Clones, Cork, Dublin, Enniskillen, Limerick, Londonderry, Portadown, Sligo, and Waterford are indicated by the first two letters in each name.

Table 8.11 *Membership of the Methodist Church in Ireland by region and triennium, 1911–26*

Number	South	North	Ratio	South	North
1911	11 388	17 973			
1914	10 581	17 426	1911–14	93	97
1917	9994	17 372	1914–17	94	100
1920	9434	17 811	1917–20	94	103
1923	8289	19 578	1920–23	88	110
1926	7827	21 495	1923–26	94	110
1911–26	*–3561*	*+3522*	*1911–26*	*69*	*120*

Note: The table shows the number of full members of the Methodist Church in Ireland, and the percentage ratio of membership at the end of each period to that at the beginning of the period. Figures for the South and North refer to circuits (not districts) centred south or north of the border established in 1921–2.

Table 8.12 *Methodist Church in Ireland: membership flow by region, 1911–26*

Triennium	Number		Rate	
	South	North	South	North
New members				
1911–14	1307	3085	47	54
1914–17	1020	2550	39	45
1917–20	984	2644	40	47
1920–23	846	4010	38	67
1923–26	956	4703	46	71
1911–26	*5113*	*16 992*	*41*	*60*
Removals				
1911–14	−31	+31	−1	+1
1914–17	−74	+87	−3	+2
1917–20	−74	+79	−3	+1
1920–23	−202	+195	−9	+3
1923–26	−123	+143	−6	+2
1911–26	*−504*	*+535*	*−4*	*+2*
Emigrants				
1911–14	894	1239	32	22
1914–17	523	629	20	11
1917–20	460	352	19	6
1920–23	736	822	33	14
1923–26	368	721	18	11
1911–26	*2981*	*3763*	*24*	*13*
Deaths				
1911–14	410	934	15	16
1914–17	397	936	15	16
1917–20	422	1026	17	18
1920–23	381	892	17	15
1923–26	343	982	17	15
1911–26	*1953*	*4770*	*16*	*17*
Ceased membership				
1911–14	705	1564	25	27
1914–17	574	1164	22	20
1917–20	488	1005	20	18
1920–23	481	917	22	15
1923–26	372	1438	18	22
1911–26	*2620*	*6088*	*21*	*21*
Net change				
1911–14	−733	−621	−26	−11
1914–17	−549	−92	−21	−2
1917–20	−461	+340	−19	+6
1920–23	−954	+1576	−43	+26
1923–26	−250	+1705	−12	+26
1911–26	*−2947*	*+2908*	*−24*	*+10*

Table 8.12 (*cont.*)

Note: Figures are based on annual returns for each Church district for the years ending in March, 1911–26 (*MCM*). 'New members' presumably incorporated reinstatements and promotions from junior membership. Figures for net internal 'removals' show the difference between the number of members in each district transferring out of one circuit into another circuit within Ireland, and the reverse (+ signifies net inward transfers; – signifies net outward transfers). 'Emigrants' were those 'removing to any place out of Ireland', whether or not they joined Methodist congregations in other jurisdictions. The returns also enumerate deaths and the number ceasing to be members for other reasons (such as expulsion, non-payment of dues, resignation, or conversion), completing the elements generating the recorded changes in membership from year to year. Thus 'net change' represents the sum of new members and net removals, less the sum of emigrants, deaths, and cessations of membership. Annual rates of flow per thousand members are based on membership in Mar. 1913 (1911–14), 1916 (1914–17), 1919 (1917–20 and 1911–26), 1922 (1920–23), and 1925 (1923–26). Aggregate figures for the South and North refer to districts centred south or north of the border established in 1921–2 (returns of flow were not published for individual circuits).

Table 8.13 *Methodist Church in Ireland: components of membership flow by district, 1911–26*

Component	Du.	Wa.	Co.	Li.	Sl.	Cl.	En.	Lo.	Be.	Po.	Total
	Components of flow, 1911–26										
New	2634	318	1032	209	343	577	1515	1659	10 875	2943	22 105
Removals	+167	−21	−164	−95	−219	−172	−254	−55	+1132	−288	+31
Emigrants	1200	240	811	223	216	291	527	686	1884	666	6744
Ceased	1166	169	409	170	219	487	574	680	3768	1066	8700
Deaths	697	160	327	179	215	375	962	584	2254	970	6732
	Components of flow, 1911–14										
New	614	79	292	81	83	158	337	410	1765	573	4392
Removals	+27	+53	−31	−19	−56	−5	−90	−18	+234	−95	0
Emigrants	335	63	248	59	81	108	180	211	622	226	2133
Ceased	248	42	183	30	41	151	163	110	1001	290	2269
Deaths	135	31	71	40	49	84	187	116	429	202	1344
	Components of flow, 1920–23										
New	454	43	162	22	52	113	309	376	2667	658	4856
Removals	+1	+14	−73	−51	−52	−41	−58	−9	+250	+12	−7
Emigrants	264	54	230	67	53	68	100	157	427	138	1558
Ceased	267	24	51	26	33	80	104	78	536	199	1389
Deaths	122	41	70	31	37	80	173	109	404	206	1282

Note: Italicised totals indicate minor discrepancies in the published returns. For definitions and sources, see notes to Table 8.12.

Table 8.14 *Methodist Church in Ireland: rate of membership flow by district, 1911–26*

Component	Du.	Wa.	Co.	Li.	Sl.	Cl.	En.	Lo.	Be.	Po.	Total
Rate of flow per thousand members per annum, 1911–26											
New	57	29	47	19	27	28	30	45	77	55	54
Removals	+4	–2	–8	–8	–17	–8	–5	–1	+8	–5	+0
Emigrants	26	22	37	20	17	14	10	19	13	12	17
Ceased	25	16	19	15	17	24	11	18	27	20	21
Deaths	15	15	15	16	17	18	19	16	16	18	17
Rate of flow per thousand members per annum, 1911–14											
New	64	32	59	30	26	32	30	51	67	68	52
Removals	+3	+22	–6	–7	–17	–1	–8	–2	+9	–11	0
Emigrants	35	26	50	22	25	22	16	26	24	27	25
Ceased	26	17	37	11	13	31	14	14	38	35	27
Deaths	14	13	14	15	15	17	17	14	16	24	16
Rate of flow per thousand members per annum, 1920–23											
New	51	21	42	12	23	32	31	51	85	58	59
Removals	+0	+7	–19	–27	–23	–12	–6	–1	+8	+1	–0
Emigrants	30	27	60	36	24	19	10	21	14	12	19
Ceased	30	12	13	14	15	23	10	11	17	17	17
Deaths	14	20	19	17	16	23	17	15	13	18	16

Note: For definitions and sources, see notes to Table 8.12. Rates of flow are based on membership in Mar. 1919 (1911–26), Mar. 1913 (1911–14), and Mar. 1922 (1920–23).

Table 9.1 *Membership of the Methodist Church in west Cork circuits*

31 March	Bandon	Bantry	Clon.	Dun.	Kin.	Skib.	Total	Residue
1911	190	106	162	124	92	244	918	907
1914	161	80	156	109	83	236	825	759
1917	129	77	146	95	87	214	748	716
1920	111	80	149	97	72	199	708	714
1923	106	72	116	79	57	171	601	559
1926	*124*	*65*	*114*	*83*	*64*	*159*	*609*	*537*
% Ratio 1926: 1911	*65*	*61*	*70*	*67*	*70*	*65*	*66*	*59*

Note: Columns give the membership for each circuit in west Cork (Bandon, Bantry, Clonakilty, Dunmanway, Kinsale, and Skibbereen), as recorded annually in *MCM*, and for the residue of the Cork district (the circuits of Cork, Youghal, Tralee, Kinsale, and Queenstown, along with Fermoy and Mallow which were discontinued in 1922).

Table 9.2 *Methodist Church in west Cork: components of membership flow by circuit, 1911–26*

Component	Bandon	Clon.	Dun.	Kin.	Skib.	Total
Components of flow, 1911–26						
New	59	42	61	34	84	280
Removals in	72	56	38	32	74	272
Removals out	80	68	61	35	124	368
Emigrants	46	31	18	42	57	194
Ceased	34	9	36	10	18	107
Deaths	37	37	27	14	42	157
Components of flow, 1911–14						
New	12	16	12	13	28	81
Removals in	27	15	12	14	20	88
Removals out	33	16	12	17	32	110
Emigrants	15	8	5	11	13	52
Ceased	7	5	16	2	4	34
Deaths	13	8	6	6	7	40
Components of flow, 1920–23						
New	19	3	4	6	19	51
Removals in	15	6	8	2	17	48
Removals out	12	16	12	3	26	69
Emigrants	17	15	7	16	22	77
Ceased	3	1	6	1	9	20
Deaths	7	10	7	3	7	34

Note: For definitions, see note to Table 8.12. 'In' and 'out' signify removals from and to other Irish circuits. Figures are derived from quarterly returns of movements in and out of each circuit, entered by superintendents in the Circuit Schedule Books, and Membership Registers and Quarterly Class Rolls: MHSIA. Various anomalies of enumeration have been resolved by comparison of these and other returns. Since returns are not available for Kinsale (1923–6), totals for 1911–26 exclude Kinsale for that triennium. No such records up to 1922 have been traced for Bantry, the remaining (and smallest) west Cork circuit

Table 9.3 Displaced Methodist families, west Cork, 1920–3

	Methodist circuit records, west Cork (1920–3)					Census schedules (1911)					
Surname	Head	Circ.	Yr	Qr	To	Fam	Age	Occupation	Co. of birth	Rms	FW
Emigrations											
Copithorne	Louisa	Sn	21	a	England	1	75	Draper's Ww	Dublin	7	3
Swanton	Charles Henry	Bn	21	a	England	5	43	Grocer	Cork	13	8
Kingston	Richard	Sn	21	b	Canada	6	49	Farmer	Cork	4	5
Nagle	William ?Moyle	Bn	21	b	Canada	1	70	Shopkeeper	Cork	8	6
Henry	John Howard	Sn	21	b	England	3	45	Commercial Trav.	Cork City	9	6
Kingston	William	Bn	21	b	England	13	43	Farmer	Cork	5	5
Sweetnam	John	Sn	21	c	Canada	3	60	Farmer	Cork	14	6
Copithorne	John	Sn	21	c	England	3	55	Pharm. Chemist	Lancs	9	7
Roycroft	William Bernard	By	21	c	Wales	5	53	Shopkeeper	Cork	11	5
Bradfield	Elizabeth	Cy	21	d	England	2	58	Farmer's Ww	Cork	11	5
Hosford	Joseph	Cy	22	b	England	3	66	Farmer	Cork	12	5
Bryan	William	Bn	22	c	England	4	49	Farmer	Cork	5	9
Jagoe	William	Dy	22	c	England	3	46	Draper	Cork	6	4
Buttimer	Mary Ann	Cy	22	c	USA	3	70	Fr-Skr's Ww	Somerset	8	6
Gallagher	Herbert	Ke	22	c		4	35	Accountant	Tyrone	6	4
Vickery	Richard	Bn	22	c		1	40	Farmer's Son	Cork	10	7
Good	James	Ke	22	d		3	76	Farmer	Cork	9	5

Table 9.3 (*cont.*)

	Methodist circuit records, west Cork (1920–3)						Census schedules (1911)				
Surname	*Head*	*Circ.*	*Yr*	*Qr*	*To*	*Fam*	*Age*	*Occupation*	*Co. of birth*	*Rms*	*FW*
Removals											
Kingston	Mary Ellen	Cy	20	d?	Wicklow	2	66	Farmer's Ww	Cork	3	9
Willis	Richard	Cy	21	b	Wicklow	4	60	Farmer	Cork	4	4
Armstrong	Caroline M. T.	Dy	21	c		1	71	Mer.'s Clk's Dau	Down	3	4
Wolfe	Mary Jane	Sn	21	d		1	70	H'ware Mer.'s Ww	Cork	9	6
Kingston	John	Sn	22	a		1	52	Farmer	Cork	5	7
Evans	William	Bn	22	b	Dublin	1	49	Grocer	Cork	12	10
Jennings	Alice B	Dy	22	c		1	74	Farmer's Ww	Cork	7	5
Buttimer	Clara	Dy	22	d	Dublin	1	64	Draper's Ww	Cork City	6	5
Deane	Kathleen A. M.	Cy	23	b	Dublin	4	46	Clk PS-Fr's Ww	Wat City	8	8

Note: For each 'displaced family' (see text for definition), the table shows surname, head of family, circuit, year and quarter of displacement, destination, number in displaced group, head's age at time of displacement, head's occupation, head's county of birth, number of rooms in family home (1911), and number of front windows (1911). Where unavailable for 1911, census returns for 1901 were used.

Index

Lightning Source UK Ltd
Milton Keynes UK
UKOW01n2209010616

275419UK00001B/14/P

Dublin City Libraries
Withdrawn From Stock
Leabharlanna Poiblí Chathair Bhaile Átha Cliath
Dublin City Public Libraries